# Republic of Egos

# Republic of Egos

*A Social History of the
Spanish Civil War*

Michael Seidman

THE UNIVERSITY OF WISCONSIN PRESS

The University of Wisconsin Press
1930 Monroe Street
Madison, Wisconsin 53711

www.wisc.edu/wisconsinpress/

3 Henrietta Street
London WC2E 8LU, England

Printed in the United States of America

Library of Congress Cataloging-in-Publication Data

Seidman, Michael (Michael M.)
    Republic of egos: a social history of the Spanish Civil War / Michael Seidman.
        p.    cm
Includes bibliographical references and index.
    ISBN 0–299–17860–9 (cloth : alk. paper)—ISBN 0–299–17864–1 (pbk. : alk. paper)
    1. Spain—History—Civil War, 1936–1939—Social aspects. 2. Spain—Social conditions—
1886–1939. I. Title.

DP269.8.S65 S54 2002

946.081'1—dc21                                                    2002002808

Individuality is the only thing that we humans have in common.

L. Namdies, *Antinomies*

# Contents

# Maps

# Acknowledgments

I gratefully acknowledge the support of a number of friends, colleagues, and institutions. An American Council of Learned Societies Fellowship and a University of North Carolina–Wilmington Research Reassignment provided resources that allowed me to spend a year in Spain conducting archival research. The College of Arts and Sciences and the Department of History of UNC–W offered grants that permitted travel to appropriate collections. I wish to express gratitude to Gabriel Jackson and Raymond Carr, who endorsed my project of a social history of the Spanish civil war. I am indebted to the cartographer, Todd Richardson. I owe special thanks to Stanley Payne both for his encouragement and deep insight. Jim Amelang and Elena López in Madrid were generous in many ways. Quím and Sara, Paco and Juliá, Coro and Pili always offered warm and intelligent refuge in Barcelona.

Michael Seidman
Kure Beach, N.C.

# Republic of Egos

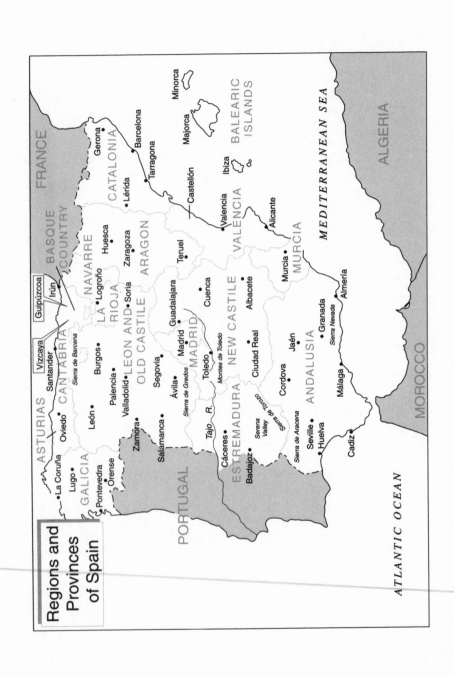

Regions and Provinces of Spain

# Introduction
## Bringing Back the Individual

It remains surprising that a civil war in a minor power on the periphery of Europe has generated and continues to provoke enormous interest. There are, it is said, twenty thousand books on the Spanish civil war—which may be as many as on the French Revolution or the Second World War, undoubtedly more significant events than the Spanish conflict. Yet perhaps because of its proximity to the Second World War and its ideological and theological scope, the Iberian conflict of the 1930s incites ongoing fascination. Unlike contemporary—principally ethnic—civil wars in southeastern Europe or in Africa, the Spanish conflict involved, to some degree, almost every important political ideology and three major religions—Christianity, Islam, and Judaism. During the conflict, opposing "isms"—Communism and fascism, anarchism and authoritarianism, republicanism and monarchism, Catholicism and anticlericalism, democracy and dictatorship—battled each other. The understandable fascination provoked by the struggles among these belief systems has marked the literature with an ideological stamp. The historiography usually explains the holy wars of right versus left, Catholics against atheists, traditionalists confronting modernizers.

The many forms of the collective have mesmerized the most recent generations of historians, including those who have studied the Spanish war. Investigation has centered on political, religious, and trade-union collectivities or has focused on social groups, such as classes or genders. This new

emphasis was a healthy reaction to the previous stress on great men who supposedly made history largely by themselves. Two major traditions, the Marxist and, more inclusively, the sociological, have inspired the shift to the
study of collectivities and social groups. Both traditions emerged from the
positivist position that sought to determine the laws of history and therefore
disregarded the unique. The Marxist tradition views the individual as a member of a social class that, in turn, struggles for survival and dominance.[1] To
resolve the class struggle, Marxism offers the tantalizing ideal of social reconciliation, a goal that still continues to inspire many. Although the sociological orientation is broader and less political, it shares the Marxist view of
men and women as social beings. This tradition argues that human subjectivity is unintelligible outside a social context. Society creates individuals,
not vice versa (Lukes 1977:177). Many who follow this orientation echo the
Marxist yearning for social reconciliation or integration.

The sociological perspective has inspired a wide variety of historical investigations, all of which celebrate the social and correspondingly neglect the
individual. Perhaps the most influential representative of the sociological orientation in historical studies is the Annales. This school's stress on climate,
geography, and demography conceded a very limited importance and reduced
autonomy to the lone human being. The disdain of Annales scholars for the
personal may be extreme, but it is indicative of what has been, until recently,
the climate in the humanities and social sciences. Indeed, the very formula-
tion, "social sciences," reveals the bias against what Steven Lukes has labeled
"methodological individualism." Do not, he and many others tell us, start with
the individual since beginning with the unique will lead to both political and
methodological failure. According to Lukes, methodological individualism
can never eliminate social explanations. It can only mask them as they return
clandestinely. Furthermore, methodological individualists, such as Friedrich
Hayek and Karl Popper, are hopelessly reactionary and capitalist.

Lukes's durkheimian objections deserve serious consideration but not uncrit-
ical acceptance. Oddly enough, it was Louis de Bonald, the classic Catholic
reactionary, who first challenged the methodological individualism of Thomas
Hobbes by arguing that the individual can be known only in society (see
Moulinié 1979:165). One of the aims of this study is to dispute de Bonald and
Lukes by showing that beginning with the individual and the personal is useful for historical understanding. There is no reason to accept a priori the
philosopher's or social scientist's argument that man is merely a social being.
Truisms, such as "human subjectivity is unintelligible outside a social context,"
can easily be refuted by claiming that the social context is unintelligible without the individual.[2] The priority of the social and the rejection of personal subjectivity should not be accepted on faith.

The following study of the Spanish civil war and revolution intends to demonstrate how individuals make history. These actors cannot be reduced to mere members of social or political collectivities. Individuals were not determined by their social class or gender or, if they were, the ways they interpreted and acted upon their class or gender identities diverged enough to dilute the explanatory usefulness of these concepts. The emphasis on the collective experience of a class or a gender assumes and even encourages the discovery or invention of a community or commonality that may not have existed.

The exploration of the individual and the personal in the following pages is a primary justification for yet another book on the Spanish civil war. Many of its most famous actors have written their memoirs from the perspective of "squabbles from above." In this type of apologetic literature, politicians and military men employed by the various collectivities defend their record (e.g., Martín-Blázquez 1938, Rojo 1974, Cordón 1977). Most historians have possessed a traditional political, diplomatic, and military orientation. They have focused with great intelligence and diligence on political parties, international diplomacy, and military confrontations. Looking back on the interwar period, many observers and participants sympathetic to the left have viewed the Spanish war as a prelude to or the first phase of the Second World War (Líster 1966:293; Modesto 1969:288).

A newer type of investigation—pioneered by Theda Skocpol—combines structural concerns with international diplomacy (see Skocpol 1979:37; Goldstone 1986:7). States in international competition have been forced to tax their people to remain competitive geostrategic players, thereby increasing social and economic tensions. In this context of internal and global pressures, certain elites subjected their own state organization to severe criticism. The lower classes, especially peasants, took advantage of divisions among elites to advance their own demands. Eventually, urban revolutionaries triumph. This model has a certain, but nonetheless limited, usefulness for the Spanish case. It underlines the importance of elite divisions, peasant revolt, and the urban/rural split, which were all central in the Spanish revolution. However, the model's stress on the influence of geopolitics on domestic policy has little meaning in Spain (see Stone 1994:16). Spain's admitted position as a second-rate power outside of the major forums of international competition does not fit into Skocpol's model, and it is not surprising that she ignored the Spanish revolution. Furthermore, structural models are concerned primarily with the origins of revolutions and do not explore social revolutions and civil wars in terms of the lived experiences of the population.[3] The structural approach privileges investigation of the state and social elites and ignores—except insofar as they are members of a social class—the people. Structuralists neglect the fact that popular experience affects outcome, which thereby becomes contingent rather than inevitable.

Until recently, there has been little social history of the Spanish civil war and revolution. The new social history of the last two decades revolves around concepts such as class and, most currently, gender. These investigations have immeasurably increased our knowledge of Spanish society in the late 1930s, but despite their valuable contributions, they often remain wedded to the collectivist and impersonal framework of traditional social history.[4] Yet Spanish society, the war, and the revolution cannot be completely understood within the conventional confines of either political or social history. Only a small minority was unconditionally political and identified with parties and unions. Much larger numbers were aware that they were members of a class, and certainly nearly everyone knew that he or she belonged to a sex or gender. Yet these identifications with broad social categories were so diffused and heterogeneous that shoving them into the conceptual bags of class or gender does not aid our understanding of what happened during the 1930s in Spain. The Spanish civil war was undoubtedly a class war, but it will be obvious that many wage earners did not identify totally with their class. They used class organizations—whether parties or unions—for their own individual purposes.

The following social history of the conflict examines the Spanish war from the bottom up. Although the militants, that is, those who identified with political and social organizations in the Republican zone, will not be ignored, equal if not more attention will be devoted to unknown and anonymous individuals who asserted their own interests against the demands of various causes and collectivities. The goal is to take history from below to a subterranean level where one's own welfare, family, and closest friends, or what may be termed the personal or intimate realm, were more important than organizations, social classes, and the future society. Kin and intimates could successfully compete for loyalties with class and gender.[5] Military historians with a sociological bent emphasize the importance of a small group of buddies to explain the soldier's performance (Holmes 1985:11; Ashworth 1980). In many cases though, the individual must choose between what sociologists call "contradictory group loyalties" of army pals or family members and the grander organizations with more abstract and futuristic goals.

I shall de-emphasize the great collectivities of party, class, and gender that historians have favored to examine the more intimate social groups of family, friends, and village. These intermediary bodies negotiated between the individual and larger society. Their complicity with the expression of personal desires permitted individualisms to flourish during the civil war. It would be foolish to assert that individuals and collectivities were completely autonomous. "Individual psychology . . . is at the same time social psychology as well" (Freud 1959:1). Class and gender will not be ignored, but more attention will be devoted to the struggles of social groups that have yet received little attention. One of the major conflicts in the Republican zone was between producers and consumers of food. The state favored the latter by imposing price controls. In addition, soldiers could use threats and violence to extort food and other goods. Conversely, peasants engaged in black marketeering or concealed their possessions.

Individualism in the singular cannot encompass precisely enough the actions of these people. Instead, they generated individualisms, which were often forms of self-help and personal advancement (Scott 1985:xvi; Fitzpatrick 1994:5). Noncommitted individualists have shady reputations among social scientists and historians who tend to identify them either with lack of class consciousness or with free-market capitalism. Yet there are several types of individualism, not all of which Adam Smith or neoclassical thinkers would have found congenial. During the war and revolution, these individualisms conflicted with union and party desires for wage earners to work and sacrifice for the Republican, Socialist, or anarchist causes. They relied on "implicit understandings and informal networks" and avoided "any direct, symbolic confrontation with authority" (Scott 1985:xvi). Symbolic and open resistance—that is, propaganda and politicking—left the relatively powerless vulnerable to repression. They preferred subtle and hidden forms of insubordination that the small group or individual left unsigned. Anonymity remained a part of protest.[6] To superficial observers, the hegemony of the state or of the elites may have appeared complete, but everyday subversive acts of resistance negated this assumption. The socially weak did not accept the ideology of the powerful or submit passively to authority. The banality and normality of subversive forms rendered them significant.

In the Spanish case, subversion adopted several configurations. Acquisitive individualists made consumption, not class struggle, their main priority. Entrepreneurial individualists ignored restrictions on overtime and deal making. They worked for themselves, not the collective or the state. They were especially concerned with overcoming the decreasing value of money. Subversive individualists refused to fight or work. Their methods were deception, foot dragging, and evasion. They violated military honor and state or private property rights. They acted in ways that both capitalists and revolutionaries would call cowardly, lazy, or even criminal. In practice, subversive, acquisitive, and entrepreneurial individualisms often cannot be clearly distinguished. Real people meshed and mingled their strands. For example, black marketeering—which both males and females commonly practiced during the conflict—synthesized acquisitive and entrepreneurial strands. Nevertheless, defining diverse individualisms has the advantage of showing a variety of motivations of historical actors. This heterogeneity demonstrates the strength and diversity of individualism. Forces of social integration had a difficult time combating these centrifugal tendencies. Shame, one of the authorities' most effective weapons for fighting against personal resistance, frequently proved insufficient.

What all individualisms shared was a rootedness in a microsociety where the personal dominated the political. They were materialist and concerned with basic corporal needs. Acts of acquisitive, entrepreneurial, and subversive individualism upset attempts to establish a controlled wartime economy. Recent historiography has often been idealist. Political historians have focused on ideologies and cultural historians on representations and symbols. Biology, though, was as important as ideology or culture. The physical condition of the body—determined by food, clothing, weather, fatigue, and illness—motivated the actions of many in the Republican zone. Historians of the Republic have often emphasized its lack of arms. Its lack of food and transportation was equally significant and has not been fully analyzed. The Earl of Cork rightly asserted that poor rations during the British civil war made for "a rich churchyard and a weak garrison" (quoted in Carlton 1992:209). Calories and clothes created as much meaning as communication or community. As the war dragged on and the prospect of the "decisive" battle faded, the political economy of each zone influenced its army's destiny.

If historians of the civil war have left material conditions of the conflict in relative neglect, they have shown even less interest in quiet fronts, that is, situations in which soldiers of opposing camps in close proximity to one another were not aggressive. Analysts have been fascinated by the major actions of the war. Whether left or right, they have pushed a kinetic vision of the conflict. Absorbed in movement, not stability, they have focused their attentions on the "decisive battles" of Madrid, Jarama, Guadalajara, Teruel, Ebro, and so forth. Just as labor historians have been continually obsessed with militancy, military historians have been fascinated with blood and guts. But battle is merely "the tip of the military iceberg," and its ubiquity has been exaggerated (quoted in Holmes 1985:76). Memory emphasizes dramatic moments of conflict instead of the commonly boring everyday existence in the trenches. Literature recalls the glory and horror of battle more frequently than the monotony of military life. It dismisses the routine grind of stabilized fronts and disregards loafing or what the U.S. engineer, F. W. Taylor, aptly called "soldiering" (see Linderman 1987:273). Spanish military historiography, usually dominated by a *franquista* bent, has too narrowly defined war by concentrating on officers' decisions and by condescending to the rank and file: "[Troops] were rested but accustomed to the relative tranquility of passive fronts. Many soldiers had a mistaken idea of war having taken part in only minor actions" (Martínez Bande 1977:75).[7] "[In the fall of 1938] the war came to a standstill [se paralizaba] in Andalusia and Estremadura and also in the Center. [It] then was reactivated at the end of 1938" (Martínez Bande 1981:285). One of the reasons given for the Nationalist victory was that they had "el ambiente y la solera [collective character] militar" (Martínez Bande 1980:103). Even quiet fronts, such as Estremadura, are examined from the standpoint of their influence on major battles, not in terms of the experience of the rank and file. In other words, outcome—not experience—has been the concern.

No one can deny that major battles had a considerable impact on the outcome of the conflict. Quiet fronts were nonetheless the background from which the celebrated clashes emerged as nonbelligerency in one area permitted the high command to plan major attacks in another. Battles were "decisive" only because stable fronts were not. To understand the supposedly decisive conflicts, some knowledge of quiet fronts is therefore necessary. Just as important, soldiers spent much more time on quiet fronts than in major battles. In the everyday life of a trench warrior, tranquility usually dominated. The comparatively rare major confrontations involved only tens of thousands of troops in a military population that eventually numbered nearly three million. For each active fighter, there may have been fifteen who were at rest on inactive fronts or at peace in the rear. Neither side was capable of simultaneously launching attacks along many different fronts, as the North was able to do in the final years of the United States Civil War. Spatially, calm also ruled. Every meter of active trench was matched by kilometers of quiet and even unguarded lines. A British World War I veteran who volunteered to fight in the International Brigades commented that "by the standards of the Great War they [Spanish soldiers] were as thinly dabbed on the ground as English mustard needs to be on English beef" (Wintringham 1939:15). General Kindelán, Franco's Air Force chief, noted that "during two years our civil war was similar to colonial wars or those between two South American countries. In all these types of conflict there were very few troops in proportion to the fronts and the territories involved" (Kindelán 1945:167).

Yet historians of the conflict—most of whom maintain a political perspective which searches for the "decisive," heroic, committed, and the militant—have ignored what constituted most of a soldier's existence during wartime. Experience and outcome are, of course, related. The harshness of everyday life of the common soldier in the Popular Army, during a war that few expected to last nearly three years, had an immensely negative effect on its performance. Historians have been much more concerned with collective winners and losers than with the happenings and reactions of individual rank and file on either side. Thus, officers, their strategies, and their equipment have exercised a continuing fascination over conventional military histories.[8] The advocacy of German historian Hans Delbrück of the integration of battle and social history has made little headway in studies of the Spanish conflict. "To evade any really inquisitive discussion of what battles might be like by recourse to the easy argument that one must stick to the point, which is decision, results, winning or losing. Against the power and simplicity of that argument, any other . . . makes slow headway in the competition for a public hearing" (Keegan 1976:61).

The literature has explored the supposedly great men and collectivities—
generals, politicians, parties, unions, classes, armies in battle, and, most
recently, genders. Social historical explorations "from below" of unknown,
anonymous, and nonmilitant individuals are scarce. Nor have historians of
Spain seen its civil war from the relatively distant perspective of the future
consumer society where the struggle for commodities replaced a variety of
wartime militancies. Consequently, the history of quiet fronts remains an informal and nonacademic oral history. Spaniards often tell stories and anecdotes
about nonaggressive situations during the civil war, but the subject has never
acquired the dignity or weight to stimulate a scholarly written history. The following pages will attempt to fill, at least incipiently and partially, this histori-
ographical gap. Although Nationalist soldiers will not be completely ignored,
the focus will be on civilians and low-ranking soldiers of the Popular Army.
The focus on the Republican zone has little to do with ideological preference.
For whatever reason, and it would be fascinating to find out why, the Republic has left a richer documentary legacy than its opponents. The possibility cannot be excluded that Nationalist officials manipulated archives by removing
documents that they perceived to have compromised them. Yet it has never been
proven, and even those who presumably had privileged access to archives during the Franco regime have noted the relative scarcity of Nationalist data
(Martínez Bande 1984:88).[9] Infelicitously, even in the Republican zone existing sources cannot explore large parts of civil war experience. For example,
numbers and regional distribution of casualties, age and rank of combatants,
attitudes toward death, and burial practices are only a few of the important top-
ics about which we have little knowledge. Nor unfortunately can I claim that
the following pages have fully integrated the vast local, national, and international secondary sources on the Spanish war. I can profess only that this social
history attempts to explore insufficiently known but absolutely essential aspects
of the conflict.

The Republican camp possessed a wealth of social experiments that aimed
to inspire sacrifice and commitment of the lower classes. These contrasted
sharply with the relative order and stability in Nationalist areas. However, the
Nationalist zone will not be totally neglected since parallels with it help to
reveal the nature of the problems of the Republic and place them in perspective. Comparisons shed light on why the Republic lost, but they do not fully
explain why the Nationalists won. In other words, Nationalists suffered the
same kinds of material and motivational difficulties as their enemies but probably encountered them less frequently and intensively. Furthermore, Nationalists were much better able to organize their wartime economy and to circulate
a viable currency. A focus on material conditions and experience will make it
easier to see the continuities between the Spanish conflict and other civil wars
in developing Western nations.

Because of its ideological nature and its supposed anticipation of World War II, foreign intervention in the Spanish conflict has received much attention. Franco's supporters believed that they could have quickly ended the war in November 1936 if not for Soviet and international Communist aid to the defenders of Madrid (Kindelán 1945:24). On the other hand, the Republican loss has often been attributed to the lack of foreign support or the "betrayal" of the democracies during the period of appeasement of the European dictators (Preston 1986:67; see also Thomas 1961:584; Graham 1999:511; Richards 1998:169).[10] This is a plausible argument, but it has the disadvantage of focusing attention too exclusively on political, diplomatic, and military history. To explain the Republic's loss it is also necessary to evaluate to what extent those in the Republican zone wanted to overcome foreign "betrayal" and to sacrifice for its triumph. In other words, how each side used its foreign aid was as important as the quantity of aid received. The Nationalists employed their support from the fascist powers much more effectively than, for instance, their counterrevolutionary predecessors, the Russian Whites.

The first chapter, "Militancy," will focus on those devoted to the Republic or to the revolution in the early stages of the war. Militancy may be defined as a willingness to sacrifice life, labor, or possessions for a cause. Communist, Socialist, and anarchist activists prevented the successful execution of a relatively peaceful *pronunciamiento* in the tradition of the nineteenth or early twentieth century. Unlike the previous coup by Primo de Rivera in 1923, the rebellious officers—who were eventually led by Generalísimo Francisco Franco—had to confront the armed activists of the various parties and unions that claimed to represent the Spanish people or, more specifically, the working class. Activists demanded arms for the masses and showed themselves willing to die for the cause. They formed militias that demonstrated enthusiasm rather than military efficiency. The emphasis in the historiography has been on the militants and their ideological divisions that endured throughout the war. It may be more fruitful, however, to view the outbreak of civil war as the ephemeral era of activism that, although it never disappeared, would decline or dissipate as the conflict endured. Militants would dominate the first months of the conflict with a thoroughness that would gradually fade.

Many if not most workers, peasants, and soldiers were not militants but rather opportunists who joined the parties and unions of the militants not from conviction but rather because a party or union card was needed to get jobs, food, and health care. As a poor Malaysian put it in his own context, "With the minority, it would be difficult, I used my head. I want to be on the side of the majority."[11] The parties and unions were hardly the mass organizations that many outsiders thought them to be. Even the famous *milicianos*, the volunteer forces that helped to save the Republic when the military rebellion exploded, often had a shaky commitment to the cause.

The second chapter, "Opportunism," will chronicle engagement in the period following the successful defense of Madrid in November 1936 to the fall of the north in the autumn of 1937. Workers engaged in subversive individualism, and authorities were forced to adopt repressive means to curb resistance to work. The governmental crisis of May 1937 ended the hopes of the most idealistic and radical anarchists. At the same time political disagreements offered respite for the noncommitted who wanted to avoid fighting and working. In Barcelona, wage earners took advantage of the political confusion to avoid the workplace. Peasants and prostitutes defied the moral and legal order of the Republican collectivity by continuing their entrepreneurial activities. Soldiers tried to avoid the line of fire and sometimes deserted. Troops often failed the test of war, which demands the highest degree of collective commitment. The Republican army had to put more and more emphasis on political indoctrination, discipline, and punishment. The repressive powers of the state dramatically expanded.

The fall of the north to the Nationalists at the end of 1937 aggravated the military and economic problems of the Republic and turned opportunism into cynicism, the subject of the third chapter. Cynicism dominated the Republican zone during 1938. Whereas opportunists were willing to work with the militant authorities, cynics acted exclusively in their own self-interest and paid the barest allegiance to higher causes. Levels of absenteeism, sabotage, and lateness persisted at the same levels or even increased in late 1937 and at the beginning of 1938. The political splits within the Republican camp were certainly not the cause of demoralization and opportunism, but they did contribute to the rise of cynicism. The rank and file did not concern itself unduly with struggles between and within the parties of the Popular Front, but the lack of unity among the left—in sharp contrast to the centralization of authority in the Nationalist zone—could only intensify an already present egotism and incipient defeatism. In the countryside, illegal black marketeering increased. In the Republican army, desertions augmented.

With continuing Republican defeats and the rise of hunger in Madrid and Barcelona, cynicism gave way to a struggle for individual survival. The fourth chapter, "Survival," will explore the final stage of the civil war and revolution. The failure of the Republican army at the Battle of Ebro in July and August 1938 turned skepticism into defeatism. Desertions became the most serious problem of the Popular Army. Most deserters did not wish to defect to the Nationalists but instead to return home. Family and personal needs prevailed over the risks and hardships of the *Ejército Popular.* The authorities responded by shooting soldiers not just for desertion but also for defeatist talk. In this context of struggle and indifference, Republican guerrilla activity—which was never a major problem for the Nationalists—nearly disappeared. In the cities, workers' productivity dropped precipitously as many abandoned the workplace to engage in personal projects, such as the Voltairean practice of cultivating one's own garden. The situation in Barcelona was so disastrous that the minister of defense wrote directly to his prime minister complaining that "workers had little desire to work." Theft and pilfering—the poaching of the proletariat—which, like the peasantry, thought it had a natural right to possess its immediate surroundings—characterized the final stage of the conflict. Subsistence farming and hoarding intensified in the countryside. "Red money," as Republican currency was colloquially known, depreciated drastically. Except for the family and most intimate friends, social cohesion disintegrated. A Hobbesian war, softened only by family solidarities, accompanied the lost civil war and a dying revolution.

The conclusion will evaluate how a social history of the Spanish civil war in the Republican zone alters the perception of both the war itself and twentieth-century Spanish history. The acquisitive, consumerist, and entrepreneurial impulses that many individuals exhibited during the conflict form the foundation for the present-day consumer society. An examination of individualisms can contribute not just to an understanding of the failure of the collectivist projects of Spanish anarchists and Communists during the civil war and revolution but also to the demise of the collectivist utopias of Falangists and fascists. This approach may encourage historians of twentieth-century civil wars and revolutions to go beyond a study of organizations and explore the desires of the large majority that identified only marginally with militant collectivities. The social historical critique of the "Great Man" theory of history is largely justified. "Great Men" and for that matter "Great Women" are merely notable militants of the nation, state, class, or gender. Returning to the personal can break new ground and, at the same time, show the limitations of the recent emphasis on race, class, and gender.

# 1

# Militancy

In order to understand the long-term causes of the civil war and revolution, it is helpful to return briefly to Spain's distant past. Spain did not follow the same pattern of development as northwestern Europe. The long Reconquest from the eighth to the fifteenth centuries helped to ensure the domination of a numerically large aristocracy linked to a church that maintained for hundreds of years a crusading mentality characteristic of the early middle ages. It was therefore hardly surprising that Spanish monarchs became the policemen of Rome and its Counter-Reformation. Militant intolerance was one of the foundations of modern Spain. The expulsion of the Moors and, perhaps even more importantly, the Jews were good lessons (if never learned) on how to destroy a potential middle class.

The Spanish monarchy compounded problems. Unlike other western European monarchs, the Spanish kings did not form an alliance with the middle classes but rather with the nobility. The suppression of the Castilian *Cortes* (parliament) after the revolt of the *comuneros* in the early sixteenth century and the discouragement of a nascent Castilian textile industry hampered the rise of a bourgeoisie in the center of the peninsula. The great movements of early modern history—the Reformation and absolutism—were aborted or adopted in less vigorous form than in other western European nations. In contrast to its British and French imperial rivals, Spain lacked the same kind of modernizing state that encouraged dynamic urban and rural sectors.

14

The eighteenth century accentuated the differences between Spain and the rest of western Europe. In the Iberian Peninsula, the Enlightenment was largely unoriginal and derivative. Its Spanish advocates were less influential than in the other major Catholic nations of the west, France, and Italy. The Enlightenment agenda of rationalism, productivism, rationalism, and meritocracy was harder to implement in Iberia. The rejection of the Enlightenment's antinoble and anticlerical agenda was most spectacular during the Napoleonic period when large numbers of Spaniards fought a bloody guerrilla war against the French invaders and their revolutionary principles. The *afrancesados*, partisans of Enlightened Despotism, were identified with the foreign enemy and forced to flee. Their defeat dealt a severe blow to Spanish economic development and liberalism. Given the large degree of illiteracy and the relatively stagnant economy, native liberalism remained weak. The First Carlist War (1833–40) showed the strength of traditionalism in the peninsula (Payne 1993:5). This war of attrition between a hesitant progressivism and bold reaction led to the death of 1 percent of the total population.

The sale of most church and common lands in the nineteenth century did not lead to an impressive increase of agricultural productivity. Demands propelled by the growing Spanish population and international markets were met by using traditional methods to extend the area of cultivated land.[1] Even though Spanish elites continued to invest in real estate, not industry, they made few improvements in agricultural productivity. The nobility usually failed to become improving landlords. Nationwide, Spanish agriculture between 1700 and 1900 was able to feed a population that nearly doubled, but this was accomplished largely by using existing technology to increase land under plow. The large sale of ecclesiastical and common property in the nineteenth century did not create an independent peasantry, as had occurred in France. It also failed to stimulate a rural outmigration, which enclosures had done in England.

On the eve of the civil war, labor productivity was only 58 percent of that achieved in many central and northern European countries. The subdivision of property in northern Spain, which was characterized by scattered holdings throughout a village, increased travel time and discouraged purchases of machinery, and the use of artificial fertilizers was limited. The abundance of cheap labor contributed to the slow pace of mechanization. Spain imported technology, but the lack of skilled mechanics and spare parts restricted its diffusion. Thus, the delay of mechanization was due not only to agrarian backwardness but also to a weak industrial infrastructure. Given the limited urban and industrial opportunities in the country, labor was understandably reluctant to leave the peninsula.

Even after the era of the Atlantic revolutions, traditionalist Spanish landlords, backed by the army and the clergy, maintained their economic and social dominance over large areas of the peninsula. In certain regions, such as Andalusia and Estremadura, landlessness was aggravated by the near monopoly of large landowners and rapid demographic growth (Maurice 1975:10). Unlike its northern European neighbors, Spain had a great mass of peasants thirsting for land even into the twentieth century. At that time, a free market in grain had yet to be created. High tariffs protected Spanish farmers from international competition, but protection had a number of adverse effects. First, tariffs generated more profits for large farmers than small ones. Modest farmers, who needed help and assistance, received little of it from a state that favored big growers. The latter preferred high tariffs to other reforms, such as an income tax or the establishment of cooperatives. Second, protective barriers reduced purchasing power that urban residents could devote to high-protein foods and manufactured goods. Wage earners bought cereal products, not dairy products or meat, thereby discouraging increased animal husbandry, which would have improved agricultural productivity. The relatively weak growth of urban centers further reduced the demand for specialized farm products. Incomplete roads and inadequate canals obstructed the distribution of milk and meat to cities and towns. Both before and after the civil war, Spanish consumers paid among the highest prices and had the worst diets in Europe.

Backward industry and lethargic agriculture contributed to the longevity of old-regime social and cultural structures. Throughout the nineteenth and twentieth centuries, the church maintained a near monopoly over many educational and welfare bureaucracies. The separation of church and state on the French or U.S. model was never fully accomplished. During the nineteenth and the first half of the twentieth century, tolerant Christian democracy remained a minor current among Catholics. The sale of church lands and the loss of its landed wealth made clerical institutions more dependent upon the rich than previously. Anticlerical attitudes proliferated in response. Just as separation of church and state proved tenuous, so did the subordination of military to civilian rule. During the late modern period, Spanish progressives frequently proved unable to limit military power. *Pronunciamientos,* that is, direct military intervention in politics, punctured the nineteenth and early twentieth centuries and encouraged confrontations between revolutionary and counterrevolutionary forces.

Except possibly in Basque Country and Catalonia, no class of energetic industrialists ever emerged. The more advanced economic development in these regions encouraged peripheral nationalisms and regionalist movements. National unity, which had originally been based upon a shared or imposed Catholic faith, was never fully consolidated, and in the wealthiest areas of the peninsula, regionalism grew during the Restoration monarchy (1874–1931). Yet demands that insisted the national government provide both economic and physical protection circumscribed both Basque and Catalan nationalisms. Even in these purportedly dynamic areas of the peninsula, until the middle or end of the twentieth century, industrial survival depended upon defense against foreign competition as well as protection from radical workers' movements. The inability of Spain's most dynamic regions to compete in world markets hindered the possibility of export-led growth. Iberia's previous history of intolerance and persecution haunted Spanish development. Catholic Spain had a difficult time opening its elites to the talented, such as Protestants and Jews, who were often in the avant-garde of economic and cultural development in other European nations. Some of Spain's most dynamic individuals emigrated from this land of reduced opportunity.

The Second Spanish Republic (1931–39) modeled itself on the ideals of the French Revolution and the French Third Republic. Simultaneously, it intended to go beyond liberty and fraternity and introduce some sort of social equality. Yet it faced special problems in trying to achieve its project in backward Spain: "On the basis of civic culture, literacy rates, and economic development ... by 1930 Spain was at the level of England in the 1850s and 1860s or France in the 1870s and 1880s. Neither mid-nineteenth-century England nor even France at the beginning of the Third Republic had to face such severe political tests as Spain underwent in the 1930s" (Payne 1993:34). The Third French Republic (1870–1940) had begun after significant spurts of industrialization and modernization during the Orleanist monarchy (1830–48) and the Second Empire (1852–70). It had also proved capable of maintaining bourgeois order by crushing ruthlessly the last major working-class revolt, the Paris Commune of 1871. Furthermore, the Third Republic took decades to secure itself politically. Only in 1905 was the church separated from the state and the military subordinated to civilian control. The Second Spanish Republic inherited even graver social and political problems and tried to solve them more quickly than its French counterpart. It faced unresolved agrarian issues that placed Spain in the ranks of underdeveloped nations. At the same time, the Iberian nation had a much stronger and better organized working-class movement that, unlike the French Third Republic, it could not or would not smash militarily. Further troubling its existence, the Spanish Republic was fighting during the 1930s against the authoritarian/fascist tide that had overwhelmed countries at similar levels of economic and social development in eastern and southern Europe.

The Second Republic heralded an age of mass politics and of higher expectations but was unable to generate the economic growth to satisfy them. The first years of its existence were characterized by a coalition of the enlightened urban middle classes—grouped in various Republican parties—with the working classes of the Socialist party and its trade unions. This alliance attempted to imitate the progressive Western model of nonrevolutionary change. However, its program of moderate but significant land reform, reduction of military spending, and anticlericalism alienated the still powerful forces of the

church, landowners, and many military officers. In fact, anticlerical sentiments
in the governing coalition were influential enough that authorities first refused
to intervene when mobs began burning churches in Madrid. The inability of
local police to engage in competent crowd control spurred the government to
create an urban and more modern national police force, the Assault Guards
(Payne 1993:46). They were eventually to number thirty thousand, approximately the same size as the Civil Guard, the traditional rural police force.

As the Republic failed to resolve the profound problems that it had inherited, the right gathered strength. In 1931 the dominance of antirepublican
components of the clerical right was uncertain, and some Catholics were willing to give the new regime a chance. However, the strength of reactionary
Catholicism grew as the Republic offered religious freedom to non-Catholics
and instituted other measures—such as divorce, civil marriage, secular education, and dissolution of the Society of Jesus—which ended the confessional
state (see Vincent 1996). The elimination of Catholic education was particularly galling to the faithful.[2] These fairly conventional steps separating church
from state were needlessly complemented by gratuitous attacks on religious
practices that alienated Catholics who were potential supporters of the Republic. New legislation that secularized burials and banned Holy Week processions
offended many believers.

The attempt to reduce the power of the military was nearly as infelicitous
as the efforts to decrease the influence of the Church. Manuel Azaña, prime
minister of the Republican-Socialist government, was highly influenced by the
post-Dreyfus French model of civilian control of the military and tried to adapt
it to Spanish conditions (Payne 1993:91).[3] Yet it was much more difficult to
impose civilian dominance on a nation whose elites had frequently depended
on direct military control of the state to ensure order and protection of property. As the Dreyfus Affair was being resolved in France, in 1906 Spanish civil
authorities gave the army the power to court-martial its critics (Alpert
1984:203). Azaña's reforms (1931–32) removed what he considered to be the
anachronistic judicial functions of the army and drastically reduced the size
of the bloated and caste-bound armed services. Despite the needed downsiz-
ing and the generosity of retirement benefits, the reforms estranged a large
number of traditionalist officers. The unpopularity of the reforms certainly
encouraged a *pronunciamiento* against the Republic. Known as the *sanjurjada*,
after one of the coup's prime movers, General José Sanjurjo, it failed to rally
sufficient military or civilian backing, and Civil Guards and Assault Guards
easily crushed it in August 1932. The Republic showed itself strong enough
to overcome the plotting of its enemies. The shattering of the *pronunciamiento*
lent the regime new prestige, and the *Cortes* proceeded to approve a Catalan
autonomy statute in September 1932. The measure granted considerable powers to the Catalan regional government, the *Generalitat,* but allowed the Spanish

state to maintain control over the armed forces, foreign policy, and tariffs. The attempt by Basques to gain their own autonomy was less successful.

Between 1931 and 1932 the Socialist labor minister, Francisco Largo Caballero, introduced wide-ranging labor legislation. The least controversial were bills that expanded accident, maternity, and retirement insurance to hundreds of thousands, if not millions, of previously uncovered workers. An array of other measures—which regulated disputes, promoted trade unions (especially Largo's own, the UGT, or Unión General de Trabajadores), limited working hours, and restricted labor mobility with the aim of reducing unemployment—aroused more opposition. Public works projects, especially a massive hydraulics program, were undertaken, but the jobs created were never enough to offset the growing unemployment of the 1930s. The solution of the Spanish governments of the late 1950s and 1960s—to export people and import foreign capital to modernize the economy—was, of course, unavailable during the Great Depression. Although the Spanish revolution and civil war were not direct results of a classic scissors crisis, they were—at least to some degree—products of the worldwide economic downturn.

Perhaps the most difficult problem that the Second Republic had to confront was that of land reform in an agriculturally dominated society. Especially in the south, landless laborers—who were often anticlerical and hostile to their bosses—worked the lands of *latifundia*. In the north, although an important number of relatively prosperous (and often Catholic) peasants farmed their own fields, uneconomical dwarf plots dominated. The overwhelming majority of farms—possibly 42 million out of a national total of 54 million—possessed less than an acre, even if some families held more than one dwarf plot (figures from 1959, cited in Payne 1993:114). Tiny farms of under twenty acres amounted to 99.1 percent of all holdings. More than fifty thousand larger holdings of over two hundred acres and more than one thousand latifundia occupied 35 percent of all cultivated land. Inefficient and absentee ownership on large estates compounded this problem of unequal distribution of land. Until the second third of the twentieth century, the backwardness of Spanish industry stubbornly restricted the opportunities of the underemployed and landless of the south to finding work in cities. This essentially captive labor force gave larger owners little incentive to mechanize production.

Spain was unfortunate compared to many other countries that have engaged in land redistribution:

Spain lacked all of the advantages that have facilitated land reform in other nations. In contrast to the new continents of North and South America, neither the state nor the municipalities possessed arable land that might be delivered to the peasantry by executive fiat and without expropriation. In contrast to Greece in the 1920s or to revolutionary France, so little land belonged to the Church that the alternative route whereby the expropriation of individual property might have been avoided was also closed. In contrast to Rumania in 1918 and Algeria in 1963, no important quantities of land belonged to foreigners, so that none of the repercussions that would follow expropriation of personal property could safely be diverted outside the political framework of the nation. Nor did enough land in Spain belong to the nobility for significant agrarian reform to be possible on the basis of an anti-aristocratic crusade alone. If land were to be distributed to the peasantry, there was only one group from which it could be taken: the bourgeois owners who in most essentials were fully integrated into the political structure of the nation and could not be expropriated except at the cost of attacking some of the basic principles of that structure. (Malefakis 1970:91)

The failed *sanjurjada* propelled passage of a moderate land reform program, but the reform ultimately proved underfinanced and inadequate. After two years, only 12,260 families had been resettled, "so minuscule a number as scarcely even to constitute a beginning" (Payne 1993:120). In retrospect, it is evident that the reforms of the first two years of the Republic alienated as many as they pleased. The progressive legislation aroused as much distrust and alienation among property owners, military officers, and Catholics as devotion and gratitude among wage earners and enlightened bourgeois. In other words, if the Republic's reforms created a social base of support that would be committed to its defense, they also provoked a counterforce that became dedicated to its destruction. The Republic's labor legislation distressed some small holders by raising wages of their workers and restricting labor mobility. Small holders who leased land to sharecroppers or rented it out in tiny parcels found that their tenants delayed payments or took liberties with landlord property (Rosique Navarro 1988:241). Angry small farmers, fearful large landowners, and devout Catholics formed the electorate of the clerical and the well-financed CEDA (Confederación Española de Derechas Autónomas) formed in 1933. It had the distinction of being the first mass Catholic political party in Spanish history. Controversy over the "fascist" nature of the CEDA was common during the Second Republic and persists today among historians of contemporary Spain. The CEDA was certainly not a Christian democratic party, such as the *Populari* in Italy. Nor was it, despite the style of its youth wing, a fascist movement. Its links to the church and the old elites were too strong. The radical right in Spain had a small popular base, and it lacked the masses of war veterans, students with dim career prospects, and ruined petty bourgeois so prominent in postwar Germany and Italy (Linz 1978:56). Only a small number of fanatical advocates of *hispanidad* convinced themselves that Spanish imperialism had a glorious future. Thus, the influence of Spanish fascism was very reduced prior to the outbreak of the civil war. Fascism as a mass movement was the creation of a *pronunciamiento*. In Spain, the counterrevolution dominated fascism, not vice versa.

On the radical left, the anarchosyndicalists of the CNT (Confederación Nacional de Trabajo) gave no respite to the new regime and provoked periodic revolts. In January 1932 the FAI (Federación Anarquista Ibérica), which largely controlled the CNT at this time, prepared to incite a social revolution and proclaimed libertarian communism in the Catalan mining district of the Alto Llobregat and Cardoner. In Sallent (Barcelona), syndicalists seized the powder kegs and dynamite of the potash factory and raised the red flag on the town hall (see Seidman 1991:61). The governor of the province called in police who easily put down the rebellion. A year later another wave of libertarian revolts erupted throughout the country. In Barcelona on 8 January, CNT bands attacked military barracks; in several Catalan villages and towns libertarian communism was proclaimed. Money, private property, and "exploitation" were abolished—until government troops arrived to suppress the revolt. Whereas in Catalonia and in northern Spain, the Republic's Assault Guards and Civil Guards acted with some restraint; in the south they brutally repressed the leftist rebels. When an anarchist-inspired rebellion broke out in Casas Viejas (Cadiz) in January 1933, Assault Guards ruthlessly killed twenty-two townspeople, twelve in cold blood. Although the Socialists stood by the government, the massacre undermined the Socialist-Republican coalition (Preston 1984:172). The scandal of Casas Viejas, the repression of the revolutionary left, and disappointment with land reform alienated radical workers and peasants. Prior to the 1933 elections the CNT enthusiastically propagated its antipolitical ideology and advocated abstention (see Vilanova 1995:18).

During the elections of November 1933, the divisions among the left prevented the Socialists from forming an alliance with the leftist Republicans. The right, especially the CEDA, profited from middle-class and Catholic fears about the collectivist and anticlerical direction of the new Republic. The misnamed Radicals—actually a centrist grouping—emerged with 104 deputies; the CEDA with 115 (Payne 1993:179). The Socialist total dropped to 60 deputies because of the split with the leftist Republicans, but the former retained their percentage of the popular vote. Alejandro Lerroux of the Radical Party formed his government in December 1933. By October 1934, the Radicals concluded that they could govern only with the support of the CEDA. Many on the left feared that the right-wing Catholic party would acquiesce in a "fascist" coup d'état in Spain. Even the moderate—and Catholic—president of the Republic, Niceto Alcalá Zamora, doubted that the CEDA leader, Gil Robles, would be loyal to the Republic and was reluctant to call him to arrange a government. Nevertheless, on 4 October Alcalá Zamora permitted the creation of a cabinet that included three ministers from the CEDA. The following day in Asturias, militant coal miners, who had been increasingly politicized by what they viewed as the failure of the "social" Republic and radicalized by deteriorating working conditions, began the famous Asturias insurrection, the prelude to the civil war that was to erupt two years later. Twenty to thirty thousand Asturian miners rebelled against what they perceived to be the "fascist" orientation of the new right-wing government in Madrid (Jackson 1965:154–58). In several weeks of intense action, General Francisco Franco and his African troops, under the field command of General López Ochoa, brutally suppressed them. Like many Third World armies today, the Spanish military proved more effective against the internal enemy than foreign foes. The United States had defeated Spain's armed forces in 1898, and the Moroccan insurgents nearly did so in 1921. The Spanish state had not sufficiently developed specialized police forces, such as the French *gendarmerie mobile,* which could control crowds without massive injuries and deaths (see Bruneteaux 1996). One of the lessons that many leftist militants drew from the Asturias repression was the necessity to eliminate the officer corps (and their civilian and clerical supporters) before it could exterminate them.

In Catalonia, at the same time as the Asturias revolt, Lluís Companys, the leader of the Catalan nationalists grouped in the Esquerra, declared the "Catalan state within the Federal Spanish Republic." This attempt at Catalan independence failed miserably, and it clearly demonstrated the limits of Catalan nationalism, whose social base was too narrow to form an independent nation. The Catalan bourgeoisie had long made its peace with Madrid and the traditionalist elements of central and southern Spain. It lacked the strength to overcome their influence and the dynamism to dominate the entire nation economically and politically. Thus, radical Catalan nationalism could not count on the support of a significant part of the large bourgeoisie that depended on Madrid for protection and favors. Without the backing of the upper class and much of the organized working class, radical Catalan nationalism in the 1930s was the province of what is called the petty bourgeoisie—technicians, shopkeepers, *funcionarios,* clerks, artisans, and sharecroppers. Their nationalism was cultural as well as political and involved a renaissance of Catalan as a spoken and written language. The economic possibilities of a nationalism that called for a separate Catalan state were severely restricted because the feeble Catalan industries depended upon tariffs granted by Madrid and on the impoverished markets in the rest of the peninsula. Catalan nationalism might mean a desirable political and cultural independence from a bureaucratic and overly centralized Spanish state, but many Catalans of varying social origins realized that, given the condition of regional industries, a separate nation might well lead to their economic destruction.

The failed insurrections in Catalonia and Asturias generated elements of severe repression of the left by the right-wing government. Various estimates placed the number of political prisoners in Spanish jails between twenty and thirty thousand individuals. Throughout 1935 the left correctly feared a continued government crackdown. In southern rural areas, numerous workers were fired, wages lowered, and working conditions changed arbitrarily (Payne 1993:237; for an example, see Maddox 1993:151). CEDA leader José María

Gil Robles, minister of war from May to December 1935, appointed extreme rightists to very sensitive and key positions in the military. More symbolically, on 14 April 1935, the rightist government decided to celebrate the fourth anniversary of the founding of the Second Republic with a public ceremony, which awarded medals to the military officers who had defeated the October revolutions in Catalonia and Asturias. The government's intention was to cre-ate—as the French had done after the Paris Commune of 1871—a republic of order that could protect private property and the church. The effort was, of course, ultimately unsuccessful. Furthermore, the ruling coalition was weak-ened by scandals that discredited the Radical Party.

The left drew together to end the right's repression. In January 1936 the Socialists, Republicans, POUM (Partido Obrero de Unificación Marxista), UGT, Catalan nationalists, and Communists formed the electoral coalition known as the Popular Front. Its program was extremely moderate since the representatives of the Republican parties made it clear that they rejected the three most significant proposals of the Socialists—nationalization and redis-tribution of land, nationalization of banks, and a vaguely defined "workers' control" (Tusell Gómez 1971:352–58; Juliá 1979:216–33). Although some conservatives were favorably impressed by the restraint of the Popular Front's program, the failure of the left to agree on some of the most important social and economic issues anticipated the ruptures that would occur during the civil war and revolution.

Although the CNT was not formally a partner in the Popular Front, it had its own reasons to dread continuation of the *bienio negro,* or the government of the right. Many of its militants had been jailed, and some were facing the death penalty, which the right had restored in 1934. In April of that year in Zaragoza, the Confederation had embarked on a two-month general strike, one goal of which was the liberation of jailed militants. The Popular Front promised amnesty for prisoners; in return, the CNT toned down its campaign for absten-tion, which affected only its most devoted militants (Vilanova 1995:22). Although some unions and leaders reiterated the official position against polit-ical participation, others—such as the influential Construction Union—deviated from the classic anarchist position. This policy of the "negation of the nega-tion," gave the green light to the rank and file to vote for the Popular Front (Brademas 1974:163). Even the famous *faísta* Buenaventura Durruti openly advocated that CNT members go to the polls (Lorenzo 1972:72).

As might be expected, the electoral campaign polarized voters. The right was divided, and its more moderate components, including a few Christian democrats, enfeebled. In February 1936 the Popular Front won an important victory. Nationwide, it captured 47 to 51.9 percent of the votes, compared to 43 to 45.6 percent for the right. The right did well in Catholic strongholds of the north and north center; the left in impoverished agrarian regions of the south and the southwest. The abstention rate of 28 percent—in comparison with 32.6 in 1933—indicated persistent apathy and only a marginal depoliticization (Payne 1993:274). The fascist Falange won merely 46,466 votes, conceivably the lowest voting percentage of a fascist party in all of Europe. The left's victory heightened rightist fears that the Popular Front would violently secure the separation of church from state, reduce the power of the military, encourage regional nationalisms, and promote land reform. In addition, the weight of the radical left in the Socialist Party and the influence of the CNT raised the specter that it would not be the moderate republicans, such as Manuel Azaña or Martínez Barrio who would secure features of the unfinished bourgeois-liberal revolution but rather, as in Russia in 1917, working-class revolutionaries who had no respect for private property.

Reports of the victory of the Popular Front in the elections of February 1936 led to riots, church burnings, and prison revolts. Public order became a major problem for the left Republican-Socialist government. Its leader, Manuel Azaña, was hesitant to use the army to jail or to shoot protesters and rioters, many of whom supported the government. On the other hand, Azaña was also reluctant to disarm the military since it might be needed to stop insurrections organized by the extreme left. The level of political violence remained acute from the electoral victory of the Popular Front in February to mid-March (Payne 1993:284; Romero 1982:56–58).[4] The Republic became symbolic of unrest and disorder to many Spaniards. Parents commonly labeled squabbling among children "a republic." A supporter of the new regime admitted, "it was idiotic to argue that Spain was a paradise. . . . Hundreds of churches were burned, hundreds were killed, many more injured, innumerable strikes. . . . Rational people knew that we were living on a volcano" (Martín-Blázquez 1938:70). The poorest sectors of the population, who had probably suffered the most from the depression, exerted strong pressures for change. Tenant farmers knew that the Popular Front government would be reluctant to move against them. Consequentially, tens of thousands of small holders and farm workers throughout Spain, but especially in the center and the south, illegally occupied land. More formally and lawfully after February, the Institute of Agrarian Reform redistributed hundreds of thousands of acres to tens of thousands of peasants. In late March in the province of Badajoz, more than sixty thousand peasants, under the direction of the FNTT (Federación Nacional de los Trabajadores de la Tierra), took over three thousand farms (Vila Izquierdo 1984:18; Rosique Navarro 1988:226). Shouting "Viva la República," they set to work on their new land.

Of course, many on the right could not share this enthusiasm. For conservatives, and even for some small and medium landowners, the Popular Front endangered private property. Strikes of Andalusian peasants and day laborers increased sharply in the spring of 1936 (Maurice 1975:65). In many cases, rural wages doubled (Payne 1993:302). At the same time, urban wage earners demanded rehiring of and back pay for wage earners sanctioned and fired during the *bienio negro*. In Barcelona, "endemic" strikes erupted for less work and more pay. Domestic and foreign capitalists reacted negatively. The Catalan capitalist elite repeated its hoary, but partly credible, warning that "the reigning anarchy" might destroy its firms. For example, in early July, the director of General Motors in Spain advised the Sindicato de Obreros Metalúrgicos that it was considering shutting down its Barcelona assembly factory because, in large part, of increased labor costs.[5] "Continual workers' demands for salary increases" made the company ponder laying off its four hundred employees. To make matters worse, "workers are not working with the same efficiency they once had. We need more cooperation from them." In provincial towns, such as Granada, attacks on shops, factories, and even the tennis club frightened both big and small bourgeois who rushed to join the Falange (Gibson 1973:27–33). In rural areas, Andalusian proletarians' wishes to expropriate the land in the spring of 1936 provoked and alarmed both large and small property owners (Garrido González 1979:25–29). In addition to threats to property, the right feared persecution by the increasingly politicized police forces of the Republic. State-sponsored police actions would culminate in the assassination of an extreme-right leader, José Calvo Sotelo. "Never before in the history of parliamentary regimes had a leader of the parliamentary opposition been murdered by a detachment of state police" (Payne 1993:357). Political and social violence in Spain was probably more severe than in other European countries—Italy, Austria, and even Germany—which experienced the breakdown of democracy in the interwar period. The extent of bloodshed reflected the underdeveloped and polarized nature of Spanish society and the inability of its weak state to control either supporters or opponents. The absence of what they considered to be a neutral and efficient state encouraged important sectors of the right to rebel.

The demands and disorders following the victory of the Popular Front promoted plotting against the Republic by a broad coalition of anti-Republican forces. Among them were Spanish fascists or Falangists; ultraconservative monarchists known as Carlists; and more "liberal" advocates of Alfonso XIII, the Alphonsines. They were joined by members of the armed forces determined to smash the Popular Front, which they associated with the "anti-Spain" of Marxism, Freemasonry, Catalan and Basque separatisms, and even Judaism. Many of these rebellious officers were *africanistas,* who had often experienced fierce combat in North African colonial wars. The insurgents' individual reputations for valor, courage, and efficiency—Mola, Millán Astray, Quiepo de Llano, Sanjurjo, Varela, Orgaz, and of course Franco himself—provided a model and a mystique for their troops that their Republican enemies completely lacked. The *africanistas*—Mola, Franco, Queipo de Llano—who led the rebellion intended to conquer the peninsula as they had domesticated Morocco and, more recently, Asturias. Their anti-Republican coalition would call itself Nationalist. Whatever the accuracy of the label, it became a powerful symbolic weapon in the hands of the right.[6] The appellation of "nationalism" may have been more mobilizing than that of "Republic." The latter was a much more ephemeral entity than the "Spain" to which the Nationalists referred when they shouted their slogan "Viva España." In contrast to the French Revolution, the left or the "progressive" forces during the Spanish civil war could not claim undisputed ownership of nationalism.

They contested the insurgent attempt to monopolize nationalism by commonly labeling their adversaries "fascist," thereby linking them to Germany and Italy. Other hostile, but possibly more accurate terms for the Nationalists were "insurgents" and "rebels." These labels stressed that the Nationalists had rebelled against the legally constituted democratic Republic. Those who sided with the insurgent officers called their adversaries "reds" or, more formally and less frequently, "Marxists." The Republic was ambivalent about its own revolution and usually did not employ the term in its sloganeering. Unlike the Bolsheviks, it never adopted the red flag. Most of those who supported the Republic preferred to be known simply as Republicans. Some favored "Loyalist" since they were loyal to the legally established Spanish state that the military rebellion was trying to destroy. Generally, I shall adhere to each side's terminological preferences for itself. In other words, "Nationalist" and "Republican" will appear frequently in the following pages. "Loyalist," "insurgents," and "rebels" will be used more sparingly. "Fascist" and "red" will remain between quotation marks.

The claims of rebellious military officers of the "movement" to represent the "real Spain" cannot, of course, be taken at face value. Nor should, contrary to much of the literature, the assertions of militants of the left that they were the "people" or the "masses."[7] The "people" are hardly ever a monolithic mass, and it is precisely the relation between the militants and the masses that needs to be explored, not assumed (see Underdown 1985:vii). It was the militants, not the "people," who were willing to sacrifice their lives to stop the 19 July military rebellion against the legally constituted Republic. In other words, although the extent of "popular resistance" was a new factor in the history of Spanish *pronunciamientos,* it should not be overestimated. Mass apathy and inattention did not disappear and, as before, remained a major factor throughout the conflict (cf. Vilar 1986:42). After all, even during the period of "mass mobilization" of the Second Republic, abstentions during national elections never dropped much below 30 percent, and many of those who voted had, at best, a marginal commitment to the party of their choice.

Ideological indifference had a long history in Spain. Prior to the Second Republic, the politics of favors had helped the Restoration to persist (Carr

1982:370). *Caciques* had endured because they could deliver at least some of the government's goodies or, conversely, were able to prevent the national state from harmful meddling in local lives. Large numbers of people—probably a majority—came to regard the civil war as an episode of unwelcome public interference in their personal existence. Like other civil wars—such as the English or, to some extent, the United States—the Spanish civil war originated as a split between two factions of the ruling classes, not as a conflict between traditional Spain and the progressive people.[8] The low reservoirs of popular commitment were quickly drained, a common problem faced by all sides in what may be called civil wars of attrition. Material incentives—which could take the form of rapine and looting—were much more potent than ideological ones. In fact, ideology often provided an excuse for plunder.

Without the militants of the left the military coup would have remained another of the *pronunciamientos* that punctured Spanish history in the nineteenth and early twentieth century. Weeks before the military uprising, General Mola—the principal organizer of the coup—worried about the high morale and "considerable offensive force" of "the proletarian masses" (quoted in Martínez Bande 1980:251). Mola would remain skeptical of the fighting ability of those conscripted and was eager to rely upon elite forces—(Carlist) *requetés,* Falangists, and, of course, professional soldiers (Fraser 1986:71). On the left, militants came from major working-class organizations. The Spanish Socialist Party (PSOE or Partido Socialista Obrero Español) was founded in the late nineteenth century. Its growth throughout the first third of the twentieth century made it a powerful force. Nineteenth-century socialists usually were committed to the temperate politics of the parliamentary road to socialism, but by the beginning of the twentieth century, especially in 1917, many began considering a more revolutionary path. The party's union affiliates, the UGT and the FNTT would also experience divisions between more moderate and radical wings. The split between reformists and more (at least rhetorically) revolutionary elements would persist throughout the Second Republic. The factions of both the PSOE and the UGT would supply large numbers of activists who were willing to risk their lives to defeat the military and rightist uprising of July 1936.

The Spanish anarchist or libertarian movement was unique in Europe for its size and strength. Libertarians believed that popular spontaneity, guided by properly conscious anarchist militants, could lead to a successful social and even cultural revolution.[9] The anarchist movement maintained two major organizations. The FAI was the vanguard group which attempted to conserve libertarian ideological purity. *Faístas* were the Leninists of anarchism and included its most famous leaders, such as the legendary Buenaventura Durruti. In its quest for revolutionary purity, the FAI exhibited a tendency toward centralism. Like the Bolsheviks, the FAI sought to keep alive revolutionary ideals by fighting against "trade-union consciousness" among the working class. One leading current within the FAI could be labeled "anarchobolshevik" (Lorenzo 1972:50). A prominent anarchobolshevik, Juan García Oliver, argued for the "conquest of power" or a kind of anarchist dictatorship. The major goal of the FAI was to make sure that the CNT stayed on a revolutionary path.

The CNT was born in Barcelona in 1910, and its birth was an indication that many anarchists continued to reject political parties but had temporarily put aside terrorist tactics to accept the union as the basis for the libertarian revolution. At its origin and throughout most of its history, the CNT had a very loose and antibureaucratic structure (Bookchin 1978:160; Lorenzo 1972:37; Gómez Casas 1973:94; and Bar Cendón 1975:222). The individual unions maintained a great deal of autonomy, since the anarchosyndicalist CNT had a horror of overcentralization. The main weapon of the CNT was to be the insurrectional general strike, the day when workers would put down their tools and take control of the means of production from a government and bourgeoisie in disarray. It supplemented this goal with other forms of anarchosyndicalist direct action—sabotage, boycott, and a virulent antiparliamentarism. The Confederation was frequently declared illegal as the government reacted to strikes, terrorism, or other forms of direct action. After the First World War, persecution of the revolutionary CNT often contrasted with official tolerance of the reformist UGT. The Spanish government and, to a lesser extent, capitalist elites were willing to accept and sometimes even encourage the existence of a union that was linked to the Socialist party and that generally advocated parliamentarism and cooperation with the state and political parties. Despite persecution in the 1920s and 1930s, the CNT was a mass organization of nominally two million members on the eve of the civil war (Thomas 1961:6). In this major trade union federation, libertarian ideology often took a back seat to bread-and-butter demands (Getman Eraso 1999). Militants from both the CNT and the FAI played a dual role as street fighters and trade unionists.

The Spanish Communist Party (PCE) was much smaller than socialist or libertarian organizations. The CNT and the radical wings of the UGT and the PSOE had preempted and largely monopolized revolutionary fervor, leaving little room—at least until the outbreak of the civil war—for yet another ideological competitor. Nonetheless, the compact size of the PCE, its Leninist-Stalinist discipline, and—above all—the support of the Soviet Union and its international network would make it a key force during the civil war. The party would gain a reputation for dedication and efficiency and contribute an increasing number of activists to the cause. More narrowly Republican parties, which eschewed socialism or communism, were much less able to provide devoted activists. However, movements in Catalonia and Basque Country that desired regional and eventually national autonomy did furnish significant cadres to the Republic.

The moderates were nonetheless overwhelmed by the dominance of the revolutionaries that, ironically, the military rebellion had provoked. The "pre-emptive counterrevolution" helped to stimulate the violence and radical social changes that it intended to stop (Mayer 1971).[10] Activists of the Popular Front revived the revolution that the rebellious officers were trying to prevent. The militants who fought against the military rebels encouraged the violation of property rights and deepened the process of collectivization of farms and factories. Activists would become the shock troops who prevented the military rebellion from triumphing in half of Spain.

They did this by using various means. One particularly brutal method might be termed the poor man's coup d'état. Radical leftists developed the technique from their bloody experience of defeat in the Asturias rebellion. Militants of both sides felt that the enemy had to be quickly eliminated. Killers of all persuasions shared a common fanaticism. A mixture of social, political, and religious hatreds and fears spurred what the poet Rafael Alberti termed the "necessary assassination" (Casanova 1999:71). Left activists would come together in small groups or squads to murder in cold blood rebellious or even potentially rebellious military officers, bourgeois, wealthy rightwingers, priests, and "fascists." A squad might knock at the door, politely ask the victim to accompany them, and, when out of sight, shoot him. These *paseos,* as they were known, seemed to have developed as a spontaneous practice among activists in the areas controlled by the Republic. Although later in the war some officials did make efforts to stop *paseos,* during the first months of the conflict Republican governments tolerated or at least did not halt them. For example, about half of the clergymen killed were executed in the first six weeks of the war (de la Cueva 1998:357). Towns of a thousand inhabitants might see several dozen killed (Borkenau 1963:97). Potential victims tried to hide their identity by going underground or disguising themselves by wearing "proletarian" clothes.

Throughout Republican Spain, iconoclastic fervor persecuted the property and people of the church.[11] Priests suffered their greatest massacre since the French Revolution. Nearly 7,000 members of the Catholic clergy were killed, including 13 bishops, 4,172 diocesan priests and seminarists, 2,364 monks and friars, and 283 nuns (de la Cueva 1998:355). Local revolutionaries might spare the lives of the rich and rightwingers, but they were usually implacable with priests. Progressives had campaigned against "superstition," which they identified with the church. As in other major European civil wars—English, French, or Russian—religion both created and revealed the gap between revolutionaries and counterrevolutionaries.[12] Priests possessed the unfortunate qualities of being both hated and easily identified. Furthermore, "fascist" clergymen gained a reputation of resisting Republicans by firing on them from church towers. In the Barcelona diocese alone, 277 priests and 425 regular clergy were assassinated (Balcells 1974:40). Nationalist sympathizers reported brutal ceremonies that recalled the rough justice of the French Revolution. On 5 September 1936 in Murcia, a Republican firing squad executed a priest, the head of the provincial Falange, and an unidentified man.[13] Their bodies were handed over to a crowd of five thousand. Its members hacked off ears and notably testicles from the corpses. This "morbid fixation on genitalia . . . must be placed within the context of both a macho culture and the age-old anticlerical obsession with the clergy's sexuality" (de la Cueva 1998:356; also, Delgado 1993:151).[14] The priest's remains were hung at the door of his church. In many towns in the Republican zone, long-buried bodies of priests and nuns were exhumed and publicly ridiculed.[15] Members of the CEDA were killed as "fascists" (Morena Gómez 1986:152).

In Ronda (Málaga) a Nationalist surgeon reported that militiamen looted and burned the towns' churches.[16] On 10 August in Aracena (Huelva) miners from nearby Río Tinto joined local leftists to attack churches and religious images (Maddox 1993:153–68). Spanish revolutionaries followed in the footsteps of French anticlericals when they recommended stripping religious edifices of brass and other metals for use in war industries.[17] The church burnings offered a spectacle of purification and initiation, which united the left around a common anticlericalism. They regenerated revolutionary feeling at a time when insurgent forces were conquering Andalusia and on the verge of taking Aracena. The destruction of images represented symbolic defiance of the elite's spiritual and artistic values. "In the long run, what the anticlericals hoped to achieve was a *reparto* (redistribution) of meanings that would outlast the temporary and doomed redistribution of land and seizure of political power by the popular forces of the town and sierra" (Maddox 1993:165). Iconoclasm also asserted anticlerical male superiority over a religion that often attracted female devotees from the working class. Several days after the church burnings, Nationalist forces easily defeated the miners and local radicals. *Franquista* retaliation in Aracena proved much more vicious and lethal than the Popular Front's terror. Leftists took to the hills where they occasionally disturbed some Nationalist soldiers (Martínez Bande 1969:19).

Albuquerque (Badajoz) was a farming town of ten to twelve thousand inhabitants that had reacted against the domination of *latifundistas* by voting overwhelmingly for the Popular Front. As in other Popular Front municipalities, its militants seized arms and arrested suspected enemies of the Republic. Twenty-four landowners and twenty businessmen—who included merchants, barbers, and shoemakers—dominated the list of the seventy-two persons the "reds" arrested.[18] According to Falangists, the town's "scum" terrorized and lightly tortured, but did not kill, their prisoners. On 17 August, Nationalist forces entered the town and liberated those whom the "reds" had not yet freed. Ensuing massacres and persecutions by Nationalists were so massive that they created a labor shortage (Pons Prades 1977:313–17). As in Aracena, the surviving leftists took to the hills. Falangists asserted that before its "liberation" by Nationalists, "red" militiamen had destroyed with gunfire an image of the Virgin.[19] In Ronda (Málaga) and surrounding towns, 623 assassinations were counted.[20] A physician who was a Nationalist sympathizer identified bodies in a Ronda cemetery and confirmed that four were local priests and three were merchants.[21] Priests, businessmen, and the "cream of (Ronda high) society" seem to have been the most outstanding victims.[22] In Baena (Cordova) women played a prominent part in the killings of rightists (Fraser 1986:130).

Other localities of Republican Spain repeated attacks on the rich. Merchants in some towns might side with Republicans against the landed oligarchy, but most shopkeepers' Catholicism and desires to protect their property rendered them sympathetic to the Nationalists (Maddox 1993:132). Indeed, the dedication of the Catholic petty bourgeois and small holder to the Nationalist cause can be compared to that of the nonslavingholding Southern yeomen to the Confederacy (see Gallagher 1997:55). In Ontiñena (Huesca), unidentified militants shot leaders of an organization of prosperous peasants (*labradores*).[23] In Cretas (Teruel, pop. 1,600), leftists of the region assassinated sixteen people from various social groups and classes—three priests, five large landowners, three peasants, four day laborers, and one merchant (Simoni and Simoni 1984:106).[24] Sometimes, an enemy provocation could set off a massacre. On 15 August, following the Nationalist bombardment of Almería, Popular Front forces in the port city assassinated more than forty military rebels who had already surrendered (Quirosa-Cheyrouze y Muñoz 1986:142).

In areas where the revolt failed in the first few months after July, Republican courts spent much time judging seditious military officers (Sánchez Recio 1990:140; Cobo Romero 1990:108). As the conflict endured, the subversive individualism of ordinary criminality reasserted itself. In Alicante, common criminals were the subjects of most proceedings, and even in Madrid in the first half of 1937, 435 out of 781 (56 percent) cases heard by Popular Tribunals (usually composed of three judges and fourteen jurors from Popular Front organizations) involved ordinary crimes, or *delitos comunes* (Sánchez Recio 1991:104). In Valencia and Asturias, crimes against property and persons constituted nearly 90 percent of court cases, whereas those that threatened the security of the Republic were approximately 10 percent. The great mass of criminals were not political but pursued their material interests through theft and pilfering.

The Popular Front in some towns, such as Burriana (Castellón), was initially divided between moderates and radicals.[25] Radicals resented the moderates' protection of "fascists" and "reactionaries." Radicals immediately shut down churches and evicted nuns from convents. By early August, they obtained full control of Burriana, burning its "useless archives" and confiscating motor vehicles. Requisitioned trucks were used to supply militia columns stationed on the Teruel front. A small minority of CNT militants "socialized" all industries in "fascist" hands. In the surrounding countryside peasants did the same with land. A million pesetas worth of food, clothing, and other goods were delivered to "heroic" Madrid. The CNT established a Burriana factory and made itself so powerful that its armed forces stymied the Republican Assault Guards' attempt to take control of the plant in March 1937.

At Graus (Huesca) in upper Aragon, the CNT, UGT, and other members of the Popular Front formed an Antifascist Committee to fight "the peculiar psychology of the mountain [people], egoist and profoundly reactionary. This was logical consequence of the influence exercised by priests and *caciques* since time immemorial. . . . The right always won elections during the Republic."[26] The Antifascist Committee did not immediately arrest those believed to be sympathetic to "fascists," but soon, faced with "rumors" of "fascist" victories, it began to detain suspects, who were eventually freed after several months of captivity. As the war endured, "economic difficulties" increased, and it became harder to feed the population. As a result, "rigorous control" was imposed on merchants. In response, they became more sympathetic to the "fascists" and tried to spark a rebellion. According to a CNT-UGT report, on 10 October 1936 merchants "deceitfully organized a seditious demonstration with some peasants" and planned to shut down the town's industry and commerce. These demonstrators "forced" local students to join them and tried to attack the post office and the office of the Antifascist Committee. The following day, a lieutenant of the *carabineros* arrived to investigate the incident. The members of the Antifascist Committee were detained but later were released when cleared of all charges of corruption. A Popular Tribunal condemned twenty-three "fascists" who were then shot by a group of soldiers sent from the front. The Antifascist Committee continued to rule Graus with a combination of terror and social works. It subsidized 360 families of *milicianos,* printed local money, controlled prices, and established a collective.

If Nationalist charges of massacre were credible, so were Republican claims that Nationalists committed bloody murders and illegal seizures. Both sides immediately terrorized civilians in towns, cities, and regions that had a tradition of social strife. The blood orgies of the summer and fall of 1936 bound together militants in each camp. Perhaps the most infamous murder was that of the Granadine poet, Federico García Lorca. Lorca had angered the right by— among other things—insisting "against what the school books say" that the Reconquest had harmed Spain by destroying "an admirable civilization, a poetry, architecture and delicacy unique in the world." In the place of this superior culture arose "an impoverished, cowed town, a wasteland populated by the worst bourgeoisie" (quoted in Gibson 1973:43; García Lorca 1967:1816–17; see also Casanova 1999:65). Lorca's vanguard multiculturalism, as well as his recognized homosexuality and unqualified commitment to the Republic, cost him his life. The Nationalists were less tolerant of the "feminine"—whether gay or female—than their enemies. They did not hesitate to kill hundreds, if not thousands, of mothers, sisters, daughters, and wives of "reds" (Casanova 1999:152).

Thousands of Republicans were also coldly murdered in the old Moorish capital. The extent and brutality of the killings on the island of Majorca led the French Catholic reactionary Georges Bernanos to begin to question his unflinching right-wing beliefs. This follower of rabid anti-Semite Edouard Drumont reported that after seven months of civil war in Majorca the Nationalists had assassinated three thousand people. The coldness of the killers, who murdered in the name of church and tradition, repulsed Bernanos, who complained that French extreme rightists were trying to make Franco into a "Christian hero" instead of the "nightmarish Gallifet [the French general who destroyed the Paris Commune]" that he really was (Bernanos 1971:547). Italian Fascists made their own bloody contribution to the Majorcan terror (see Coverdale 1975:140). Other lesser-known massacres occurred throughout the Nationalist zone, and they seem to confirm the impression that the Nationalist repression was colder and more extensive than its Republican counterpart. In Quinto de Ebro (Zaragoza), nine Falangists and *cedistas* were accused of directing the seizure of the town hall, assassinating the mayor, and shooting more than one hundred Popular Front sympathizers, most of whom, it seems, were members of Izquierda Republicana.[27] This is one of the few occasions in which charges can be verified. A report by the Nationalist Civil Guard confirmed fifty-seven of these deaths.[28] Those murdered were from various social strata, showing the broad support that existed for the Popular Front in this Aragon town. Some of the executed were relatively well off peasants (*labradores*), demonstrating that "the civil war was also to a very significant degree a fratricidal conflict of peasant against peasant" (Malefakis 1972:192–227). Others murdered were petty-bourgeois militants of Izquierda Republicana who had served on the town council or other official bodies. A few were propertyless CNT activists.

In the same province of Zaragoza, Belchite—later to become famous as the site of a bloody summer battle—experienced a similar massacre. In that town, a peasant who had joined the Falange confessed that he had executed fifty men and five women by the end of July.[29] At least 150 other Republicans were shot, and some of them tortured. In Quinto, females sympathetic to the Popular Front were forced to shave their heads, a common humiliation imposed on leftist women, or were handed over to Falangists "for amusement." In a Huelva *pueblo* similar treatment was administered to socialist women (Collier 1987:35, 146). Leftist activists—and their brothers and sons—were physically eliminated. A total of thirty-eight Socialist men—12 percent of Belchite's adult males—were killed in the first year of war. In this town not all who were shot were proletarians or small holders. The massacred included merchants who had aligned with Socialist agrarian unions to contest the power of the landed oligarchy. The latter hated the Second Republic because of its land reform policies and were even more hostile to its labor laws that had given workers considerable power to determine wages and working conditions.

Throughout Nationalist Spain, officials persecuted and sometimes physically eliminated Protestant clergy and closed, if not destoyed, their churches (Bautista Vilar 1990:171). The Nationalist harassment of a half-dozen Protestant communities in the Sierra de Gredos (Ávila) showed dedication to the perpetuation of the Inquisition (Pons Prades 1974:233–36). In Piedralaves and El Barraco (Ávila), Protestants were shot as casually as leftists. Additionally, local authorities converted the Protestant church into a prison and refused the dead proper burial. A Protestant minister and mason, Atilano Coco, was executed (Fraser 1986:206–7).[30] These killings inspired Professor Miguel de Unamuno to alter his analysis of the uprising. Unamuno had initially supported the insurgency, but before his death in December 1936, the professor—who was Coco's friend and had unsuccessfully tried to help persecuted Protestants—became disillusioned with the Nationalists. He would classify the new state as "an imperialist-pagan African-type militarization" that had instituted a "stupid regime of terror" (quoted in Fraser 1986:208; Casanova 1999:99).

In response, hundreds of leftist militants formed defensive and offensive militias. Without these female and male fighters of the CNT, UGT, FAI, PSOE, PCE, and POUM, the military rebellion would have easily succeeded. *Milicianos'* guerrilla warfare stopped it with enthusiasm and bravery. They defeated rebellious officers in Madrid, Barcelona, and in parts of the north, thus keeping the most urbanized and advanced parts of the peninsula in loyal hands. Colorful names reflected the political devotion of *milicianos:* UHP (Unión de Hijos del Proletariado or Uníos Hermanos Proletarios), reminiscent of the Asturian revolt (Alpert 1989:35; Thomas 1961:241). Three units took the name of the German Communist martyr, Ernst Thaelmann. An anarchist column called itself Tierra y Libertad (Land and Freedom). La Pasionaria was also a popular appellation since she inspired martial, if not Marian, devotion. The appearance of this Stalinist icon provoked sentimental "tears. [She was] the most sublime of beauties, the beauty of divine maternity" (Martín-Blázquez 1938:135). The Battalion Aida Lafuente adopted the name of a young Communist woman who had perished during the Asturias revolt of 1934. Female activists sometimes joined the fight: "The war broadened female agency and opened up new fields of activity. . . . Women appeared, un-chaperoned, in the streets by the thousands. . . . They engaged in multiple war activities—building barricades, nursing the wounded, organizing relief work, sewing uniforms or knitting sweaters" (Nash 1995:58). These young women were socially and professionally heterogeneous. "Large numbers wore pants and carried weapons"

(Cleugh 1963:100). Only small numbers of female activists joined the militia of their party or union, and fewer found themselves fighting on the front.

Although militias were indispensable to the survival of the Republic and in many instances helped to spark a revolution, they displayed not only bravery but also egotism. Militias inflated membership lists in order to get more food and pay from government and military organizations (Alpert 1989:34, 39; Salas Larrazábal and Salas Larrazábal 1986:87; Martínez Bande 1970:276). According to a prominent Republican officer, "Never in any war at any time was there so much waste" (Martín-Blázquez 1938:190; Gallardo Moreno 1994:76). Even though some Nationalist units were as profligate as their enemies, Republican squandering gave Nationalists a considerable, if not decisive, initial advantage (Tagüeña Lacorte 1978:87). The Madrid's quartermaster's office supplied 250,000 daily rations for only thirty thousand troops. Neither the famous Fifth Regiment, which prided itself on Communist discipline and efficient antifascism, nor the almost equally renowned Iron Column, known for its ultrarevolutionary stance, were exempt from exaggerating numbers to wrest more from state coffers (Alpert 1989:50; Bolloten 1991:335). It is difficult to know how many men belonged to the Fifth Regiment, but it is considerably less than the sixty to seventy thousand PCE luminaries claimed (Líster: 1966:62; see Blanco Rodríguez 1993:245–47). The pay of real and fictitious militiamen placed an enormous burden on the public treasury.[31] On the other hand, less fortunate militias lingered for months without receiving their remuneration.[32] Supplies were dependent not on fighting ability but on the influence of the militia's parent organization on the government.[33] The whole business of regularizing the status of at least thirty thousand militiamen was a monumental administrative task, which the Republic was obliged to accomplish.[34] According to Antonio Cabrera, secretary-general of the Militia Liquidation Commission, more than ten thousand "incompetents and do-nothings" eventually were taken off the payrolls.

Many militias would take what they needed and glibly assure the owners— whether businessmen or local governments—that they would be reimbursed in the future (Salas Larrazábal 1973:416). Few paid in real money. In Madrid partisans confiscated almost every commodity, including radios, typewriters, watches, and even bras (Martín-Blázquez 1938:115–17, 231).[35] Before November, Madrid militiamen enjoyed comfortable lodgings and free gasoline (Martínez Bande 1976:33–34). In certain stores looters left only the vacant display tables that they had stripped of all items. Likewise, workers who did not show up for work nevertheless received their salaries. By October 1936, the uncontrolled requisitioning of militia columns in Aragon threatened the "total ruin" of the region (Bolloten 1991:524). Pillaging must have scared the swing group of small holders and tenant farmers who were torn between Nationalists and Republicans. If they were attracted to the Republic by its de facto abolition of rents owed to large landowners, they were also repelled and frightened by its inability to protect property, its failure to secure goods, and the quartering of its troops in their villages. Disrespect for property alienated small holders, renters, and sharecroppers and negated the Republic's attempt to win them over by its 7 October decree that guaranteed their inalienable right to farm the land they worked. As in the English civil wars, "nothing alienated local support faster than plunder" (Carlton 1992:151). Uncontrolled requisitioning might have worked if the Republic had been able to achieve a quick victory, but it was disastrous in a long war.[36] In response to the early requisitions, the provinces surrounding Madrid soon refused to supply food to the capital. Many unprivileged *madrileños,* that is, those without access to loot, became doubtful of militia bravery.

In other regions, the situation was similar (Gallardo Moreno 1994:22). In 1937, the Aragon town of Puertomingalvo (Teruel) was still waiting for its promised compensation.[37] Antifascist authorities admitted that the use of coupons by *milicianos* had nearly ruined Valencian commerce and industry.[38] Republican vouchers proved as unredeemable as Royalist ones emitted during the English civil war (see Kenyon 1988:130, 202; Carlton 1992:285). The Republic, despite its progressive reputation, could not match the feat of the New Model Army that won friends by promptly reimbursing those who lodged and fed it. Even in his 1649 Irish campaign, Cromwell issued a guarantee of cash payment for any goods supplied or requisitioned. Also, in contrast to the U.S. Civil War, looting developed immediately in the Spanish conflict (Linderman 1987:184–85). The enemies of militias accused them of pillaging private homes, businesses, and farms (see Bray 1937).

Not only food and supplies but also essential transportation was requisitioned in a haphazard manner. Committees confiscated the one or two vehicles from owners of minuscule trucking or bus firms (Souchy Bauer 1982:119). Even though the army procured thousands of cars and trucks, it never possessed a sufficient number of vehicles or an adequate organization to move and supply troops. A transportation shortage persisted and was the main cause of supply bottlenecks (Martín-Blázquez 1938:119, 206).[39] Political and union priorities took precedence over military necessities. Rational resource allocation was rare since each party or union placed its own needs first and sometimes stole the vehicles of its rivals (Bolloten 1991:259; Aróstegui and Martínez 1984:325–26). A commander of the (Communist) Fifth Regiment admitted that it hijacked CNT conveyances. In the opening days of the conflict in Madrid, doctors treated more inexperienced drivers hurt in automobile accidents than soldiers injured in battle (Estellés Salarich 1986:42).

Throughout the Republican zone, the conduct of war often resembled a regression to an early period of Western history when plunder took precedence over trade (Duby 1990:59). In the first few weeks of the conflict, the Málaga militias became notorious for disorder and theft (Martínez Bande 1969:91). Workers went on strike even though leftist organizations controlled the town. Groups of "uncontrollables" incinerated sectors of the city and assassinated suspected "fascists" (Woolsey 1998:57; Casanova 1999:151). The largely Catalan militiamen under Alberto Bayo, who led the expedition to conquer Majorca, were—according to a fascist admirer—"hordes of pillagers" who stole or ate everything that they touched (see Bray 1937:63, 65, 67, 80, 84, 85, 122, 133). The time the "reds" devoted to looting permitted Falangist troops to mobilize. Bayo finally ordered his officers to take severe measures against plunderers. Other observers agree that Majorca was not so much vanquished by the Nationalists and their Italian allies—including the flamboyant and legendary "Count Rossi" who spurred local fascists into battle—but rather was lost by an inefficient Republic (Coverdale 1975:137). The island remained the key, and only, Nationalist (and Italian) naval and air base in the Mediterranean until the end of the war.

The amateurishness of militias was confirmed by their neglect of logistics. On the Aragon front in early September 1936, Nationalists reported that the enemy's paucity of regular meals for two days had caused its morale to falter (Martínez Bande 1970:260). The Battalion of Mieres (Asturias) complained about administrative disorder and the resulting scarcity of bread and meat.[40] The militias' irrational and egotistical use of resources would corrode the Republic and contribute greatly to its ultimate demise. Insecurity of property discouraged sutlers, who feared confiscation and distrusted Republican currency, from accompanying Republican troops.[41] As the Popular Army grew larger, so did requisitions. The friction in the Republican zone between soldiers and peasants with a surplus should be contrasted with the relative confidence that existed in Nationalist regions. Nationalists—unlike their counterrevolutionary predecessors, the English Cavaliers and the Russian Whites—could be trusted to protect property. They followed the model of the Duke of Wellington's Peninsular army, which Spanish and Portuguese peasants favored because it compensated them for goods and services (McNeill 1982:204). In Navarre, for example, during the first weeks of the conflict "purchases were paid in cash," thereby encouraging production for the market (Aragón 1940:46). "Requisitions were no longer allowed since we had enough money. Moreover, requisitions disturbed the agrarian economy." The Spanish counterrevolutionaries avoided following the example of Kolchak's White army whose forcible confiscations alienated Russian peasants who, in turn, rejected White banknotes, withdrew their foodstuffs from the market, and avoided military service (Figes 1996:654). In contrast, Spanish farmers welcomed Nationalist currency and rejected the Republican militas' promissory notes. When Nationalists did requisition items, they usually provided indemnities (Viñas et al. 1975:145). In addition, the *franquistas* seem to have depended on regular collection of taxes, thereby providing soldiers with steady pay rather than unpredictable plunder. Franco proved more successful than his opponents in meshing money with military power (see McNeill 1982:25). Although Nationalists quickly annulled popular Republican land reform projects, medium and small holders appreciated their protection of property rights. Their defense of property and soundness of currency may have overcome their failure to sanction even moderate land reform. The most popular Republican *guerrilleros* realized the advantages of fair exchange and always paid peasants in cash (Pons Prades 1977:354).

Given the real and potential antagonism between civilians and military, the militias were not the "people." In neither zone did the "masses" volunteer to fight. Political and social programs and promises motivated very few. The highly controlled press in the Republican zone repeatedly asked for volunteers and was no doubt disappointed with the response. The lack of enthusiasm revealed the low percentage of workers who were firmly committed to a Popular Front organization. The overwhelming majority of wage earners—80 to 85 percent—joined a party or union only after the civil war erupted (see Seidman 1991:93–94; cf. Richards 1998:34). Their motivation was less ideological than practical. To keep their jobs, housing, health care, and other benefits, they had to possess a membership card. At the same time, an overwhelming majority wanted to avoid participating in the violence of the conflict.

The reluctance to pitch in was not limited to the Republican zone, and the number of volunteers in areas controlled by the insurgents was comparable (Salas Larrazábal 1973:538). Only Navarre with its Catholic and Carlist traditions was exceptional, furnishing according to some accounts, 10 percent of its population or even one-third of its men (Casas de la Vega 1977:1:245; Martínez Bande 1980:48).[42] Even here, though, "there were more that applauded those who were going than who actually went themselves" (Salas Larrazábal and Salas Larrazábal 1986:120–24; Thomas 1961:359). A number of Navarrese signed up for noncombative positions (Aragón 1940:40–41). A few crossed the fluid lines to fight for the Republican Army.[43] Despite the fact that that Burgos had always elected monarchist and Carlist deputies, its "masses" did not immediately volunteer (Fraser 1986:56). The future Duke of Medinaceli was surprised to find that very few of the Sevillian bourgeoisie offered themselves to the local condottiere, the garrulous General Quiepo de Llano. Many on both sides preferred to leave the dirty work of war to the military or militiamen. In Madrid and its suburbs, which had a population of 1.5 million, fewer than ten thousand offered their services (Salas Larrazábal 1973:423). In the capital itself, recruitment was difficult. For example, in August when Franco's forces were advancing up the Tajo River, hundreds of *madrileños* promised to fight but only 150 actually fulfilled their pledge (Salas

Larrazábal 1973:472). In Catalonia and Valencia, regions that were indispensable to Republican Spain, enlistment was "remarkably low," given population densities and their supposedly firm regional commitment to the Republic (Alpert 1989:45, 63). A Catalan journalist concluded that it was the militants—mostly of the FAI, CNT, and POUM—and not the "masses" who were responsible for defeating the military in Barcelona (Fraser 1986:107). A FAI activist agreed: "2,000 of us libertarians rallied to put down a fascist coup. . . . By 8 A.M. the next day there were 100,000 in the streets," who claimed the victory as their own. Only eighteen thousand volunteered in Catalonia, and perhaps twenty-five thousand were on the Aragon front in 1936 (Salas Larrazábal 1973:330; Alpert 1989:45; Casanova 1985:107). Franz Borkenau, who arrived in Barcelona in August, reported that none of the villages in Catalonia that he visited had sent a single man to the Aragon front (Borkenau 1963:94). The number who volunteered to fight was insufficient to break the stalemate in the east. In Basque Country and in the north in general, the response was more enthusiastic. Although the "masses" of Asturias, Santander, and the Basque provinces supposedly possessed "political fervor," conscription was nevertheless imposed between October and December 1936 when authorities mobilized age groups from nineteen to thirty-five.[44]

To attract more men, the Republican government promised to hire volunteers as policemen and low-level functionaries. Most of those who joined the militias were males between twenty and thirty years old, unskilled, and unmarried: "It would be incorrect to say that the masses enrolled in the Militias" (Alpert 1989:41). The majority were not members of political parties and were probably enticed to join by the very attractive salary of ten pesetas per day, more than three times as much as the daily pay of foreigners in Franco's *tercio*. They became "the best-paid common soldiers in the world" (Payne 1970:318). Their families were guaranteed the wage in case of death or injury. In contrast, during the Second Republic, an agricultural day laborer in Aragon earned five pesetas per day (Simoni and Simoni 1984:32). The high salary attracted relatively large numbers of Andalusian and Castilian peasants (Salas Larrazábal and Salas Larrazábal 1986:123; Martínez Bande 1976:33). *Manchegos* from Albacete acquired a reputation for being particularly willing to serve (Pons Prades 1977:386). From Aragon, Orwell reported that "boys of fifteen were being brought up for enlistment by their parents, quite openly for the sake of ten pesetas a day" (Orwell 1980:12). Those who had signed up because of monetary and careerist incentives were probably less motivated fighters than their more ideological comrades. One committed Spaniard estimated an International Brigadier to be worth many indigenous soldiers (Tagüeña Lacorte 1978:191; Lamas Arroyo 1972:275). Motivation based upon material rewards has proven less effective in revolutionary wars than normative compliance, which is founded upon the soldier's loyalty to some collectivity or cause beyond himself (See Lynn 1984:24).[45]

Both camps paid a grotesque homage to the value of volunteers by executing captured ones. In the first few months of the struggle, 120,000 volunteered for the Republic compared to approximately 100,000 in the Nationalist zone (Salas Larrazábal and Salas Larrazábal 1986:120–24; Alpert 1989:63). As the supply of "active citizens" dried up, officials in both zones had to resort to conscription, although the Republican draft came sooner and involved younger and older men than its Nationalist counterpart (Casanova 1985:85; Hermet 1989:155, 181). During the conflict, the Republic mobilized twenty-seven age groups, ranging from eighteen to forty-four years old and totaling 1.7 million men. The Nationalist government conscripted only fourteen or fifteen age groups, ranging from eighteen to thirty-two years old, totaling 1.26 million men.[46] Given the long tradition in Spain of draft dodging (e.g. Tragic Week of 1909), the figures on both sides may be inflated. The International Brigades had an even wider age expanse, with one volunteer fifty-six years old (Wintringham 1939:115).

At first glance, larger Republican numbers might seem to give them the advantage, but Nationalists were better able to equip and train a smaller number of younger troops. Nationalist professionals provided key reserves that capably countered many initially successful Republican offensives.[47] Franco preferred to rely upon professional soldiers for the toughest operations, and only in 1938 began employing conscripts in major engagements. The *generalísimo* may have feared repeating the mistakes of the Russian Whites, whose military effectiveness was diluted by draftees, who often had little commitment to any side (Pons Prades 1974:212). Like the "masses," large numbers of apolitical commissioned and noncommissioned officers were forced to serve the camp that dominated the city or the region in which they happened to find themselves after 18 July. They were geographically, not ideologically, loyal.[48] Approximately 50 percent of officers on active duty happened to be in the Republican zone, and perhaps half of these worked for the legal regime (Coverdale 1975:67). A similar phenomenon occurred during the Russian civil war when the desire to survive by serving led former Czarist officers to join the ranks of the Bolsheviks (Figes 1996:591).

The local climate of hostility or acceptance often determined the success of the military rebellion (Martínez Bande 1969:13). The loyalty of police and Civil Guards was a decisive factor. In the major urban centers, professional Republican forces of order often joined amateur militiamen. Sensing the feelings of their fellow urban residents, soldiers and police in the principal cities were often wary of supporting the military rebellion. For example, fifteen companies or three thousand Security and Assault Guards stationed in Barcelona declared themselves unconditionally loyal to the *Generalitat* (Martínez Bande 1970:23). In one town, Iglesuela del Cid (Teruel), a large number of Civil Guards abstained during a vote to determine whether their local detachment would support the Republic or the rebellion.[49] In Almería, the military rebels would have been successful but for the intervention of soldiers and sailors faithful to the Republic (Quirosa-Cheyrouze y Muñoz 1986:117–18). On the other side, armed soldiers or police who opposed the Republic mercilessly eliminated virtually unarmed leftist militants.

Throughout the war, both camps were obsessed with the possession of provincial capitals. Despite its vaunted reputation as a libertarian fortress, rebellious officers dominated Zaragoza where the local CNT proved to be a paper tiger (Casanova 1985:86). In that city—unlike Barcelona, Madrid, and Valencia—the left failed to win any amount of collaboration from the forces of order (Cifuentes Chueca and Maluenda Pons 1995:18). Disappointed and puzzled militants blamed the urban inhabitants for their "inertia" and "passivity" (Lorenzo 1972:113; Sanz 1978:261). Likewise, activists were frustrated that Oviedo, the capital of famously militant Asturias, remained in rebel hands. Despite a significant presence of the left, Nationalists were able to capture the Andalusian capitals of Cadiz, Algeciras, Seville, Cordova, and Granada (Moreno Gómez 1986:23; Gibson 1973:chapter V). The conquest of Granada gave them control of the El Fargue factory, which, at the time, was the only plant in this zone able to produce gunpowder, bombs, and grenades (Martínez Bande 1969:82). The centralization and cruel efficacy of the Seville command of General Queipo de Llano greatly contrasted with the bumbling of his enemies. According to a CNT militant, "the Seville proletariat was not the organized proletariat of Barcelona. There was a lack of cohesion, a lack of consciousness. Seville was underdeveloped" (quoted in Fraser 1986:52). Nationalist bloodletting was enormous. In Cordova, at least 2,543 were shot during the war; in Granada minimal figures were 4,000 for the capital and perhaps 26,000 for the province (Gibson 1973:167–69). In Cordova province, only the mining and industrial district of Peñarroya-Pueblonuevo remained loyal to the Republic.[50]

Algeciras offers a good example of how outnumbered, but not outgunned, insurgents were able to achieve success. This port city was the key to the control of Andalusia and the rest of Spain. If the Republic had been able to capture Algeciras, it could have stopped or at least delayed the landings of thousands of Moorish troops. The Nationalists quickly dominated the entire Campo de Gibraltar—Algeciras, Tarifa, Los Barrios, San Roque, and La Linea. Their success was an initial demonstration of how small groups of well-trained soldiers who had the support of a broad sector of the middle classes could defeat a larger but poorly organized popular movement.[51] Insurgents admitted frankly that the "people" or at least "the working masses" were against them. "A few good Spaniards" under the proper command were able to smash "the red hordes." On 18 July, several infantry companies and the Civil Guard—aided by the active assistance of sympathetic employees of the telephone company—frustrated a larger group of militants of the Popular Front. "Elements of order who offered themselves to military authorities" broke an Algeciras general strike called for Sunday, 19 July. Scabs allowed most public services—especially telephone and electricity—to function without interruption. Trains, however, were halted, and the port remained isolated until the arrival of the Nationalist cruisers, *Canarias* and *Cervera*. Even though the "working mass" was initially hostile to the military rebellion, once its militants were defeated, it adjusted to the new situation and began to cooperate with Nationalist authorities.

In the Campo de Gibraltar (and frequently in the rest of the country), inexperienced militias raised Loyalist morale but were unable to defeat smaller forces of professional soldiers.[52] Until 27 July, Nationalist Civil Guards and small groups of infantrymen controlled without much opposition San Roque, a village halfway between Algeciras and Gibraltar. On that day, a column of two thousand men arrived from "red" Málaga. They proved capable of defeating a much less numerous group of rebellious Civil Guards and infantrymen. Shortly thereafter, the column was in turn vanquished by Nationalist soldiers sent from Algeciras. Nationalists claimed that during the short Popular-Front domination of San Roque, the "reds" assassinated military officers and landowners. In Andalusia, the latter remained among the principal supporters of the military uprising (Moreno Gómez 1986:39). As in Algeciras, workers called a general strike, but it too was ultimately unsuccessful, in part because of gender division. The *señoritas* of the telephone company immediately cooperated with the rebellious military.

Loyalists also briefly controlled La Línea de la Concepción, which abutted Gibraltar. The republicanism or neutrality of army and Civil Guard units stationed in La Linea led to an ephemeral period of leftist dominance. Nationalists claimed that their enemies looted the drugstore, photography studio, jewelry shops, and five medical and dental offices. Military rebels with the aid of a Moroccan unit killed or wounded dozens and captured the town in several hours. The local bourgeoisie regarded the insurgent military as saviors. As in much of the rest of Andalusia, the "working mass" was hostile to the revolt, but its general strike evaporated after eight to ten days. Nationalists also seized Tarifa without a struggle, despite the Popular Front majority that controlled the municipality. In Los Barrios on 23 July, Popular-Front militants abandoned their weapons when troops and Civil Guards approached the town.

Insurgent success in southern Spain sheds light on the nature of the radical right. Politically, "fascism" in this part of Andalusia meant a military revolt to which frightened sectors of the middle classes adhered, not a mass radicalization that had been able to rally broad sectors of the population, as in Italy and Germany. In other words, unlike the great fascist powers, Spain would not expe-

rience the combination of mass political party and elite sympathy that would
lead to the fascist control of the state. Instead, immediate fears of revolution
and disorder led the middle and upper classes to support eagerly the *pronunciamiento*. In Spain, the military took the initiative and dominated the party.
The traditional authoritarianism of the Spanish right proved far stronger than
any radical or revolutionary fascist movement (see Payne 1980:139–57; Laqueur
1996:84; for Alava see Ugarte 1990:2:63). In Andalusia and Estremadura, the
Spanish civil war began as a variety of colonial war with foreign mercenaries
and foreign troops under Nationalist control reconquering the civilian
population.

The Republican loss of the Campo de Gibraltar in particular and Andalusia
in general provided the Nationalists' crack African troops easier access to the
peninsula. These combat-wise soldiers gave the insurgents a decisive advantage even if in the first days of the war the number of professional soldiers on
both sides was roughly equal—eighty-seven thousand Nationalists and seventy-
seven thousand Republicans (see Payne 1970:315). Italian planes secured
Nationalist air superiority in the Mediterranean. Rightist domination of the
skies between Africa and Andalusia was to persist throughout the conflict. In
addition, the disorderly incompetence of the Republican navy allowed Franco's
maritime forces to control the straits of Gibraltar after July (Jackson 1965:266).
The inability to secure the straits showed the ineffectiveness of the Republican military, which could have obstructed the transfer of Moorish forces by
stationing in Málaga only a few squadrons of aviation fighters (Kindelán
1945:187). Nationalists benefited from the friendly neutrality of the British who
refused to let the Republican navy use facilities in Gibraltar and Tangiers.

The insurgents received the immediate and effective aid of the Germans and
the Italians in the first crucial months of the war; whereas the Republic obtained
substantial Soviet assistance only beginning in the fall (Viñas 1979:42; Howson 1999:19). The fascist powers initiated the first major airlift in history. In
the late summer German and Italian planes helped to ferry twelve to twenty
thousand Moors (often referred to as *regulares* and legionnaires) and hundreds
of tons of material across the straits (See Coverdale 1975:86, 108).[53] Approximately sixty-five hundred men were airlifted to the peninsula during August.
Skeptics have often stressed the irony of Nationalist use of Muslim mercenaries
to conduct a supposedly Christian crusade. The Moroccan army may well have
been, as a number of perceptive observers have labeled it, "the decisive factor" of the war. The Nationalist utilization of the German and Italian airlift
anticipated the effectiveness with which Franco's forces would employ foreign
aid throughout the conflict. Many historians have taken this efficacy for granted.
In contrast to the *franquistas*, counterrevolutionary Russian Whites and Chi-
nese Nationalists proved incapable of using Allied supplies, much of which
ended up on the black market.

Over the course of the Spanish conflict, seventy-two thousand Italian ground troops assisted the Nationalists (Coverdale 1975:396).[54] German and Italian assistance to Franco was more timely, more persistent, and more regular than Soviet aid to the Republic. By the end of the war, Nazi Germany was Nationalist Spain's primary trading partner (see Whealey 1989:87). The Republic tried to narrow the foreign assistance gap by employing forty to sixty thousand International Brigadiers, who were more interested in ideology and less in booty than Franco's Moors. The Internationals became a generally well trained force that was organized into small and coherent units (Wintringham 1939:62). In fact, they often felt themselves superior to Spanish Republican soldiers.

Nationalist authorities quickly had come to an agreement with Moorish notables who provided Franco's forces with many thousands of aggressive mercenaries (Payne 1967:369). This Nationalist success in recruiting North Africans has stimulated debate over the Republic's colonial policy. The Republican government apparently discussed the option of promoting a revolt in Morocco but ultimately rejected it. Republican officials in Tanger believed that they had had an opportunity to enroll Moors in their military.[55] Several hundred fighters in the Anyera zone were ready to serve the Republic against the "military traitors" who they believed were oppressing them. Loyalists in the colony thought that properly armed Moors might have been able to liberate the colony from Nationalist rule. Yet it did not enter these Republican officers' minds to recommend that Spanish Morocco be promised independence. Instead, they offered mercenaries arms, five pesetas per day for recruits, and five hundred per month for the chieftains and their men. However, the overwhelming majority of Moorish mercenaries and their leaders chose the Nationalist side. Possibly they remembered the successful Asturias campaign and reasoned that the chance of booty and victory was greater with the established military leadership of the colony. Over 60,000 to 70,000 North Africans—often organized in *tabors* of approximately 250 men—fought for Franco and became "the vertebral column of the Nationalist Army," which distinguished itself in the battles of Madrid, Teruel, and the Ebro (Salas 1989:30; de Madariaga 1992:80). They were Franco's Gurkas and constituted "the single most important source of reliable manpower" (Payne 1967:389).[56] During the last two years of the war, Nationalists recruited almost as many Moors as had already served in the peninsula.

The Nationalists had significant successes in the first days of their movement, but in the largest cities and more industrialized regions where working-class organizations and their militias were strong, the rebellion failed. As in the English civil war, the cities sided with the "progressive forces," but, contrary to the winning sides in the English, French, U.S., and Russian civil wars, the Republic's control of urban centers did not provide the margin of victory. Nevertheless, it would retain urban bases in Madrid and Barcelona until the end of the war. Militia columns sent from urban Catalonia conquered eastern and lower Aragon, approximately half of the region. In the Valencia region, the CNT and UGT dominated the rebels in several weeks (Bosch Sánchez 1983:18–19). At the end of July 1936, Catalonia, Basque Country, Asturias, Santander (Cantabria), and the Levante remained in Republican hands. Although this gave the Republic a definite numerical superiority, it was not nearly as great as the four to one or five to one advantage that the Bolsheviks possessed over the Whites during the Russian civil war (Pipes 1994:11). Nevertheless, the Republicans possessed an overwhelming initial advantage of arms, textiles, and manufactured goods. For example, two-thirds of motor vehicles and an even greater percentage of gasoline and oil stocks were in Republican hands (Martínez Bande 1990–91:29; Martínez-Molinos 1990:221, 228). However, it should be remembered that Spanish industry had survived because of high tariffs and that Spanish manufactures were not competitive on the world market. To gain foreign currency to buy raw and finished materials, both bands would have to export agricultural products, whose revenues would be insufficient to finance the war. The battle to earn foreign currencies was a standoff (Viñas 1984:267). Republicans held the citrus-growing regions and thus the most profitable and largest food exports of the early 1930s. During the war, Loyalists would trade them for other food products—flower, eggs, milk, potatoes, and sugar—that their zone lacked.[57] However, oranges—which constituted less than 3 percent of Spain's agricultural output—could never provide the monies that would enable the Republic to overcome its material shortages (Simpson 1995:219). The Republicans also had a distinct advantage in olive oil production, the second-largest prewar export. Indeed, as before the war, they expected both to supply their own population with oil and to export it.[58] Loyalists too controlled 57 percent of Spanish vineyards (Ministerio de Agricultura 1936:4). Olives, nuts, and tobacco were evenly divided among adversaries.

The exports of Andalusia (wines, oils, and ores) and the Canaries (fruits and vegetables) quickly fell into insurgent hands. Nationalists traded Rif iron ore, pyrites, cocoa, raw wool, and coal (Viñas 1984:276). The Nationalists, possessing the Castilian plains, had more than twice as much wheat as their adversaries (see Salas Larrazábal 1973:2435). They were also much better supplied with beef and pork, and this was a key to their victory. They could feed their army and their rear, an accomplishment never matched by the Republic, which had to provision a bigger army and the largest cities of Spain. During the war the Nationalists were more likely to put into effect the *franquista* propaganda slogan, "no family without bread." In contrast to their enemies, the Nationalists would not have to import food from abroad (Viñas et al. 1975:142). From the beginning, Burgos—the official seat of government from October 1936 to the end of the war—forbade the exportation of foreign currency and fixed the peseta at its prewar level. This helped to stabilize prices in the Nationalist zone at least until between 1938 and 1939. Republican attempts to freeze prices by decree were much less successful.

Foreign investors and markets had faith in a Nationalist victory as well as a fervent desire for it. Fears of communist influence and practices in the Republican zone pushed sectors of the international bourgeoisie to help the insurgents. The loss of investments in Russia that had occurred during the previous decade was fresh in the minds of businessmen all over the world (Thomas 1961:273). The Republic's failure to convince owners that it could protect property rights plagued it internationally and domestically. Although the Republic sporadically attempted to protect foreign interests, both foreign and domestic owners stayed skeptical about its ability or desire to preserve private property. It could not float bonds attractive to domestic or foreign lenders. British and U.S. banks sabotaged its efforts to transfer funds to purchase desperately needed supplies, forcing it to turn to the Soviet banking system and its branches in America and Europe in order to overcome Western financial hostility (Viñas 1979:218–27). Conservatives used Russian intervention in the war—in the form of an irregular flow of supplies and approximately three thousand military advisers—to argue against aid to the Republic. The British, French, and U.S. banks refused to advance it substantial credits; whereas, German, Italian, and Portuguese banks, as well as General Motors and the Texas Oil Company, generously offered them to the insurgents (Hermet 1989:184).[59] Credit was indispensable to Franco's victory (Viñas 1984:280; Howson 1999:56). It compensated for the Nationalist lack of gold and precious metals. The insurgent triumph—like those of Parliament in the English civil war or of the North in the U.S. Civil War—rested upon healthier and more fortunate finances. Unlike the Republic, Franco's forces did not have to pay their main suppliers in foreign currencies (Eguidazu 1978:157). This partially explains why the Nationalists never suffered from the fuel and transportation shortages that so handicapped their enemies.

In August and September, the most significant action took place as the Army of Africa, composed of crack-Spanish legionnaires and indigenous troops, advanced north from Seville to Mérida and Badajoz, then continued up the Tagus (Tajo) valley towards Toledo and Madrid (Jackson 1965:266). The Nationalists wanted to connect their Andalusian stronghold with their northern armies. In addition, the advance would cut off the Republican zone from Portugal. The Republican militias' main task was to conserve the initial Loyalist control of urban and industrial regions, but militiamen often had few arms or military training. They lacked experienced leaders who could organize the various militia "tribes," who remained uncoordinated even when they belonged to one organization, such as the CNT (Aroca Sardagna 1972:26). Andalusian militias acquired a reputation for incompetence and were reported "running away like cowards" (Borkenau 1963:160). Apparently, individual militiamen had not internalized the military ethic and did "not feel guilty in the least." General José Miaja's attempt to capture Cordova in the summer of 1936 failed because of the inexperience and indiscipline of his forces (Martínez Bande 1969:63, 195). As the troops of the Falangist officer, Juan Yagüe, advanced through Estremadura in August, many leftist militiamen lost their enthusiasm for fighting. Selected *milicianos* had to be posted in the rear to halt or shoot retreating comrades.[60] The seemingly unstoppable victories of the African troops resulted very quickly in a sharp drop of Republican enlistments (Salas Larrazábal 1973:256–58).

The Nationalists used terror to discourage their real and potential enemies. One of the most infamous massacres occurred at Badajoz, near the Portuguese border (this account follows Jackson 1965:268 and Vila Izquierdo 1984:50–60). The city of forty thousand was fiercely defended by four thousand militiamen—who, although outmanned and outgunned by the enemy—offered real resistance to the African columns. After losing well over one hundred men, the legionnaires captured the town on 14 August. When African troops entered, they looted small businesses and sold the booty to the Portuguese.[61] More shockingly, according to foreign journalists, Yagüe's troops executed at least several thousand men who were suspected of fighting for the Republic.[62] The bullring was drenched in the blood of the victims. In nearby Mérida, legionnaires, Falangists, and Moors reportedly assassinated several thousand (Vila Izquierdo 1984:44–46). In the rest of the Nationalist-conquered province, repression and terror were equally severe. In addition to great landowners, in Estremadura an estimated ten thousand wealthier peasants—along with their workers and servants—fought and killed for Franco (Pons Prades 1977:322). The Nationalist subjugation of Badajoz and Mérida achieved the objective of severing rail and road communications between Portugal and the Republic.

The number of victims in Badajoz province may have surpassed those of Badajoz city. For example, Almendralejo was a relatively prosperous town of nearly eighteen thousand residents, the majority of whom voted monarchist. However, during the Second Republic the town experienced a high level of labor unrest and protest. Large, medium, and even small owners united against highly class-conscious and militant wage laborers. The property owners' association threatened to shoot any landowner who employed anarchist workers. When Nationalists took the town, over one thousand people were executed.[63] As in Andalusia, the Nationalist bloodletting in Estremadura decapitated the workers' movement and terrorized its remaining sympathizers. If some of them took to the hills and plotted attacks against the *franquistas,* others chose to desert or to surrender without resisting.[64]

It was not in the Nationalists' interest or within the realm of possibility to execute all members of left unions and parties. Throughout the peninsula (and in the Canary Islands), a CNT or PCE card had often been necessary to get or

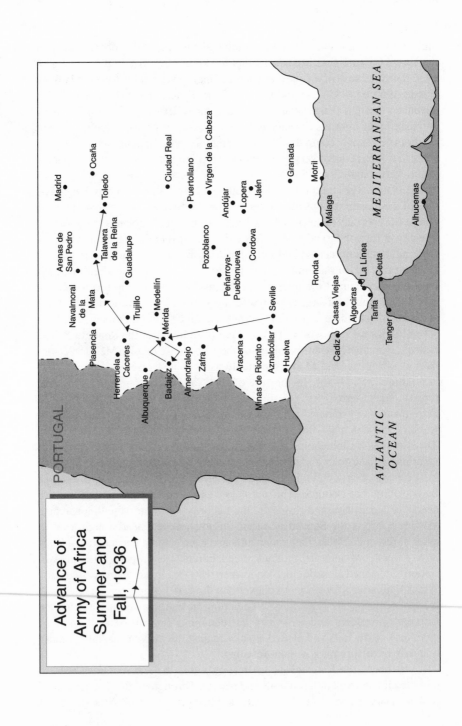

Advance of
Army of Africa
Summer and
Fall, 1936

PORTUGAL

MEDITERRANEAN SEA

ATLANTIC
OCEAN

Madrid

Ocaña

Toledo

Ciudad Real

Arenas de
San Pedro

Puertollano

Virgen de la Cabeza

Andújar

Lopera

Jaén

Granada

Motril

Talavera
de la Reina

Navalmoral
de la
Mata

Guadalupe

Málaga

Pozoblanco

Cordova

Trujillo

Medellín

Peñarroya-
Pueblonueva

Ronda

La Línea

Ceuta

Plasencia

Mérida

Seville

Casas Viejas

Algeciras

Tarifa

Herreruela

Cáceres

Zafra

Aracena

Cadiz

Tanger

Albuquerque

Badajoz

Almendralejo

Minas de Riotinto

Aznalcóllar

Huelva

Alhucemas

retain a job during the Popular Front.[65] Entire regions, such as Asturias, were
thus considered to be totally "red."[66] It was inevitable that many card-carry-
ing Communists and others would—through luck or misfortune—end up in
Franco's camp. A few of the most politicized *"rojos"* found themselves serving in the Nationalist Army. Ironically enough, their knowledge of ideology
enabled them to survive by giving them political cunning and rhetorical ability to mask their real views. In response, Nationalist authorities took the prudent step of investigating the political antecedents of their soldiers. Often,
prisoners were not immediately executed after capture but investigated for
"crimes" and interrogated to discover if they were committed "reds." In particular, officials were especially vigilant if any of their soldiers were suspected
of having rightist blood on their hands. The insurgents, like their adversaries,
tried hard to distinguish believers from opportunists.

The "indiscipline and cowardice" that produced the "shameful flight" of
many *milicianos* contributed to the Nationalist capture of Talavera (Toledo) on
3 September (Salas Larrazábal 1973:258). General José Asensio Torrado,
Largo Caballero's favorite, attributed flights (*desbandadas,* literally a de-
grouping) to "a lack of means and a lack of social and political discipline, given
that military discipline was completely absent."[67] Disdain for manual labor
stimulated refusals to dig trenches (see Thomas 1961:248). Even foreign help
had limited utility. A squad of French aviators and mechanics serving the
Republic acted "with absolute independence degenerating into anarchy."[68]
Their "disorder" did more harm than good.

Nationalist victories in the south enabled them to launch an offensive in the
north (Jackson 1965:273–75; Thomas 1961:249–51). They wanted to close the
French border at Hendaye and eliminate the Basque threat to their rear. After
the bloody triumph at Badajoz, General Franco ordered seven hundred legionnaires to reinforce the troops of the Carlist commander, Colonel Beorleguí, who
was directing the campaign to take Irún. Between 26 August and 4 September, the two-thousand-man force of attackers—including legionnaires, Carlists,
Falangists, and Civil Guards—opposed an equal number of defenders. These
Irún defenders—Anarchists, Basque Nationalists, Catalan Nationalists, and
simple republicans—were as politically heterogeneous as Nationalist forces.
Superior organization and armament gave the victory to Colonel Beorleguí,
who was mortally wounded in action and provided another example of Nationalist valor. His men succeeded in cutting off the Republic from the French border at the western end of the Pyrenees. In addition, they gained important
supplies of linseed oil, which was used for waterproofing and for making soap.
The latter commodity would be sorely lacking in the Republican zone as the
war endured (Aragón 1940:108). On 13 September, the insurgents took San
Sebastián (Guipúzcoa) without a fight from militias demoralized by the Irún
defeat. The Basques may have vacillated and permitted aesthetic concerns, that

is, the preservation of their most beautiful city, to take precedence over its all-out defense (Thomas 1961:280). Basque Nationalists, Socialists, and Communists negated the anarchists' offer of last-ditch resistance (Martínez Bande 1980:91). The ferocity that marked warfare in southern Spain was largely absent in the Basque campaign. Neither side made a policy of shooting prisoners. Maybe their shared Catholicism acted to restrain the most brutal aspects of war.

In early September, in addition to the nearly simultaneous fall of Talavera and the capture of Irún (Guipúzcoa), the Nationalists forced an initially successful Republican invasion out of Majorca with the decisive help of the Italian air force and navy. Similarly, the "frequent and important *desbandadas* [which occurred] without apparent motive" troubled a militia commander near Sigüenza (Guadalajara).[69] These unruly exoduses endangered the stability of the fronts. According to the commander, a number of factors produced flights. First, militiamen overreacted to artillery and aviation bombardments and abandoned their positions. They could not stomach the danger of explosions and accompanying noise. The sounds of bombs seem to have been more frightening than any other audible experience (Dollard 1943:24). Second, many irregulars could not tolerate hunger, thirst, and cold. Third, soldiers in newly formed units lacked confidence in their colleagues. Almost all flights "began with a spontaneous retreat of a few groups of scared men" whom the rest then followed. The commander recommended a number of changes: construction of well-dug trenches that would give soldiers "a feeling of security" and improvements in Republican aviation, which "despite what our papers say," was deficient. The officer believed that enhancement of supply services and intelligent use of reserves could limit the flights and defections that exhaustion had encouraged. Militiamen must be instructed that those who fled to avoid their own death or injury created situations that magnified the possibilities of casualties. Soldiers should be drilled to instill confidence, strengthen obedience, and induce group trust. He called upon each battalion to organize its own police to arrest and, if necessary, execute those who fostered discontent or indiscipline. The presence of military repression would silence "irresponsibles" forever.

At the end of September the loss of Toledo, where the Loyalist effort had begun auspiciously, capped a series of Republican defeats. In July, those supporting the military rebellion had been forced to retreat into the Alcázar, the fortress-castle of the medieval capital (Jackson 1965:272; see Malraux 1937 for the novelist's view). Under the leadership of Colonel Moscardó, more than one thousand Civil and Assault Guards, Falangists, and a few military cadets took the women and children of known leftists as hostages and withstood a two-month Republican siege. The string of victories by the advancing Army of Africa bolstered their morale. Franco himself decided that relieving the

Alcázar was a top priority, even though it might cost him a quick victory in Madrid (Thomas 1961:282; Thomas follows Kindelán 1945:23). He believed that the propaganda benefit of a rescue of the Alcázar defenders justified a delay in capturing the Spanish capital. On 26 September as Colonel Varela and the Army of Africa approached the fortress, a few hundred *milicianos* offered only token resistance and retreated toward Madrid.[70] They fled before the enemy or disappeared from the city. Militias abandoned the entire contents of the Toledo arms factory to the Nationalists (Thomas 1961:284; Martínez Bande 1976:13). They also left tons of wheat and thousands of heads of livestock in enemy hands. The capture of the Alcázar on 27 September ended the ten-week siege, and Moscardó subsequently became another symbol of resistance and courage for the insurgents. Most of the besieged were undoubtedly heroic, but it has been largely forgotten that several dozen low-ranking soldiers escaped and deserted the nearly two thousand trapped inside.[71] As the war endured, in each camp anonymous antiheroes like the dozens came to outnumber heroes like Moscardó. After the fall of Toledo, the province became so quiet that committed Nationalist volunteers yearned to leave it to see some real action (Kemp 1957:49).

Republican defeats led to increasing pressure to reorganize the militias and even to replace them with a new Republican army that could effectively resist Nationalist professionals, volunteers, and foreign allies. The tensions and distrust that characterized relations between Republican professional officers and militiamen delayed reforms (Alpert 1989:137–38). Officers loyal to the Republic had difficulty controlling *milicianos* who suspected—sometimes correctly—that their commanders were sympathetic to the Nationalists and might betray their men. Social as much as political differences divided them. Officers distrusted the breakdown of order in the Republican zone, and men suspected that their commanders, who possessed superior education and social rank, secretly disdained them (Alpert 1984:213).[72]

Colonel Mariano Salafranca revealed the problems of commanding militias. In late August, in an atmosphere of strain between regular officers and militiamen, Salafranca reluctantly took control of a column whose mission was to guard the main southwest road to Madrid. Morale was low, and the men had recently killed an officer who had tried to stop a *desbandada*. Salafranca tried to make the *milicianos* respect the chain of command and attempted to halt the very unmilitary practice of abandoning one's post to dine in a nearby village. He claimed that his men were a mixture of noble and base (Alpert 1989:57). The "mass" was "amorphous" and acted "egotistically" and sought only personal survival in moments of danger (quoted in Alpert 1989:57). Militia fighters were ignorant of the most elementary military practices, seldom concentrated their fire, and had to be reminded of the value of surprise and the virtues of last-ditch resistance (Salas Larrazábal 1973:524–25). They were unaware that advancing in a horizontal line and clustering in a group provided excellent targets to enemy gunners. Their retreats lacked order. They panicked, especially during artillery and aviation attacks, and bunched together on roads where hostile aircraft—armed with machine guns—could easily mow them down (Payne 1967:363; Thomas 1961:292; Wintringham 1939:131). "Untried troops most need the sense of security provided by bunching. Experienced soldiers usually bunch less. This is partly because they realize, at a purely rational level, that a clump of soldiers offers a good target. It also reflects a deep-seated trust in their comrades: They have confidence in a support that may be invisible but is nonetheless perceptible" (Holmes 1985:159). Showing inadequate training and professional consciousness, they frequently abandoned their weapons to the enemy, a habit that persisted into 1937 and beyond (Holmes 1985:39; Martínez Bande 1984:81; Martínez Bande 1970:176).

Republican Guards and regular Spanish soldiers could be equally amateur and inexperienced. Several dozen Republican (formerly Civil) Guards scattered in terror when encountering one unidentified plane near Valdemoro (Madrid) at the end of October 1936.[73] Investigators revealed that although none of the guards were wounded, they felt incapable of resisting the enemy. It remained unclear whether political alienation from the Republic or military inadequacies caused their failure to fight. The disappearance of their officers encouraged the soldiers of Ninth Infantry Regiment to flee when the enemy attacked the Talavera front in mid-September 1936.[74] Nor in Talavera itself did militiamen or the National Republican Guard fight more competently. In an operation near Guadarrama in early August, soldiers of the Second Infantry Division revealed a striking deficiency of training and fear of combat.[75] After their sergeant was injured, no corporal emerged to provide leadership in his place. Indisciplined soldiers tended to hide from the enemy rather than fight. Nor were they supplied adequately with either food or workable weapons. On the Madrid front, those in the rear received arms only when their comrades in the front were killed and injured (Gárate Córdoba 1976b:93). Even Communist troops—reputedly the best supplied—were said to have suffered from constant lack of guns and munitions (Líster 1966:158). It has been argued that the Republic possessed a generally adequate supply of weapons in the first months of the war, but shortages remained because of faulty distribution, mismanaged allocation, and thoughtless abandonment (Salas Larrazábal 1973:524–25, 617). Unsatisfactory standardization stymied Republican forces. A brigade might possess rifles manufactured in three different nations, each requiring distinct cartridges. The nearly fifty thousand rifles that the Soviets delivered in 1936 were of ten different types, from eight different nations, and of six different calibers (Howson 1999:138).

In Aragon, the front quickly became "stabilized." In other words, it became a quiet front. Despite considerable gaps and unguarded areas of a very irregular line, militiamen—as George Orwell and others have pointed out—became unaggressive (Orwell 1980). In three weeks, Orwell fired only three shots. Even in the early months of the war, each side agreed "not to plug one another" and conducted conversations with the enemy (quoted in Bolloten 1991:258). A journalist sympathetic to the anarchists was astonished that men took no cover and wandered about in full view of the enemy (Gabriel 1938:55–56; see also Aroca Sardagna 1972:43). Vehicles traveled in close range of the foe without being molested. In this context, it is not surprising that some observers reported that the "presence of prostitutes . . . caused more casualties than enemy bullets" (Martínez Bande 1970:65–97).[76] So did friendly fire. All-day bombardments produced not a single injury. Soldiers of the Karl Marx Division abandoned the front with impunity.

On the Nationalist side, local militias often proved unassertive and had to be supplemented by devout Navarrese *requetés*. General Mola himself ordered troops to maintain an active defense by constantly raiding the enemy, but his commands were largely ignored. Nationalist deserters abandoned their side not to fight for the Republic but to return to their hometowns (Aroca Sardagna 1972:99). Ultimately, the quiet front in Aragon benefited Nationalists more than Republicans since the latter initially outnumbered the former ten to one. By January 1937, the Republican prevalence had dropped to four to one, but still—as on other tranquil sectors—Republicans did not take advantage of their numerical superiority to conquer enemy territory. Largo Caballero concluded that "discipline, morale, and leadership can multiply military effectiveness by four" (cited in Martínez Bande 1970:273).

Anarchists and *poumistas* blamed the lack of aggressivity on inadequate support from the Republican government, especially the shortage of arms and the absence of an offensive plan. On the other hand, soldiers of the various columns in Aragon refused to surrender their arms when ordered to the rear (see Fraser 1986:134). The passivity of Aragon fighters hardly encouraged the Republican leadership to launch eastern offensives in 1936. A U.S. volunteer reported that prior to the arrival of the Lincoln Brigade in Aragon in August 1937, only two soldiers had been wounded during the year (Landis 1989:69). This volunteer, like many other U.S. citizens in Spain, was philo-Communist and blamed quietude on Anarchist nonaggressivity. However, his political explanation for the calm was superficial. On other fronts, where anarchism had little influence, Republicans and Nationalists fraternized.[77] General Mola, Nationalist commander in the north, warned his troops in October that they should not let the quiet fronts in Viscaya and Guipúzcoa render them passive (Martínez Bande 1980:190). Observers reported that both sides respected the siesta (Cleugh 1963:60). Opposing camps allegedly arranged football games. In a trench war, as in any other situation, it is usually much harder to kill your enemy if you know him personally.

By wasting great quantities of munitions, which were usually in short supply, militias precociously revealed what would become one of the Republic's major difficulties.[78] To overcome this problem, the Ministry of Defense suggested that marksmanship awards be given on the basis of economy as well as accuracy. All soldiers, especially militiamen, were told to learn basic rules of holding fire. In addition, their waste of gasoline motivated authorities to establish a system of rationing.[79] Troops tended to monopolize transportation that was needed for civilian food supply. Some units selfishly overordered stocks of clothing, forcing others to tramp about half-naked or barefoot during the winter of 1936–37. Even where the militias were competent and disciplined, they gave little thought or effort to the big picture. Localism, or what is called in Spanish history *cantonalismo,* characterized the early months of the war in both zones and was never fully eradicated. Just as the individual or personal realms took precedence over the political party or class, the local dominated the national.[80]

Generally, the militias were incompetent, but in specific situations and in certain localities, they fought heroically and efficiently. The discipline of the Basque militiamen and that of the Communist Fifth Regiment was, according to most observers, superior to others. In the Sierra north and west of Madrid, militias held off the Nationalist advance to the capital and stabilized the front (see Tagüeña Lacorte 1978:89–90). They confounded Italian Fascist and German Nazi views of the inevitability of a quick Nationalist victory. Even after the Battle of Madrid in November 1936, militiamen continued at great personal and financial risk to man the trenches.[81] Near Cordova at the end of September, the "brave" resistance of the Battalion of Alcoy, under Miaja's leadership, to the assaults of the Foreign Legion astonished the Nationalists (Martínez Bande 1969:71). Then in November and the first half of December, the Cordova front remained quiet. In the south during the summer and fall, militias resisted ferociously around the Río Tinto mines, Almendralejo, and Mérida (see Martínez Bande 1976:32, 1969:70, 110). The latter towns were in Estremadura, where hundreds of *guerrilleros* occasionally disturbed Franco's forces (Vila Izquierdo 1984:95). Some peasants in Badajoz province refused to return to the status quo ante and took to the hills. The guerrilla movement in the province was not "pacified" until 1937 (Martínez Bande 1969:19). Given the stiff resistance of the local militia, it was no accident that some of the fiercest guerrilla fighting of the war would take place around the Río Tinto mines. As in Asturias, the miners had a long tradition of commitment to the left, and a good number had participated in the revolutionary movement of October 1934 (Collier 1987:47; Bolloten 1991:7).

On 4 September the desperate military situation spurred the formation of a new Republican government. The left-socialist leader Largo Caballero composed a cabinet of six Socialists, four Republicans, and one representative each

of the Catalan Republicans and the Basque Nationalists. In addition, for the
first time in western European history, two Communists joined the government.
In its first weeks in office, this "Victory Government" proved no more capable of winning battles than its predecessor. In October, Caballero issued a series
of decrees that disbanded the militia and formed, under the control of the general staff, "mixed brigades," that is formations of thirty-five hundred to four
thousand men that intended to be versatile and self-sustaining (Payne
1970:330). Mixed brigades were, however, much smaller than a division, a unit
that had been formulated in the eighteenth century to provide armies with a
flexible, self-sufficient force of up to twelve thousand (McNeill 1982:163).
Critics charged that the mixed brigade slavishly copied the Soviet model and
that it generated an overly high proportion of noncombatants. On paper, its
3,500 hundred men and 150 officers manned four infantry battalions, one cavalry squadron, one antitank battery, a communications company, a hospital
company, sappers, a munitions section, a motor section, and a company of reinforcements. It planned to manage its own communications, transportation,
supplies, and medical services.

The militias underwent what was called "militarization" and were placed
under a central command. The new officer corps would include both former
militiamen and the professional officers whom militants continued to distrust.
Militarization produced increasing Communist domination over many sectors
of the Popular Army, which introduced the red-star emblem of the Soviet Army
on its uniforms, decorations, and weapons (Payne 1970:321). The clenched fist
salute of the Popular Front became the common salutation. Militarization also
brought a renewed assertion of male dominance. Women directly involved in
war—traditionally the most macho situation of all—became unduly suspected
of betrayal and espionage. During militarization, the head of the Popular Army
of the Center imposed a "total ban" on their presence at headquarters.[82]
"Female personnel . . . delayed and hindered the positive course of operations."
Based upon this sexist hostility, "women were rarely addressed in their own
right as rational beings who could reject fascism as individuals but rather as
mothers and spouses to whom fascism was presented as a threat to home and
family" (Nash 1995:73). The war disturbed but did not profoundly transform
traditional gender divisions. The expulsion of women from the military may
have also signaled that men were finally getting down to the business of killing
other men.

By October, Largo Caballero and other senior government officials had witnessed the collapse of militia morale and discipline on a number of fronts. To
remedy these failures, they established a War Commissariat to "exercise political and social control over soldiers, militiamen, and other Republican armed
forces" (see Alpert 1989:176–94; Martínez Bande 1974b:55). A commissar system was quickly instituted to direct and guide officers and men. All parties,

except the moderate Republican ones, would share positions within the Commissariat. Communist experience, interest, and organizational ability quickly gained them a preponderance of authority in this new bureaucracy. The precedent of the Russian civil war and growing Soviet influence during the Spanish conflict led to PCE domination of the Commissariat (Bolloten 1991:275). Instead of commissars, Nationalist forces employed chaplains. They ministered to supposedly anticlerical Falangists: "Every day at dusk, we said our rosary [rezaban el rosario]. Then we sang the Falangist anthem and shouted "Franco, Franco, Franco" (Colmegna 1941:177).

Militarization and the establishment of a commissariat had little immediate effect upon the fortunes of war. At the beginning of October, the Republic was still enduring an unbroken chain of defeats and had yet to achieve its Valmy. The insurgents sustained their assaults on several fronts. With the Duce's aid and assistance, the Nationalists dominated the Mediterranean (Coverdale 1975:127). On 16 October, after weeks of hard fighting, the Nationalist garrison in Oviedo, which was being besieged by militant Asturian miners, was finally relieved. As in 1934, professional Moroccan forces played an indispensable role in its capture (Martínez Bande 1980:139, 148). The rescue of Oviedo repeated Nationalist success in relieving beleaguered garrisons, such as Moscardó's at the Alcázar of Toledo. Republican aviation had alienated potential supporters by indiscriminately bombing the city (Fraser 1986:249). The Nationalist capture of Oviedo was a real and symbolic blow to the Republic because it meant defeat for the Asturian miners who had volunteered to fight in relatively large numbers and had a history of tough resistance (Salas Larrazábal 1973:358).

In October, the Nationalists seemed unstoppable as they conquered town after town and village after village south of Madrid (Thomas 1961:307–8). Reputedly "fascist" prisoners paid the price for their side's victories. Republican military authorities learned that a group of three hundred militiamen had executed "various" adult inmates who were snatched from the reformatory in Ocaña (Toledo).[83] Northeast of the capital, in Sigüenza, militias "without exception" abandoned the town as the enemy approached.[84] A number of militiamen near Madrid had the habit of leaving the front for the rear in search of another unit that was in a less dangerous situation.[85] These "slackers" (*desaprensivos*), as they were called by the high command, were reluctant to sacrifice their bodies but were anxious to retain the free meals and the ten-pesetas-per-day stipend. They were especially interested in joining hometown militias, which were stationed away from the front.[86] The homing instincts of both urban and especially rural residents would be evident throughout the conflict. In other words, even at the beginning of the war, some militiamen wanted to serve on quiet fronts. The proliferation of committees and militias made control difficult and centralization necessary. Severe punishment, including life imprisonment, was imposed to stop individuals' switching to cushy units. Certain groups were absolutely forbidden to move from their positions between sunrise and sunset.[87] They were told not to ask for sick leave that was granted only with the approval of a military physician.[88]

The miserable military record of the Republic did not lead to optimism about the prospects of the battle for Madrid. Nationalist bombardments, in which the German-controlled Condor Legion participated, terrorized the urban population, including thousands of refugees fleeing the rebel advance. By the end of 1936 at least seventy thousand refugees had flooded into the capital (*Rapport de la mission* 1937?:21). Their influx balanced those who left the city; thus Spain did not experience the massive de-urbanization that occurred in Russia during its civil war (Figes 1996:609). In late October, between twenty and twenty-five thousand Nationalist troops—mainly Moroccans and legionnaires—under the command of General Varela, approached the capital. On 5 November the Republican government decided to abandon Madrid for securer Valencia. The decision to move the capital divided the government, which now included, for the first time in history, anarchist ministers. The latter chose their practical need for cooperation with other Republican forces over their stateless utopian project of the future. The four newly appointed CNT ministers opposed the transfer of the capital, but libertarian leaders silently accepted in the name of government solidarity what they considered to be an unwise move. The shift of the national government to Valencia and later to Barcelona limited Valencian and eventually Catalan hopes for autonomy (Bosch Sánchez 1983:69).

At the same time, many *madrileños* proved reluctant to follow their government to the new capital. The ties of geography and family were stronger than those of politics and ideology. For personal reasons, sixty-two communications workers refused orders from their director to leave Madrid after the national government had abandoned the city.[89] Management felt justified making the transfers since the Nationalists had cut telephone and telegraph lines to the capital while the volume of communications work in the provinces had increased. Thus, leaving Madrid became a patriotic as well as a professional duty. In fact, after the Nationalist bombings of the city in the fall of 1936, the government had encouraged nonessential personnel to depart in order to mitigate growing shortages of food and housing (Aróstegui 1988:143–44). Nevertheless, these sixty-two employees insisted for their own reasons that they should remain in the city. Almost all the disobedient workers had joined the CNT or UGT well after July 1936, indicating a degree of opportunism since—as we have seen— a union card had become a prerequisite for survival in wartime Madrid. In a plea to its militants, CNT telephone officials commented bitterly on the indifference to the union exhibited by the "majority of comrades." They accused the inactive of "scientifically sabotaging antifascism and the Republic."[90]

The overwhelming majority of the sixty-two who refused the transfer had joined the UGT after July but then switched to the CNT, believing that the latter organization would defend them against the transfer order. These "butterflies" (*mariposas*) were not, in general, right-wingers. Five had been members of the monarchist Acción Popular and only one had belonged to the Falange. To gain members, the CNT local supported the refusals of the disobedient wage earners, subsequently embarrassing the CNT regional.[91] According to militants from both unions, the saga of the telephone transfers indicated that most of the rank and file and many of their leaders were not revolutionary but merely opportunistic. A CNT activist pessimistically concluded his short history of the Spanish workers' movement: "In reality, neither union is dominated by revolutionary militants but rather by people who had to have a union card for practical reasons. . . . In the telegraph section, except for a small number of revolutionaries, the rest don't really care about the union."[92] In other sectors, workers would switch from one union to another for personal or financial reasons, not because of ideology.

Largo Caballero appointed General José Miaja to lead the defense of the threatened capital. The Republic's history of defeats at the hands of Franco's regular forces led many to believe that Miaja had taken on an impossible job.[93] Yet Miaja proved himself a highly capable organizer, and Franco acknowledged his rival's bravery and ability (Cantalupo 1951:97).[94] In the evening of 7 November, Nationalist troops at the Casa de Campo on the outskirts of the city center met the stiffest resistance yet encountered as they tried to cross the Manzanares River. The threat to the capital stimulated one of the worst massacres of the conflict. On the nights of 6 and 7 November, prison guards removed from the Model Prison over one thousand inmates, identified as being pro-Franco "Fifth Columnists," and coldly executed them in wide ditches in the town of Paracuellos, northeast of Madrid (see Cervera 1999:90–100). Other murders of political prisoners followed on succeeding nights. A week later, Republican militias were ordered not to execute prisoners of war.[95]

On 7 November, an Italian tank was blown up, and on the body of one of the dead officers, Republicans found a copy of General Varela's operational orders for the conquest of the capital. Loyalists therefore knew where Nationalists would attack. Colonel Rojo moved his best troops to the Casa del Campo and the University City, and on 8 November they proved able to turn back the enemy. When they hesitated, officers stepped into the gap. As the Moroccans broke through near the Model Prison, General Miaja himself visited the threatened sector, drew his pistol, and harangued retreating soldiers, "Cowards, die in your trenches. Die with your General" (quoted in Jackson 1965:327). Miaja's example—which was reminiscent of the valor of Moscardó—was effective, and his men eliminated the Moroccan vanguard. Nationalist officers reported that the enemy's resistance was "fierce" and "tenacious" (Martínez Bande 1976:249–51).

One Nationalist column reported losing 284 men, many of them Moors. Desertions were relatively minimal as troops on both sides displayed commitment.[96] During the Battle of Madrid, even if some self-inflicted wounds were reported, Republican retreats never turned into routs (Salas Larrazábal 1973:599; Martínez Bande 1984:28).

The successful defense of Madrid, summarized by the well-known slogan "no pasarán (they shall not pass)," was the greatest military achievement of the militants, both Spanish and foreign. Republican forces met the challenge of the Army of Africa and stymied the enemy's attempt to capture Madrid. In the history of Western civil wars, no side has won without conquering the capital. London remained in the hands of Parliament; Paris was controlled by revolutionaries; Washington by the federal government; and Moscow (and Petrograd) by the Bolsheviks. Franco could not expect to win quickly without Madrid. On 8 November, the first units of the International Brigades—some three thousand men, mostly antifascist Italians and Germans—arrived in the city. Many were veterans of the First World War, and they impressed citizens with their military bearing and professional marching. Their examples of digging foxholes, using cover, and economizing ammunition were models for Spanish militiamen. The first few hundred Internationals who were ordered into the Casa de Campo were disseminated in the ratio of one brigadier to four Spaniards. They bore the brunt of Nationalist attacks in University City, and many observers from various political persuasions have long regarded them as the key to Republican victory (Borkenau 1963:226; Bolloten 1991:316; cf. Jackson 1965:326). Their courage was real and their officers were killed or wounded in much larger numbers than other Republican troops (see Wintringham 1939:252). The Internationals came to embody the Republic's major military success of 1936. The U.S. volunteer, Alvah Bessie has well expressed their collectivist and anti-individualist mission: "It was necessary for me, at that stage of my development as a man, to work (for the first time) in a large body of men; to submerge myself in that mass, seeking neither distinction nor preferment (the reverse of my activities for the past several years) and in this way to achieve self-discipline, patience and unselfishness—the opposite of a long middle class training—and the construction of a life that would be geared to other men and the world events that circumscribed them" (Bessie 1975:182). To many of Bessie's generation and political orientation, Spain represented "the chance to make one grand, uncomplicated gesture of personal sacrifice and faith which might never occur again" (Lee 1991:46).

The arrival of a shipment of Soviet arms and supplies, especially first-rate tanks and planes (for which the Republic would pay dearly) bolstered the defenders (Whealey 1989:22; Howson 1999:138). Tanks were insufficiently numerous and sophisticated to play a major role in the conflict. The November shipment of Russian aircraft, however, gave Republicans air superiority

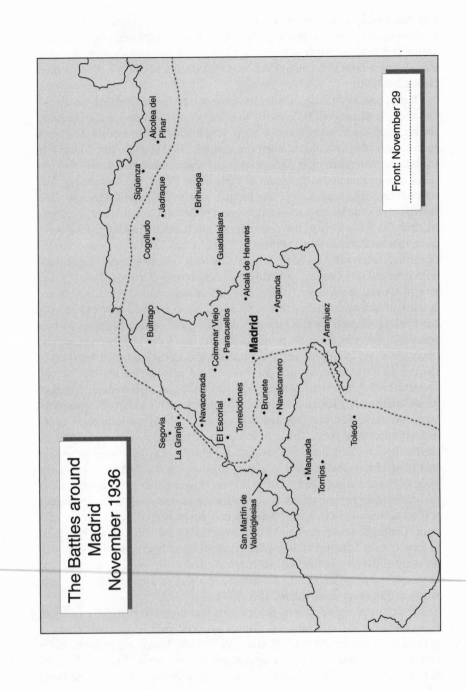

The Battles around Madrid November 1936

Front: November 29

Alcolea del Pinar
Sigüenza
Jadraque
Brihuega
Cogolludo
Guadalajara
Alcalá de Henares
Buitrago
Colmenar Viejo
Paracuellos
Madrid
Arganda
Aranjuez
Navacerrada
Torrelodones
El Escorial
Brunete
Navalcarnero
Segovia
La Granja
Toledo
San Martín de Valdeiglesias
Maqueda
Torrijos

possibly for the first time, and Nationalist troops sometimes proved as panicky under air attack as leftist militiamen (Martínez Bande 1984:36; Durán
1979:66; Coverdale 1975:109). On occasion, Moorish *regulares* fled and abandoned their equipment as quickly as Republican militiamen.

Madrid, however, was not saved by its residents (there were very few fighting battalions of *madrileños*) but rather by forces that arrived from its Sierra,
Levante, Andalusia, Catalonia, and, as mentioned, from abroad (Martínez
Bande 1984:25). Catalan nationalists and anarchists came to help the defense.
On 14 November, Durruti, the anarchist legend, entered the capital at the head
of his three-thousand-man column. He asked Miaja for a tough assignment and
was given a sector of the University City. On 17 November, his anarchists could
not prevent Varela's insurgents from penetrating his lines and entering the Clinical Hospital. Once again, Miaja rushed to the front and successfully rallied
its defenders. Miaja's mission was helped by the growth of Republican forces
from ten thousand defenders at the beginning of the month to forty-thousand
at the end (Martínez Bande 1984:25, 262). In mid-November the Republic's
demographic advantage allowed it to mobilize thirty thousand armed men to
defend the capital. Recalling the massive participation of Londoners in erect-
ing urban defenses during their civil war, an estimated eighteen thousand
Madrid workers constructed formidable fortifications, a relatively rarity in the
Spanish conflict. It is important to point out that this civilian contribution
occurred before the months of hunger that would dampen urban desires to sacrifice for a Republican victory. Although the Nationalist offensive exhausted
itself, the insurgents stepped up their bombing and shelling of the city, which
killed an estimated five hundred people on the night of 17 and 18 November.[97]
Hundreds more would perish in succeeding nights. Franco's German allies,
especially officers of the Condor Legion, wanted to gauge the reaction of the
civilian population to mass destruction. The five- to six-thousand-man aircraft
group, which was assembled in Spain in November, would be one of the
Führer's contributions to Nationalist victory (Coverdale 1975:113; cf. Howson 1999:19). German experiments in mass bombing would set a precedent
that would culminate during World War II in the devastation of London, Ham-
burg, Dresden, and Tokyo (Thomas 1961:329).

Republican success came at a high price. On 21 November, Durruti died in
mysterious circumstances.[98] Several conjectures circulated to explain his death.
Some argued that he was killed accidentally when a gun unexpectedly fired.
Others assumed that he was shot by one of his own men as he attempted to
halt their flight before advancing Moors. Whatever the case, his body was
returned to Barcelona where his funeral became the greatest ceremony of the
war. A crowd of two hundred or three hundred thousand (depending on estimates) attended. Many of them pledged to carry out Durruti's principles, even
if it was unclear what these really were (Thomas 1961:329).[99]

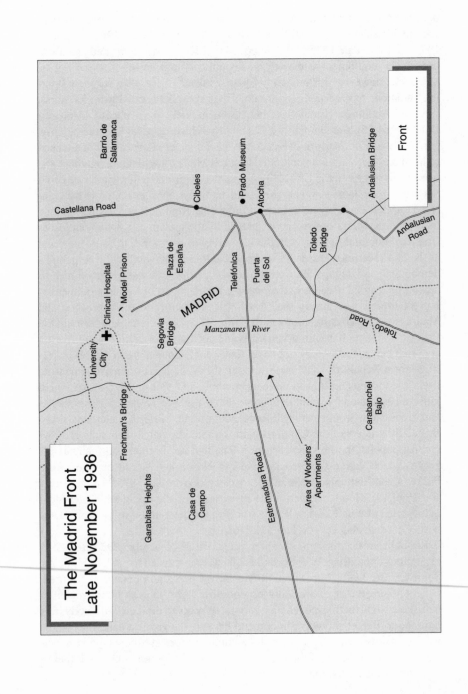

The Madrid Front
Late November 1936

Front

Barrio de Salamanca

Castellana Road

Cibeles

• Prado Museum

Atocha

Andalusian Bridge

Andalusian Road

Clinical Hospital

Model Prison

Plaza de España

Telefónica

Puerta del Sol

Toledo Bridge

Toledo Road

University City

MADRID

Segovia Bridge

Manzanares River

Frechman's Bridge

Garabitas Heights

Casa de Campo

Estremadura Road

Area of Workers' Apartments

Carabanchel Bajo

The Republican high command estimated that the battle cost nine thousand of its best fighters.[100] Their replacements did "not have the same fighting ability." The toll was particularly acute among officers. Madrid was a great defensive victory but also a dangerous bleeding of militants. From 6 to 11 November, Republican forces lost at least 2,369 men (Martínez Bande 1976:136). The early casualties of some of its most devoted fighters would make it difficult for the Republic to win a long war. The success of the Loyalists in Madrid ended Franco's desire for a rapid victory. His failure to capture the capital would mean a war of attrition that the more efficient side would win.

Most of the English-language literature has emphasized the heroism and sacrifice of the *madrileños* in preventing the Nationalists from storming their capital. According to Hugh Thomas (1961:322), "the urban mass" opposed the Moroccans and legionnaires. The victory of the Republic was a "victory of the populace." Paul Preston (1986:88) agrees that the defense of Madrid was "a heroic effort which involved the whole population." Wartime Madrid has remained the prime example of popular antifascism (Serrano 1991). Many were willing to sacrifice to save the capital from Nationalist forces. Tens of unions and factory committees reported the deaths of dozens of poorly armed and underclothed militants at the front. In the opening months of war, rank-and-file workers seldom objected to deductions from their paychecks to finance measures of solidarity designed to assist families of the fallen. A 5 percent salary deduction destined for militiamen was standard in many enterprises. Wage earners donated to organizations such as Socorro Rojo Internacional (a politically "red" Red Cross) and Solidaridad Internacional Antifascista. War widows and their children received priority of employment in many firms. At the beginning of the conflict, those who missed work usually did so for what was considered to be a legitimate reason, for example, to aid an injured family member or to help evacuate children from a city subjected to constant Nationalist attacks. The committed gave their time freely for the cause. In Barcelona also, many responded. People willingly donated their blood during the first months of the war (Broggi i Vallès 1986:18). Collectives lent thousands to militia columns.[101]

Yet even at the start of the war, solidarity was not universal, and there were many workers who could be classified as egotistical. Most wage laborers seem to have had a marginal allegiance to their union, whether the CNT or the UGT. In many regions and cities, they joined one or the other organization because it guaranteed employment and insured them against harassment or imprisonment by the various official police forces, which were anxious to take measures against those not affiliated with a Popular Front organization (Bosch Sánchez 1983:29). Azaña (1982:88, 1990:3:502) commented bitterly, "The syndicalist spirit dominates factories, including munitions factories. [Socialist leader Indalecio] Prieto has made it public that when there were no pursuit planes in Madrid, workers of the repair shop in Los Alcázares refused to lengthen the workday or to work on Sundays." He also noted: "The construction strike—which had begun in May, imposed and directed by the CNT—persisted after the war started. It did not finish until August" (Azaña 1990:3:449).

The new Republican capital became known, not for its fighting prowess, but rather for its nightlife. "There was much justification for the comment of new arrivals in Valencia . . . that the Levante capital 'didn't seem to know there was a war going on.' . . . Cabarets were crowded from opening hour early in the afternoon until long after midnight" (Knoblaugh 1937:164). Madrid maintained its amusements. Its female performing artists gave benefit concerts in return for a safe-conduct pass out of the city (Calleja Martín 1991:119–20).

Lack of commitment promoted scandal. Nationalist intelligence reports asserted that the CNT and various committees in Barcelona were selling antifascist identity cards.[102] In other parts of the Republican zone, Popular Front organizations were insubstantial. In a number of *pueblos,* union organizations arose only after the *pronunciamiento.* In other words, like the Spanish revolution itself, local organizations of the left sprang into existence as a reaction to the military revolt. In the province of Teruel, in the villages of Puertomingalvo (1,200 inhabitants) and Escorihuela (675), all organizations—UGT, CNT, JJLL (Juventudes Libertarias), and Izquierda Republicana—formed after 19 July.[103] In most towns in the orange-growing areas of the Levante, neither the CNT or the UGT existed prior to the military uprising.[104] New members may or may not have agreed with the ultimate collectivist goals of the organizations but felt that only the unions could defend their material interests (Casanova 1985:3). The uncommitted chose either the CNT or the UGT according to pragmatic, not ideological, criteria. They would join the organization that could either guarantee employment or required lower dues.[105] *Ugetistas* could be "elks in a community of buffaloes" (Woolsey 1998:86). The UGT was a minority union in Barcelona (6,000 members) and in Catalonia (10,000 members) and was forced to confront the hostility of the more powerful CNT. In small Aragon towns, Izquierda Republicana members might switch to the CNT because it was more powerful and influential in the region.[106] Autonomous locals, which had not affiliated with any major labor federation, thought it advisable for reasons of antifascism or opportunism to join one of the newly empowered organizations.[107] For instance, it was publicly announced that all Madrid newspaper vendors had to join either the CNT or UGT by 20 October 1936, if they wished to continue to receive their allotment of the daily press (*El Liberal,* 9 October 1936). A CNT postal worker complained about new adherents, concluding that "from the beginning the CNT and UGT have erred in admitting unknown comrades."[108] Many did not pay their dues, and on May Day in 1937 militants checked each member's union card to make sure that it was up to date.[109] Workers who were too far behind in union dues might lose their jobs.

In one major graphics firm, the Unión Bolsera Madrileña, delegates were requested to keep a list of all workers who had not joined a Popular Front organization.[110] Yet in this firm the control committee itself was hardly a paragon of revolutionary or even trade-union virtue: none of its members had joined a union until after the *pronunciamiento* erupted.[111] It seems that the truly devoted were not in the rear but fighting at the front. As a way of ensuring loyalty to the cause, both unions were reluctant to allow members who had joined after 19 July to serve in positions of responsibility.[112] To circumvent these restrictions, one worker falsified his union card.[113] A chauffeur, who was a bit too eager to hedge his bets, was expelled from the CNT transportation union for belonging to four political parties.[114] Throughout the war the unions pressured the nonaffiliated to join in order to increase each organizations' financial base and political power.[115]

Acquisitive individualists showed almost immediately that they were more willing to struggle for higher wages than for the Republic. Early in the conflict, the Graphic Arts Union, an important organization in the largely service economy of the Spanish capital, discouraged demands for pay hikes.[116] To avoid difficulties for management, it asked the rear not to request higher wages.[117] One militant considered all wage hikes "antisocial" and believed— with the "most advanced" parties and unions—that wage earners should labor extra hours without remuneration. Yet the control committee of the Unión Bolsera Madrileña was forced to deal with what were, according to at least one of its members, "immoral" and "mean-spirited" demands for higher pay and more overtime.[118] Their comrades' egotism at the workplace so frustrated some militants that they departed for the front, only to find their fellow soldiers' indiscipline equally repulsive (Vilanova 1995:56).

Street vendors, who had been organized by the UGT, had been excellent *milicianos* at the beginning of war and had acted with "true heroism," despite scarcities of arms and food.[119] By January, several factors had cooled their initial enthusiasm. Their more apathetic colleagues had been able to avoid military service by joining the CNT that, at least in this branch, did not push its members to fight for the Republic. Nonmilitants, who constituted an overwhelming majority in every industry, searched for and adhered to the less rigorous and less demanding union. Thus, much to the chagrin of UGT militants, the CNT vendors were hawking daily in the streets and making handsome profits. This demoralized committed colleagues, who were forced to ask the UGT to allow their wives to peddle papers. By the beginning of 1937, commerce had triumphed over valor: The *milicianos* abandoned their battalion to return to their businesses on the streets.

Ironically, the nascent war economy led many wage earners to ignore leaders' pleas. Food shortages stimulated inflation throughout the urban economy. The extended strike that protested the *pronunciamiento* aggravated shortfalls

(*De julio a julio,* cited in Martínez Bande 1970:38). Once prerevolutionary stocks were used up, food deficits became more acute. The war created a crisis in the Barcelona construction industry.[120] In general, prices of materials increased much faster than wages. The UGT urged its members to renounce trade-union demands concerning wages or hours. All workers, they argued, should sacrifice for the war effort. So did the legendary Durruti before his death (quoted in Martínez Bande 1976:179). Another famous *faísta,* Juan García Oliver, told his comrades "not to talk about the six-hour day or the eight-hour day or even of any fixed number of working hours. How many hours do we have to work now? As many as are necessary for the victory of the revolution" (quoted in Borkenau 1963:92).[121]

In a number of regions and cities, workers who took over their factories avoided the tutelage of unions or regional, let alone national, economic organizations. As in the Russian civil war, committees of wage earners divided profits among themselves and refused to pay taxes (Bosch Sánchez 1983:31; see also Figes 1996:611). In Valencia, a CNT militant repeatedly noted the "egoism" of wage earners (Noja Ruiz n.d.:11, 1937:16). Some industrial and urban collectives were able to turn themselves into largely self-sufficient units by providing their employees with gardens. Acquisitive individualists often doubled as entrepreneurs. The main priority of entrepreneurial types was not consumption but rather earning wages or making deals. Working overtime was one form of entrepreneurial individualism. In watchmaking and repair, "many union members and bosses" disregarded the legal forty-four-hour workweek.[122] In the midst of the battle of Madrid, milkmen established regulations that punished those engaging in unauthorized overtime by ordering them to perform fortification work.[123]

Entrepreneurial and acquisitive individualisms, although obstacles to revolutionary or Republican solidarity, were much less damaging to the cause during 1936 than was subversive individualism. Included under this rubric were asocial and antisocial phenomena such as absenteeism, petty theft, apathy, indiscipline, and refusals to work or fight. These actions revealed the failure of revolutionary social projects to induce workers to sacrifice.[124] They showed workers' and soldiers' rejection of the secular religion of labor, invented by the Enlightenment and shared by both republicans and Marxists. Revolution and war increased the pressures of the workplace, but workers resisted this intensified socialization by avoiding work time. Anonymous individuals interpreted the revolution in their own subversive ways. Perhaps the most important example occurred among Madrid wage earners who did not produce but took advantage of union power to pick up a paycheck (Salas Larrazábal 1973:472–73; Martín-Blázquez 1938:190–91). Few fortification workers really dug trenches, but many received a ration (cf. Líster 1966:86). A case of faking illness appeared among linoleum workers at the beginning of the conflict:

inspectors did not find the "sick" worker at home during their visits and reasonably concluded that he was pursuing his own interests.[125] Very early in the war, the workers of the UGT-affiliated Unión Bolsera Madrileña were subjected to stringent penalties for lateness.[126] In both Barcelona and Valencia, workers returned to work slowly and irregularly.[127]

What concerned the first meetings of the council of the collectivized General Motors assembly plant was not the hostile attitude of the former bosses but rather the behavior of its own workers. The factory was urged to produce trucks for the Republic, and its council agreed that "all comrades who are not absolutely necessary for union organizations must return to work immediately. They will be strictly controlled."[128] The personnel delegate was to evaluate all leave demands "in order to avoid any possible abuses." Sickness would be "severely watched to avoid any tricks or lies." All absentees were to be investigated, and union physicians assigned to pursue "doubtful" cases. If they found deceit, the guilty worker would be expelled from the factory. Guards were posted in workshops. Throughout November, demands for leave continued to provoke repression from the committee. The doorman was ordered to halt the departure of any employee who did not have a correctly signed pass. The council intended to stop trafficking and favoritism in the use of company automobiles. Throughout the war those, such as the employees of General Motors, who had access to cars often abused their privilege. In addition, pilfering persisted and may have increased. In the repair workshops "quantities of materials of significant value have disappeared." Thefts reached the point that the doorman employed in this department asked to be transferred since he wished to avoid responsibility for his colleagues' pilfering. To reduce lateness, all workers would be required to punch in.[129] Special permission was required to leave early.

To intensify production a sixty-hour week was planned. In early September 1936 all the delegates of factory committees involved in war production agreed "to give the strictest orders to the entire defense-industry workforce. It is necessary to work as many hours as needed. Those who don't carry out these orders will be treated as enemies."[130] In early October committees invigorated the fight against absenteeism by requiring prior authorization for any days missed.[131] The following week the committee posted a note on the time clock "in view of the fact that production is declining and to increase the collective good, it is necessary that each person work with interest and enthusiasm."[132] Discipline problems—lateness, faking illnesses, and unauthorized leave—persisted throughout the conflict.

In cities of the Republican zone, many owners had fled or had been eliminated. The Spanish civil war introduced the "servant crisis" that more advanced nations had already experienced before or during World War I. The relatively prosperous who were lucky enough to escape with their lives lost their maids, who were "liberated" from domestic service. For example, Madrid's active population of three hundred thousand persons included seventy thousand maids, or *criadas* (Cervera 1999:152). The flight of the wealthy also compelled working-class organizations to take over factories and workshops. Apathy and indifference plagued revolutionary attempts to establish industrial democracy. Rank-and-file Barcelona workers believed that a new set of rulers had replaced the old and that the workplace was still unfriendly territory (Vilanova 1995:54). In Madrid, despite collectivization of 30 percent of industries, many wage earners remained without commitment to the cause (Hermet 1989:123). Fines and threats to discontinue food coupons punished Madrid linoleum workers who missed meetings.[133] Several were fined for indiscipline.[134]

Given individual priorities, the bombing of Madrid did not inspire in all workers the sacrifice that novelists and historians have depicted. For instance, the committee of a firm working for the arms industry felt compelled to move its machinery to a new location despite an order from the Defense Committee that discouraged transfers of plant equipment during periods of enemy bombardments.[135] Although the firm was located in a "dangerous area," which was presumably vulnerable to attack by *franquistas,* the move was made in response not only to the Nationalist danger but also from a less identifiable internal foe that was stealing "machines, tools, and materials." Looting and theft continued to harm the firm's efforts to produce for the Republican effort. Workers in another company were warned that repeated acts of indiscipline would result in expulsion from the factory. Furthermore, they were expressly forbidden to indulge their curiosity by leaving the shop floor to observe air battles over Madrid.[136] Both office and manual workers had to carry a pass in order to exit the workplace.[137] In Cartagena enemy shelling inspired workers to abandon their jobs and to exit the city. "After the cannon bombardment of Elizalde in Guipúzcoa, no one wanted to work at night. When the government left Madrid, Valencia came close to welcoming it with cannon fire. Her citizens feared that its presence might attract air raids. Until then Valencians hadn't felt the war. They received refugees grudgingly because they ate up provisions" (Azaña 1982:89, 1990:3:427).

Examples of everyday egotism abounded. At the very start of the struggle, con artists posed as CNT militants to fleece subscription money from a gullible public that thought it was supporting the official organ of the Confederación (*La Libertad,* 1 August 1936). Swindlers posted signs on gambling machines falsely indicating that the proceeds were destined for the antifascist Red Cross (*La Libertad,* 18 September 1936). In a situation in which the unions had in many cases confiscated the property of landlords who had fled, many workers refused to pay rent.[138] Laborers were suspected of inflating their expense accounts.[139] Some shop clerks divided the available victuals among themselves and ignored the needs of remaining comrades.[140] The offenders were punished, and steps were taken to stop unauthorized members who claimed to represent the collective from acquiring food.[141] By late 1936, courts in the Republican zone began to be much more concerned with common criminals than with military rebels (Sánchez Recio 1991:104).

In the city and the countryside, proletarians confiscated the property of "fascists" and bourgeois.[142] Expropriation by *braceros* and their supporters in militias did create a material basis of support for the Popular Front. Land redistribution heightened enthusiasm for the Republic among numerous farm workers (Pons Prades 1977:227). On 7 October 1936, Vicente Uribe, the Communist minister of agriculture, gave peasants the right to farm individually or collectively land confiscated from those who supported the uprising (Bolloten 1991:236). However, changes in property relations might produce disorder as well as enthusiasm. Republican confiscations endangered the Valencian harvest (Bosch Sánchez 1983:38). According to Uribe, "no one was working the land." In the eyes of many peasants in the Valencian region, Popular Front organizations abused their power by using coercion, abolishing money, and sacrificing animals. Peasants called the collectives "el muntó," or the Valencian expression for riot (Bosch Sánchez 1983:57). The result was a decline in production.

In Aragon, as in Valencia, many individualistic peasants were forced to join collectives even though they wanted to leave them to farm their own land. At Tamarite de Litera (Huesca) farmers who owned less than 3.5 hectares of land had to belong to the collective (Leval 1975:216). Those with more property were offered a choice, but all had to turn over their working animals to the collectivity. Many of the more prosperous opted out of the collective at the earliest possible moment. Agricultural collectives had considerable autonomy, and early in the revolution some turned toward self-sufficiency. Their autonomy became in the words of the CNT ex-secretary-general, Horacio Prieto, "permanent egoism" (speech of 15 January 1938, quoted in Bosch Sánchez 1983:280). Usually CNT and UGT members had to orient collectives. The theme of collectivization has fascinated observers, but it must be remembered that although total confiscation may have amounted to approximately one-third of arable land, only 18.5 percent of the land in the Republican zone was collectivized (Payne 1970:240–41; Garrido González 1988:100).[143] Thus individualists on the land were overwhelmingly dominant, especially in comparison to the situation of Soviet agriculture in the same period. More than three hundred thousand Spanish peasants acquired land in one form or another. Half of these peasants resided in the provinces of Albacete, Ciudad Real, Cuenca, Toledo, and Madrid. Perhaps the extent of land reform in the center helps to explain why much of that region resisted repeated Nationalist assaults against Madrid in 1936 and 1937. For example, the famous and reputedly fierce Fifth Regiment was said to be composed of approximately 50 percent peasants (Líster 1966:62; see Blanco Rodríguez 1993:341–48). In March, Uribe announced that nearly 9 percent of total Spanish farmlands had been distributed to the peasantry. By the end of the year, the Communist press claimed that over a third of private holdings had been redistributed or confiscated (Bernecker 1982:146–48). The peasants, the PCE asserted, had largely opted for individual use. Unfortunately for the Republic, the break up of large estates usually encouraged self-sufficiency rather than production for the market. In Catalonia, collectives were islands in a sea of medium and small property holders (Balcells 1968:280). An inquiry conducted by the *Generalitat* at the end of 1936 revealed that only sixty-six localities had taken some collectivist measures, and over one thousand municipalities had not (Bernecker 1982:194–96). Small owners, it seems, formed the relatively few collectives that did exist (Bernecker 1982:170). In Catalonia, the *Generalitat*'s decree of 5 January 1937 reinforced the family farm by granting legal usufruct to those who had cultivated the land as of 18 July 1936 (Payne 1970:259). Even in Aragon, supposedly the most revolutionary and anarchist of regions, where the CNT was often the most powerful organization, most of the land was not collectivized. Notwithstanding the presence of militias who encouraged it, only 40 percent of the land of the region was expropriated. In February 1937, 275 collectives had 80,000 members; in June, 450 collectives held 180,000 members, less than two-fifths of the Aragonese population in the Republican zone.[144] In Castile, collectives often started late and were formed in 1937.

Collectivization occurred both spontaneously and unwillingly. As in the French Revolution, joyful bonfires of property deeds and documents symbolized the end of the old economic order (Borkenau 1963:102). Poorer peasants were willing to give collectives a chance (Leval 1975:91; Collectif Equipo 1997:57). At the same time, though, most peasants remained apolitical and uncommitted to any utopian visions (Simoni and Simoni 1984:140). They may have been attracted by the "welfare-state image of the good life" that various forms of communism or socialism promised (Fitzpatrick 1994:10). In other words, peasants wanted the advantages and perks that urban industrial workers had gained. Many who were not entirely destitute may have felt that collectivization might help to solve the problem of dispersed plots. Thus, collectivization could lead in theory to a needed rationalization of Spanish holdings, which were scattered, tiny, and farmed without machinery. As in the Soviet Union, numerous Spanish collectives seem to have allowed their members to work personal plots or to raise animals (Leval 1975:146, 217). Furthermore, collectives were not communes and did not force or even encourage their members to live together.

In part, though, collectivization was forced. The atmosphere of execution of "fascists" encouraged obedience to radical authorities. Anarchosyndicalist militiamen believed that collectives were the best way to feed the troops. Their columns gave a needed boost to a feeble local militancy. Individualists also resented the prohibition that existed in some villages on employing wage labor (Fraser 1986:355). In a number of towns, they resisted threats to their property.[145] They found that the collective, which in some settlements enrolled the majority of inhabitants, tended to boycott them. An anarchosyndicalist source reported that "the small owners who don't wish to join a collective . . . had to wage a difficult struggle to survive" (Souchy and Folgare 1977:27). On 2 January in Albelda (Huesca), tensions between property owners and a "thieving" antifascist committee stimulated an owners' street demonstration against the committee that an angry crowd believed had unfairly arrested a woman.[146] In retaliation, a few demonstrators were jailed. Yet in comparison to the Soviet precedent, Spanish collectivization was largely voluntary.[147] A powerful state did not force peasants to combine literally at gunpoint. Nor did they slaughter their animals en masse.

Acquisitive individualism was not specifically bourgeois but a popular and international phenomenon that occurred in the countryside, the city, and abroad. Few, regardless of politics, had confidence in Republican money, and all wanted to be paid in hard coin. This was confirmed very early in the struggle, when France (which may have eventually received more than one quarter of Spanish gold reserves) provided some goods and services in exchange for Spanish gold (Viñas 1979:78). The USSR was enticed to support the Republic not only for strategic and political reasons but also because it had the fourth largest gold reserves in the world (Viñas 1984:267; Sardá 1970:435; Howson 1999:128). Nearly five hundred tons of Spanish gold arrived in the Soviet Union in November 1936. Given the hostility of Western financial institutions, Spanish Republican officials believed that the "workers' state" was the safest place for their enormous deposit, even while they reserved the right to transfer it from Moscow or to sell it to any nation they wished. The Spanish government reasonably feared that if its gold were deposited in banks of a Western nation, the latter might restrict or block its use. By the beginning of 1937, the Soviet state refused to advance more credit and began to insist that the Republic pay for arms and materiel with the gold deposited on its territory. The Soviets continued to make loans backed by Spanish gold in Moscow. The precious metal assured them that their aid would not rest unremunerated and encouraged further assistance. Although the USSR was only great power to substantially aid the Spanish Republic, its support was nonetheless "measured."[148] The Republic was never certain if the Soviets would continue to advance credit or even to supply material.

Several factors constrained Soviet assistance. The Russians had to take into account their own international position and the parlous situation of their ally. After the Nationalist capture of Málaga in February 1937, they became more reluctant to make loans. Furthermore, fears of provoking the Germans and Italians into a general European conflict restrained the level of Russian help. In order to fill Republican aid requests, the Soviet Union had to purchase raw materials from foreign countries. From February 1937 to April 1938, Spanish gold was sold and liquidated to pay for the war. The Russian sales illustrated the major difference between Republican and Nationalist finances. The former had to compensate its suppliers and allies with precious metals or hard currency; the latter received major credits from the fascist powers and others (Viñas 1979:328–29). Possibly a "realistic" or skeptical assessment of the Republic's chances for victory led the Russians to limit credit much more strictly than Franco's allies.

Individuals in the Republican zone distrusted their own money as much as the Soviet and other states did. One of most common acquisitive practices was the hoarding of coins. Those with limited silver content were almost immediately stashed away. "The egotism of certain people" triumphed over repeated calls by both the Basque and other Republican authorities not to stockpile silver, gold, or other metals (Santacreu Soler 1986:50; González Portilla and Garmendia 1988:70).[149] The owners of the means of production were not the only hoarders and speculators. As Richard Cobb (1987:289) has suggested in another context, "almost everyone was a hoarder at times, and the country people always were." In Alicante, it seems, nearly everybody wanted to keep small change. This practice disrupted daily commerce, an intrinsic part of everyday life in many towns.[150] Orwell (1980:198) reported that the lack of coins intensified the food shortage for the poorest people, who had to wait in long lines to find merchants who could break their bills. Some had to resort to barter or, for small transactions, to ad hoc script printed by localities. When authorities confiscated stockpiles of coins and returned them to circulation, they were immediately stashed away by another speculator. This speculative procurement of metallic currency contradicted what was supposedly a major aspect of the Spanish revolution—the abolition of money. Savers ignored patriotic pleas from Popular Front newspapers and emptied their accounts even from financial institutions that had the solid backing of working-class organizations. The rivalry between the CNT and the UGT compounded the problem. Neither organization would deposit its own collectives' cash in its rival's bank (Bolloten 1991:126). The distrust of Republican currency spread to the military. Some Republican soldiers resented being paid in "paper money."[151] Militiamen were threatened with severe punishment if they were caught in possession of "fascist" banknotes.[152] By January 1937, Republican money could not buy everything. As in the Russian civil war, peasants were reluctant to trade real goods for government paper (Figes 1996:608). For example, the municipality of Altea (Alicante) forbade trading pork for Republican currency (Santacreu Soler 1986:67).

The Nationalist zone also suffered from the lack of coins, but geography, not hoarding, was the major cause. The mint remained in the Republican zone.

The Nationalist shortage was resolved by contracting an Italian firm to print bills of one and two pesetas (Banco de España 1979:335). Faith in the Nationalist peseta was stronger than its Republican counterpart (Sardá 1970:440). Nationalist authorities refused to recognize Republican money and decreed in November 1936 that all bills circulating in its zone be stamped with the seal, "Spanish state, Burgos" (Banco de España 1979:309). This allowed Nationalist financial officials to undertake an exact accounting of the amount of money in circulation. In contrast, the Republican zone experienced the proliferation not only of bills of the Bank of Spain but also of coins and paper money issued by a host of uncoordinated organizations—regional authorities in the north, the *Generalitat,* municipalities, and even unions. These bills were not usually accepted outside of the areas where they were issued. Given their aversion to money, some CNT organizations did not denote their bills in pesetas but rather in what were called "unities" (*unidades*). This semantic sleight of hand did not change the fact that "unities," like pesetas, represented value (Banco de España 1979:348). The printing of local moneys was also designed to prevent villagers from hoarding the official Republican currency (Souchy and Folgare 1977:153). The loss of confidence in the *moneda roja*—by its own workers and peasants as well as international capitalists—would be one of the major reasons for the defeat of the Republic. Wealthy Spaniards bet on the Nationalist peseta and—unlike their Russian White counterparts—provided "vast sums" to the insurgents (Richards 1998:107). They also imposed upon themselves taxes on luxury goods (wine and tobacco) and on incomes higher than sixty thousand pesetas (Cervera 1999:125).

# 2

# Opportunism

As the war endured, increasing opportunism diluted militancy. By early 1937, what one author has called popular "passionate interest" in the civil war had transformed itself into rank self-interest (Borkenau 1963:212). Around Madrid, desertions became a growing problem for the militias that had played such an important role in the defense of that city.[1] Militiamen continued to shift to less dangerous units, and in January, this practice of switching was outlawed.[2] In one battalion in Barajas—currently the site of the Madrid airport—nearly one hundred militiamen, most of whom wanted to be transferred to units in other provinces, refused to accept newly imposed military discipline.[3]

Self-interest also meant sex. Madrid soldiers ignored propaganda that warned them not to frequent prostitutes. An entrepreneurial activity that accompanies nearly all wars (and peaces), authorities discouraged pleasure professionalism. The UGT labeled prostitutes "the principal element of the fifth column."[4] The anarchists asserted a puritanical group morality and reasoned, "The man who frequents houses of ill fame is not an Anarchist. . . . He who buys a kiss puts himself on the level of the woman who sells it. Hence, an Anarchist must not purchase kisses. He should merit them" (*Revista Blanca* quoted in Bolloten 1991:69). *Claridad* identified prostitution with "the old regime . . . robbery, deceit, crime." At the outbreak of war, it was claimed, prostitutes had enthusiastically joined the people's militias; however, sex professionals were soon accused of following the dictates of fascism by selling their bodies to male

74

comrades. Ladies of leisure exerted an unsurprisingly powerful attraction over well-paid soldiers of the regular army. Militants regretted that at a time when gasoline and public transportation were desperately needed for the war effort, long lines of cars awaited their turn in the suburbs of "immorality." From these encounters with "thieves and spies," Republican soldiers would contract diseases that would keep some of them out of action longer than battle wounds. As in the Russian civil war, numbers of prostitutes probably increased dramatically in major cities (Nash 1995:156). In Madrid, "a considerable number of professional prostitutes . . . mingled with other female militants" (Cleugh 1963:100). Sex professionals were reported on the Aragon front where Durruti himself felt compelled to charter a truck to return them to Barcelona so that they would no longer "destroy young men" (Gabriel 1939:26–27). The Fifth Regiment undermined its reputation for superior morale and morality by reporting a serious problem with venereal disease (Castro Delgado 1963: 337–38). At the same time, some pleasure proletarians were reported in the Nationalist capital, where prostitutes expressed an unsubtle antifascism. Ladies of leisure working at the *maison* La Luisa, which was located directly behind the celebrated cathedral of Burgos, were reportedly hostile to insurgent aviators who frequented their bordello.[5]

These women seemed more committed than the disorganized Republican Army of the south, which had been created on 15 December and had thirty-six thousand men by the beginning of January 1937. The general supervising the active sector of the front in Cordova province admitted that the Milicias Andalucía Extremadura (CNT) disbanded "almost without being attacked and went into the village where they committed all kinds of excesses." Failure in battle was "caused fundamentally by the lack of morale," which had degenerated since early December.[6] The scarcity of aviation support demoralized troops, who felt that they had inadequate arms to fight the "fascists." The Madrid general staff was willing to provide, when available, the necessary support and equipment but was reluctant to dispatch vast resources to local militias. It feared that assistance to Republican forces in the south would create a vicious circle: to send resources to demoralized troops might mean throwing good money and men after bad, but to refuse aid would lead to further demoralization and flight. The general staff realized that battle desertions were contagious. To restore discipline, it absolutely insisted upon the disarming of defective units and punishment of the disobedient. Their weapons would be turned over to more reliable forces in the area. Madrid ultimately sent arms, equipment, and an International Brigade of machine gunners but was unable to send antiaircraft weapons that it did not possess. In total, five thousand men with "abundant equipment" were transferred to the Cordova front. The general staff thought that the reinforcements would be sufficient to reestablish the formerly advanced positions. The bolstering of the Cordova front meshed with a Republican strategy designed to take pressure off Madrid by planning offensives in other zones, such as Teruel on the Aragon front and Vitoria (Alava) in the north.[7]

In Cordova province the strategy failed, and Nationalists maintained the initiative. The initial performance of supposedly experienced Internationals sent by Madrid was little better than that of Republican and CNT militias who retreated when enemy horsemen attacked. Republican aviation officials reported that the enemy had only three hundred men on this sector of the Cordova front. The Republican operational general, Fernando Martínez Monje, countered that the enemy possessed four to five thousand men but admitted that they were not "frightening." His superiors nonetheless insisted that the adversary was very weak and should not have been victorious. Apparently, Nationalist aviators had scared Republican militiamen. Planes continued to frighten more than they killed. One company of volunteers fled to the village of Lopera where they executed four persons who were imprisoned in the town jail.[8] Authorities ultimately decided to disarm and punish two battalions of militiamen, two companies of Cordova volunteers, and other militiamen from Jaén and Estremadura. Their weapons were recycled to soldiers of a new battalion that, commanders hoped, would use them more competently than their former owners. The defeat "greatly worried" Minister of Defense Largo Caballero. The Republic lost a rich agricultural area on the verge of harvesting its bumper olive crop of 1936 to 1937. It also forfeited a hydroelectric plant (El Carpio) and two important flourmills. Nationalists claimed to have killed more than three hundred and to have captured a great quantity of war material. Insurgent aviation remained unchallenged, but the Internationals—who suffered casualties of 30 percent—rallied and managed to halt the enemy at Andújar (Toribio García 1994:12). Republican officials concluded that there was no certainty that such troops could hold the line with new air and material support, but they were virtually sure to collapse if help was not forthcoming.

At the beginning of 1937, Republican authorities faced similar dilemmas in Málaga, a city of over one hundred thousand that even then catered to international tourism. After the military rebellion was defeated, the situation in that coastal capital became literally anarchic, and muddle characterized the war effort (Jackson 1965:342; Thomas 1961:370; Bolloten 1991:343). Militias created "the independent republic of Málaga" (Martínez Bande quoted in Salas Larrazábal 1973:804). Shops were looted, fashionable residential quarters burned, and hostages assassinated in retaliation for Nationalist air raids. An urban population victimized by insurgent aviation attacks responded by hastily murdering any available "fascists." Militants of the left remained divided on party and union lines. The Málaga militia—which numbered forty thousand (mostly Andalusian) men—had attracted a wide range of opportunists who merely wanted a party or union card to facilitate their everyday existence or, in extreme cases, to save their lives (Asensio 1938:47, 75). Málaga militiamen wasted their limited supply of munitions and failed to construct roadblocks or trenches (Martínez Bande 1969:93). A key bridge remained unrepaired until insurgents conquered the city. The makeshift system of acquiring medicines with official coupons (not with currency) could not meet demand (Gracía Rivas 1986:107). In January 1937 the Republican government sent Colonel José Villalba to reorganize the defense, but given the absence of cooperation and the indifference of the *malagueños*, he could do little (see Cordón 1977:247 for a critical portrait of Villalba). Far from Madrid, Málaga militias remained untouched by national reforms that aimed to militarize and centralize them. Largo Caballero was aware of the disorder and refused to commit more resources to what he considered an ill-fated effort (Salas Larrazábal and Salas Larrazábal 1986:182).

To conquer Málaga, the Nationalists employed approximately ten thousand Moors, five thousand *requetés,* and fourteen battalions (over 11,000 men) of Italian "volunteers" under the command of Mussolini's trusted supporter, the Italian General Roatta. So that the glory of their victories in Spain would reflect favorably upon his Fascist regime, the Duce insisted on organizational auton-omy for his nearly fifty thousand combatants (Coverdale 1975:168–207). Franco's forces generally retained a considerable numerical advantage in for-eigners fighting for their side (Whealey 1989:24). Nationalists were mightily impressed by the Italians' possession of "real luxury of all kinds of equipment" (Martínez Bande 1984:297). The Fascists had plentiful supplies of trucks and artillery. They also possessed small numbers of tanks and planes and a navy that was able to bombard Málaga during battle. Certainly, in the early stages of the war, aid from Germany and Italy outweighed that of the Republic's allies. However, the quality of Italian troops varied. Most Italian "volunteers" were recruited from the ranks of Fascist squads of Black Shirts. Some came from the regular armed forces and had experienced combat in Ethiopia, whereas oth-ers had been pressured or deceived into going to Spain. Even members of the Fascist Party had varying levels of commitment. Like many Spaniards in the armed forces, a large number were opportunists. They had come to Spain more anxious to advance their careers than to fight "reds."

The Battle of Málaga would show diminishing Republican militancy. Nation-alists and their allies controlled air and sea, and leftist militiamen departed before them, causing historians sympathetic to the insurgents to judge the retreaters harshly as "cowards who were incapable of undertaking collective action" (Salas Larrazábal and Salas Larrazábal 1986:184). In this context, cowardice meant putting one's own life before the great causes of Republic and revolution. In the final hours of Republican Málaga, it was every person for himself or herself.[9] Nationalist attackers captured the city confronting only minor resistance. "Forgetting completely about military objectives," military,

civilian, and union officials fled in disorder and fear with their families
(Martínez Bande 1969:222). General Asensio pointed out, "Málaga was not
won by the enemy but was abandoned without a fight by our [Popular Army]
forces" (Asensio 1938:82).[10] A U.S. woman who lived among them argued
that "Malagueñans . . . were a people of peace and wanted to take as little part
in this unnecessary struggle as possible" (Woolsey 1998:95). On 6 February,
about one hundred thousand people began a mass exodus along the coastal road
to Almería, where Nationalist aircraft heartlessly harassed and strafed them.
Some died from exhaustion, and others committed suicide (Martínez Bande
1969:168). According to an official Republican inquiry, the retreat was "mad."
Its depiction in André Malraux' *L'Espoir* rendered it infamous. Even less fortunate than fleeing refugees were militants of the left who remained trapped
in the city. Approximately five thousand of them were put to death (see
Coverdale 1975:192). Málaga won the unenviable reputation for undergoing
the worst repression that *franquistas* had to offer, the Badajoz massacre
excepted (Pons Prades 1977:117). Ten thousand prisoners and almost all of
their equipment were seized (Martínez Bande 1969:172). The captured who
were not executed were eventually integrated into Franco's army.

The fall of Málaga was the lowest point of the many Republican misfortunes in Andalusia. The Popular Front had allowed the Nationalists to capture
a major city virtually intact. The Málaga fiasco was a significant psychological blow to a Republic that had successfully defended Madrid. Asensio himself was forced to shoulder much of the blame. The failure to defend a major
Andalusian city bade ill for the left. Nor did the defeat provoke a patriotic rush
to Republican recruiting offices. Instead it increased pressures to conscript more
men (Bolloten 1991:347). Given its social structure of impoverished
proletarians—many of whom desired land redistribution—southern Spain
should have been a bastion of revolution. Observers expected the Spanish peasantry of the south to become staunch defenders of a new Republic committed
to land reform, as had peasants of central Russia during their civil war. The
latter fought against Russian Whites to preserve changes undertaken at the
expense of the gentry. Spanish peasants were likewise predicted to participate
enthusiastically against an enemy that at the end of September had annulled
all post–Popular Front agrarian reform and had returned the land to its original owners (Fraser 1986:202).

Yet the impoverished masses of the south were not particularly aggressive
against the Republic's enemies. Authors on the left have argued that the revolution in the Republican zone could have been accompanied by guerrilla warfare: "The proletarian revolution had not developed its own revolutionary
instruments and strategies of war; it had suffered defeat as a result" (Fraser
1986:501).[11] The many mountainous regions of the Iberian Peninsula were
quite suitable for irregular warfare. From the very beginning of the conflict in

Andalusia, Estremadura, and Aragon, the front lines were extensive and usually poorly guarded and fortified. Neither side had enough qualified officers (Martínez Bande 1981:147, 159, 163, 196). The possibilities of infiltration, raiding, and bushwhacking were enormous. On both sides, the spade was neglected even more than the sword (Kemp 1957:76). Perhaps the failure to use the shovel reflects either an aristocratic disdain of manual labor or a self-fulfilling fatalism. At the end of 1936, Franco had only 130,000 battle-ready troops to man the extensive twelve-hundred-mile lines (Coverdale 1975:156–57). Furthermore, Nationalist soldiers in the south were of "poor quality" and even more reluctant to build fortifications than their Republican counterparts. Leftists have argued that a revolutionary guerrilla war would have motivated the masses and forced Nationalists to combat on the Republic's terms. A constant guerrilla would have disrupted Franco's strategy and ended or at least restricted the conventional trench warfare that Nationalist officers had been trained to fight. Franco's advantage in preparation and execution of major battles would have been neutralized (Abad de Santillán 1977:227; Pons Prades 1977:157, 316).

The failure to give full support to irregular warfare is often blamed on Communist influence in the Popular Army. On the other hand, Líster (1966:277) ascribed the neglect of guerrilla war to "Caballero, Prieto, and other high military leaders." The argument that guerrilla warfare would have turned the tide may be correct, but the way that both Communists and anti-Communists have attributed its failure to each other ironically reflects an elitist spin that has granted virtually unlimited power to policy-makers and thus clashes with the populist initiative characteristic of guerrilla conflict. Furthermore, the putative partisan strategy assumes that guerrilla warriors were available in sufficient quantity and quality, ignoring that many blamed the inadequacies of the Popular Front militias in the summer and fall of 1936 on the "natural inclination" of Spaniards for disorganized and irregular warfare. Lastly, proponents of irregular warfare neglect the tendency of Republican troops to loot. Republican *guerrilleros* might have plundered even more than regular troops. General Robert E. Lee's remarks on partisan warfare as a strategy may be pertinent: "[Confederate soldiers] would have no rations, and they would be under no discipline. . . . They would have to plunder and rob to procure subsistence. The country would be full of lawless bands in every part" (see Gallagher 1997:142).

In fact, Republican officials did encourage a very modest level of guerrilla activity. Rojo, the chief of staff of forces defending Madrid, created two fifty-man companies of guerrillas whose task was to attack the enemy rear.[12] According to one highly placed psychiatrist in the Popular Army, the *guerrilleros* had to meet rigorous selection requirements (Mira 1943:71). Some spontaneous irregular activity occurred in parts of Andalusia and Estremadura.

On 28 December 1936, in search of food, sixteen "hungry fugitives" attacked the train station of Herreruela (Cáceres).[13] The governor of the province was not terribly concerned and believed that only police (not the military) were needed to deal with the situation. Several weeks later, members of a larger armed group of forty men, twenty-eight of whom were on horseback, assaulted a large landowner's isolated farmhouse in search of supplies.[14] They were intercepted by ten Falangists, five Civil Guards, and three Carabineros. A bloodless skirmish ensued, and the guerrillas fled toward Badajoz. Leftist *guerrilleros* in Estremadura sabotaged Nationalist installations, attacked Falangists, and daringly raided farms owned by "fascists" (Vila Izquierdo 1984:99–108; Pons Prades 1977:314). Leftist partisans would engage in livestock raids in the enemy rear (Pons Prades 1977:157). They pursued notorious Nationalist executioners, such as a certain Agustín Ramos, who became known as the "butcher of Albuquerque."

In 1937, the guerrilla war in the province of Huelva was more serious. Once again, in search of supplies, a small group, whom Nationalists labeled *marxistas,* attacked the train station of El Cerro de Andévalo (Huelva) in April 1937 and killed the station master as he was attempting to inform the Civil Guard. The assaults increased in July. The "red" miners of Río Tinto, Aznalcollar, and Pozoblanco were prominent in these attacks. They were resourceful in the rugged and hilly terrain, and their refusal of the partial amnesty offered to them by Nationalists showed either their skepticism or commitment to the cause.[15] In the fall of 1937, they scattered small mines in Nationalist territory in the province of Granada.[16] In the spring of 1938 when civilians supplied them, they were still capable of sabotaging Nationalist railroad, power, and telephone lines.[17] They were seconded by a regular unit of Republican *guerrilleros* who were attached to the Army of Estremadura.[18] By May 1938, Civil Guards and other police forces organized in small patrols (from two to forty men) were sufficient to neutralize the activities of the irregulars, many of whom had already surrendered to authorities. Guerrilla activity picked up in the south at the end of 1938 as the Nationalists gained more territory, but once again the latter repressed the irregulars without a major engagement of troops (Martínez Bande 1981:286). It should be noted that not all guerrilla activity was Republican. In the area of the Sierra de Bárcena (Cantabria), civilians and deserters from Republican ranks awaited the arrival of Nationalist forces to participate in the campaign against "Marxists."[19]

The presence of Spanish *guerrilleros* in the mountains and cities of Spain from 1936 to 1960 was unprecedented in modern Western Europe. Irregular warfare over more than two decades was another indication that Spain was indeed different. In Andalusia, Estremadura, Galicia, and Asturias, fighters received support from the local population, especially women, and were able to divert some Nationalist forces. Andalusian and Asturias partisans fought most intensely (Pons Prades 1977:433; Cordón 1977:261). Yet during the civil war, guerrilla warfare never became a vital military problem for the Nationalists (Cuesta Monereo 1961:232). Indeed, General Kindelán was surprised "by the completely new phenomenon in the history of Spain that in a war of great passion and intensity . . . no spontaneous or self-taught guerrilla leader [*caudillo*] emerged" (Kindelán 1945:199). Part of the reason was that—with some exceptions—guerrillas seemed to be isolated from peasants and country people in areas in which they operated. Nationalist terror and torture made civilians reluctant to cooperate with partisans. To get supplies, the latter had to raid farmhouses and small towns and regularly exposed themselves to enemy forces. To obtain information, they were obligated to bribe shepherds and others. Sometimes the locals—either because of intimidation by guerrillas or in sympathy with them—seem to have been hesitant to betray them to Nationalist authorities, but blanket Nationalist repression was efficient enough to keep threats under control. In contrast, for instance, to the Russian Whites, the insurgents were able to impose elementary, if not terrorist, order over the population. Nationalist authority was easier to impose because the old elites who supported Franco had not undergone the degree of disruption that their Russian counterparts had suffered during World War I (Pipes 1994:37–38).

In the province of Cáceres, Nationalist officials managed to smash a well-organized plot that, they claimed, aimed to take over the provincial capital.[20] Hundreds of "reds" and their sympathizers were supposedly conspiring to assassinate Nationalist leaders. To prevent the "conspiracy" from succeeding, Nationalist authorities arrested former mayors, town councilors, and officials who had belonged to Popular Front organizations, to the Casas del Pueblo (socialist centers), and to "extremist" unions. Between 25 December 1937 and 20 January 1938, 196 persons were executed.[21] The toll confirms Republican claims of nearly indiscriminate Nationalist bloodletting. A similar massacre seems to have occurred in Zaragoza (Payne 1967:390). In that former anarchist stronghold, hundreds of CNT activists had been compelled to join the Tercio to avoid the retribution of the White Terror. The leftists in one *bandera* (a unit of 500–600 men) plotted to seize the center of town. They were discovered and then machine-gunned on the parade ground.

Instead of constant activity and aggression, Andalusia became a locus of quiet fronts until the end of the war. Exceptions that may have proved the rule were the Battle of Pozoblanco in March–April 1937 and the siege of the Sanctuary of the Virgen de la Cabeza. The Republic was victorious in both of these confrontations. The attack on the Sanctuary on 1 May put a definitive end to the live-and-let-live situation during which Republican forces had tolerated the "neutral" Civil Guard that had retreated into the fortress (Cordón 1977:269). Quiet then returned to the south. In 1937 the Twenty-first Division—composed of three mixed brigades (76, 79, and 80) that were stationed around Granada—

engaged primarily in "a few small operations and raids."[22] Throughout the year, the Twenty-first managed to capture or injure only several dozen Nationalists. The division lost even fewer troops. On certain sectors of the Andalusian front, near Ugíjar (Granada), "numerous" Republican and Nationalist soldiers exchanged newspapers, tobacco, and information.[23] Enemies were on friendly terms. "Comrades" from both sides sang songs, gave nicknames, and circulated news of mutual friends. Most of 1938 passed without significant fighting or battle injuries. The shortages of supplies (barbed wire, concrete, and transport) and training encouraged tranquility and nonaggressivity.[24] But a technological explanation cannot account for a lack of belligerency that has been termed "live and let live."[25] Soldiers often restrained themselves from exercising the possibilities for aggression that always existed.[26] The Twenty-third Division engaged in a raid, but it revealed a mediocre level of Andalusian militarism.[27] Several factors caused the raid's failure. Most of the soldiers and officers were recruits from nearby Motril (Granada) and were unwilling to fight. Furthermore, they were indiscreet and gossiped with their relatives in town concerning Republican military plans. These relatives, in turn, revealed valuable information to Nationalists.

Thus, poor equipment was only a contributing factor in the establishment of informal truces in which both sides agreed not to attack. After all, using only knives the Moors gained fearsome reputations for silently surprising and slitting the throats of their enemies (Martínez Bande 1984:114, 1980:142; Pons Prades 1974:241; Jackson 1965:266). If North Africans wished to intimidate the enemy, their well-earned notoriety and bloodcurdling cries were sufficient.[28] Like the Johnny Rebs of the U.S. Civil War, the Moors knew the intimidating value of shrieks and collective shouts. If troops wanted to be aggressive, high tech was not necessary.

The Republican Army of the center proved far superior to its comrades in the south and was prepared to take on the attackers. Nationalist assaults in January showed that Franco wanted to tighten the siege around Madrid (Jackson 1965:345). He persisted in hoping for a quick end to the war by capturing the capital. Nationalist attempts to cut the Madrid–La Coruña road in January had come close to success. Republican defenders continued to abandon weapons and positions to the attackers, but improved Popular Army organization and discipline stopped Nationalists from scoring an easy victory (Martínez Bande 1984:85). In January in Madrid, the Republican army sacrificed 503 dead, 6,169 wounded, and 4,112 sick.

The Jarama battle at the beginning of February 1937 coincided with the Nationalist victory at Málaga. The goal of the Nationalist offensive at Jarama was to consolidate the Madrid siege by cutting the Madrid-Valencia road and therefore to intensify an already acute food shortage.[29] General Orgaz, the Nationalist tactical commander, had some forty thousand troops at his command, many of them African. To maintain discipline and morale, Nationalist officers mixed uncommitted and potentially unreliable conscripts with combat veterans and political militants.[30] Prisoners with leftist sympathies whom the insurgents had conscripted found themselves fighting on the same side as dedicated Falangists and *requetés* (Martínez Bande 1984:277). The planes of the Condor Legion supported Orgaz's heterogeneous forces. German aid to the Nationalists was largely devoted to supporting this aviation unit, which proved to be the most ruthless and effective in the war.[31] Rains forced the Nationalists to wait until 6 February to launch their assault. At first, it appeared that the insurgents would attain their objectives. Their intelligence service functioned well and enabled them to attack the weakest and least experienced units who put up little resistance and fled. A U.S. volunteer reported that that the "new Spanish battalion on their [Lincoln's] left broke in the face of the tank attack" (Landis 1989:26; Rosenstone 1969:46; Wintringham 1939:255–57). From 12 to 16 February, "the intensity of enemy [Nationalist] attacks was extraordinary. The mass of artillery fire thrown against our positions and men was the most powerful we have known throughout the war. Because of this and because some of our brigades were inexperienced, several *desbandadas* occurred."[32] Heavy bombardments convinced soldiers of the enemy's formidable power and persuaded them to surrender without a fight (Holmes 1985:322). Individuals concluded that authorities who exposed them to such overwhelming dangers no longer deserved their loyalty. The defection of a captain to the enemy broke his brigade. Fortification workers from the CNT and UGT labored inadequately.

Nevertheless, the Popular Army recovered and achieved a degree of coordination and combativeness that it seldom equaled. Certain Republican units fought bravely, notwithstanding the depletion of munitions supplies and the failure of the quartermaster to provide food and drink for two days.[33] Forty new Russian planes helped them to achieve air supremacy. The Republic's aerial success stimulated its troops. The intervention of the International Brigades blunted the offensive. They were more militarily experienced and probably more motivated than many Spanish Republicans (this is the interpretation of Herrick 1998). Often, as in the defense of Madrid, "they taught the cheerfully incompetent Spanish militiamen what modern fighting meant" (quoted in Wintringham 1939:183). Toward the end of the battle, "they were thirsty, hungry, and had not washed for five days. At night the brave kitchen staff defied artillery barrages and supplied bread, canned food, a bit of sausage, and cheese" (quoted in Martínez Bande 1984:140). Internationals were posted to areas of extreme danger where various battalions were annihilated. El Campesino's brigade lost one thousand men. Officers, especially commissars—who had demonstrated "considerable heroism" and remarkable discipline—also suffered severely (Martínez Bande 1984:278).

The largely Communist forces under El Campesino, Modesto, and Líster performed admirably (Líster 1966:102). As the battle endured, Republican health, transportation, and quartermaster services improved. By 16 February it was clear that Orgaz had failed to achieve his goal of cutting the highway. Republican forces on other fronts around Madrid—Carabanchel, Cuesta de las Perdices, and El Escorial—launched raids that diverted some potential Nationalist reinforcements from the Jarama arena.[34] By 23 February the exhausted fighters on both sides could no longer carry on the battle. Jarama showed that both camps needed foreigners to supplement their insufficient native militancy. In the Republican case, foreigners were usually militants, not professionals or mercenaries who fought for the Nationalist side. Nearly three thousand Internationals were killed or wounded, including many of the best volunteers. The Fifteenth International Brigade lost half its men.[35] The Internationals' courage was equaled by the *regulares* of Ceuta and of Alhucemas, who also suffered extremely heavy casualties. The Nationalists lacked reserves to pursue the offensive, but the bravery of their elite troops blunted Republican efforts (Martínez Bande 1984:119; Kemp 1957:80). Nationalists suffered over six thousand killed or wounded; Republicans over seven thousand (439 dead, 6,929 wounded, and 3,310 sick) (Martínez Bande 1984:149).[36] By the end of February, the Republic had nearly forty thousand men at Jarama and outnumbered Nationalists three to one. The sacrifices of the Army of the Center arrested the despair caused by the Republican defeat at Málaga. Notwithstanding, a Nationalist general believed that the Republic never recovered from this deprivation of its bravest and most aggressive infantrymen (Kindelán 1945:66).

Injured Republicans found that they had special problems. An antifascist-U.S. nurse reported two to three patients per bed (de Vries 1965:120–21). Madrid Hospital 14 (Calle de la Puebla) recorded so many self-mutilations in the left hand and arm that health-care personnel assumed that any injuries in these areas were self-inflicted.[37] Hospital workers considered men with these injuries "fascists" and treated them as cowards. When a genuinely heroic soldier who was wounded in action during the Jarama struggle was admitted to this hospital for treatment, the personnel assumed that he was another slacker, insulted him, and forced him to room with the self-mutilated. To terminate this sort of treatment of the brave and the courageous, commissars recommended that battalion doctors inform hospitals regarding the precise circumstances under which soldiers had been injured. Significant numbers of *automutilados* also turned up during the battles of Brunete and of Teruel. Most had shot themselves in their left palm, an injury that became known to doctors as "a contagious wound" since it usually occurred in large numbers among men of the same unit (Picardo Castellón 1986:196).[38] Because of its frequency, political commissars issued orders that no soldier with such an injury was to be evacuated. Only iodine and gauze were available to treat them. Thus, many developed gangrene, and if lucky enough to survive, they did so because their arm was amputated.

Conversely, certain hospitals did not inspire confidence. One had "a great quantity of faults" that went uncorrected because "certain unions and parties" protected their employees.[39] The night guards were never at their posts, and ambulances—forced to motor through often muddy or impassable roads— sometimes had to wait forty-five minutes for hospital doors to open. The long wait caused the death of one injured soldier. Elevators functioned, but operators worked only from 8:00 A.M. to 1:00 P.M. Thus, during most of the day and throughout the night, stretcher-bearers carrying the wounded had to climb stairs. This exhausted the former and was not beneficial for the latter. The morgue opened for longer hours—from 7:00 A.M. to 6:00 P.M. When it was closed, however, cadavers were left in the halls. This display of piled-up corpses did not hearten new arrivals. While Republicans learned to improvise needed items—such as protective rubber gloves and even ambulances—and improved their treatment of the sick and injured, their health care system remained inferior to the Nationalists (Estellés Salarich 1986:41).

Shortages caused Republican spirits to suffer. Even in the Lincoln Brigade, which had gained a fearsome reputation among Nationalists, ideology was second to individual creature comforts: "The morale, the political line, etc. that a commissar is responsible for . . . depend on proper food and proper cloth- ing, and bandages for the feet when the shoes rub, and soap and towels and newspapers and cigarettes and sufficient instruction and not too much instruc- tion and seeing that the canteen carries the favorite drink of each and that the toilets flush and sufficient disinfectant is on hand, etc., etc., etc." (Dallet 1938:42).[40] Soldiers of the Popular Army found themselves saddled with the same material shortages as Johnny Rebs who had had "to sleep in the open under a captured blanket, to wear a tattered . . . uniform, and to march and fight barefooted" (McPherson 1988:319).

The limited success of the Popular Army at Jarama did not resolve the dif- ficulties of feeding nearly one million *madrileños,* and the evacuation of many from the city did not significantly diminish the problem. Communist supply ministers on the Junta proved no better stocking Madrid than their anar- chosyndicalist counterparts in Barcelona. Although Miaja's Defense Junta had managed to defend Madrid and Miaja himself would be promoted to the com- mand of the 150,000-men Army of the Center, the continuing food shortage in the city led to a steep decline of the popularity of his Defense Junta (Martínez Bande 1984:152).[41] In response to revelations on torture practiced in makeshift Communist prisons in Madrid, the Junta would finally be dissolved in April 1937 (Fraser 1986:298). Largo Caballero referred to the continuing "problem of food supply." Nor was Barcelona adequately nourished, and the productivity of defense workers—a privileged group of wage earners—dropped as a result of their constant search for food.[42] Personnel changes did not overcome the difficulties of provisioning major urban areas.

The Battle of Guadalajara was yet another attempt by Nationalists to rupture the post-Jarama stalemate around Madrid. After Jarama, troops adopted defensive strategies. Near Usera both sides agreed not to fire at each other. This unwritten accord frustrated the Republican commissars who wished to agitate among enemy troops and convince them to abandon their lines. The *franquistas* knew "that our defensive lines in the Guadalajara sector were weak and without fortifications since 10,000 men guarded a front of 80 km. They lived peacefully, discipline was poor, and there was little communication between high-ranking officers and men" (Líster 1966:106). Franco also wanted to relieve pressure on General Orgaz's tired and discouraged forces near Jarama. In early March, the *generalísimo* concentrated approximately fifty thousand soldiers around Sigüenza (Guadalajara). Twenty thousand of them were legionnaires, Moroccans, and some Carlists—led by Moscardó, the hero of Toledo's Alcázar. Nationalists lacked sufficient numbers and depended upon Italian forces—General Roatta's thirty thousand well-equipped Italian "volunteers" of the CTV (*Corpo Truppe Volontarie*)—to take the initiative (Jackson 1965:349; Thomas 1961:383). The Italian Fascists' easy success at Málaga encouraged overconfidence. The Duce expected a spectacular victory since the Republican troops facing them had earned a lackadaisical reputation. Near Jadraque and Almadrones, the Popular Army had done little to improve defective fortifications and trenches (Martínez Bande 1984:176, 293). On 8 March, the Italians broke through the front and quickly dominated the heights, but bad weather slowed the Nationalist advance and limited the use of the Condor Legion. The poor Spanish roads delayed Italian convoys. Once the offensive was under way, the insurgents and their Italian allies had to face some of the best Republican forces, who had been hastily assembled to halt the threat of the encirclement of Madrid. Líster's Eleventh Division, which was composed of the German XI International Brigade, a Basque Brigade, and the ex-Communist First Brigade, was stationed between Trijueque and Torija. The well-considered anarchist commander, Cipriano Mera, headed a division that included XII International Brigade led by the Garibaldi battalion. For five days, from 12 through 17 March, the CTV contained with difficulty counterattacks from a Republican elite immeasurably aided by a revitalized air force. Republican airfields at Alcalá and Guadalajara were close to the battle zone, and their hard surfaces made them less dependent upon inclement weather.

Nationalist support services broke down. Treatment of the insurgent wounded was deficient (Martínez Bande 1984:296). Some reports criticized the effectiveness of the Nationalist quartermaster for not providing hot meals, warm drinks, and alcoholic beverages. Disheartened and demoralized Italians, who were inadequately clothed for a winter battle, abandoned their equipment, brutalized local villagers, and fled in small groups of two or three. They jumped on the running boards and mudguards of already overflowing trucks that were heading towards the rear (Martínez Bande 1984:214). Nationalist observers criticized the faintheartedness of both Italian officers and men. Fascist generals and their staff refused to get out of their cars to try to stop their troops from breaking and running. For his part, Roatta was angry that his Spanish allies never launched even a minor counteroffensive that would have tied down Republican reserves and prevented them from massing against him (Coverdale 1975:233). On 18 March, the flights of individuals and small groups of Italians turned into a collective collapse. Republican aviation dropped leaflets promising safe-conduct to all Italian deserters and offered a fifty- to one-hundred-peseta reward if they defected with their weapons. The Garibaldi Battalion of the International Brigades sent a special invitation to their Italian "brothers" in Mussolini's expeditionary force. Yet the stiff resistance and the dominance of Republican aviation contributed more to the CTV's defeat than antifascist propaganda.

The Italian retreat, which was sudden enough to be termed a rout, stopped a few miles short of the bases from which their advance had started. General Roatta complained that a good number of men were "older married men who are not very aggressive" (quoted in Coverdale 1975:256). Many lacked the most elementary military training. In other words, elements of the Italian expeditionary force suffered the same lack of motivation as their allies and enemies. The Republican victory at Guadalajara may be attributed in part to the commitment of the peasant-soldiers of the center, who profited more than peasants elsewhere from Republican land distribution. The ill-named Battle of Guadalajara (which was untouched by the fight) once again confirmed the stalemate around Madrid. Both sides suffered important casualties. About two thousand Republicans were killed and four thousand wounded (Coverdale 1975:248). Four hundred Italians died, eighteen hundred were injured, and five hundred were captured or missing. The Popular Army snared hundreds of prisoners and large quantities of weapons and supplies during the battle.

International contributions to Guadalajara were even more significant than at Jarama. The presence of tens of thousands of foreign activists and mercenaries once again bolstered the militancy of both sides. Without their heroism and sacrifice, the Spanish war would have ended much more quickly and with less blood. The defensive victory at Guadalajara, which Rojo called "the most rapid and orderly concentration of forces ever carried out by the Republic," sparked elation among antifascists all over the world (Rojo quoted in Coverdale 1975:252). Finally, it seemed, the string of Nationalist and fascist victories had been broken. Famous war correspondents—Ernest Hemingway and Herbert Matthews (of the *New York Times*)—waxed euphoric. Even for a good number of insurgents, the Italian defeat represented a triumph of Spanish bravery over Italian arrogance and pretensions. At Franco's headquarters, the Italian defeat created an "absurd sense of satisfaction" (Coverdale 1975:263). Spanish Nationalists gloated over the failure of a Mussolini who had made little secret of the contempt he felt for Franco and his Spaniards who, according to the Duce, "had a weak desire to fight and lacked personal bravery" (quoted in Martínez Bande 1984:168).

As at Jarama, the Nationalists had once more failed to encircle the capital. Franco was again forced to abandon his plans for a quick end to the war through the conquest of Madrid. In early April the Republican attempt to capture the Casa de Campo likewise failed to break the Madrid stalemate. Lt. Col. Rojo concluded that during this attack, "a growing number of men frequently abandoned the field of combat without any excuse" (quoted in Martínez Bande 1981:95). The Republicans too had been unable to win a clear offensive victory. During the Battle of Guadalajara, continuing Nationalist pressure at Jarama may have prevented the command of the Popular Army from calling up more reserves (Martínez Bande 1984:216–18).[43] Organizational problems, such as the failure of the quartermaster to provide a steady flow of food, weakened Republican efforts.[44] Fortifications were ineffective. Officers of building battalions grumbled that they were more than willing to sacrifice, but their soldiers were slackers.[45]

The struggle for Madrid would not resume on a large scale until the end of the war. On other fronts, commissars charged that officers were incompetent and uninterested, whereas troops, although underfed and underclothed, labored unselfishly and engaged in heroic acts. The charges against professional officers were plausible. Most regular army officers in the Republican zone, like their men, had joined antifascist organizations after 19 July.[46] Some were frankly hostile to the regime and would eventually be purged. A head commissar estimated that 40 to 45 percent of fortification officers were opportunists who were unable to maintain discipline; 35 to 40 percent were competent and committed; and 10 to 15 percent were outright enemies of the Republic.[47] Commissars tried to ensure political loyalty and to raise low output in a context where considerable tension existed between fortification soldiers and combat troops. The latter felt that the former were lazy.[48] On fronts in the Madrid area, absenteeism among civilian fortification workers was high.[49] In response, orders restricting unauthorized leave were issued for both military and nonmilitary personnel. Officers monopolized the services of productive units. They disobeyed transfer orders of "their" fortification battalions by refusing to permit them to leave their sector of the front.[50]

Following the Battle of Guadalajara, attention once again turned from the stalemate around Madrid to the war in the north (Jackson 1965:375–88; Thomas 1961:399–423). In the fall of 1936, the inability to capture Oviedo had demoralized Asturian militias, which were some of the best that the Republic possessed. An important offensive of February 1937 to take the provincial capital had resulted in the mobilization of all men between the ages of twenty and forty-five (Martínez Bande 1980). Moreover, massive mobilization did more harm than good. The inability to seize Oviedo led to "frequent desertions [and] self-mutilations" that forced the Socialist leader of Asturias, Belarmino Tómas, to issue a March 1937 decree that condemned deserters to death (Salas Larrazábal 1973:975; Murillo Pérez 1990:219). Tómas understood the lesson that men fight from fear: "Fear of the consequences first of not fighting (i.e. punishment) then of not fighting well (i.e. slaughter)" (Keegan 1976:70). Many Asturian miners, belying their international reputation for aggressive antifascism, tried to avoid the front by remaining in or returning to the mines.[51] They may have regretted the days of *caciquismo* when the local boss knew ways to exempt them from military service (see Carr 1980:14–15). They struggled to obtain work-related exemptions. The Basques who participated in the unsuccessful attempt to take Oviedo also became discouraged and blamed their Republican allies (Martínez Bande 1980:247).

After the fall of San Sebastián on 12 September, Basque Republicans maintained thirty to forty thousand militiamen of their own, along with several thousand anarchist and UGT volunteers (Jackson 1965:375–88; Thomas 1961:399–423). Compared to their enemies, the Basques were poorly armed. Their weapons, especially small arms, were so varied that it was difficult to supply them with the appropriate ammunition (Martínez Bande 1980:174–79). The services of the Army of the North functioned poorly, and soldiers and sappers possessed only sandals and summer clothing in the winter of 1936 through 1937 (Martínez Bande 1980:183). Many became ill. Jealous of their autonomy, they were reluctant to cooperate with the national government. The Basque president, José Antonio de Aguirre, absolutely refused to integrate Popular Army commissars into the Basque forces. For its part, Madrid was reluctant to aid the region (Martín-Blázquez 1938:267). In addition, there was considerable friction and distrust between the Basques and the Popular Fronts of Asturias and Santander. The Basque leadership was bourgeois and Catholic; the Asturian and Santanderian were proletarian and anticlerical. The latter were isolated from central authorities and developed into *taifas* (divided kingdoms) that made it difficult for the Republican military to develop and coordinate its forces.[52] For example, the head of the Seventeenth Corps claimed that the Council of Asturias obstructed his plans for the draft.

Paralysis of the northern front began after the unsuccessful Republican attempt to capture Vitoria. At the end of November and beginning of December 1936, Nationalist troops had stopped the Republican forces at Villarreal (Alava). Incomplete figures show that the Basque Army suffered well over six thousand casualties—54 percent of whom were wounded, 17 percent killed,

and 29 percent ill. Inattention to medical and quartermaster services hindered
the attackers (Martínez Bande 1980:218). From December to March 1937, the
northern front was quiet and stable, "being disturbed only by an occasional
exchange of shots that was without consequences."[53] Officers did not bother
to discipline their troops. It should be noted that desertions plagued both the
Republican and Nationalist armies in the Basque Country during this four-
month period of passivity.

As had occurred in the Russian civil war, in the north many rank-and-file
soldiers on both sides were unclear about what they were fighting for (or
against). They calculated the risk of being sent to prison or a concentration camp
and deserted when it was opportune (on Russia, see Pipes 1994:9; Best 1986:45).
General Mola's forces experienced "continuous" desertions which—like their
adversary—generally affected common soldiers, not officers.[54] The frequency
of desertions limited psychiatric casualties on both sides. Some mentally disturbed soldiers simply went home. Others were admitted into hospitals where
they constituted 2 to 3 percent of patients.[55] From 12 to 22 January, forty-five
soldiers, four Falangists, and one requeté fled the Nationalist Army of the
North. Many, it seems, were Asturians who returned to their native villages. In
February, five carabineros abandoned Nationalist Spain because they were
about to be sent to the front.[56] The onset of bad weather in the fall of 1936
tested the commitment of Franco's troops. As the climate became colder and
wetter, more troops deserted.[57] The colonel of the Sixth Division, whose headquarters was in Vitoria, complained of "repeated" desertions, whose numbers
were relatively insignificant but whose frequency was "highly demoralizing"
in certain units. Most deserters were from specific regions—such as Galicia—
where "great and secret leftist propaganda" was spread in the rear.[58] Nationalists were more fortunate than Republicans since their deserters were often
limited to Galicians and Catalans. Four of the latter who had been stationed on
the Aragon front abandoned the Nationalist camp. Officers, including the hero
of the Alcázar, José Moscardó, were frustrated that the extensive and sparsely
covered front prevented competent surveillance and enabled the Catalans to
defect. Their treason disheartened remaining soldiers.[59] In the Basque Country, Nationalist officials recommended ceaseless vigilance and the establishment
of a system of informers to stop enemy propaganda. Astute Republicans wished
to enact a policy to attract Nationalist deserters by offering them, not Republican propaganda nor even paper money, but hard coin (el premio en metálico).[60]
Nationalists retaliated by threatening to deport family members of any known
deserters or "red" sympathizers.[61] Peasants became resigned to serving on the
Nationalist side, especially when they believed that Franco would win. Some
also feared that the "reds" who attacked the church would also deprive them of
their plots and livestock (Fraser 1986:466). On the very quiet Aragon front,
where Líster complained that "anarchist bosses preferred playing soccer with

the enemy rather than fighting him," desertions of dozens of soldiers (not officers) occurred monthly on both sides (Líster 1966:120). Nearly half defected
without firearms, indicating a significant shortage even among Nationalist
troops.[62] Possibly, as in the Russian civil war, deserters would sell their weapons
(Figes 1990:169). Individual and small-group flights lengthened the conflict and
helped to turn it into a war of attrition.

After the Battle of Jarama, the Nationalist leadership temporarily accepted
the deadlock around Madrid and began to concentrate forty to fifty thousand
troops under the command of General Mola for an offensive in the north. They
included Carlists, Moroccans, and Italians. Just as importantly, the Condor
Legion once again provided air support. It was virtually unopposed since its
Basque adversaries had no antiaircraft artillery and few planes. German aviation was able to terrorize at will civilian populations and untrained troops. The
latter, lacking experience and weaponry to fight planes, deserted from even fortified positions. On 5 April in a message to the Spanish ambassador in Moscow,
Prieto admitted "the superiority of enemy aviation is creating a situation of
extreme gravity in the Basque fronts" (quoted in Viñas 1979:340). He asked
his ambassador to plead for more Russian planes. Observers agreed that the
preeminence of fascist aviation was key to the Nationalist victory in the north,
but it was by no means the only factor.[63] The lack of confidence and cooperation between the Basques and their Asturian and Santanderian allies hindered
the defense of Vizcaya.[64] Political struggles disorganized and divided the rear
(Rojo 1974:32). The government of each region "cordially hated" the other
two. All three governments allowed many young men to avoid dangerous military service by assigning them to rear-guard duty. Youth especially favored
the customs service that offered them the possibility of confiscating food and
other items. Each regional authority printed its own money, and several types
of currencies circulated. Branches of the Bank of Spain in Bilbao, in Santander,
and in Gijón issued bills (see Banco de España 1979:290–307). The lack of a
single currency discouraged commerce. It also promoted town vouchers and
city currencies, which could not be exchanged beyond municipal limits. Peasants refused to accept local currencies and wanted only Bank of Spain script.[65]

The Basques planned to defend the provincial border of Vizcaya while con-
structing a defensive "Iron Ring" around the city of Bilbao, their industrial
base. The ring had been conceived in October 1936 as a way to utilize Basque
industrial expertise and manpower. According to one expert observer, the ring
was "more for show than effect."[66] "Officers, who were incompetent and
lacked preparation, spent their time in Bilbao. Simultaneously, commanders
and quartermasters . . . lamentably abandoned the care of their troops."[67] Soldiers ate badly, and the civilian population starved. Defeatism led important
politicians and military men to send their closest relatives to France in postal
planes.

In April the Nationalists took the mountain passes with few losses on either side. It was during this month that the Condor Legion destroyed Guernika (Vizcaya), foreshadowing the mass destruction initiated by the Third Reich and intensified by the Allies during World War II. The center of the town was reduced to rubble; 1,654 people were killed and 889 wounded. Conceivably the goal of the bombing was to intimidate the population of the industrial towns of the Ría de Bilbao so that they would offer minimal opposition (González Portilla and Garmendia 1988:83). The Madrid/Valencian government was able to send the Basques a few planes, but they still proved incapable of seriously challenging Nationalist air superiority (Salas Larrazábal and Salas Larrazábal 1986:275). Many Basques felt that the Republic had abandoned them.

Nationalist intimidation may have helped to discourage resistance. If soldiers were not lucky enough to get an honorable wound that could serve as a passport to home, many would manufacture one. By May self-mutilation had proliferated so much that Aguirre, president and defense minister of Euzkadi, recognized that he had to punish it more forcefully and made it equivalent to desertion.[68] On 25 May, the Basque Military Tribunal confirmed the decision (Salas Larrazábal 1986:1422). Under the threat of punishment, commanders were warned to report all desertions.[69] Perhaps they wanted to conceal the numbers in order to acquire extra rations. On 30 May the head of the Third Army Corps chastised "repeated cases of abandonment of positions for inexplicable reasons" (quoted in Almendral Parra, Flores Velasco, Valle Sánchez 1990:194). These caused "catastrophes on the fronts." Republican soldiers left their positions "without a fight, in disorderly retreat."[70] According to Buzón, the Basque Nationalist forces were especially to blame. Although they were the best armed, they were also the most likely to run. Aguirre's attempt to combine the roles of president and commander in chief of the armed forces was no help. His vanity earned him the ridicule of the population, which gave him the nickname of "Napoleonchu." The victorious Navarrese quartermaster had no trouble recuperating large quantities of unused or hidden Republican weapons and ammunition (Aragón 1940:112–15).

The material and moral deficiencies of Republican forces in the north resembled those that had been responsible for the earlier defeat in Málaga. The Nationalist advantage in artillery and aviation, the ineffectiveness of the Republican plan of defense, and the demoralization of Loyalist troops permitted the penetration of Iron Ring on 12 June. Bilbao was ordered to put up a stiff defense but did not do so. Two hundred thousand fled before the Nationalists entered the city on 19 June. The abandonment of the provincial capital by much of the civilian population made its military defense less likely. Basque, Asturian, and Santander militias retreated westward. Both officers and men deserted massively. The flights of the latter are usually blamed on the distrust and pessimism of the former, but the reverse could also be true. At any rate,

Bilbao would not be Madrid, and its capture more than compensated for the Nationalist setback at Guadalajara. So many soldiers of the Basque National- ist Party (PNV or Partido Nacionalista Vasco) fled that military authorities took the precautionary measure of withdrawing them from the front and replacing them with more reliable Asturians and Santanderians.[71] Bilbao's capture fur- ther diminished the Basque interest in fighting (Fraser 1986:410; Colmegna 1941:93). To reach a less Carthaginian peace, the PNV bargained its surren- der with Franco's Italian allies rather than with their Spanish compatriots. In fact, after the fall of Bilbao, Nationalist commanders believed that more and fresher troops could have conquered the entire Republican army in the north (Kindelán 1945:86).

Republican defeat led to infighting. On 23 September and 4 January, Ger- man air raids on Bilbao so enraged militiamen that they expressed their hatred of the enemy by storming the jails and lynching large numbers of political pris- oners.[72] Eighty were massacred in September, and more than two hundred in January. After these incidents, the Basque police tried to prevent prison mas- sacres and stopped any scorched-earth practices. Basque leaders decided to guard the jails with their own policemen and soldiers, thus alienating their pro- letarian allies. The Basques opened fire at the Asturians who wanted to blow up the ammunition depot at Deusto to prevent the Nationalists from capturing it. By permitting supplies and factories to fall intact into Nationalist hands, this Basque prudence allowed the insurgents their first major industrial base.[73]

When the *franquistas* entered Bilbao, they put into practice their policy of "practical generosity" and fed a city that was starved for food (Peers 1943:6). Price controls and rationing had not prevented hunger in the northern Repub- lican zone. The population had allegedly assaulted trains carrying food sup- plies (Aragón 1940:245). A British volunteer who fought with the *requetés* reported that "we were constantly besieged by pathetic, emaciated figures— men and women of every age and class, with wasted flesh, sallow skins and eyes bright with famine, begging piteously for a little bread" (Kemp 1957:94). One of the great weaknesses of the Basque defense was its inability to nour- ish its troops. They depended nearly totally on foreign, especially British, ship- ments of victuals. Basque dependence inspired the witticism that Bilbao would never fall to the Fascists because the Basques would give it first to Great Britain. The Nationalist blockade was far from complete, but nonetheless it discouraged normal trade and regular fishing activity. Furthermore, it was hard for the Basque government to pay for supplies. Its financial situation became so difficult that on 3 May 1937 the "bourgeois" government of Euzkadi expro- priated all precious stones and metals in banks and safe-deposit boxes in its territory (González Portilla and Garmendia 1988:74). Its expropriations repeated those of the Republican and Nationalist governments that also raised desperately needed foreign currencies by selling any valuables that they could

confiscate. Authorities invaded homes and safe-deposit boxes that they suspected contained convertible assets.

Republican soldiers in the north lacked bread and meat. The quartermaster
(Intendencia) warned that their diet was inadequate for combatants and could
produce physical disorders.[74] The effects of hunger are similar to those of tired-
ness (Holmes 1985:125; Dollard 1943:52). Hungry men are more susceptible
to cold and exhaustion. In addition, they quickly become indifferent to the cause
and are more likely to go on scavenging missions than to fight the enemy.
Almost as many veterans (34 percent) of the Abraham Lincoln Brigade blamed
situations of demoralization on poor food, clothing, and shelter than on defeats,
retreats, and heavy casualties (39 percent). Studies have noted that men who
go without coffee or some breakfast do significantly worse in target practice
than men who eat even a light snack. "The lack of food constitutes the single
biggest single assault upon morale. . . . Apart from its purely chemical effects
upon the body, it has woeful effects upon the mind. One is in the dismal condition of having nothing to look forward to" (Fergusson 1946:194). "For soldiers, meals are not just sustenance . . . but security that they are not isolated
from the rest of the world. They reinforce the men's confidence in their officers and strengthen combat readiness" (Líster 1966:282). Food shortages created unbounded resentment against those, often including officers, that others
perceived as better fed.[75] An expert criticized the quartermaster service of the
Basque forces as inefficient and overly decentralized. "The demand . . . for
meals was exaggerated. . . . It reached the point that for every rifle fired, there
were two mouths to feed. The waste of food and clothes was great. Go-
betweens and middlemen were so numerous that food often never reached combatants."[76] Likewise, in Asturias civilians were improperly fed because of
waste and dishonesty (Martínez Bande 1974b:114). Furthermore, "immoral"
officials were seldom punished for their misdeeds. In contrast, elite units of
the Republican army boasted of their ability to provide warm coffee and
cognac to their troops (Líster 1966:117).

The Nationalists remained logistically more successful than Republicans.
The Navarre quartermaster of the Nationalist Northern Army was proud of its
ability to feed and clothe its forces, thereby "improving their health and spirit.
The proof of this was the very low percentage of the sick during the hard winter."[77] Proper uniforms helped to build an esprit de corps, and regular meals
offered not only an opportunity for reinforcing group cohesion but also psychological certainty in a highly insecure environment. The ability to provide
three meals per day reinforces the military community. Only sleeping together
creates stronger bonds among strangers. "The preparation and consumption of
food is as much a social ritual as it is a physical necessity. Cooking and eating take up slack time, break an interminable day into tolerable spans, and provide high spots whose anticipation lends point to an otherwise bleak existence"

(Holmes 1985:128). The Navarre quartermaster claimed that he was also able to feed the rear, spending over 124 million pesetas in the month of June alone (Aragón 1940:241). Supplying hungry towns was of incalculable political importance. The women of the Auxilio Social often undertook the job, which reflected the traditional female role as nurturer (Colmegna 1941:247). In the Nationalist zone, a strong peseta limited inflation, and while a few capitalists and entrepreneurs violated accords on food and transportation, most seemed to cooperate in the collective effort.[78] Except in rare cases, "the patriotism of merchants and industrialists made sanctions unnecessary" (Aragón 1940:52; Rodríguez García 1990:381; cf. Barciela López 1986:392). At least until 1938, Nationalist quartermasters established reasonable prices that, they believed, could provide a decent profit to growers and merchants. Military authorities maintained wide powers to punish "those who impede supplies, raise prices unjustly or contribute to scarcity" but seldom used them (Berdugo et al. 1990:251).[79] Other decrees issued at the end of 1936 forbade speculation in currency, precious metals, and commodities (Pedraz Penalva 1990:365; see also Arranz Bullido 1990:205–14).

The extent of cooperation of property owners is not surprising since most recognized that Franco's forces were fighting for property rights, not social justice. Furthermore, rightwingers had much more experience administering wealth than their counterparts on the left. Observers reported that the insurgents were able to feed the front and the rear (Oudard 1938:20–21, 56).[80] In fact, Nationalists imported little food from abroad and could export wheat to Germany, Italy, and Portugal (Viñas et al. 1975:1:142; Barciela López 1983:670). This organizational superiority and consequent logistic advantage more than neutralized the loss of many of the most important Nationalist generals (Peers 1943:5). Sanjurjo and Mola were killed in airplane crashes. Goded, Fernández Burriel, and Fanjul were executed, and López Ochoa was eliminated in a prison hospital. Cabanellas and Martínez Anido died before the end of the conflict.

Poor rations must have reduced desires to sacrifice for the Republican cause. Despite ambitious official recommendations, soldiers of the Thirty-seventh Mixed Brigade stationed near Madrid, received twenty grams of meat, forty of oil, twenty of sugar, and ten of salt in November 1937.[81] In contrast, Nationalist soldiers in 1937 had a normal daily ration of two hundred grams of meat, sixty of oil, fifty of sugar, and fifteen of salt.[82] In every food group, except dried vegetables (i.e. beans), Nationalist soldiers were better fed. Their diet was also much more varied, and they were able to consume coffee and wine— even though the Republic had a considerable advantage in vineyard acreage— much more regularly than Republican soldiers (Ministerio de Agricultura 1938?). Franco's quartermasters made special efforts to supply their soldiers with regional dishes, hot meals, and alcoholic beverages during periods of cold and bad weather.[83] Supplying troops with foods that they know and like offered a physiological and psychological boost. Partaking of what is aptly called spirits often bolsters morale. Soldiers in many wars have recognized that drinking—and more recently in Vietnam, taking drugs together—initiates and reinforces the group. In the nineteenth and twentieth centuries, the French Army was happy to provide brandy to its warriors; likewise, the British Army offered rum (Holmes 1985:249). Caffeine and alcohol have helped many a man go over the top. In contrast, Republican meals were so repetitious and unappetizing that soldiers frequently refused to eat them when they had the possibility to scavenge in surrounding villages (*Servicios de Intendencia* 1938:24). The Republican logistic disadvantage was not erased despite the massive shipment of thousands of tons of food, fuel, fertilizers, and raw materials from Russia. In the first five months of 1937, the Soviets sent 22,153 tons of wheat, 6,621 of rye, 4,686 of oats, 154 of lentils, 4,332 of flour, 4,516 of sugar, 625 of salt pork, 54 of bacon, 776 of butter, 381 of cod, 1,001 of peas, and hundreds of thousands of canned foods (Viñas 1979:349). Veteran Republican soldiers were tipped off that a major offensive was in the offing when meals dramatically improved in quantity or quality (Pons Prades 1974:263–64). "Like pigs," a country boy commented, "being fattened for slaughter." Brecht's Schweyk would have added, "Where the bullets fly, the grub stands by."

Nationalist officials replaced vendors (who were usually Moorish troops) with cooperatives that offered nonessential items at regulated prices and whose profits were limited to 10 percent.[84] Once cooperatives satisfied soldiers' needs, suppliers turned to the civilian population. The Navarrese quartermaster financed its entire supply effort by deducting two-thirds of soldiers' wages. Nationalist soldiers may have had nominally less discretionary income than their Republican counterparts, but they were better fed. The insurgents' reputation for dietary attentiveness was apparent when four Spanish soldiers, who served with the quartermaster of Mussolini's Italian forces, deserted in January 1938.[85] Normally, deserters were immediately shot, but these men were given a formal hearing. The Spaniards argued that Italians had discriminated against them. Their most severe complaint concerned the difference between their diet and that of their Mediterranean allies. The latter received wine and *café con leche,* whereas Spaniards got only black coffee. They claimed that their meals were worse than any in the Nationalist army. It is not known what happened to these deserters, but the fact that they based their defense on food shortage showed that Nationalist authorities were concerned about nutrition and considered desertion an understandable response to dietary discrimination.

Nationalist troops received ten times more meat than Republican soldiers. Of course, Nationalist zones were rich in grazing, but this does not entirely explain the superior diet of their troops. Other explanations—in keeping with the dominant tradition of political history from above—have blamed the Republican food deficits on incompetent leadership. Whether the fault was attributed to anarchists, Communists, or Socialists has depended upon the ideology of the observer.[86] Yet the problem involved political economy more than politics per se. Narrowly political explanations have failed to examine soldiers' and civilians' everyday existence.

As has been seen, peasants with livestock distrusted soldiers whom they rightly feared would rustle what they wanted. Small holders in the Sierra surrounding Madrid protested against troops who did not respect property. Near Colmenar Viejo (Madrid) nine soldiers belonging to Líster's column stole hundreds of heads of sheep.[87] Although they would be required to return them to their lawful owners, the thievery created an atmosphere that damaged both the Republican economy and the reputation of Líster, who had taken great public pride in his ability to control—and if necessary shoot—"bandits" whom he claimed had exploited the peasantry (Bolloten 1991:241). When Líster's soldiers entered Gálvez (Toledo), they learned that Republican units had mistreated local peasants.[88] In response to numerous soldierly abuses—requisitions, forced labor, and sexual harassment—women led thirty families with their twelve hundred animals to the Nationalist side. According to Santiago Alvarez, a veteran of the Asturian revolt who became Líster's political commissar, "most peasants [did] not know how to distinguish our forces from those of the fascist army." The continual stealing and destruction of soldiers stationed in the Sierra de Guadarrama terminated "any desire of peasants to work for our cause."[89] Both officers and men were notorious for their thefts of livestock and potatoes. Shortages aggravated a lack of confidence. Hungry soldiers were tempted to steal. Near El Escorial, troops confiscated animals and offered peasants little or no compensation.[90] They extorted food and other property with violence and threats. Soldiers' deliberately destructive and careless behavior, peasants charged, had damaged their crops.[91] The commanding officer denied the accusations, but dozens of municipalities complained that "excesses took place too frequently." Municipal councils asked military authorities to stop the abuses. The mayor of Tejadillos (Cuenca) complained of soldiers' unauthorized requisitions.[92] The commissar and the colonel agreed that "opportunistic (*despreocupados*) individuals . . . use these times of social change for their personal benefit." In the Spanish conflict, as during the French Revolution, soldiers had few "scruples when it came to wine, *eau-de-vie,* and chicken. Everything drinkable and edible was fair game, a kind of *taxe de guerre,* a duty on *incivisme"* (Cobb 1987:135).

Just as significantly, price maximums (*tasas*) did not encourage peasants who wanted to produce a large surplus and sell it legally.[93] A decree of 4 August 1936 established *tasas* that prohibited prices of food and clothing that were higher than those of 15 July 1936. Fines ranged from a thousand to a hundred thousand pesetas. This policy showed a basic continuity with the early years of the Republic when Marcelino Domingo, minister of agriculture and a prominent leftist Republican, refused to increase the price ceiling on wheat in order to keep bread cheap (Maurice 1975:66–67; Tió 1982:68). Throughout its history the Republic—however ineptly—would attempt to protect consumers. Azaña (1990:3:520) noted that immediately after the wartime maximums were established, food products disappeared from stores.

Early in the conflict, it was clear that the Republic would have a hard time provisioning its troops. The unplanned waste and overconsumption of the first few months of the conflict, when many believed that the war would be short and the rising would soon fail, had led to a precipitous slaughter of livestock. For example, hens, which should have been nurtured and used to produce eggs, were instead butchered (*Servicios de Intendencia* 1938:24). In many cases, the imprudent slaughtering resulted in a meat shortage that forced Loyalists to choose between a vegetarian diet or the continued killing of draft and milking animals. The rash carnage was both a cause and an effect of transportation bottlenecks. The disappearance of livestock made sure that Republicans would have less recourse to animal transport and pack trains than their enemies. Meat, alive or dead, could not get to the troops or into the cities. Even though Republican officials in Valencia tried to help municipalities by regulating butchering, local authorities in the Sierra of Madrid wanted to maintain their own control over the remaining livestock and were reluctant to export to other regions.[94] In turn, the quartermaster distrusted peasants and local unions whom, it suspected, might independently or secretly produce cheese or other products.[95] It took over most cheese-producing dairies in the region.

Valencia encouraged a project to produce massive amounts of *queso manchego* (cheese from sheep's milk), and it began auspiciously.[96] Local officials believed that if they overcame "exchanges, hoarding and speculation," they could help solve the Republic's food shortages and enable it to reduce imports.[97] At first, peasants and their cooperatives collaborated and profitably made cheese for the military and civilian populations of Madrid province. Problems, nevertheless, quickly appeared. Producers sometimes succumbed to the temptation to create cheese of poor quality under less than sanitary conditions. "In certain localities," cheese was hidden from military authorities, and peasants exchanged it directly for products that they needed. They persisted in hoarding and bartering, despite authorities' pleas that they were harming soldiers at the front. Commissars were unable to carry out their mission of "defeating the resistance of politically uneducated peasants who refused to declare their stocks" (*Servicios de Intendencia* 1938:21).

Bread production was also problematic, in large part because of the inexperience and irresponsibility of bakery workers.[98] Workers abandoned the Villalba (Madrid) bakery "without authorization or permission," ignoring demands for increased productivity. Neither the quartermaster nor union delegates, it seemed, could control their members who had little "love or faith in the

Republican cause."[99] In June 1937 the Ministry of Agriculture issued regulatory decrees that required permits for the circulation of goods.[100]

Food was not the only commodity in short supply. The clothes-distribution system needed to be rationalized and centralized since some units had adequate clothing while others lacked shirts and (as in the Confederacy) shoes. Soap was also badly needed, especially in hospitals which, however, were charged with making "exaggerated" demands for many commodities.[101] Military hospitals operated "with perfect anarchy" and never paid their bills. Some ignored their patients, offered only leftovers, and were unsanitary, despite large numbers of cleaning personnel (Ferrer Córdoba 1986:136).

The rampant alcoholism Spanish eugenicists detected among "thousands" of wounded men disturbed them (Carreras Panchón 1986:14). A prominent Nationalist psychiatrist asserted that these wounded "heroes" nonetheless dedicated themselves to "a life of laziness and dissipation" in the rear. Alcoholism, he argued, posed a great danger for the "race." He fretted that his side had a more serious problem than the enemy, even if the lower quality of alcoholic beverages in the "Marxist" zone inflicted on the Popular Army more cases of "chronic psychosis." Women were also exposed to the danger: "Young women [of both sides] . . . were frivolous, impertinent, irritable, erotic, but incapable of taking care of the home and raising children" (Vallejo Nágera 1939:72–75).

Barter and not devalued Republican money was needed to obtain goods ("pues con el dinero no se va a ningún lado").[102] In the first year of the war, the Republican peseta lost approximately half its value on foreign exchange markets.[103] But this decline abroad was less important than domestic loss of confidence. Prices in Catalonia rose 6 to 7 percent every month, and barter had to be used to obtain desired items. Collectives could and did exchange goods. The prohibition or absence of money in many towns has been portrayed as a socialist or libertarian measure since CNT militants were in theory against trading with "individualists" and the state (Collectif Equipo 1997:64). While ideologically inoffensive, barter also enabled collectives to adhere to the official price and thus not break the law. At the same time, barter allowed collectives to avoid the effects of devaluation of Republican currency. It was therefore a rational method of exchange among villages and collectivities (Leval 1975:141–42; Souchy Bauer 1982:55, 84). Yet barter also meant a regression to a more primitive economy where the local took precedence over the national and even the regional (see Simmel 1991:18). The money economy's more sophisticated and complex division of labor regressed to a simplified exchange of wares between producers. Those without direct access to real goods—in theory, workers in much of the secondary and tertiary sectors—were left out of the loop and literally in the cold. Furthermore, the distrust of "red money" also revealed the failure of the Republic to create a centralized state that "is an important political correlate of a developed money economy" (Poggi 1993:152).

By April 1937 in certain regions, transportation had become the most acute bottleneck. Rationing of transport came tardily (Leval 1975:256–57). The Republican Ministry of Agriculture blamed some of the decline of agricultural production on the inability to ship chemical fertilizers. If it was difficult to convey victuals to the troops, to supply civilian populations was nearly impossible, especially the more than one million refugees in the Republican zone.[104] Civilians were desperate enough to become "an enemy within" and to create "serious conflict." The inhabitants of Valencia, now the capital city, were hungry, fearful, and depressed (Bosch Sánchez 1983:132). At the end of the year, women, frustrated by hours in queues, engaged in street protests against high prices. They were unhappy that in major cities a medical prescription was required to obtain eggs, fish, meat, and milk (Nash 1995:143). To overcome supply problems, Valencian officials recommended that one flourmill (fábrica de harina) be employed exclusively for the needs of civilians but worried whether they had enough transportation to carry out the plan. Only if automobile use was rigorously controlled and "frivolous trips" avoided, could the shortage be eased. Lack of transport contributed to the rotting of Valencian citrus and rice in the fall and winter of 1937. As in the Russian civil war, the failure of the transport network intensified the crisis of the market and ultimately of political authority: "If it is true to say that the breakdown in transport was a central cause of the food-supply crisis, it is just as true to say that the food-supply crisis was a central cause of the breakdown in transport" (Lih 1990:57). Likewise, the Confederacy's formidable agrarian capacity was severely handicapped by the decay of its transport network (McPherson 1988:319).

In this context of civilian and military deterioration, Loyalists felt compelled to act. In May and June, Republicans launched several attacks to divert Nationalist efforts in the north, especially the threat to Bilbao (Thomas 1961:443). Catalan units disturbed the normally quiet Aragon front by conducting a June assault against Huesca, a town of fourteen thousand. It was a complete failure, and the Loyalists suffered ten thousand casualties. The other diversionary effort occurred on the Segovia front (Navacerrada), where Republicans tried to capture the provincial capital. The Popular Army's offensive on Segovia in the last days of May was initially successful. Its troops displayed considerable bravery, and its support services were efficient.[105] Quartermasters supplied the soldiers, and hospitals functioned better than at Jarama.[106] Nevertheless, Nationalists put up a tough defense. On the Segovia–La Granja line they possessed efficient artillery, dominant aviation, and African troops. "The resistance and action of the [Nationalist] enemy were greater than ours."[107] According to José María Galán, a committed Republican and commanding officer of the Thirty-fourth Division, in early June two Republican brigades (3rd and 69th) demonstrated heroism in operations but lacked experience and technical ability.[108] The Spanish conflict—like other twentieth-century wars of artillery, armor, and aviation—demanded a degree of coordination that Republican units did not possess. They did not know how to employ machine guns or to mesh their actions with other companies. "An enormous percentage of shells did not explode. This had a disastrous effect on morale."[109] These failures had the unexpected benefit of making friendly fire, which tumbled down on the Fourteenth International Brigade, less dangerous than expected. Republican airfields were too far from the front to lend effective support. In some units, officers lost control of their men. Troops of the Third Battalion assassinated their commander. "Many" soldiers and some officers of the Twenty-first Brigade defected to the enemy. The Thirty-first Brigade remained "passive," suffering "only" fifty-four injuries and five dead. It disobeyed orders to attack and spent its time filling out "false reports." By 3 June it was clear that the Segovia operation had failed. Better morale and increased commitment among Republican soldiers might have changed the outcome.[110]

The food shortage deepened in the middle of 1937 throughout the Republican zone. Soviet sources reported a steady decline of calorie intake of Republican troops as the war endured (Payne 1970:358). The chief medical officer of units stationed near Chinchón complained of the "insufficient rations" allotted to his men.[111] A CNT union representative in the province of Cuenca noted "that in some villages our stores (*economatos*) have been looted because we refused to sell to everyone."[112] CNT locals in Motilla del Palancar (Cuenca) complained that the official ration of 300 grams of bread per day did not provide enough calories for peasants engaged in hard physical labor.[113] At other times, the official ration was supposed to be 630 grams of bread, which was only a "distant fantasy."[114] "Thousands" of trade unionists from agricultural regions of La Mancha were obliged to spend time in other regions searching for food supplies.[115] "Small peasant proprietors" refused to cooperate with collectives and hoarded what they had. The enemy was well aware that the lack of food weakened the morale of the Popular Army.[116] Quiepo de Llano's nightly radio talks from Seville mocked the "red" leadership for its failure to feed its people (Quiepo quoted in Martínez Bande 1973:272; Souchy and Folgare 1977:115). Nationalist agricultural experts did not trust the Republic's figures for food production and believed that the extensive trenches and accompanying no man's lands had considerably reduced arable land on both sides (Dirección General de Agricultura 1938). *Franquistas* knew that the looting and "destruction" of the soldiers of the Popular Army had further diminished Republican edibles.

Hunger and military setbacks provided additional context for the May revolts in Barcelona. As has been noted, in November 1936 four CNT leaders had joined the government of Largo Caballero. Even earlier in the revolution, the

CNT had participated in—if not dominated—the *Generalitat,* the Catalan regional government. Libertarian participation in both the *Generalitat* and the central government ended shortly after the famous May Days of 1937 when CNT and FAI militants fought Communists and Republicans in the streets of Barcelona and in other towns throughout Catalonia. This is not the place to describe in detail the political struggles and violent skirmishes between the libertarians and the Communists, which have been amply reported elsewhere (see Orwell 1980). Suffice it to say that May has been viewed as a conflict between revolutionary (CNT-FAI-POUM) and counterrevolutionary (PSUC-PCE) forces. Libertarian dockers, for instance, refused to unload Soviet ships to protest the Communist attempt to assert hegemony in Barcelona and elsewhere (Pons Prades 1974:134). This revolutionary/counterrevolutionary struggle explains much of the fighting but omits the context of economic crisis and material shortage (see Bricall 1978:1:336). At the end of 1936 and the beginning of 1937—when it was clear to foreign observers that the Catalan provinces would have difficulty feeding their populations—women demonstrated against the shortage of bread. Other protesters maintained the Barcelona tradition of popular seizure of food supplies. On 6 May 1937, "a large group of women descended on the port of Barcelona where they looted a number of vans filled with oranges."[117] These riots recalled the appropriation of food supplies by desperate females in Southern cities during the U.S. Civil War (McPherson 1988:617). Basic foodstuffs were rationed, and Catalan householders forced to spend time in long lines. Barcelona may have received more refugees (100,000) than Madrid (70,000) (*Rapport de la mission* 1937?:21–28). It should be noted that the majority of workers of one of the most supposedly radical CNT affiliates, Madera Socializada (Carpentry Union), had expressed their self-interest by staying home during the May skirmishes. After the street fighting had ended, members did not demand political or social changes from union officials who had personally participated in the melee but instead requested lost wages (Pons Prades 1974:138).

The May conflict, which pitted the radical forces in the CNT who were joined by the POUM against the rest of the Popular Front coalition, had some minor repercussions in the Popular Army. In a few units, tensions between Communists and *cenetistas* erupted.[118] More significantly, unconfirmed reports blamed *cenetistas, poumistas,* and *faístas* for abandoning the front, assaulting Aragon villages, and assassinating Communist and other political foes. Vandalism led to the massive exodus of peasants from their villages.[119] Whatever the truth of these charges, antianarchist and anti-POUM elements portrayed the activities of their enemies much like the Nationalists described the "reds." Adversaries saw each other as bloodthirsty, evil, and prone to commit atrocities and engage in torture. In May 1937 the divisions within the Republican camp were at moments as irreconcilable as those between the Nationalists and the Republic. On the other hand, in towns where cooperation among all elements of the Popular Front—including the CNT—was the rule, the political struggles of May in Barcelona and elsewhere were of little import.[120] More consequential were the political effects of May at the national level. Juan Negrín replaced Largo Caballero as Prime Minister. Negrín had won PCE support and would pursue the centralizing mission that his predecessor had initiated. Catalan autonomy was restricted, and CNT influence curbed. Communists augmented their sway in the military and government. Soviet/PCE secret police were given a freer hand repressing and even eliminating Trotskyist and anarchist militants. The most infamous example of Communist lawlessness was the arrest and subsequent execution of the POUM leader, Andrés Nin, in June 1937 on phony charges of treason.

Nationalist intelligence agents reported that masses of recruits in Barcelona and Catalonia ignored Republican conscription, forcing the Popular Army to face the dogged and worsening problem of draft dodging.[121] On the quiet Jarama front in the summer and fall of 1937, officers were much less likely to desert during either quiet (or active) periods than lower ranking troops.[122] In July, 146 privates, 18 corporals, and 8 noncommisioned officers fled. No commissioned officers were among them. To stop defections, commissars sought volunteers to patrol the trenches and shoot their less committed comrades who abandoned their positions.[123] On the Madrid front (El Pardo–Las Rozas), seven "fascists" were caught trying to flee to the enemy and executed in front of their battalion.[124] Their capture and death raised suspicions of a larger plot involving more potential deserters. To counter the threat and to restore discipline, officers imposed strict controls on movements of men and vehicles.[125] They planned to jail disheveled or drunken soldiers.[126] These measures did not stop three men who still managed to flee to the enemy in September.

Nor did it halt the return to Nationalist lines of two Moors who had originally deserted from the insurgents at the beginning of 1937. Moroccans had a long tradition of desertion from the various pre-1936 Spanish armies (de Madariaga 1992:69). The duo had become disillusioned when the Popular Army refused to promote them to sergeant or lieutenant.[127] Their defections surprised officials since the two had been excellent soldiers, at least "until this egotistical desire to be promoted arose." Perhaps the Republic could have neutralized or won over many more of Franco's sixty to seventy thousand North African troops if it had promised not only national independence for Morocco but also better pay and quick promotions of indigenous soldiers in the Popular Army.[128]

Desertions by Moroccan soldiers to the Popular Army were rare. Instead of fleeing to the enemy, dissatisfied Africans either transferred to other Nationalist units or returned to Morocco to join family members.[129] In other words, Moroccan flights occurred for personal—not ideological—reasons. Of thirty-two deserters in the Tenth Tabor of Ceuta, only one defected to Republican ranks. Their officers concluded, "these desertions are a result of individual choice." Nationalist authorities had recruited Moroccan soldiers with generous subsidies and treated them with great care. Moors received two months' pay in advance, four kilos of sugar, a five-liter tin of oil, and a family bread ration fixed to the number of children they had fathered (de Madariaga 1992:78). Authorities paid Moroccans on time and promptly sent half their salary to their wives in North Africa. The Office of Indigenous Affairs rapidly handled their complaints and requests.[130] The quartermaster was especially proud that meals of *regulares* contained a considerable quantity of meat, which North Africans were allowed to butcher themselves according to Muslim rite.[131] Authorities permitted Moroccan butchers to supervise operations in their canning and meatpacking factories. During holidays each *pelotón* (unit) was given a lamb. Muslim troops were offered well-spiced meals and tea with large quantities of sugar. In sharp contrast, a good number of Republican soldiers fell ill when, to supplement their unspiced diet, they consumed poisonous plants that apparently resembled parsley and other edible herbs (Estellés Salarich 1986:49). North African mercenaries had complete uniforms, including helmets, gloves, and boots. This treatment resulted in a generally "excellent military spirit." At times, the Moors, whose aversion to fortification work was well known, even agreed to dig trenches. Even though Nationalist propaganda proposed a Christian crusade against an atheistic, godless, Masonic, and even Jewish republic, Christian intolerance quickly was overcome when it served Nationalist military interests (Martel 1938:51; *Los regulares de Larache* 1940:7). Of course, this careful treatment of the mercenaries did not preclude everyday racism. One Nationalist psychiatrist equated Moors with "the mentally weak" (Vallejo Nágera 1939:141).

After the battle of Guadalajara (March 1937), the center was generally quiet. For example, "calmness and stability" characterized the Guadalajara front from the end of March to July (Martínez Bande 1984:312). Although Republicans significantly improved their fortifications in the center, which probably became the most formidable of any Loyalist structures in the war, in the capital itself sacrifice seemed to have declined among troops. Soldiers of the mining battalion neglected to care for expensive equipment.[132] Officials regarded their carelessness as equivalent to sabotage. Laxness combined with corruption when the commanding officer, accompanied by a few of his men, violated leave policy and ventured to Valenicia on a buying spree.

The tranquil line may have encouraged right-wing civilians who felt trapped in Madrid to find professional help to attempt escape from the capital. They could employ an open-minded but venal goatherd who, for a fee, might be more than willing to aid those of any political persuasion.[133] However, the expert help of a mountaineer was no guarantee of success. The enemy would bribe or threaten the country folk in the Sierra to induce them to betray refugees and their helpers.

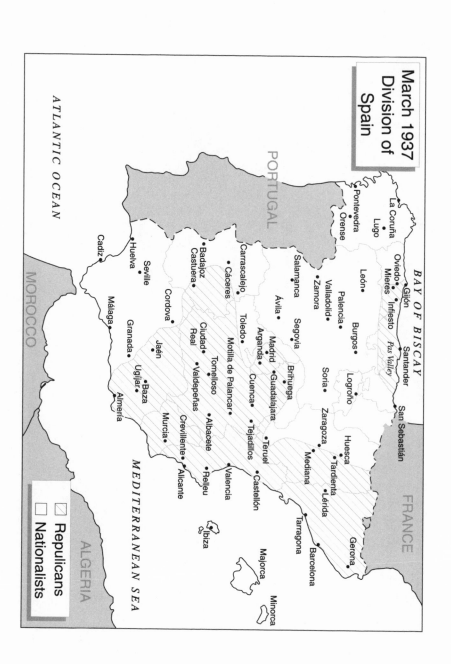

**March 1937
Division of
Spain**

ATLANTIC OCEAN

PORTUGAL

BAY OF BISCAY

FRANCE

MEDITERRANEAN SEA

MOROCCO

ALGERIA

La Coruña
Pontevedra
Orense
Lugo
Oviedo
Gijón
Mieres
Infiesto
Santander
San Sebastián
Pas Valley
León
Burgos
Logroño
Soria
Zaragoza
Huesca
Tardienta
Lérida
Gerona
Barcelona
Tarragona
Mediana
Teruel
Castellón
Valencia
Relleu
Alicante
Crevillente
Tejadillos
Albacete
Cuenca
Guadalajara
Brihuega
Arganda
Madrid
Segovia
Ávila
Toledo
Ciudad Real
Motilla de Palancar
Tomelloso
Valdepeñas
Murcia
Almería
Baza
Ugíjar
Jaén
Granada
Málaga
Cordova
Seville
Huelva
Cadiz
Badajoz
Castuera
Carrascalejo
Cáceres
Salamanca
Zamora
Valladolid
Palencia
Majorca
Minorca
Ibiza

Republicans
Nationalists

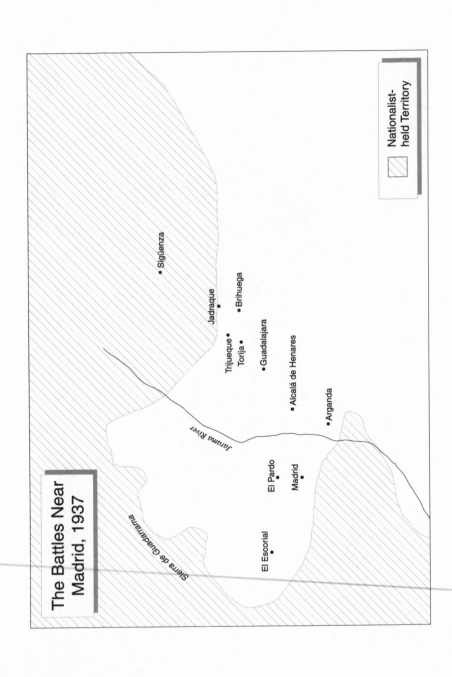

The Battles Near Madrid, 1937

Sigüenza

Jadraque

Trijueque
Torija
Brihuega

Guadalajara

Alcalá de Henares

Arganda

Jarama River

El Pardo

Madrid

El Escorial

Sierra de Guadarrama

Nationalist-
held Territory

An important minority of deserters on both sides was killed as they attempted to flee. One Republican soldier from the Army of the Center almost reached enemy lines before he was shot dead. He had left a pathetic note explaining his decision: "I am not a fascist. I am leaving because we have lost the war. I am not stupid and don't wish to be cannon fodder."[134] In the following weeks, eight more soldiers tried their luck and proved much more successful than their unfortunate predecessor. On the Aragon front, Nationalist authorities adopted the venerable policy of punishing family members of deserters.[135] When two deserters from the province of La Coruña fled with their arms to the Republican camp, Nationalist officials ordered the arrest of adult male members of their immediate families "as a just reprisal and an example." The flights of five others, who were from Navarre, also resulted in the detention of their adult male relatives. While the motives of these runaways were unclear, some Nationalist soldiers resented what they perceived to be iron and arbitrary discipline that their officers imposed. Others were presumed to be "extremists" or "reds" who hated the poor treatment and ostracism reserved for their families in the Nationalist rear.[136] To stop these "frequent desertions," Nationalist commanders recommended both the carrot and the stick. They endorsed the establishment of a network of informers within certain militia units, and they also suggested that village authorities pardon "any previous errors" of relatives of all enlisted soldiers. Officials of the Spanish Foreign Legion, it should be remembered, had experience with wiping the slate clean and insisted that once an individual volunteered for service, his past mistakes were erased.[137] Officers were disturbed that local authorities persevered in penalizing families of volunteers who had a leftist history. For example, the mayor of Cornago (La Rioja) refused to give a subsidy to a legionnaire's family. Cases of unfair treatment or persecution of soldiers and their relatives were numerous enough that high-ranking legionnaires requested that the *generalísimo* himself issue a directive imposing "forgive and forget" on all local authorities. Insurgent officials seemed to have been surprisingly successful in enlisting or conscripting numerous men with a leftist past (Payne 1967:390).

In the Sierra de Guadarrama, "a remarkable tranquility" had reigned for several months.[138] Only an occasional aviation or artillery attack or an even rarer raid interrupted the calm in the mountains. When the latter was attempted by inexperienced Republican troops against able Moors, backed by *requetés,* the results were negative.[139] For example, although the raid on La Atalaya during the early morning hours of 4 June injured or killed thirty of the Nationalist foe, the attackers lost more than they gained. In the face of "enormous [enemy] resistance," the Republican raiders failed to capture enemy positions and provoked a ferocious counterattack by one thousand Moors who forced them into an embarrassing retreat. The battle-hardened blamed the withdrawal on "extremely nervous" recruits who had panicked. The soldiers who retreated justified their flight by claiming that they had exhausted their munitions. Yet investigators found their apology unconvincing and asserted that the retreaters had abandoned to the Nationalists not only the bodies of killed or wounded raiders but also nine boxes of hand grenades and six boxes of cartridges. The incursion and its consequences cost the Republicans at least twelve dead, thirty-one injured, and twelve missing in action. On other fronts in Castille, raiding by volunteers was more successful, but raids risked creating confused conditions that allowed potential deserters, especially new recruits, a chance to escape to the enemy.[140] Shooting unsuccessful runaways and imprisoning the uncommitted effectively restored discipline.[141]

Such draconian policies increased the defensive posture of the rank and file. The calm on the El Escorial front in the fall of 1937 shocked a Republican volunteer and reminded him of a similar peace in Aragon.[142] He observed that enemy soldiers immediately in front of Republican positions "came and went" as they wished. They "calmly served themselves coffee, washed their clothes, and dried them in the sun." On this section of the front, enemies would unexpectedly meet during explorations for dietary supplements, such as raisons and figs. For the CNT militant who observed the action (or rather the lack of it), the culmination of live and let live was his fellow Republican soldiers' tolerance—in their full view—of enemy construction of fortifications "as though they were building a [swimming] pool." Nationalists reciprocated by not interfering with preparation of Republican machine-gun nests. In the months prior to Brunete, fortifications near El Escorial seemed largely symbolic. Officers were aware of mutual tolerance and did not terminate it. Indeed, when a Republican soldier accidentally fired at the enemy, both officers and fellow soldiers severely sanctioned him. His captain threatened his transfer to a disciplinary battalion. Those truly dedicated to the Republican cause wondered if the officers' promotion of live and let live would destroy the weeks of ideological instruction preached by devoted commissars.

On quiet fronts affected by live and let live, sickness and disease were much more dangerous enemies than Nationalists. For every battle injury, there were four, five, or six who had to be discharged or hospitalized because of illness.[143] In comparison, Nationalist ratios of sick to injured were two or three to one.[144] After the flu and other common illnesses, malaria and scabies were most widespread. Lack of soap exacerbated the latter. At times, Republican soldiers received no more than a bar per month.[145] The Twenty-third Mixed Brigade on the tranquil Jarama front in September 1937 reported 224 sick. Malaria (60 cases, or 27 percent) was the first cause of illness, followed by digestive disorders (41, or 18 percent); flu, colds, and rheumatism (29, or 13 percent); skin diseases (27, or 12 percent); exhaustion (12, or 5 percent); and miscellaneous illnesses.[146] Most illnesses could have been prevented by better diet, soap, and, of course, quinine for malaria. Improved nourishment and common medications enabled many to return to the front. This explains why—despite the lack of antibiotics and sulfa drugs—Republican military physicians achieved such a high recovery rate (Estellés Salarich 1986:53–54). To the numbers of the sick should be added those who injured themselves, an indication of the failure to integrate individuals into their unit. On a quiet sector near Lérida in September 1937, commissars recommended public shaming and severe punishment, including death sentences, for *automutilados*.[147] The proclamation of the death penalty revealed that self-inflicted injuries were a serious problem that could not be treated with indulgence. Even on more active fronts, the numbers of the sick far outweighed—by at least two to one—those who were killed or wounded. Insufficient or low quality food supply and inadequate shelter against rain increased the numbers of the ill.[148] In certain battalions serving near Brihuega, illnesses of the digestive tract and fatigue—which were often caused by inadequate food supply—may have touched almost one quarter of the men.[149]

Commissars realized that "a soldier's valor depends on his stomach," but were helpless to resolve the many material shortages that plagued the quartermaster's office.[150] In these situations, only care packages from home could alleviate hunger.[151] Voluntary shipments to the front by collectives and other organizations proved insufficient (cf. Simoni and Simoni 1984:114). A year after the successful defense of Madrid, the key problem for troops defending the city in the northern Sierra was the lack of food. The chief health official of the Second Corps reported that calorie intake was insufficient.[152] Furthermore, troops lacked the essential vitamins that vegetables and fresh fruits could furnish. Experts thought that more cases of vitamin deficiency (*avitaminosis*) would appear in the near future and fretted over their inability to treat them. With the onset of winter, colds and respiratory diseases were expected to increase. The normal diet of these troops provided only two thousand calories, when at least twenty-five hundred and even four thousand were needed during periods of activity and cold weather. A distinguished military historian has argued that "before a commander can even start thinking of manoeuvring or giving battle . . . [he] had—or ought—to make sure of his ability to supply his soldiers with those 3,000 calories a day without which they will soon cease to be of any use as soldiers" (van Creveld 1977:1).[153] The return of hunger, which had been a constant of Spanish history and had not been eliminated by the uneven modernization of the peninsula, must have been especially disheartening for the poor drafted to defend the Republic.

Hygiene was also substandard. Latrines and sewers functioned badly, resulting in an increase in the number of rats. The lack of underwear, infrequent washing, and shortage of disinfectants helped fleas to thrive. The bath, which relieves not just the body but also the soul, seemed virtually nonexistent: "The removal of uniform, and the reversion to a natural—and rankless—state reminds men of happier times when they splashed together with their boyhood friends or showered after a game. The bath provides time out of war in more than one sense: it not only cleans a grubby body, but it also affords a temporary relief to the hard-pressed mind" (Holmes 1985:113). In January 1938, the injured were less than 5 percent of the ill in the Sixty-seventh Brigade of the Second Army Corps.[154] The lack of clothes especially troubled new recruits on the Madrid front and elsewhere. The inability to provide them with uniforms created a ragged appearance that weakened military spirit and discipline. It was no accident that the antimilitarist and pacifist hippies of the 1960s cultivated a scruffy look. The quartermaster of Guadalajara considered the lack of clothing "the most serious problem" as winter approached.[155] The newly conscripted had no coats or blankets and frequently became ill. They also lacked spoons and plates for eating. Units that had originated as militias sometimes had access to stocks of garments; those that had been formed in the regular army did not.[156] Despite regulations, newcomers were almost never equipped with complete uniforms. Nationalist servicemen also experienced clothing shortages, but they seemed less acute. Their female textile workers produced millions of socks, sandals, pants, shirts, blankets, belts, and coats. The insurgent quartermaster claimed that his office efficiently mobilized women wage laborers in the traditional textile towns, such as Béjar (Salamanca), and militarized scattered workshops in the provinces of La Rioja, Palencia, and Navarre.[157]

The lack of everyday pleasures, especially tobacco, further demoralized the many smokers in uniform.[158] It would have been in the interest of the Popular Army to make tobacco supplies a top priority since smokers worry less about eating than nonsmokers. Cigarettes are appetite suppressants and help to relieve stress (Holmes 1985:129). Instead of the real thing, Spanish soldiers were forced to puff on ersatz joints made from fallen leaves that were rolled in old newspapers or brown wrapping paper (Alvarez 1989:105). The most desperate smoked only the paper itself. Of course, substitutes made many sick. Líster's loyal commissar, the twenty-four-year-old Santiago Alvarez, who had been wounded at Jarama, concluded—along with most contemporary drug experts—that tobacco caused the most powerful addiction.[159] As in many wars, tobacco—and alcohol—kept the warriors going psychologically. The fondness for the brown leaf also showed—like the hoarding of coins—that anarchist rejection of "vices," such as smoking, coffee, and perfumes—had little appeal outside of small circle of the most convinced militants. U.S. cigarettes that were sent in care packages to antifascist volunteers were often intercepted and stolen by Spaniards whose addiction overcame their antifascism (Landis 1989:31). Franco's soldiers were just as hooked. Nationalist "heroes" under siege on the Aragon front in early September 1936 demanded that Burgos immediately send them tobacco.

The quest for momentary pleasures is understandable in a climate of sickness and disease. Inadequate drainage and standing water in the trenches caused rheumatism. In addition, omnipresent vermin and potential outbreaks of malaria convinced many to take advantage of fleeting opportunities for fun. During June, July, and August in certain battalions stationed close to Madrid, venereal and sexually transmitted diseases affected approximately 5 percent of the troops.[160] In contrast, during World War I the venereal disease (VD) rates among Allied soldiers ranged from 8 to 15 percent (Holmes 1985:95).[161] However, in certain Republican units at certain times, VD downed more soldiers than the enemy.[162] This was also true for Nationalist forces on quiet fronts. For example, in the province of Badajoz in February 1938, VD (157 cases) was more common among the four divisions than serious wounds (150 cases) or deaths (88).[163] Furthermore, VD has serious military consequences since it usually entails relatively long hospitalization. At the end of 1937, soldiers in the center were risking their lives and health not for the Republic but for personal pleasures.[164]

Commanders worried about the overly defensive proclivities of their troops. They reasoned that only those that attack win wars.[165] In May, Nationalist authorities had already strictly forbidden "the exchange of newspapers and conversations between our forces and certain elements of the Red Army."[166] The prohibition on fraternization was in response to an incident in which, according to the Nationalists, five hundred Republican soldiers emerged from the trenches to talk and trade newspapers with their adversaries, even as they refused Nationalist invitations to desert.[167] The Fourth Brigade listed 104 soldiers, including one captain and one lieutenant, who "fraternized with the enemy on 1 June (1937) near the Frenchmen's Bridge."[168] *Franquistas* feared that friendly contact with the foe would reduce discipline. They worried that many soldiers in their army did not possess an unwavering right-wing ideology and were as uncommitted as the enemy rank and file. Several weeks before the Brunete offensive, Prieto, the Republican minister of war, and Manuel Matallana Gómez, an apolitical professional soldier serving as chief of staff (Jefe de Estado Mayor) of the Army of the Center, had condemned "the frequency of fraternizing on certain fronts."[169] These acts "ate away at the morale of our troops, diminishing willingness to combat and increasing desertions." The general prohibited the various forms of live and let live: "Talking with the enemy, exchanging press or periodicals, and establishing any agreement concerning the interruption of hostilities." He threatened that those who violated these orders would be punished quickly and severely. Officers were warned that they would be held responsible for the desertions of their men. Commanders were authorized to disarm unreliable units.

In this context of live and let live in the center, Republicans prepared an attack to counter Nationalist victories in the north (Jackson 1965:394–98; Thomas 1961:460–66). Even though it was well known that Republican forces in Estremadura were inexperienced and disorganized, Largo Caballero pushed for an offensive in that province. He hoped to undo what Yagüe's advance in

August 1936 had accomplished. If the Republic could recapture Mérida, Nationalist forces would then be divided and their communications with Portugal threatened.[170] Communists and their supporters opposed the Estremadura thrust and instead argued for an attack in the center where a successful offensive, they believed, would encourage the French to reopen the border. An overland supply route was urgent since several Russian freighters had been sunk during the spring (Jackson 1965:394). The Communists successfully overruled Caballero, and the battle would take place near Brunete, fifteen miles west of Madrid and a quiet front since the January struggle at the Coruña highway.

According to a German military expert, the Republican plan was well prepared and conceived.[171] In early July, about fifty thousand of the best troops of the nearly six hundred thousand strong Ejército Popular were concentrated for the attack that was supposed to envelop the besieging army from behind and thus lift the Nationalist grip on the capital. Some of the toughest units of the Popular Army were present: the divisions of Líster and El Campesino and three International Brigades. Other less reputed units had made considerable efforts to improve their undistinguished performance. For instance, the Tenth Division suffered many desertions before competent officers had whipped it into shape and prepared it for the Brunete battle.[172] Republican troops had sufficient weapons and were supported by Russian aircraft and tanks (presumably superior to Italian and German models). They made an initial breakthrough on 6 July, but, as in other consequential confrontations, the small force of Nationalists mobilized quickly to check the attack. The Nationalist defense of the village of Boadilla was so firm that Republican officers, armed with loaded revolvers, had to stand behind their men and compel them to attack.[173] The enemy's bravery and skill in defending positions around Majadahonda earned the admiration of Republican forces and their commissars.[174] Throughout the war, the heroism of the small groups of Nationalist soldiers provided a model for the rest of the insurgent forces. One Republican commander at Brunete, Gustavo Durán, reluctantly concluded that Nationalist forces generally showed more discipline and more capacity for maneuver than his side (Durán 1979:49). By 13 July, Nationalist reinforcements had stemmed the offensive. The *franquistas'* rapid mobility recalled, oddly enough, the unusually nimble armies of the French Revolution. The fortitude and tenacity of small garrisons of Moors and Falangists who were stationed in small towns and villages surrounding Brunete allowed Nationalist officers enough time to call up reinforcements that were able to check assaults. This pattern repeated itself in major battles throughout the civil war and reinforced trust between front-line garrisons and a high command that spared no effort to support its besieged.[175] If the Nationalist army was somewhat less mobile during major offensives in 1938, it nevertheless was able to pour its reserves into trouble spots with surprising rapidity.

The inexperience and lack of training of many Republican officers and men weakened their effort.[176] In the second half of July 1937, the Popular Army was no longer capable of sustaining the sacrifices it had made in the first half of the month.[177] Brunete became a struggle for individual survival of the Republican soldier. Uncoordinated attacks, which constituted a major problem for the Popular Army throughout the war, tipped off the enemy and lost the advantage of surprise.[178] Infantry and noncommissioned officers were particularly incompetent. The Popular Army suffered from an acute shortage of the latter, in contrast to the Nationalists. The inadequacy of support services—transportation, communications, and fortifications—demonstrated that the whole organizational structure of the Republican military needed revision.[179] The system of mixed brigades, which combined fighting and support troops, gave too much weight and resources to noncombatants. "Its hodgepodge formation left it scarcely able to put half its men on the firing line" (Payne 1970:330). Bureaucracy consumed the Popular Army (see Alpert 1989:77, 307–8). An enormous number of trucks were employed wastefully moving much unnecessary material and many unneeded men. The essential could have been transported on a simple regimental train.

Some Republican units fled, abandoning "without any good reason" their arms to the enemy.[180] In certain brigades, officers lost control over panicky troops.[181] Soldiers assigned to fortification battalions were especially tempted to desert to nearby Madrid.[182] After several days of battle, Nationalists transferred planes from the northern campaign, and Republicans lost control of the skies (Kindelán 1945:92). Yet enemy aviation—the Italians dropped 106,000 kilograms of bombs—was once again more destructive of morale than of men. As in the early days of the militia, a "simple artillery bombardment" could cause frenzy. On 25 July, a *franquista* air attack created "a terrifying and contagious panic" that allowed the Nationalists to recapture Brunete (Líster 1966:138). "The side which turns and runs does so not because it has been physically shaken but because its nerve has given" (Keegan 1976:69). Friendly and quite inaccurate fire from artillery and aviation dampened any desire to fight. Promises given on the first day of battle that troops would be relieved quickly were not fulfilled. Bad food and lack of water during the extremely hot Castilian summer demoralized other Republican soldiers. To supply troops with sustenance was even more important in a time of stress, which dramatically increased the metabolic rate thus making men hungrier and thirstier (Holmes 1985:129).[183] The stink of decaying bodies and the bleach that was used to disinfect them dampened appetites and spirits.

The commander of the Eighteenth Corps was especially critical of the inefficiency of medical services. Evacuation of the wounded was slow, and some turned up in hospitals with insects and worms multiplying in their lesions (Picardo Castellón 1986:193).[184] The injured who were evacuated to the rear sometimes went hungry (Herrick 1998:209). Casualties were extremely high, and healthcare personnel remembered the Battle of Brunete as among the bloodiest of the entire struggle. Líster (1966:140) argued that it began a new, more violent stage of conflict. The Nationalists lost approximately ten thousand men; the Republicans twenty-five thousand, many of whom were among the best and most militant troops. The International Brigades, especially their American members, were greatly affected. Certain heroic units suffered 80 percent losses. The destruction of 40 percent of the Eighteenth Army Corps devastated and exhausted the remaining fighters. Segismundo Casado, appointed on 11 July to command this corps, concluded that its enormous losses of officers and men during the first days of battle diminished any subsequent desire to attack.[185] Casado—who would lead the rebellion against the Negrín government at the end of the war—discovered that his officers continually filed false reports and engaged in wasteful and ritualized artillery exercises with the enemy. The corrupt administration of rations resulted in an unhealthy diet that, in turn, led to sickness among many fatigued and passive soldiers. Casado's solution was to employ more and better reserves. The offensive's lack of success reduced the prestige of the Communists who were unable to show that their strategy was more effective than their political opponents. The Battle of Brunete may have retarded the fall of Santander, but it failed to break the siege of Madrid. In the end, the Republic lost more than it gained.

One of the results of the failure was a shakeup of the commissar system of the Army of the Center. Commissars had not been sufficiently energetic to stop massive desertions and, in some cases, had fled themselves. Francisco Antón, a top-ranking commissar of the Army of the Center who won fame or notoriety as the twenty-something lover of La Pasionaria, reacted to these disappointments by recasting the commissar's role.[186] He assigned the main responsibility of preventing panics and reestablishing order to brigade commissars. To accomplish this task, Antón recommended that some of the most disciplined and conscientious soldiers be stationed in the rear to shoot retreaters and the officers who had allowed them to flee. Commissars were to ensure that soldiers would never abandon conquered positions. As a practical matter, he counseled commissars and political delegates to remove distinctive badges and markings, which had become easy targets for enemy sharpshooters who often favored sniping at recognizable militants. Antón was given a personal but probably unwelcome opportunity to put his own recommendations into practice when Minister of Defense Prieto ordered all commissars of his age group to the front (Alpert 1989:184).[187]

Fighting switched from the center to the north and to Aragon. Action in the last region occurred during the Battle of Brunete and showed the difficulty that the Popular Army had fighting simultaneously on two fronts. In Aragon, Republican officers had to confront insubordination. Soldiers of a battalion of the 119th Mixed Brigade refused orders to take several hills near Zaragoza.[188] They declined to become, they proclaimed, "cannon fodder." Believing the enemy to be well fortified, the rank and file turned nervous and fearful. The rebellious soldiers were ordered to the rear. The following day they once again rejected participation in the operation. Commissars from divisional headquarters were sent to the scene of the mutiny but the men surrounded, insulted, and nearly shot them. Two hundred twenty-five soldiers were later arrested and disarmed.

Coinciding with the beginning of the battle of Brunete, another incident of disobedience erupted at Albarracín (Teruel).[189] A group of libertarian militiamen refused orders to attack. They claimed that months in the trenches without leave, without arms, and without aviation and artillery support had exhausted them. They were victims, they argued, of superior enemy weaponry, friendly fire, and unfair courts-martial—which threatened some of them with twenty-years imprisonment. They correctly suspected and resented that many pistols and other weapons remained in the rear.[190] Militants of all persuasions refused to relinquish their guns.[191]

On the Aragon front unquestioned bravery mixed with selfishness. Near Albarracín, several battalions fought "magnificently," and examples of sacrifice were numerous.[192] Terribly desiccated machine gunners sacrificed drinking water for their guns. However, officers recognized that the Popular Army might have been victorious if troops had fortified positions around the town. Instead of devoting their efforts to future victory, they combated everyday hunger by looting houses in a search for food. The lack of communications equipment, the absence of aviation support, and the malfunctioning of medical services disheartened the men. One battalion's disorderly retreat so depressed its commissar that he attempted suicide. The bravery of some commissars inspired their troops, whereas others had to force their men to return to their parapets at gunpoint. In the second week of August, enemy pressure and artillery led to more orderly retreats from positions near Teruel.[193]

At Yesero (Huesca) the lack of leave demoralized the 517th Battalion of the 130th Mixed Brigade.[194] Its men had received no *permisos* for six months. Furthermore, Nationalist raiders who easily penetrated their lightly guarded lines harassed them. "A great number" of soldiers wanted to leave the battalion to join units stationed in the rear. In similar circumstances, the 519th Battalion rebelled. According to a Communist informer, their punishment had been, "a repulsive spectacle" reminiscent of old-regime tortures. Three arrested soldiers and a sergeant had their wrists tied together and then were forced to march thirty kilometers. Sixty-nine soldiers of the Second Battalion of the 125th Mixed Brigade disobeyed orders to transfer to another unit.[195] According to a commissar, their officers were too frightened to sanction this group of largely professional soldiers who had remained loyal to the Republic and had previously conducted themselves well on the Huesca front. A malaria epidemic had added to their discontent.[196] Ultimately, Communists—whose units spearheaded the Aragon offensive—proved no more effective against the thinly-held

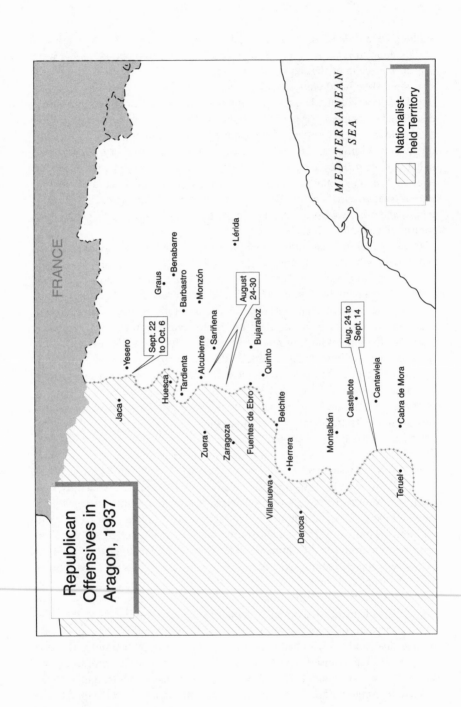

Republican Offensives in Aragon, 1937

FRANCE

MEDITERRANEAN SEA

Nationalist-held Territory

Yesero
Jaca
Huesca
Tardienta
Alcubierre
Sariñena
Graus
Benabarre
Barbastro
Monzón
Lérida
Sept. 22 to Oct. 6
August 24-30
Zuera
Zaragoza
Fuentes de Ebro
Quinto
Bujaraloz
Belchite
Herrera
Villanueva
Montalbán
Castellote
Cantavieja
Cabra de Mora
Aug. 24 to Sept. 14
Daroca
Teruel

Nationalist lines in this region than the anarchists whom they so disdained and to whom they had denied Soviet arms.[197]

On 23 August, the Popular Army initiated a series of actions that aimed—as had the Battle of Brunete—to divert Nationalist efforts in the north. The goal was to capture Zaragoza, an important regional center of almost two hundred thousand inhabitants. It had been a former Anarchist stronghold whose quick seizure by Nationalists at the beginning of the conflict had more than embarrassed libertarians. Zaragoza had become one of the few urban capitals of an essentially rural Nationalist Spain (Martínez Bande 1973:16–17). Both sides tolerated the quiet and frequently unguarded front near the city for almost a year (Martínez Bande 1973:79). Juan Modesto noted, "In this sector of the front, there were none of our men or any trenches. Going along the Zaragoza road, you can see a handful of our men in primitive trenches. . . . A little further along, there was a pocket of the enemy, but they were so far from each other that you could travel between them in a car without the least danger" (Modesto 1969:125–26). After Brunete, many of the best remaining Loyalist troops, such as Líster's Eleventh Division and several International Brigades, had been transferred to the Aragon front (Thomas 1961:472–75). Significant desertions from the Nationalists seemed to have encouraged a Republican attack (Payne 1967:397).

From the very beginning, the Republicans paid a high price for any territory they captured. Between 26 August and 6 September the Zaragoza offensive transformed itself into a battle for the much less significant town of Belchite (3,000 inhabitants) in a climate of extreme heat, dust storms, and terrible thirst (Cordón 1977:305). Ten thousand Republican soldiers surrounded about seven thousand defenders—Requetés, Falangists, and Civil Guards—who desperately fought off the attackers. They were supported by Nationalist aviation that bombarded Republican forces while airdropping supplies. The defenders' water resources were cut off during the appallingly hot summer. Ricardo Sanz, head of the Twenty-sixth Division and a CNT militant, was impressed with the enemy's "gutsy resistance" in defense and "enormous pressure" in attack. The commitment of small groups of Nationalist soldiers on quiet fronts was once again evident. Desertions from insurgent ranks seemed to have declined somewhat during the Aragon fighting.[198] Their engagement showed the combat effectiveness of what has been called "primary group cohesion," that is where buddies in a unit take priority over other collective and individual loyalties, including family ties (see Lynn 1984:34; Holmes 1985:91; Grossman 1996:149). It is this melding of the individual into a small community of comrades that is the essential building block of the military. Ninety-four percent of interviewed veterans of the Abraham Lincoln Brigade agreed that they fought better knowing that weakness would endanger the lives of their friends (Dollard 1943:60). Nationalist small-group cohesion was reinforced by the confidence that their command would spare no effort to relieve or rescue tiny units. It was further stiffened by the reputation that Nationalist officers—such as Quiepo de Llano, Yagüe, Mola, Moscardó, Beorleguí, and, of course, Franco himself—had gained for courage and valor either in Morocco or at the inception of the civil war. On the Republican side, outfits such as the Abraham Lincoln Brigade and the Fifth Regiment inspired their own men and others. According to a Nationalist intelligence report, the dedicated U.S. soldiers of the International Brigades resolutely attacked from the Fuentes de Ebro but were "almost destroyed because they were not backed up by Catalan battalions on the flanks who refused to budge from the trenches when the attack order was given."[199] Catalans were sometimes reluctant to sacrifice for any army. The tendency of Catalan artillery crews stationed near Madrigalejos (Cáceres) to desert corrupted remaining soldiers, including officers.[200] During the Battle of Zaragoza other non-Catalan brigades dissolved at the first contact with the enemy (Cordón 1977:308). Rojo complained that the Popular Army knew how to fight defensively but could not maneuver well (Rojo paraphrased in Martínez Bande 1973:124). On the other hand, the Twenty-eighth Division, for example, lost eighteen lieutenants, two captains, a commander, and several political delegates in the first days of battle.

Although Belchite's defenders—short of food and water—finally surrendered to the Popular Army on 6 September, Prieto was understandably depressed that so many Republican troops at Belchite captured so little. His discouragement was understandable since Aragon was one of the least fortified of all Nationalist fronts. Local resistance at Belchite had slowed down, if not stopped, the offensive. Nationalist commanders transferred reinforcements from Castile—many of whom were veterans of Brunete—who blocked the Republican offensive's main objective of capturing Zaragoza. Republican efforts in Aragon did not succeed in diverting sufficient Nationalist troops from the north to alter the outcome there. The deficiencies that were evident during the battle of Brunete resurfaced (Líster 1966:165). The CNT concluded that PCE soldiers were much better conquering defenseless towns in the rear than fortified ones on the front.[201] According to a CNT activist, the libertarian units—Twenty-fifth, Twenty-eighth, and some of the Twenty-sixth—distinguished themselves, whereas the Communist performance was comparatively disappointing (Aroca Sardagna 1972:182–83). Part of the problem was that Republican recruits needed training and could not handle machine guns. Others—deprived of food, pay, leave, mail, and clean clothes—lacked the will to fight and retreated without orders (Líster 1966:168–69). Nationalist intelligence reported that "to take Belchite, Assault Guards from Barcelona and Valencia had to be called up with the goal of stopping desertions."[202]

Following the offensives of Brunete and Aragon, Vicente Rojo, the chief of staff of the Army of the Center, reflected on the offensive capabilities of the

Republican army.[203] Rojo envied the Nationalist example of small but determined units holding out until reinforcements arrived.[204] Among his most important criticisms concerned the employment of reserves. Although officers were told to ensure that their troops were not exhausted and to relieve them when necessary, he assigned reserves a function other than relief: they should remain in the rear to interrogate all soldiers who were behind the lines "without justification." Rojo repeated the orders of Union officers in the U.S. Civil War who instructed their men to fire on those who faltered during attacks (Linderman 1987:171). As in the U.S. Civil War, orders to shoot were often ignored, but Rojo wanted every Republican soldier to know that shirkers would be arrested and prosecuted as deserters. He repeated earlier criticisms that panicky commanders called for reserves too quickly.[205]

After the capture of Belchite, desertions continued on the long and thinly held Aragon front. At times, deserters lost their way. One from Republican ranks mistakenly took a trail back to his own lines and, as luck would have it, yelled out "Viva Franco" to members of the 100th Brigade of the Popular Army. It was an error that he would never repeat since his former buddies responded by shooting him dead.[206] The ease of losing one's way and ending up in enemy hands rendered many fronts dangerous (Cordón 1977:258). However, in this Aragon sector, most deserters sneaked back to the rear rather than over to the enemy. Some found it hard to return to their former jobs since factory committees often demanded proof of an honorable discharge as a condition for reemployment.[207] As in the Russian civil war, supply problems encouraged desertions (Figes 1990:198). In the 143rd Mixed Brigade, "agents provocateurs encouraged desertions by claiming that the enemy ate better and did not suffer from cold."[208]

By the fall, quiet had returned to many Aragon lines. Republican authorities asserted that "the enemy has tried to fraternize with our forces."[209] They reminded all commissars that previous secret orders had prohibited exchanging with the enemy not just newspapers but even personal letters from families separated by the conflict. Restrictions did not prevent Nationalists from "organizing something like an armistice" supplemented by informal truces under the specific pretext of recovering corpses. In Aragon, the 105th Division of the Nationalist Army was wracked by desertions. In September 1937, an officer attributed them to "extremism," or, in Nationalist parlance, leftist ideology of whatever variety.[210] He called for a "purge of leftists" and greater surveillance of all soldiers. Desertions persisted in November, and officials planned reprisals against deserters' families.[211] By early 1938, senior officers concluded that the problem was as much regional as political, a finding that confirmed the rule that nonpolitical reasons for desertion are usually far more common than political ones (Holmes 1985:86). The 105th was loaded with recruits from coastal areas of Galicia who had little desire to sacrifice for their fellow Gallegan, Francisco Franco. Galicia, it should be noted, returned more Popular Front deputies than any region (Payne 1993:438). It was the only Republican region that the insurgents immediately captured, and it provided the Nationalists with perhaps the most important contingent of troops, 237,385 or one-fourth of Rebel manpower (Payne 1967:519). General Yagüe himself felt that Gallegan numerical domination of the 105th made it useless.[212] Divisional officers asked Burgos for "180 Falangist volunteers ready to carry out a special mission." To prevent desertions they were to be dispersed among twelve battalions of the Army of the North. General Franco decided to send twelve hundred men, none of whom would be Gallegans, "to clean out" (sanear) the division. Many Gallegans would end up in labor battalions.[213]

While Gallegans achieved fame or notoriety for desertions, they were not the only group reluctant to serve the Nationalist camp. In October 1937, in response to "the growing number of seventeen year olds who are emigrating to America," (the draft age was eighteen), the generalísimo himself—like the Communist dictators that he purportedly detested—imposed severe restrictions and prohibited all males sixteen or older from leaving the country.[214] Neither side repeated the pattern of the Russian civil war, where desertions often corresponded with the demands of agricultural labor—possibly because Spanish agriculture and growing seasons were more varied, and many regions needed agricultural labor throughout much of the year (Figes 1990:182).

After the Battle of Brunete, practices of live and let live—for example, exchanging newspapers—also resumed in the Madrid region.[215] The end of Brunete initiated a one-year period during which the center, like the Andalusian and the Estremaduran fronts, became inactive (Martínez Bande 1981). The calm of the Madrid front surprised journalists (see Oudard 1938:130). The south was even more tranquil. A posting to the Army of Estremadura was one of the cushiest jobs an officer could get (Gárate Córdoba 1976b:86). In Pozuelo (Madrid), a message in one Nationalist shell that failed to detonate read, "Surprise! Comrades, . . . don't worry. These won't explode. We are with you. UHP."[216] Whether by design or, much more frequently, by accident and technical incompetence, "many" Republican shells also failed to explode and may have contributed to an atmosphere of live and let live.[217] On the western Madrid front, near El Pardo, half of the grenades launched by grenade-throwers did not detonate.[218] Duds, common on both sides from the beginning of the war, were also widespread in urban bombing raids. In Madrid and Alicante, Nationalist forces estimated that 40 to 50 percent of bombs dropped by aircraft did not burst.[219] One failed shell contained the message, "Spaniards, we are your brothers and don't wish to cause any harm." Another shell had the inscription, "Antifascist workers of Palma de Mallorca send greetings to their brothers."[220]

Sometimes, though, the results of technical incompetence were not so humane. In the center, unreliable grenades blew up whoever attempted to employ them.[221] During 1937, 2,546 civilians in Madrid were victims of bombs that—unfortunately for them—did work.[222] From July to December 1936, 1,890 civilians were victims, most occurring during the Battle of Madrid in November. In other words, as the war progressed in Madrid, Nationalist bombings became less dangerous. The overwhelming majority of victims, from 60 to 90 percent, were wounded, not killed. Minors (under 15 years old) had a mortality rate much greater than adults. It may be, in accord with much of the literature, that bombings were targeted at working-class areas. But according to health officials, even more harmful was the "suicidal frivolity" (*despreocupación*) of Madrid residents who had a tendency "to take advantage of the good weather" and strolled near exposed and dangerous areas.

In October, officers in the Army of the Center felt it was absolutely essential to instill an "offensive spirit" among their troops.[223] Soldiers must lose their "most lamentable" habit of remaining in the trenches. To increase aggressivity, the high command of the Army of the Center encouraged raiding, which should have been popular among ill-fed and poorly clad soldiers who might have been eager for enemy booty. But live and let live undermined its effects. On a cold night in December 1937 in the sector of Quijorna-Brunete, it would have been easy for Nationalists to gun down newly stationed Republican troops. Instead, insurgents offered a warm welcome by allowing them safe passage to their dugouts "so that they wouldn't catch cold" (Pons Prades 1974:231). An invitation to share hot coffee with their adversaries pleasantly surprised green and shivering Republicans.

Commissars fretted over the commitment of the conscripted. Some promised to become more punitive with deserters.[224] At the same time, political delegates tried to understand the apathetic. They realized that individuals had different reasons for not volunteering for service and concluded that most did not "comprehend" political and social issues. The commissar's job was to "dominate" this "mass" and mold it into a fighting force. In general, commissars devoted much more time to the prevention of desertion and the creation of an acceptable level of military discipline than to ideological policing. The Tenth Division, which had experienced defections before Brunete but had performed bravely during that battle, quickly returned to its lax precombat habits.[225] Officials blamed commissars for poor political indoctrination and thus for the revival of desertions, whose direction was commonly toward the rear to join family members in Levante.[226] Officers were dismayed that a few soldiers who had been wounded or even decorated at Brunete defected to the enemy.

The organizational difficulties of feeding and clothing the Popular Army disheartened even political delegates of the Forty-forth Division on the Mediana-Quinto-Azaila sector of the Aragon front.[227] In the fall of 1937, the most serious health problems were acute rheumatism caused by damp living and sleeping conditions, intestinal problems brought on by bad food, and colds.[228] Chief medical officers argued that troops should be given a period of rest and recuperation in the rear. Only eight doctors, instead of the required twenty-one, served the entire division. Competent surgeons were rare. Most military physicians had sided with the insurgents.[229] The major advantage of this medical disorganization was that doctors had a great deal of autonomy to experiment without bureaucratic obstacles (Broggi i Vallès 1986:22–23).

By the middle of winter, the situation had gotten worse. Many soldiers did not have coats or blankets, which they had abandoned during hot weather.[230] A "plague" of parasites—especially fleas and lice—infested nearly every man in uniform. Vermin did not respect rank. As a World War I soldier put it, "We were beset by an itch that was barely tolerable except when fear overshadowed all bodily discomforts" (quoted in Holmes 1985:112). The lack of soap and clean water made washing difficult, and it was nearly impossible to cure skin diseases since men could not change or disinfect their underwear.[231] Quite different was the experience of an Argentine physician serving with the insurgents (Colmegna 1941:54). His *bandera* of eight hundred men was inspected monthly for parasites and venereal disease, and they received a weekly change of clothes.

In the winter of 1937, illness caused over half the *bajas* in the 143rd Brigade and in other components of the Popular Army. In some units, the majority of soldiers had scabies (*sarna*) or other dermatological afflictions.[232] Another skin disease, which affected 40 percent of personnel in the First and Third Battalions, could not be treated because it could not be identified. The contaminated water of the Ebro spread typhoid fever, but men were too weak to receive the vaccination, which produced a dangerously high fever.[233] Scarcities of fresh fruits and vegetables containing vitamins B and C increased threats of gingivitis and stomach disorders. With body defenses weak, minor cuts and injuries developed into serious infections. Trench soldiers were especially angered that quartermaster personnel ate more and were in better physical condition than they were. At the end of the year, the 145th Brigade did not repeat the aggressive attacks against the enemy and the consequent heroic deaths that had occurred in September and October. Instead, its soldiers disobeyed their officers and fraternized with the enemy.[234]

Rifles—old Winchesters—proved unreliable. The only dependable weapon was the hand grenade. The result was a "defensive not offensive posture." The enemy, soldiers feared, might retaliate with munitions that worked. The wounded died waiting for nonexistent stretchers and broken-down ambulances, or they perished on bumpy and muddy dirt paths. Nationalist propaganda advertised Republican material deficiencies—often aggravated by the lack of transport, unpaved roads, and bad weather—to demoralize their adversary. At times, more than half of Loyalist bombs and mortars did not explode. As Nationalist soldiers went on leave, they vocally flaunted their good fortune and shouted at their Republican counterparts that they would rot in the trenches. Republican civilian authorities took the precaution of criminalizing listening to Nationalist radio broadcasts. They even tried to alter radios so that they could receive only Republican stations (Quirosa-Cheyrouze y Muñoz 1986:210).

The lack of military training was also harmful to the Popular Army. Even when fortifications were constructed with great effort, they often served little purpose. Commissars recognized the superiority of enemy entrenchments in every region except the center.[235] Ineffective fortifications led to more frequent and more intensive guard duties that fatigued the troops.[236] Building brigades were scorned and maltreated by other soldiers.[237] In certain regions, they had to confront both the indifference of locals and the presence of scorpions.[238] They suffered late pay, inadequate calorie consumption (despite the fact that they had the right to 10 percent more than the normal ration), and lacked uniforms or even basic garments.[239] Some had worn the same civilian clothes for ten months. Others could not work because they were shoeless. Shortages of tools, explosives, and canteens reduced their productivity. In summer, they had only winter pants and the same pair of underwear issued at conscription. Their motley and colorful attire made them easy targets for enemy sharpshooters. As winter approached, doctors worried that workers might fall sick. Yet despite official neglect, they were desperately needed. Certain officers maintained their refusal to obey orders to permit the transfer of "their" fortification workers to other fronts. By force or subterfuge, they kept them under their own command.[240]

Thousands of volunteers were needed to put building brigades at full strength. Although most construction workers initially proved to be solid antifascists and provided "numerous examples of abnegation," the risks and intensity of fortification work led fewer and fewer to volunteer.[241] Only in Madrid—but not in other urban areas, such as Barcelona—did Republicans match previous examples of sacrifice in civil wars: for example, the sacrifice of the unpaid Puritans who worked with "hectic enthusiasm" to fortify London in 1643 (Kenyon 1988:64). Many enrolled in certain fortification brigades assumed they would be stationed in the rear and became discouraged when posted near the front. With the goal of increasing numbers of active builders, commissars asked authorities not to permit workers between the ages of twenty-eight and forty to labor on public works projects. Some localities that were initially far from the front used sappers to construct roads that benefited the local economy but had little military purpose.

The CNT blamed failures on the PCE and consistently complained about Communist influence and favoritism in the army.[242] Libertarians were especially bitter about Soviet advisors and Líster, all of whom they considered to be incompetent. Only the Communist propaganda machine, they thought, kept the truth of PCE inadequacies from emerging. Whatever the verdict on these allegations, (Hugh Thomas considers Líster one of the best Republican

officers, and Ramón Salas Larrazábal calls him a natural leader), the egotism of many CNT members prevented them from countering PCE power.
The CNT Defense Section accused military tribunals of leniency toward disobedient Communist troops, and it charged the PSUC (Partit Socialista Uni-
ficat de Catalunya) with stuffing the automotive unit (*parque movil*) with
UGT affiliates. Yet it had to admit that its own union, Sindicato Sideromet-
alúrico, had shown no interest in filling with its own adherents the slots in
the automotive unit or in other sections of the military.[243] The CNT only
gradually overcame its reluctance to participate in government and in official organizations. At the end of 1937, an overwhelming majority of CNT
peasant organizations of the center—which claimed eighty-eight thousand
members—mastered the opposition of more radical members, who thought
that the formation of a corps of labor inspectors was counterrevolutionary
and agreed to participate in the creation of an association that would inspect
the work of both labor and management.[244]

In the summer of 1937, Communists reorganized the Aragon rear and tried
to destroy the collectives that had been established at the beginning of the war
(and temporarily legalized in June 1937) in parts of the expropriated land of
the region (Casanova 1988:51). The collectives originated when urban militants, who were mostly anarchist, marched through Aragon and imposed their
idea of libertarian communism or socialism (Casanova 1985:96, 111, 122,
195).[245] They felt that collectivizing the means of production and distribution
was the best method to feed the troops. The militiamen ignored the complaints
of villagers and took what they needed or wanted. Some locals, especially
medium property owners and even a few renters and *braceros,* felt compelled
or coerced into joining collectives.[246] Militiamen concluded that young male
villagers had no interest in fighting on the front.[247] They assumed that locals
had food supplies hidden at home. The overwhelming majority of Aragon peasants owned some property, although it was not sufficient to allow them to feed
their families or to provide any degree of financial security (Simoni and Simoni
1984:16, 31). Most did not show much gratitude to a Republic that had done
little to improve their situation, but many were willing to give collectivization
a chance. "Indifferent" citizens opportunistically joined collectives just as they
had joined unions. In the village of Cretas (pop. 1,600, Teruel), two-thirds of
the inhabitants became members. They included wageworkers, small owners,
and wealthy families whose property had been confiscated. The relatively
comfortable owners who farmed individually found that it was hard to do business with the collective, which tended to boycott them.

The conflict between Communist soldiers and anarchist activists in the villages of Aragon has become one of the most controversial issues of the war.
The Communists have argued that the CNT and its followers coerced peasants
into unproductive collectives. They made specific charges that, for example,

in Albalate de Cinca (Huesca), a CNT stronghold whose collective contained over a fifth of the sixteen hundred inhabitants, and in Poleniño (Huesca) collectivists destroyed trees and were responsible for sharp declines in production.[248] It is noteworthy that accusers were not afraid of putting their allegations in letters that they knew had a good chance of being intercepted and read by enemies.[249] Militiamen enrolled in the Battalion Largo Caballero accused the CNT-dominated town council of their hometown, Cantavieja (Teruel), of forcing small holders into collectives and expropriating property of their friends and families in an effort to impose "libertarian communism."[250] They charged the town council with exiling or arresting members of Izquierda Republicana (IR). Because of poor management and corruption, Cantavieja's meat supply and animals had disappeared. Food in the village was scarce. To end the "terror," five militiamen planned to return to the town and shoot the councilmen. The town council denied the charges and claimed that it had acted in accordance with the directives of the Council of Aragon, which was dominated by the CNT and the FAI. Cantavieja councilmen argued that meat had become rare not because of their own expropriations but rather since militia columns had consumed too much of it.

Anarchists defended themselves from PCE charges by accusing Communists of illegally jailing antifascist militants and disrupting production. A libertarian source estimated that 30 percent of the Aragon collectives were completely destroyed (Leval 1975:336). In Aragon, the dissolution of the collectives and the repression of CNT activists disrupted the status quo and, in certain cases, production (Bolloten 1991:523, 529). This is not surprising since after more than a year of operation, many villagers had found a modus vivendi with their collective. This is not to argue that peasants were intent upon building a socialist or libertarian future. Peasants lacked the utopian perspective of many militants (and historians) sympathetic to collectivization. Instead, rurals used the collectives for their own purposes. For example, collectivization eliminated debts to larger landowners (Souchy Bauer 1982:90; see also Souchy 1992, ch. 11). In addition, some members of an extended family might join a collective and use its rations to feed less fortunate members. Collectives reported that individual farmers had their elderly parents sign up to avoid providing for them (Leval 1975:210). The new policies imposed by the army in the summer of 1937 were more favorable to private property and encouraged some owners to return to reclaim their land from the collective.[251] Village conservatives regained the upper hand and their confiscated land, animals, and tools. Furthermore, the army and assault guards prevented the Aragon regional police from aiding collectivists.[252]

In many villages, CNT militants were jailed or forced to flee. In October 1937, the CNT Peasants' Union estimated that six hundred of its Aragon militants remained incarcerated. The Communist-inspired repression was nationwide. The CNT claimed that "thousands" of its supporters were imprisoned and that hundreds were assassinated (Bolloten 1991:499). In Castille and La Mancha, the CNT Peasant Federation of the Center needed significant financial contributions from its members to defend itself against repression.[253] The funds were mainly devoted to legal expenses for imprisoned militants. Tensions between libertarians and Communists lasted into 1938.[254] Many activists remained in hiding, rendering the collectives leaderless for a considerable period. Some preferred to stay with CNT forces at the front.[255] The Communist offensive against the collectives and their political supporters in the Consejo de Aragón had the secondary effect of alienating CNT militants in the army, whose units seemed to have retained considerable autonomy.[256] They simplistically blamed their material and military deficiencies on Communist domination.

A dispassionate examination of the charges and countercharges leads to the conclusion that both anarchists and Communists were correct. The former used illegal coercion to initiate collectives, and the latter used it to destroy them. Collectivization meant trying to put everyone to work. Anarcho-syndicalists advertised that in their collectives each member had the obligation to labor (Souchy Bauer 1982:20). Miguel Chueca of the CNT, Labor Minister of the Aragon Council, was proud that his department had forced "an endless number of people who lived off the rest" to produce.[257] "Liberated Aragon" no longer offered the "lazy" any opportunity to be parasitic. Chueca was satisfied that he had leveled salary differentials and had raised pay for women. By the summer of 1937, the Aragon Council realized that it was counterproductive to force "individualists" to remain members, and many of them left collectives.[258] In other regions, in 1937 peasants also abandoned collectives to farm on their own (Garrido González 1979:62). Their withdrawals created sticky problems of property rights since it was sometimes difficult to evaluate how much land and, in particular, labor the former collectivists had contributed to the general effort. For example, the Spanish collectives—like Soviet ones—had to confront the issue of ownership of the harvest of a field that was "donated" to the collective, sowed by it, and reclaimed by its former owner.[259] In most collectives and in certain towns, such as Caspe, wage laborers were forced to join either the CNT or the UGT and to pay their dues on time in order to remain members.[260] A system of fines and sanctions compelled them to attend assemblies.[261]

Even after more than a year of collectivization, a *faísta* complained that villagers remained "materialistic" and "uncivil."[262] Other militants reported that collectivists wasted bread and other items when offered free or at artificially low prices (Fraser 1986:354; Simoni and Simoni 1984:114). In the district of Almansa (Albacete), the district secretary reported that "the members of unions which call themselves CNT could call themselves anything. . . . They throw out the letters and messages we send them."[263] The growing influence of Communists and their alliance with the propertied peasantry undermined the few collectives that existed in this area. For anarchists, there remained the "painful task" of educating workers who acted so selfishly that militants in many collectives eventually agreed that the egotistical should be permitted to leave.[264]

Historians have highlighted the tensions between the individualists who wanted to exit the collectives to farm on their own and the collectivists who supported communal agriculture. In a number of towns, the sociology was predictable. The propertyless preferred to support the collective, whereas small property owners desired independence. The poorest villagers of Castellote (Teruel) protested to the governor of Aragon that Communist-inspired changes had destroyed the collective and forced it to return property to former owners.[265] The four or five reactionary absentee landlords, who had possessed nearly the entire village, had reestablished control over it. Their sharecroppers (*medieros*) recaptured the exclusive right to farm, thereby "dispossessing half the village and leaving it without means of support." Merchants, all of whom were rightists, resumed their commercial monopoly. Prosperous farmers in other areas of Spain resented the obligation to market their products through the collective and had less privileged access to loans from the Agrarian Reform Institute (IRA) (Rodrigo González 1985?:82). It should be noted that even after the Communist assault on collectives, restrictions remained on individual farmers. In some Aragon villages, such as Calanda (population 5,000, Teruel), they were still unable to employ wage labor (Collectif Equipo 1997:79). Nor could landlords—big or small—appreciate the Republic's official moratorium on rent payments, decreed in August 1937 and lasting until September 1938 (Bernecker 1982:149).

Yet a large number of modest or poor *arrendatarios* and *medieros* (renters and sharecroppers) were not enthusiastic about collectivization and felt that the collectivists had unfair advantages—such as access to food supplies—that other villagers were denied (Casanova 1985:195–97). Collectivization destroyed the higher status and income that some sharecroppers had enjoyed. In the small town of Cabra de Mora (Teruel) with ninety inhabitants, sharecroppers (*masaderos*) were relatively prosperous and, according to their enemies, sympathetic to their "feudal lords."[266] They strongly opposed collectivization. Nor was this town unique. Where prominent landowners could offer long-term or advantageous contracts to the propertyless, they could create loyal supporters (Collier 1987:42). The collectives' proponents were forced to call in Aragon police to take over sharecropper land. In response, sharecroppers left Cabra de Mora and put themselves under the leadership of a sympathetic militia chief and the UGT. Aragon Communist officials skeptically observed that "the petty bourgeoisie, *medieros* (poor sharecroppers) and *arrendatarios* . . . don't have a revolutionary spirit and if they enrolled in unions or parties, they did so to defend their bits of property and their petty interests against the attacks and pillaging of elements [i.e., anarchists] that have dominated Aragon during the last year."[267]

Even some *braceros* had no interest in joining CNT collectives and feared confiscation of their few possessions.[268] Among themselves in private, Aragon Communists did not show great respect, let alone solidarity, for many rural proletarians: "Day laborers who were not in unions were always slaves of the *caciques*. They feared losing their miserable wage or being thrown in jail." *Braceros* were more concerned with the recuperation of the back wages of July and August than in plans for future collectivization (Borkenau 1963:156). PCE militants accused "the masses" of Monzón (Huesca), where the CNT exercised considerable influence, of being "extremely disoriented."[269]

In certain professions (such as resin makers) and some districts (for example, Priego in Cuenca province) peasants seemed uninterested in collectivization.[270] In four Cuenca villages collectives were not formed; in another the collective functioned poorly; and in only one was it considered to have worked well. Although many CNT members were apathetic about collectivization, UGT adherents in this district—some of whom "possessed the card of every party"—resisted even more. Depending on the village, there could be either violence or cooperation between the two unions. In Gascueña (Cuenca) which was divided between 201 CNT members and 242 UGT adherents, some of the latter had tried to kill one of the former. Madrid province also experienced tension between the unions. Even so, cooperation of rivals was possible. In Valdeolivas (Cuenca), where 145 were in the CNT and 150 in the UGT, the unions reached an agreement "to oblige all physically fit townsmen to work the harvest" and to find suitable jobs for others (cf. Bernecker 1982:170). In Cardenete (Cuenca) landless laborers formed a relatively autonomous collective which abolished money, established rations based on work, and traded its surplus with a neighboring village.[271]

In the battle for sugar, CNT collectives gained an upper hand because of their political influence in Aragon, where they tried to monopolize sugar-beet production for the Monzón factory.[272] Libertarians took charge of seed distribution and allocated little for individual farmers. Sometimes they confiscated crops and produce of individualists who were forbidden to employ wage labor. However, the high price set for sugar beets awakened peasant "egotism" and encouraged their efforts. On the other hand, delays and illiquidity discouraged farmers, but they were eventually paid. For some, it was the first significant sum they had received since the beginning of the civil war. Payment delays dismayed individualists and ultimately convinced them to become subsistence farmers, a turn that would prove counterproductive for the Republican economy.

Some sugar-refinery workers sympathized with small producers. The proposal of Aragon's Minister of Labor, Chueca, to reduce their salaries from twenty-five pesetas per day to less than eighteen angered the highest-paid wage earners of the Monzón refinery. They could not publicly protest since to do so would risk their being labeled "fascists." Policies that reduced salaries of the skilled in times of inflation risked provoking industrial collapse by encouraging irreplaceable workers to leave the factory. Ideology—no matter how libertarian—could not overcome acquisitive individualism. An informant who was hostile to the CNT recommended that the influence and authority of the CNT-dominated Aragon Council—which had been legalized by Largo Caballero at the end of 1936—be reduced. He also proposed that the Valencian government nationalize sugar refineries (*azcucareras*) to lessen tensions and to increase production.[273]

Undoubtedly, resistance to leveling and collectivization was a central issue in towns and villages, but this conflict has hidden another dimension. The collectives often practiced organized selfishness on a local level. This helps explain why large numbers of villagers remained committed to them even after the Communist sweep into Aragon. Localism also explains why even Communists were eventually forced to restore some of the dismantled farms in order to increase production (Bolloten 1991:531). The collectives themselves often acted greedily. Prosperous ones refused to aid the less affluent.[274] In his letter of resignation, the *consejero de economía y abastos* complained about the increasingly "autarkic nature" of the Aragon villages.[275] It is ironic that this complaint came from an official of a council that itself was accused of attempting to establish an autarky (Maurice 1975:76). Collectives intransigently refused to share the vehicles at their disposition and thus intensified a serious transportation shortage.[276] For example, beets destined for sugar-processing plants had to be left in the fields and eventually used as animal feed because of a lack of transport and containers. This local independence and egotism made information gathering impossible: "In spite of our appeals, no one, absolutely no one" in the villages responded to statistical inquiries.[277] The flow of data did not improve even though on 28 January 1937 the Aragon Council threatened to confiscate all unreported stocks. At times, the government made good its threat and expropriated unauthorized goods and fined their owners, even if they were cooperatives or collectives.[278] But usually Republican authorities—like the Bolsheviks during their civil war—proved unable to overcome peasant reluctance to reveal what they had harvested (Figes 1996:622).

The lack of data became a national problem. In the center, CNT peasant groups lamented failures to inform them about the creation of collectives, gathering of harvests, and sowing of fields.[279] The National Peasant Federation wrote to all of its regional organizations demanding, as they had agreed, "the most exact and concrete information" on peasant production and possessions.[280] It argued that "CNT wealth in the countryside belonged to all libertarian peasants. It was not the property of groups and collectives that have authored absurd parochialisms [*cantonalismos*] that are absolutely contrary to what we believe." Regional federations that repeatedly asked their locals and collectives to provide the needed statistics were ignored "1001 times."[281] The collectives' refusal to provide statistics and Nationalist control of the capitals of certain provinces made the Agricultural Ministry's task of collecting data especially difficult. It remained ignorant of production in large parts of Loyalist-controlled Badajoz, Toledo, Asturias, León, Burgos, Huesca, Zaragoza, and Teruel.[282] Refractory centrifugal and localist forces—similar to those that the Confederates, Cavaliers, and White Russians confronted during their respective civil wars—weakened Republican war efforts.

The refusal to provide statistics and the concealment of goods enabled the villages and collectives to avoid paying their debts. "The most typical case" was the village of Angüés (Huesca), which asked for a large quantity of fertilizers and used only a third of what it was loaned.[283] This wasted not only the fertilizer itself but also transportation. In general, the Aragon Council accumulated great debt because the *pueblos* made almost no effort to repay what was loaned to them. A similar situation developed in Valencia (Bosch Sánchez 1983:291–92). It is not surprising that members of collectives had to be forced to pay their personal arrears.[284] Deficits made it impossible for the regional organization to lend money to many collectives. Personal and local refusals snowballed into a national problem.

UGT collectives were no better at reporting than those of the CNT (Mintz 1977:217). Negrín was said to have distrusted collectives because as finance minister in Largo Caballero governments from September 1936 to May 1937, he had found it impossible to collect taxes from them (Fraser 1986:450).[285] Even after the Communist attacks in the summer of 1937, collectives still avoided taxation. In its inability to raise revenue, the Republic of 1936 resembled its predecessor of 1873. A de facto taxpayer strike seemed to have existed throughout the Republican zone. The Spanish Loyalists never matched the ability of English Parliamentarians to assess the most prosperous areas during their civil war (Kenyon 1988:75). Nor is there any evidence that the Republic would have been able to collect a progressive income tax, as the North did during the U.S. Civil War. The failure to raise revenue increased pressures to print money and therefore accelerated inflation.

The parochialism of collectives is why observers had such varied views of them. They may have functioned well on the local level but less so on the regional or national.[286] Many were uninterested in assisting those outside their village. The seventeen delegations that failed to attend a full meeting of the CNT peasant locals of the province of Madrid outnumbered the fifteen that were present.[287] Representatives who were in attendance "unanimously registered their disgust at the absentees" who, they charged, had demonstrated a lack of responsibility and disregard for libertarian ideals. They planned to investigate "collectives [that] have transformed themselves into businesses that practice financial manipulations, forgetting union solidarity." The district committee reminded its affiliates to return statistical inquiries. Without them, it could not run an efficient organization nor eliminate the lazy.

The absence of trust between regional and local officials made it difficult to arrange deals and trades, which would have been mutually beneficial. Towns and hamlets feared—sometimes with good reason—that union officials would rip them off.[288] The dearth of trustworthy militants created the impression among peasants in the district of Belmonte (Cuenca), which claimed nine collectives and over three thousand union members, that union representatives were just another group of predatory officials. This feeling was acute in Sisante where "some small landowners" did not want the union to use their draft animals to work confiscated lands.[289] The CNT local was told to ignore peasant desires and employ the beasts. Cuenca earned a "reactionary" reputation because its peasants refused to deliver their wheat (Fraser 1986:488).

The reluctance to report was an indication of the hiding of goods, which revealed that war had revived old-regime fears of scarcity and shortage. Hoarding also reflected the traditional agriculture of the Spanish countryside with its closed, family-based production (Casanova 1988:12). Concealing information and goods—which Republican law declared a crime under certain circumstances—was a major problem because it hindered efforts to feed other regions.[290] Smuggling merchants and traders, especially those from Catalonia, gained a reputation for exploiting Aragon peasants. Catalan merchants supposedly made enormous profits buying Aragon agricultural products at low prices and exporting them abroad.[291] The Catalans then used the foreign currency to purchase Spanish products at a discount. Similarly, smuggling of men and commodities over the border became a big business.[292] Dozens of mountain guides were eventually imprisoned for conducting several hundred "deserters and fugitives," who included draft dodgers and rightwingers, over the border.[293] The motivation of the guides was monetary, not political, but they nevertheless risked the death penalty. As early as November 1936, fears of improper profiteering motivated the Department of Agriculture of the Council of Aragon to prohibit all wheat exports without its consent.

Aragon officials also forbade the export of meat to ensure the region's own supplies (Simoni and Simoni 1984:123). Meat quickly became scarce for the front-line soldiers and the civilian population. *Labradores* (middle-class farmers) and shepherds who engaged in unauthorized trading of animals were arrested and fined.[294] Whatever its intentions, prohibition disrupted the economy of certain districts. In a sparsely inhabited area in the district of Benabarre (Huesca), inhabitants lived off the proceeds of livestock grazing, especially goats.[295] When the number of animals surpassed the capacity of the land to support them, they were sold to those outside the district. Furthermore, wise land-use policy mandated the reduction of the number of goats to preserve recently planted trees. Nevertheless, restrictions on sales were rigorously enforced. Police, or those posing as police, caught a widow and her son trying to sell nine goats. They forced them to pay immediately a two-thousand-peseta fine. When the unfortunate couple opened their safe-deposit box in the presence of the alleged "officers," the latter expropriated its entire contents, amounting to at least twenty-five hundred pesetas. In some towns bordering Catalonia, the Aragon Council's interdiction seemed to have disrupted the normal exchange of local agricultural products for Catalan manufactured goods.[296] Even front-line soldiers sometimes had difficulty acquiring food because of interference by the Aragon Council's police.[297]

Villages that bartered sometimes risked penalties. In April, Cogul (Lérida) exchanged its 2,296 kilograms of olive oil for Sena's (Huesca) 6,888 hecto-liters of wheat.[298] During the return trip to Cogul, police—claiming that the wheat lacked a proper travel authorization—confiscated it in the village of Fargo (Huesca). Months later, Cogul was still waiting for the return of the wheat that, it asserted, was desperately needed to feed dozens of refugees in the village. Another village, Alcampel (Huesca), was much luckier. It transported three church bells to Barcelona where it traded them to the Ford collective for a 1929 truck (Souchy Bauer 1982:142).

Towns hid knowledge of what they possessed for fear that Republican police or soldiers, like the militias of the early days, would confiscate it (Casanova 1985:173, 181). The fear was not unrealistic since police and soldiers sometimes did "abusively" take what they wanted.[299] A series of scandals involving transportation implicated police of the Aragon Council, one of the major institutional supports of the collectives. At gunpoint, they forced the attendant of the gas pump of the Antifascist Militia Ebro Column to fill up their tank.[300] The Column protested that gas should be used exclusively for the war effort. Three incidents of police extortion during one day convinced the militia to assign a machine gunner to prevent fuel hijacking.

Police also requisitioned the car of the physician of Arén (Huesca), a small town that, like many in rural Spain, had few private automobiles and lacked telephones and telegraphs.[301] Towns suspected the political police of acting in their own personal interest and requisitioning too much food and too many possessions from "fascist" villagers.[302] Police arrested and fined many, leaving to town councils and collectives the responsibility for feeding and clothing the families of those detained. In general, the Aragon Council won a reputation among some for corruption and favoritism (Fraser 1986:393). In contrast, Nationalist quartermasters claimed that gasoline, automobiles, and livestock were carefully measured and rationally distributed (Aragón 1940:74–76).

In Tardienta (Huesca), the CNT, UGT, and IR members of the Antifascist Committee accused a militia column, which seems to have been composed of

PSUC members, of completely trashing and looting the town.[303] Tardienta, which possessed an anarchist collective and between one and five hundred CNT members who had played a major role in defeating rebellious Civil Guards in July, had agreed to house the militiamen in peasant homes. The latter used the furniture and tools of the peasants as fuel for cooking and heating. They stole what they could easily sell, ate the livestock, and shipped dozens of wagons of wheat to Catalonia. In Ribaroja (Valencia) soldiers gratuitously destroyed a collective's trees and consumed its Mediterranean stashes of nuts, olives, fruits and vegetables.[304] Plundering may reflect soldiers' secular resentment of civilians' relatively cushy lives. In addition, Spanish *campesinos,* many of whom had been drafted into the army, had a tradition of appropriating landlords' crops during times of dearth (Rosique Navarro 1988:240). In June 1937, the Ministry of Defense lamented soldiers' looting of civilians and warned that such acts would be severely sanctioned.[305] As in other civil wars, pillaging may have been linked to inflation in the Republican zone and to the inability of the Popular Army to pay its troops at regular intervals (see Kenyon 1988:126). The Spanish Republic's incapacity to remunerate its forces resembled Royalist difficulties during the civil wars in the British Isles. Soldiers, like workers, may have felt they had earned the right to supplement low wages through pilfering. In Brihuega (Guadalajara) in the summer, a typewriter, radio, and cash from the CNT-UGT Comité de Enlace became soldiers' spoils of war.[306] They also took the peasants' tractor. As cold weather approached, they confiscated blankets and mattresses from the civilian population. The troops' behavior repulsed a high-ranking commissar who feared that a "regime of terror" against peasants would convince them to join the fascists and destroy Spanish agriculture. Looting aggravated the already acute problem of feeding the Republic.

Soldiers' belief that peasants were price-gougers tended to justify troops' depredations.[307] Peasants were more than happy to sell them whatever they wished above the price of the *tasa.*[308] In Castille, soldiers occasionally looted what others considered the nation's artistic treasures.[309] When the general staff of the VI Corps was transferred from its headquarters at the El Pardo Palace, it removed truckloads of antique furniture.[310] The Army of the Center observed that "troops unjustifiably damage the structure and furniture of the buildings that they occupy" and urged officers to prevent such destruction.[311] Anticlericals in uniform did not always appreciate the artistic value of religious buildings. If not plundered or vandalized, they were used for lodging and storage.[312]

In this context, assaults on collectives can be seen from a new angle. Historians have often interpreted the attacks by certain units of the Republican Army in political terms. Communist troops, it is said, wanted to destroy the revolution in the countryside. This may be true, but these assaults were also another episode in a secular history of peasant/military confrontations. If some soldiers were convinced Communists, others were mere looters. In June

in Aragon, they held up trucks at gunpoint and confiscated the vehicles and
their contents (Leval 1975:334–35). As the CNT Peasants' Union put it: "The
outrages against the collectives must stop. The government should take the
necessary measures so that the military quartermaster or another official
organism can reimburse the collectives and individual farmers for the products that troops of the Popular Army have requisitioned without the approval
of the military quartermaster."[313] For CNT peasants, the violation of their
property rights was as scandalous as the repression of libertarian militants.
Commissars warned soldiers on a quiet section of the Aragon front that they
would be shot if caught looting.[314]

The dissolution of the collectives coincided with that of the Aragon Council, which the government announced on 11 August. These acts reflected the
Republic's centralizing drive that aimed to reduce regional autonomy (Broué
and Témine 1970:305–15).[315] Urban interests attempted to dominate the countryside, splitting both the CNT and UGT into urban and rural factions.[316] The
"unchecked egoism" of hoarders caused high prices and scarcities in cities and
towns where abundance had normally reigned. The governor-general of Aragon,
José Ignacio Mantecón, a Leftist Republican sympathetic to Communism,
believed that the treatment of black marketers, speculators, and monopolists
had been too lenient. He wanted to subject them to the same punishments as
other enemies of the Republic. In addition, he suspected the collectives of
engaging in economically and morally shady activities and forbade them from
"trading in food." In September 1937, Mantecón ordered an all-out battle
against "speculators" and "monopolists."[317] Municipal authorities would be
responsible for controlling, inspecting, and, if necessary, confiscating the stocks
of collectives. Little wonder that black marketeering and regressions to subsistence farming proliferated. During the first two years of war in Catalonia
and Valencia, peasants must have felt discriminated against by an increase of
600 or 800 percent in prices of manufactured goods (such as textiles) and a
mere 30 or 40 percent price increase of agricultural produce (Bernecker
1982:162).

The major cause of the difficulties experienced by female or male peasants
after the Communist attempt to dissolve the collectives was not organizational
conflicts over legitimacy of property rights but rather what the peasants considered the artificially low price that the state established for their olive crop.
Communist militants debated "the discontent of the peasants concerning the
price of olives."[318] Agrarians continued to feel that the political economy of
the Republic discriminated against them by setting maximums on agricultural
but not on industrial products. Agricultural wage laborers in Aragon further
objected to low wages. Workers—including some from the UGT and probably
many females—had fought against the official wage scale and apparently had
refused to work or, at least, had slowed output until a new agreement was

reached. Communists were in an uncomfortable position since to support the government meant risking unpopularity among wage earners. They came down on the side of production, calling for "shock brigades" and "piecework to stimulate the output of the day laborers."

The pressures of the outside world compounded internal difficulties. As the war endured, collectives became more selective about their membership. Perhaps this explains, in part, the decline of the ratio of members per collective. From mid-1937 to the end of 1938, the number of collectives increased by 25 percent while the number of collectivists dropped by 50 percent (Fraser 1986:393; see Mintz 1977:148). New collectives in the summer of 1937 issued rules designed to limit the admission of unproductive members. They excluded those past the age of sixty who had not previously joined, widows without children in collectives, and minors whose parents were not adherents. All who joined were told to stay for at least a year and had to become union members. At a meeting of CNT peasant organizations of the center, a delegate from Toledo believed that support for the unproductive—that is, widows, orphans, physically impaired, and elderly—was the most divisive issue among members.[319]

The CNT Regional Federation of Peasants of the Center debated the issue of incentives versus the fixed (family) wage. The latter was viewed by many as the main guarantee against the revival of prerevolutionary inequalities (Leval 1975:192). In the fall of 1936, the CNT regional unions of Catalonia and Levant had introduced the "family wage," to be paid to the father according to the number of children (Bernecker 1982:185). In 1937 the fixed salary began to be questioned. Delegates from Guadalajara, where fourteen collectives had over six hundred members, and Villarejo asserted that "the family wage does not motivate workers."[320] The delegate from Sonseca (Toledo) disagreed because collectives in his area had "totally abolished money" (thus, in theory, preventing private accumulation) and distributed the harvest according to familial need. In response, the secretary of the Federation objected that "it was certain that peasants did not have a revolutionary spirit." Sometimes, he maintained, new members worked better than veteran militants. After considerable discussion, representatives agreed to a vague formula that maintained the family wage but applied it "with flexibility," that is with the possibility of monetary incentive. In Graus (Huesca), the collective had commenced with a family wage but by the fall of 1937 felt compelled to introduce an incentive based on production.[321]

In the province of Madrid, there was a consensus that collectivists who committed serious errors should be punished but not expelled. Nevertheless, the need for sanctions was such that certain delegates admitted that collectives in their districts were excluding disobedient members. Usually, expulsions had to be approved by a general assembly of collectivists. Many other collectives issued "producer's identity cards" that detailed the individual's work record.

Observers have often interpreted the common program of the CNT-UGT of 18
March 1938 as a sellout by libertarians who agreed with counterrevolutionary
Communists and Socialists to end the family wage (cf. Bernecker 1982:137).
However, pressures from the base were often responsible for ending the fam-
ily salary and tying pay to productivity.

The collectives in the province of Ciudad Real (renamed Ciudad Libre)
encountered major obstacles. In a number of its districts and towns, the UGT—
which CNT members claimed was composed of "bourgeois exploiters"—opposed
any CNT collective or union.[322] The conflict between hostile municipal authorities and CNT locals and collectives existed throughout La Mancha, even
though in some towns, such as Las Labores, Tomelloso, and Argamasilla de
Alba, the UGT and CNT cooperated and formed harmonious collectives.[323]
Other collectives experienced internal difficulties arising from "a current of
particularistic egotism of the comrades."[324] Many members, who were either
wage laborers or small property owners before the revolution, were not interested in or knowledgeable about libertarian or socialist ideals. On both collective and private lands, regional CNT officials reported that "agricultural
production is declining and livestock is being rapidly consumed."[325] In the
area east of Valdepeñas (Ciudad Real), "in the middle of the harvest, the union
locals that controlled all the wealth of these towns did not do their job, and
local union leaders had to be forced to work." Men and machinery were unpre-
pared or inadequate. One farm, which had been electrified and mechanized,
was abandoned even though—with proper treatment—it could have become
the breadbasket of the province. The productivity of laborers and harvesters
had fallen well below the level it had reached during "the bosses' era. . . .
Almost all workers don't care about anything but getting their daily wage.
They treat the controlled economy as though it were privately held." To
increase output, incentives and piecework were recommended. CNT regional
authorities also suggested assigning to each union and collective a militant
chosen by higher ups to restrain the "egotism . . . of some comrades" that
was destroying the economy.

In the Valdepeñas region, a transportation shortage obstructed the wine harvest of the fall of 1937.[326] The acquisitive drivers of the Federación Regional
del Transporte took advantage of this situation by demanding—and receiving—
salary supplements. The shortage of trucks led to the rotting or abandonment
of food shipments destined for troops defending Madrid.[327] The insufficiency
of the trucking fleet made it difficult to collect milk for dairy production. Peasant proprietors tried to solve the transportation deficit by using horse-drawn
vehicles, and unions and collectives were instructed to attempt similar ad hoc
solutions.

To avoid "egoisms," union organizations wanted to fix higher commodity
prices. Producers argued for a new wine rate well above the *tasa* and asserted

that they had to sell other crops below production cost. The price of grapes did indeed double from 1936 to 1937 (Ministerio de Agricultura 1936). In Sueca (Valencia), which claimed to produce one-sixth of Spanish rice, UGT growers protested a decree-law of 27 August 1937 that seemed to fix what they considered to be an overly modest price for rice.[328] Unionists also wanted to centralize sales and reduce the role of intermediaries and private merchants, but they were unable to do so since they lacked the capacity to market to consumers.

The problem of organized selfishness on the local level was also evident in the Valencian region. This area was essential for the Republican future since it produced the most valuable exports (Bosch Sánchez 1983:104–5). Sixty percent of its agricultural produce was sold abroad. With the exception of the gold deposit, exporting oranges remained the principal means for the Republic to obtain indispensable foreign currencies. During the winter of 1936–37, despite opposition from Communists and small property owners, the CLUEA (Consejo Levantino Unificado de la Exportación Agrícola), which the CNT and UGT dominated, took control of citrus exports. The CLUEA was supposed to coordinate the local committees or CLUEF (Consejos Locales Unificados de Exportación de Frutos), but the autonomy of many of the latter hindered the execution of a coherent policy (Abad 1984:332–38). The CLUEA's guidelines were ignored not only by its own local committees (CLUEF) but also by unions, cooperatives, and peasant organizations. The situation was "anarchical."[329] It was estimated that at least 20 percent of CLUEFs functioned badly. Riots protesting the local CLUEA broke out in Carcagente in January 1937 and Cullera in February (Bosch Sánchez 1983:122). In these two towns, small property owners had been forced into joining collectives that, it seems, the CNT largely dominated. In at least five towns in the spring of 1937, CNT militants were attacked.[330] A few local committees sent their own representatives to negotiate abroad, thereby undercutting the official CLUEA prices. They too were suspected of corruption (Abad 1984:344). Some officials did indeed become venal and embezzled proceeds destined for others. Workers reacted by attempting to kill them. Farmers without a strong union or political influence had their land confiscated, were refused jobs, and were left unpaid for their produce. The delays in payments for exported citrus threatened to provoke more riots.[331] In many cases, the union-controlled CLUEFs' first priority was to remunerate workers, not owners. Farmers considered the CLUEFs thieves and became reluctant to produce for the market.

Workers' main concern was to be paid on time, but even when paid regularly, they sometimes labored with "disinterest." In Oliva in April 1937, UGT laborers were assigned to the harvest but "they did not show up since they were offered another job at a slightly higher wage. Lately in the port of Gandía tens of thousands of kilos of oranges were lost since shippers refused to load the merchandise because they were owed money."[332] Some wage earners threatened to strike if payday was late. The situation was even worse for females, who received 30 to 50 percent less pay than males and who, in some cases, had difficulty getting maternity insurance.

Where CLUEFs functioned well, bourgeois elements—former exporters and technicians—were often in control. Given the problems of union management, the state took charge of exports in September 1937 (Bosch Sánchez 1983:144). To carry out their policies against libertarian opposition, national and regional government officials often employed Communists and Socialists. For instance, in Alborache—where 342 persons (27 percent of the population) reportedly belonged to the CNT collective—the governor promoted those that the CNT considered rightist municipal officials whom the PCE, PSOE, and the UGT had protected.[333] During the rice harvest in early September 1937, the town council of Cullera, following orders of the national government, requisitioned all trucks, including the two from the CNT collective.[334] The collective protested that without its vehicles it would be unable to bring in the harvest. Other collectives in the province—in Sollana, for example, which held over a quarter of the residents, or 940 people—objected to similar requisitions.[335] Yet the number of collectives in Valencia continued to grow throughout 1937, even though they exhibited a lack of solidarity and remained isolated from each other.

Labor shortages further hindered production. The civil war created what may have been the first significant scarcity of workers in the history of modern Spanish agriculture. By the fall of 1937, the labor deficit was becoming more serious. Many men had been conscripted into the army; others were attracted to urban areas because of higher salaries and greater opportunities in certain trades, such as chauffeuring, which provided ample occasions to engage in potentially profitable petty entrepreneurialship.[336] According to male trade unionists, women of the Infantes district (Ciudad Real) "held such deep prejudices" against wage labor that an active campaign by female militants was necessary to get them into unions and working the fields.[337] Collectives established severe controls to ensure that females performed fieldwork (Leval 1975:115). One reason for this resistance to work was that, as winter approached, both female and male peasants lacked clothing and shoes. One solution was to use (threshing) machinery, but it had to be imported. Necessary foreign currency was scarce, and local authorities in the Council of Aragon fought over priorities with the national government. The latter did not regard machinery as sufficiently urgent and vetoed its purchase.

By early 1938 the female presence was dominant in many villages. Unions maintained discrimination against women by paying them less and even, in the village of Berbegal (Huesca), expelling single females from the collective.[338] A CNT official protested the attempt to eliminate long-standing female members. Yet the most lucid union leaders realized that female cooperation was absolutely essential in a period of labor shortage. They supported professional training programs and opportunities for women, although new jobs should be "biologically" suitable and not contribute to the "degeneration of the race."[339] Despite their sexism, collectives sometimes found women were their strongest defenders. In Peñalba (Huesca), they protested when local authorities confiscated the collective's milk.[340] Young women might also prefer the relative freedom from religious domination, especially with regard to sexuality and coeducation, that collectivization brought to certain villages (Thomas 1971:252). Parents appreciated the emphasis on childhood education and literacy training in many collectives (Prats 1938:93).

The Lérida farming collective, the only one in this town of thirty-five to forty thousand, is one of the few agrarian collectives for which we have fairly complete documentation.[341] The lack of information has been attributed to rural illiteracy, but it may also be due to a desire not to wash dirty laundry in public (Bosch Sánchez 1983:191–92). In the fall of 1936, the CNT was the moving force behind the formation of the Colectividad Campesina "Adelante" of Lérida.[342] Apparently, in Lérida, CNT followers usually held less property than UGT adherents, who were relatively uninterested in joining collectives.[343] The collective was created on land that had been confiscated from or abandoned by "fascists," who had suffered disproportionately in Lérida during the early months of the revolution (Casanova 1999:128). Until the end of 1936, the collective seemed to have operated without great friction. By the spring of 1937, it comprised one hundred families, four hundred members, three hundred hectares planted with corn and grain, and had access to tractors, trucks, and other machinery (Bernecker 1982:111; Peirats 1971:1:277). Members initially performed their jobs satisfactorily, but soon problems appeared. For example, before Christmas of 1936, a woman—who had to tend the feeding and clothing of ten to twelve comrades—complained about overwork. Conflicts over labor led the collective to pass more rules: any comrade who was absent during working hours would be expelled on the third violation. The reluctance to sacrifice made the imposition of local foremen a necessity, and the leadership was awarded authority to discipline those who did not do their duty.

The most important difficulty concerned how much collectivists should work. Some argued for infinite sacrifice; others wanted to define precise working hours. When the latter were established in January 1937, "those who did not show any real interest and came late or left early" ignored them. The problem of tardiness persisted throughout the year. In fact, in Foucauldian fashion, lateness stimulated new control and accounting procedures. A comrade was given the task of recording all comings and goings of personnel. One member noted "we need statistics for those who do not know what work is and do not want to work." The assembly assigned one person "who could more or less read or write" in every farm (*finca*) to catalogue its possessions and register daily entrances and exits of its wage earners. By June 1937, the cooperative store was tightly monitored.

Some members violated rules on revenue reporting by failing to declare the income of wages of their children who worked outside the collective. They wanted the cash that wage labor provided but, at the same time, did not wish to lose the benefits of collective membership. When discovered, their furtiveness resulted in their expulsion. Other collectives enforced strict regulations concerning the reporting of outside income and demanded that members turn over all wages in excess of the standard collective salary (Souchy and Folgare 1977:151). In August 1937 several members who worked undeclared second jobs were excluded. A few collectivists appropriated collective food for noncollectivist family members.

By April 1937, tensions, which reflected the growth of the refugee population, had developed between old and new members.[344] The original members—who felt that they possessed the true collectivist spirit, that is, "everything is for everyone without any class distinctions"—believed that newer members "did not understand what a collective is." They complained that the laborers referred by the Placement Office of Lérida were "not conscientious in their work for the collective." The collective, it was said in June, "should not become a sanctuary." By July, it had "too many people." From their perspective, newer members—who were refugees—deemed that they were victims of discrimination. When they organized their own clandestine meeting in the summer of 1937, the leadership reacted aggressively. The general assembly removed refugees' right to speak, to vote, and permitted their expulsion. Tensions continued into the fall of 1937 when several members circulated a petition, which they sent to the *Generalitat,* that accused the leadership of stealing and corruption, a frequent complaint of members of other collectives (see Fraser 1986:368–69). The leadership credibly refuted the charges and won firm support from the CNT's local federation. Management was helped by the family history of one of its detractors: his wife and daughter had been caught at the border trying to flee with "thousands of pesetas." The petition's defenders were excluded from the collective.

The divide between "those who work a lot and others who hardly do anything" became the major impediment in this and other collectives.[345] Collectives made the obligation to labor universal, but in Lérida certain farms were notorious for doing little. Throughout 1937, workers left early and abandoned their tools by the roadside. Propositions for elimination of the work shy proliferated: "They all should be expelled for not doing their work. They don't have the right to do what they want." Those who claimed that they were sick were told to get medical proof of it. At the end of May, the General Assembly decided to award itself the right to discharge "comrades who don't do their work" and "those who are intoxicated." One of the latter was excluded in August 1937. The assembly also banned workers who made false accusations and had to expel a violator on least one occasion.

By May, the problem of political purity arose. The collective was CNT-AIT, but it was hard to find officers who had belonged to the Confederation throughout their adult lives. To elect officials, one member recommended that "we look forward not backward because if we look towards the past, we shall find only four comrades who have been loyal to the CNT." The relationship between workers and those who were in charge of output and quality was hostile. The former continually insulted the latter, calling them "bourgeois" or "dictators."[346] Some workers threatened managers, and others complained that the delegates in charge made them work as hard as the bourgeois had.[347] Managers' and delegates' own irresponsible acts undermined their authority. Some abandoned their jobs for the attractions of town. Another hid gasoline and motor oil in his home, justifying himself by claiming that obtaining the proper documentation was too difficult. The growing state bureaucracy and "its innumerable laws" were common complaints of peasants—whether collectivist, individualist, CNT, or UGT.[348] The assembly was obliged to pass measures mandating inspection of the work of delegates and managers. The most important and divisive issues facing the collective involved individuals' willingness to contribute to the community.

A veteran militant, who was one of the most active and respected of the collectivists, proposed that "we expel the gypsies. They are very young and have alot of children."[349] Gypsies, of course, never adopted the productivist lifestyle propagated by activists of various modern "isms." As Orwell (1980:6) noted, they continued to beg on the streets of Barcelona during the apex of the revolution. The family wage scale made large families financially burdensome for the collective. Struggle erupted between big families who took advantage of the collective's social and medical services and those with fewer or no offspring. A similar problem concerned the exertions of the elderly and their contribution to the community. The assembly approved a complex wage scale that aimed to base pay on the needs of various age groups and genders.

Still, gender strife persisted. Women were almost always paid less and sometimes treated as second-class members. In many collectives, they could not vote (Bosch Sánchez 1983:356). Females were hardly ever elected as officials of collectives (Nash 1995:133). On one of Lérida's farms, they struck to protest the order to sleep on straw. However, it should be mentioned that mattresses were scarce in a number of collectives, and in certain cases, a woman had to be pregnant to obtain one.[350] A female comrade refused wage labor that paid fewer than eight pesetas per day. Gender conflict heightened the struggle between female individuals and social demands. The sexist male leaders of the collective concluded that "the problem of women is similar in all the collectives. It is a result of egotism and lack of spirit of sacrifice. Unfortunately, there are few that are conscientious collectivists. Female comrades must do certain jobs, such as cleaning and washing." A woman who refused to work in the dairy was threatened with expulsion. Females were warned that if they did not attend an assembly (to be held on a Sunday in August 1937), they would be penalized.

Gender discrimination was tied to an often unspoken but pervasive bias against all those—women, elderly, and gypsies—who were not considered full-fledged producers. Historians have often attributed the difficulties of collectives to outside forces, that is, the pressures of the war and the attacks of the Confederation's political enemies (see Bernecker 1982:130). Certainly, without the support of an efficient and unified government, it is difficult to see how collectives could have prospered. However, selfishness and internal divisions among the workers themselves compounded political tensions and economic deficiencies.

As in other regions, in Valencia agricultural collectives—a reduced sector comprising only 4 percent of usable land (*superficie util*)—exhibited "total autonomy" and ignored both state and union directives (Bosch Sánchez 1988:34–45). Solidarity—whether anarchist or socialist—was often nonexistent. The CNT collective of Oliva (Valencia) sold potatoes at .75 pesetas per kilo, considerably above the *tasa* price of .55.[351] Authorities confiscated and sold its supply. Few people—whether collectivists or ordinary union members—paid union dues. Members of the CNT Oliva collective, where the unauthorized extraction of melons or farm animals was common, had to be reminded not always to take from the collective but to give back in return.[352] In fact, the UGT-affiliated Spanish Union of Commerce Workers noted that it was necessary to "clean up" union membership lists and expel those who joined "in first moments (of July) when there was an avalanche of demands to sign up."[353] These new members wanted only a union card and never paid dues.

In the spring of 1937 police and *guardias* attempted to reassert state power and attacked CNT militants and important collectives in various villages—Carcagente, Benaguacil, Lullera, Catarroja, and Utiel (Bosch Sánchez 1983:134–35). Sporadic assaults on libertarians and their organizations occurred throughout the summer. In June in Burriana (Castellón), Socialists and the UGT fought against the CNT. Former bakery bosses who had been forced into collectives in 1936 rebelled and demonstrated in the streets.[354] CNT collectivists of Fuenterrobles (Valencia) and Almazora (Castellón)—the latter collective enrolling about 10 percent of the town—reported that local authorities harassed and persecuted them.[355] In Horta de Terra Alta (Tarragona), the CNT collective was accused of cutting down trees without authorization.[356] *Rabassaires* and UGT militants charged that the collective was confiscating rents and evicting tenants.[357] Even though the number of CNT and UGT collectives grew during 1937, problems of "lack of solidarity" and isolation persisted. A considerable gap remained between rich and poor collectives. CNT militants complained that many collectives were "egotistical" businesses in disguise (Bosch Sánchez 1988:45). In Alicante, the Institute of Agrarian Reform—with the approval of the UGT and CNT—stipulated that all who joined the collectives must be "enthusiastic."[358]

In Cuevas de Vinroma (Castellón), the municipal council had to deal with the difficult problem of refugees, tens of thousands of whom had flooded the province.[359] As in other areas of the Republican zone, the poor sanitation and health of the refugee population raised the specter of epidemics, such as typhoid and typhus. The latter had been the scourge of camp and barracks life since the old regime and had affected nearly one third of the Red Army during the Russian civil war (Best 1986:33; Figes 1996:598). A severe outbreak of typhus was reported in a field hospital near the Ebro front in 1938 (Nash 1995:151).[360] Cuevas de Vinroma, although prosperous, had to struggle with the issue of how much aid it should offer to potentially contagious nonnatives. Officials claimed that some of the supposedly sick who had been evacuated from other regions were taking unfair advantage of the meat ration provided by the municipality. In late 1937, when supplies of grain became more difficult to acquire, the problem of feeding outsiders deepened. Although the council awarded itself power to requisition all wheat, it was nevertheless obliged to form a commission to seek and purchase the commodity throughout loyalist Spain. Its mission met with only limited success in part because of hoarding and the general decline of wheat and cereal production. In October the bread ration was reduced and its cost increased. In November a six-month minimum residence requirement was imposed to obtain a ration card. Bread rations would first be distributed to natives of Cuevas de Vinroma, then to outsiders. The reduction coincided with a widespread bread shortage and its consequent high price throughout the Republican zone. The village argued that it did not have the resources to feed and clothe refugees, and it established a tax earmarked for refugee needs. It was levied on nonnative merchants who subsequently attempted to evade it. The town's greatest source of revenue remained a 4 percent levy on the sale of all food and energy. Although local supply-siders criticized the tax by asserting that it would discourage production for the market, the Cuevas council retained it since it was easy to collect and hard to dodge. In this case the supply-siders may have been correct since at the end of 1937 revenues from the 4 percent tax declined substantially. Natives of other provinces, such as Jaén, also resisted taxing themselves to feed refugees (Cobo Romero 1993:464).

Shortages encouraged defeatist attitudes. Army commissars planned to overcome them by organizing shock brigades dedicated to counterespionage. They would be composed of the most "conscious" comrades whose mission would be to categorize "fascists," "opportunists," and the "indifferent." Their task was to suppress gossip that subversively criticized the official line. The goal was to "eliminate" the authors of rumors of an armistice or a compromise. This subversive talk circulated by word of mouth and in letters from the rear. Shock brigadiers were to make sure that only Republican and antifascist ideologies were disseminated. A special propaganda effort was planned to convince skeptical peasant recruits.[361]

On this issue, Communists were joined by the rest of Popular Front, which included all the parties and unions of the Left, not excluding the FAI. The entire spectrum called for Stakhanovites to sow and harvest in the countryside.[362] Despite controlled wages, rural workers tried to use the labor scarcity in the countryside to push their own agenda. The peasants and workers in Mas de las Matas (pop. 2,300, Teruel) and more generally in the district of Valderrobres, where anarchists were the principle political force and often enrolled majorities in CNT collectives, were not reticent about making bread-and-butter demands a top priority. They felt they were not being adequately compensated for their labor and seemed to be reluctant to work the fields.[363] The Valderrobres district had many small farmers and a valuable olive crop. But given state power to set wages and prices, agricultural wage laborers, many of whom were women, had difficulty taking advantage of the labor shortage.

To stimulate peasant production, the CNT Regional Federation of Peasants requested that prices for agricultural goods be raised.[364] Without increases, it implied, the *campesinos* would not produce. The decreasing purchasing power of the peasantry, at least of those peasants who were not black-market entrepreneurs, would persist in Aragon throughout 1937.[365] For example, by the end of the year, a pair of sandals, which had cost the equivalent of one kilo of oil, was worth four.[366] Everyone, whether collectivists or individual owners, worried that the government would confiscate their olive oil, which they could profitably use for barter, and compensate them with devalued scrip.[367] Union members asked that the government pay for the collectives' oil (a commodity valuable not only as food but also as lighting fuel) not with paper money but rather in kind.

In fact, anarchosyndicalists suspected that the main objective of rebels' military operations in Andalusia was to conquer the olive oil harvest (Souchy and Folgare 1977:118–19). In early 1937 the Republic still possessed more than half of the Spanish olive oil crop and could, in theory, supply its entire population and even export, if transportation and containers had been available in sufficient quantities (Ministerio de Agricultura 1936). Both sides knew that "to take oil is to stockpile gold." To discourage peasants from selling until Nationalists conquered the area, insurgent radio constantly promised a much higher price for oil than the Republicans offered. Many peasants took the bait and refused to sell when under Republican control. The desire for real goods and the corresponding economy of barter were not limited to Andalusia and Aragon but occurred throughout the war in towns and villages of Alicante (Santacreu Soler 1986:68). Soldiers with access to commodities speculated with them and with Republican currency.[368] The devaluation of "red money" put pensioners, including those who had lost a husband or father in the conflict, in a precarious position.

The *tasas* of the Republic favored the urban masses, which had defended it when the military rebelled and remained its firmest basis of support.[369] In contrast, the more flexible price controls of the Nationalists, which allowed farmers larger profits by assuring them that the state would purchase their wheat crop at a reasonable price, reflected their peasant base, especially in Castile (cf. Richards 1998:134). Moreover, industrial goods in the Republican zone were largely unregulated and sharply increased in price. However, the loyalty of many urban workers declined as government controls were unable to prevent the de facto rise of food costs. The president of the Republic reported that in Valencia and Catalonia the promulgation of price controls resulted in the complete disappearance of food from the marketplace (Azaña cited in Martínez Bande 1973:28–9; Azaña 1990:3:520). Azaña was disappointed that the populace refused to denounce speculators and hoarders. Instead, "it was every person for himself." Urban residents engaged in a bidding war with their neighbors for edibles. In this context, workers ignored official calls to delay demands and continued to seek higher wages.[370]

In Barcelona, the workforce of Hispano-Suiza, one of the few and most important of Spanish automobile companies, demonstrated its alienation. Forty wage earners refused orders from both the CNT and UGT to work on Saturday afternoons.[371] They were sanctioned by pay deductions. Several months later, a disgruntled Hispano-Suiza worker complained of the "technical and administrative incompetence of comrades who make up the factory council (Consejo de Empresa)."[372] "The uncoordinated and ridiculously diminutive production of a factory with 2,000 workers" led to the militarization of the plant in September and the sharp reduction of the powers of the factory council and the union committee. Three months of militarization (September to November), however, failed to bring the desired increase of productivity. Although the factory had been supplied with all necessary raw materials, it had produced no aviation motors, cars, or trucks since the outbreak of civil war. Nor could any finished goods be expected until February 1938. Managers' (*cuadros*) incompetence, it was asserted, lowered the morale of workers and employees. Problems of indiscipline also persisted in Madrid.[373] A worker from the Cooperative of Wholesale Fish Workers who showed up inebriated was suspended without pay for one month. Other absentees or those who trafficked in fish were expelled, suspended, or subjected to heavy fines. A go-getter who held two jobs was ordered to choose one or be dismissed. The inability to prevent indiscipline led to the resignation of the coop's vice president.

Republican war industries' persistent inability to supply the fronts increased an already dangerous reliance on imports. In early November, following the failed Zaragoza offensive, military and civilian leaders of the Republic—who included General Vicente Rojo, Foreign Minister Julio Alvarez del Vayo, Air Force chief Ignacio Hidalgo de Cisneros, and others—were aware of the inadequacy of food supplies and unaffordable prices, but they did little to redress the situation (document cited by Martínez Bande 1973:278–88). The army needed at least a thousand more trucks, which could have been supplied by requisitioning vehicles from other branches of the military and the unions. The shortage limited its ability to conduct operations. The officials' proposed solution was the "declaration of a state of war" that would allow military and civilian authorities to centralize control and increase police power.

In the north, the frivolous attitude that had been a factor in the collapse of Bilbao was not corrected in Santander.[374] While battles raged in Aragon in August, Santander was contested. In that province, desertions had begun to increase in May.[375] By June, soldiers from the "difficult-to-police" Valley of Pas (Cantabria) abandoned their weapons and drifted back to their homes.[376] Divisions among the Loyalists continued to hamper military effectiveness. Early in the war in July and August 1936, Largo Caballero wrote of the situation: "I had to deal with four independent and autonomous fronts. The Catalan one which the Generalitat and CNT ran; the Teruel front of the Valencian [CNT] confederation; the North of the Basque government and the Center of the central government. Each one had its own general staff and promoted its own officers. Catalans and Basques sent their own missions abroad to buy arms, which the central government later paid for. . . . Such independence and autonomy were a great obstacle for the conduct of the war" (quoted in Viñas 1979:105).

Coordination did not improve as the conflict endured. The Basque and Asturian governments resisted the centralization that the national government attempted to impose on them. They conceived their interests narrowly and were sometimes reluctant to help other Republicans.[377] They failed to coordinate their efforts when they sent delegations—which local branches of the Bank of Spain supplied with gold—to purchase supplies and equipment abroad.[378] Neither members of these delegations nor, at the beginning of the conflict, representatives of the central government had the skills to bargain in the tricky world of international arms sales, which was peopled by notoriously shady characters. Separate and competing regional trade delegations did not possess the knowledge or experience to distinguish honest businessmen from con men, obtain export licenses, hire a ship and a reliable crew, and avoid unwanted anti-Republican publicity, which might kill the deal. Unscrupulous Republican agents abroad found ways to line their own pockets (Viñas 1984:269). Aguirre, president of Euzkadi, protested against the "immorality" that characterized arms purchases (quoted in Martínez Bande 1980:258).

The victories in the north tipped the scales and reinforced the Nationalist advantage in resources. In July 1937 the insurgents controlled approximately 60 percent of Spanish territory (555,719 sq. km.) and population (14,615,927 inhabitants) (Carro 1938:2). Franco's army held areas that produced 65 percent of Spanish wheat, 50 percent of oil, 68 percent of potatoes, 75 percent of cows, 70 percent of sheep, 67 percent of goats, 70 percent of pigs, and 67 percent of fish. In the summer of 1937 rice production was the only major food product where Republicans retained an advantage.

The campaign for Santander began on 14 August. Republicans controlled the heights of the Cantabrian range, but Nationalists possessed the advantage in weaponry, especially in artillery and aviation. Quickly, on 16 August, the Nationalists captured the armaments factory at Reinosa where desertions had been "very numerous" in July (Salas Larrazábal and Salas Larrazábal 1986:257). Next, the Italian and Spanish Black Arrows broke through the front by the sea. With Italian help, Nationalists were able to gather forces that were far superior to those used in their Basque campaign.[379] On 26 August the Nationalist Army of the North walked into Santander and captured Castile's only port (Thomas 1961:468; Jackson 1965:389). Resistance collapsed quickly, and thousands of men fled, discarding all kinds of weapons and materials. The loss of Santander constituted another major defeat for the Republic.

Since early August its population had been facing starvation.[380] The Nationalist blockade was partially responsible for this situation. So was Republican corruption. The livestock department (Dirección General de Ganadería) in Santander suffered from "administrative immorality."[381] "Dirty deals" were consummated, and bills worth nearly four thousand pesetas were left unpaid. Communists expelled a member who had been in control of the department because he had used its resources to help himself and his friends flee to safety to France or to Valencia. Other PCE members were excluded for similar reasons. In May and June, the insufficient daily diet of 200 grams of rice, 150 grams of bread, and 100 grams of canned goods left many without the energy to go to work. The civilian population had gone meatless since the beginning of the year. Queues became longer and those who arrived late could not be sure if anything would remain in the shops. Since nearly all homes had family members who received soldiers' pay, money was not scarce, but little was available for purchase. The "desperation" that had led authorities to reduce rations for military and war-industry personnel had stimulated protests by workers of various factories. Residents of the province, whose numbers were inflated by the nearly two hundred thousand (mostly

Basque) refugees, could no longer tolerate the unending sacrifices. As Azaña (1990:3:519) pointed out, when the "masses" lost all hope of victory, they also shed any desire to sacrifice.

Nationalists inherited a starving population to which they administered thirty-eight thousand meals.[382] The insurgents had deep contempt for their enemies. The "reds" in their "cowardly flight" had abandoned "an alarming number of women, children, and the elderly." On 23 August the majority of the Basque forces had withdrawn to the small port of Santona, thirty kilometers to the east. Thousands of those trapped in Santander itself tried to escape by boat to France or Asturias. High-ranking officers and others ignored orders to retire to Asturias to carry on the struggle and, instead, went to Bordeaux or Bayonne and then on to Valencia. They were welcomed in the last city not as deserters who deserved punishment but as heroes who merited cushy jobs in the bureaucracy.[383] The Popular Army was no longer able to replace the eighty-six battalions that were lost, in large part because of desertion, with new recruits.[384] The defection of the Basques was especially discouraging for CNT militants in Aragon and Barcelona.[385]

Recriminations against Basque combativeness and willingness to sacrifice were particularly divisive. Many concluded that outside of Euzkadi, most Basques had little desire to fight for the Republic. The Basques deeply resented the popular perception that they were unwilling soldiers of the Republic.[386] In June 1937, the formation of a special Basque Brigade (numbered the 142nd) did not end doubts about Basque military performance.[387] The unit had been established with the approval of the Minister of Justice—the Basque politician, Manuel de Irujo—to enroll his compatriots in the Popular Army. By December, desertions had more than decimated it. For example, "collective panic" had seized it after its second battalion had lost ten men to an enemy aviation attack. Although many "brave fighters" had joined, some had bribed their way into what they believed to be a cushy unit. The brigade's quartermaster service was made up of these *enchufistas,* and its health section was nonexistent. Transport was in "total confusion," and its artillery did not even possess a cannon. The disappearance of the paymaster and the lack of remuneration angered nondeserters. Basque nationalists objected that the takeover of the unit by Communist officers at the beginning of 1938 would further discourage Basque combatants.

It should be noted that the Fascist Black Arrows also suffered from desertion. Eight recent Spanish draftees, all sailors from La Coruña, who were thought to be CNT members, abandoned the Nationalist camp.[388] However, their commander believed that the deserters' politics was less important than their geographical origin. The *gallegos* went to the rear to see their families, not to the front to fight for the "reds." Their flight recalled the emigration and self-mutilation men had used to avoid conscription by the Restoration state

(Carr 1980:69).[389] To avoid more unauthorized departures the commander of the Black Arrows recommended that the 525 conscripts be transferred from the north to another region, such as Estremadura, which would be far from their hometowns. The First Division of the VI Corps also experienced the Gallegans' subversion when twenty-seven nominal "Falangists" from La Coruña deserted ranks.[390]

Certain groups of soldiers were doubly tempted to desert. A *gallego* who was gay must have found the army extremely inhospitable.[391] His companions amused themselves by mimicking stereotypical voices and gestures of homosexuals. Mocking gays was then—as it is now—an intrinsic part of Spanish popular humor. Orwell (1980:19) recalled that soldiers of the POUM ragged the enemy facing them by shouting "Fascists-Faggots" (Fascistas-maricones)." Gay bashing could take a nastier form. The murder of the Andalusian poet, Federico García Lorca, may be attributed not only to the poet's total identification with the leftist Republic but also to violent homophobia (Gibson 1973:10). Mediterranean culture especially detested the gay who adopted the passive, "female" role (see Brandes 1980:96). After all, *machismo* is a Spanish word and *maricón* a favorite term of abuse. Spaniards, especially Andalusians, want to prove publicly their manliness (Gilmore 1990:32). Homosexual baiting was an accepted form of doing so.

The final chapter of combat in the north took place in Asturias (Thomas 1961:480). The outbreak of civil war had led to a revolution that, according to one observer, had profoundly disrupted the Asturian economy.[392] "[It] ruined agriculture and decimated livestock. Small industry and commerce disappeared. . . . Heavy industry [iron and coal] could survive because of war needs, but produced very expensively." Communists had become increasingly influential in the Asturian regional government, which earned a reputation for meddling in military as well as civilian matters. Its Commerce and Provisioning Departments impounded substantial cargoes but were unable to distribute them to troops. The local police were accused of arresting attractive girls, accusing them of complicity with fascism, and raping them in prison.

The Nationalist campaign in Asturias began on 1 September but progress was slow. The terrain and certain Asturian units were tough and bravely battled a clearly superior enemy. The heroism of Asturian troops surpassed the Basques or Santanderians and became a model for commissars on other fronts.[393] Bravery, though, could not compensate for the failure of the distribution system in the north. The lack of communication with the center reinforced the Nationalist advantage in supplies and weapons. Franco's Navarrese units were particularly well equipped with tanks. Early in the struggle it was clear that many Asturians, including the famous miners, were more interested in protecting themselves than the Republic. After all, the region fell to the insurgents in seven weeks: "The miners were a disappointment. At the beginning they took up arms and fought. When they saw that the war did not end and demanded discipline, they returned to the mines claiming that they were irreplaceable workers. They did not leave the mines until August when they began to build fortifications. If they and other shirkers had been mobilized and provided with arms, 20,000 additional men would have been available."[394]

Of the six hundred trials studied in Gijón between November 1936 and October 1937, 58.5 percent concerned desertion and another 9.5 percent self-mutilation to avoid military service (Almendral Parra, Flores Velasco, and Valle Sánchez 1990:189–90). In the nearby towns of Avilés, Mieres, and Trubia, the percentages were similar. Most of the remaining cases also involved subversive individualism—abandoning one's post (5.5 percent), insulting or threatening superiors (4.3 percent), and theft (3.6 percent). All of these offenses violated the codes of the great collective bodies of army and nation. Their transgressions were not especially political since the overwhelming majority of the accused in Gijón were not active members of any parties or unions. In nearby towns, many deserters were affiliated with Popular Front organizations, but their desertions merely showed their tenuous commitment to their organization's ideals. Crimes (*delitos*) classified as "actions against the means and the ends of the [Popular] Army" amounted to 75.6 percent, 10.8 percent "against the security of the Army," 9 percent "against military discipline," and 3.6 percent "against the security of the Fatherland." It should not be assumed that subversives were fascist or *franquista* since more than 80 percent of desertions were not considered treasonous. In other words, more than four-fifths of Gijón deserters did not go over to the enemy. The great majority left the military for personal reasons—to see their family, to recover from illness, to get a change of clothes, and to eat a decent meal. It has often been emphasized that the civil war was a period of mass mobilization when national politics dominated the lives of Spaniards. Yet in many cases family solidarity continued to prevail over other group loyalties.

The material reasons for desertion indicate that the Republican army in the north was often unable to adequately feed or clothe its troops, let alone provide them with weapons. In contrast, the Nationalists claimed that the daily meat ration for its soldiers during the northern campaign was 300 grams per day, instead of the normal ration of 250 grams (Aragón 1940:158). The chief of staff, Vicente Rojo, pointed out that Republican industry "was not able to finish a single kind of rifle or machine gun or cannon" (quoted in Payne 1970:344). Given substantial material reasons to desert, Republican courts were reluctant to punish offenders severely. Nationalist deserters shared with their Republican counterparts the desire to be with their families.[395] Around Jaca, the handful of Nationalist deserters fled either to join loved ones or, more rarely, to enlist in elite or shock units.[396] Peasants on both sides wanted to work their land, and desertions may have increased during harvest time.

Although many analysts have blamed the demoralization of the rank and file on the untrustworthiness of the Republican officer corps, a study of court records shows that officers in the north seldom fled (Almendral Parra, Flores Velasco, and Valle Sánchez 1990:191). One captain, 7 lieutenants, 4 sergeants, 9 corporals deserted compared to 440 low-ranking soldiers. Fifty-three others were unclassified, but most were probably from modest ranks. Deserters' professions were peasants (27.5 percent), miners (11 percent), day laborers (11 percent), and carpenters (3 percent). The rest (47.5 percent) had held a variety of jobs. The number of working-class deserters appears to have exceeded the number of peasants, who evidently had no monopoly on subversive individualism. In April in Somiedo, the movement of *evadidos* was "constant" (Salas Larrazábal 1973:1520n. 38). In Balmori only three or four out of twenty-two recruits reported. Following the loss of Bilbao (19 June), desertions in Gijón skyrocketed. In other Asturian towns, flight and self-mutilation increased substantially.

Mutiny and desertion often began not at the front but in the rear (Holmes 1985:329). In August and September, many recruits were not interested in fighting or even reporting to their units (Salas Larrazábal 1973:1476). Instead, they fled to the mountains. According to the head of Republican forces in Asturias—Adolfo Prada—poor morale in the rear, desertions, and flight were the principal causes of the defeat (1484). A Socialist who went on an inspection tour of eastern Asturian towns reported instances of petty corruption among the remaining male residents and "enormous ignorance" among women who demographically dominated certain towns.[397] The party planned to assign female militants to "educate" them. Few in the region, including most Socialist activists, knew anything about Marxism. Communists were equally opportunistic, and several of their officials were expelled from the party because they had used connections to get "disability certificates," which enabled them to flee besieged Asturias.[398] Some of the most outrageous cases of disobedience went unpunished.[399] The following were not brought to justice: A commissar who tried to shoot his superior and missed but wounded one of his colleagues; officers of the Isaac Puente Battalion who abandoned the front "in outright rebellion"; and a number of other officers who defied orders.

As the sixteenth-century Spanish monarchy had learned during the Dutch Wars, Republicans discovered that late pay could spark mutinies (Parker 1973:37–52). Retarded remuneration—in October, Asturian soldiers were owed four months back wages—contributed to demoralization, especially when the men were aware that unions in the rear were hoarding large amounts of cash.[400] Republican authorities in northern Spain ignored the precedent of the seventeenth-century English civil war. The Spanish Republic could not produce a Cromwell who realized that prompt pay was a key to victory. "Old Ironsides" knew that regular remuneration would prevent much indiscipline and that even partial pay would guarantee the loyalty of troops (see Kenyon 1988:224). Nor did the Popular Army follow the seventeenth-century adage, "pay well, command well, hang well" (quoted in Carlton 1992:81). Late pay, irregular food, and poor medical care led to a "broken contract" that encouraged soldiers to refuse to sacrifice for authorities who could not supply their needs.[401] Oddly enough, Republican soldiers resembled Philip II's host, who in 1576 attacked the richest city in northern Europe, Antwerp, when they did not receive the back pay that the king owed them (McNeill 1982:106). Twentieth-century mutinies were less organized than in the sixteenth and often took the form of soldiers' sit-down strikes during which fighters refused to wage war aggressively. Even more common was an individualized revolt in which the grunt looked out for himself more than any common cause.

In contrast, Nationalists paid their men regularly. Just as importantly, they were prepared for the mountain war that Asturian geography imposed, even though their progress was slow.[402] Their columns could not use the roads that Republican forces had "carefully destroyed," but Rebel mule trains, composed of herds of hundreds, overcame this obstacle. In contrast, Republican forces lacked both mules—animals that had the advantage of being calm during bombardments—and horses to supply their mountain forces. Nor could they easily evacuate the wounded or the dead. Some of their forces guarding mountain passes near León perished from cold. The loss of nearby Santander and the Basque provinces limited Loyalist reserve manpower. Unquestioned initial Republican heroism evaporated throughout September. Although the Condor Legion remained in Aragon, Nationalist aviation, composed almost entirely of German planes and personnel, went unchallenged and was extremely capable during the Asturian campaign. On 15 October Nationalist forces linked up in the mountain town of Infiesto, and panic spread among the Asturian defenders. The Condor Legion returned from the Aragon front and carpetbombed the trenches of the Asturian miners. Republican munitions became scarce, and weapons wore out.[403] Sixty percent of shells of artillery batteries of the XIV Corps did not explode. In the second half of October, some battalions had three hundred rifles for four hundred men, and others possessed seven different types of guns. Thus, furnishing them with proper ammunition was no simple task.

On 17 October, exhausted Republican units were relieved by troops from quiet fronts, but desertions of newly incorporated recruits endangered Loyalist positions. New battalions, "lacking antifascist leadership," dispersed on their first contact with the enemy, and entire units defected to the Nationalists.[404] Even before meeting the enemy, at least 20 percent deserted to the rear where a sympathetic civilian population provided them with food and shelter. Enemy aviation and artillery bombardments eliminated another 10 percent. When a chief commissar confronted deserters and told them that they should return to the front since the enemy was approaching Gijón, they self-interestedly replied that the enemy executed only officers, not men. These defectors were immediately shot, but their deaths "did not provoke a favorable reaction among the troops."[405] The shooting of deserters and the execution of officers was "not exceptional."[406] Despite the enemy's huge advantage in troops and supplies, orders were given (and carried out) to shoot any commander responsible for abandoning a position before suffering the loss of half his men. On the night of 17–18 October, the highest military authorities in the north concluded that "the moral and physical state of our forces" made further resistance impossible. Consequently, they planned escape. Asturian troops were asked to delay the enemy so that an orderly evacuation could take place, but "everyone was primarily concerned with his own safety, and they struggled to get on board the boats" (Salas Larrazábal 1973:1483). Top-ranking officials, including Belarmino Tomás, had "cowardly" planned the evacuation of themselves or their immediate family members.[407] Soldiers and sailors who remained in Asturias were demoralized by rumors, which apparently proved true, that Communist officials had arranged their own maritime transportation to avoid Nationalist capture.[408] Ten thousand ex-combatants reached French ports.[409] On 21 October, the insurgents entered the port city of Gijón which they sacked and looted (Fraser 1986:425). As in Santander, they found large stores of unused supplies (Jackson 1965:390). The civilian Consejería de Comercio had apparently expropriated reserves and had sold them to the Popular Army (Salas Larrazábal 1973:1487–88). Hoarders had stashed significant amounts of clothing. Concealment, which synthesized acquisitive and entrepreneurial impulses, damaged the Republic's northern operations.

The Nationalist victory in the north was a major turning point in the war. It was the wealthiest and most densely populated region but, at the same time, the weakest of Loyal fronts.[410] The Republican northern army surrendered en masse, and 230,000 combatants were lost or quickly recycled as Nationalist soldiers (Martínez Bande 1974a:16). The captured north would provide insurgents with sufficient reserves to counter Republican attacks and offensives elsewhere. Nationalists were able to exploit the Asturian coalfields and the industries of Basque Country. Very quickly, the *franquistas* mobilized the northern war industries that had remained stagnant and unproductive under Republican control (Richards 1998:111–12). Within six months of their capture, iron-ore output well exceeded that fabricated under the Euzkadi regime (Fraser 1986:409). The whole northern coast fell to the Nationalists, who could henceforth concentrate their naval efforts in the Mediterranean. At the same time, their entire army could move south. Given the history of Asturian militancy, it is not surprising that a number of devoted Republicans, adventurers, and the apolitical fled to the Leonese mountains and remained there as guerrillas.[411] Without plans, supplies, or radios, they were largely ineffective against the Nationalists, who needed only small numbers of troops and civil guards to neutralize them (Solé i Sabater and Villarroya 1999:219). Fear of reprisals against friends and family made them reluctant to engage in offensive actions, and they often limited themselves to avenging assassinations.

In addition, the defeat in the north forced the Republic to institute a counterproductive *levée en masse* that drafted skilled workers and peasants and thus aggravated growing labor shortages.[412] Conscription of young sons and brothers alienated village women. On 18 September in Manresa (Barcelona) "a great number of women" gathered "to protest against the war."[413] Their goal was to prevent the call-up of their boys and, more ambitiously, "the return of frontline soldiers to their homes." The female demonstrators refused police orders to disperse and insulted the forces of order. Their ringleader was arrested but was lucky to receive the minimum sentence—six years in a labor camp—since she lacked a criminal record and was not known as a rightwinger.

Many historians have commented that the loss of the north was the severest blow to the Republic, which forfeited approximately 25 percent of its manpower, much of its aviation and pilots, and more than 50 percent of its industrial potential (Salas Larrazábal 1973:1496–97).[414] The way the north was lost, especially the lack of commitment by the rank and file to the grand causes of the revolution or the Republic, anticipated the rest of the conflict. In what remained of the Loyalist zone, individuals would be more concerned with the fate of the *patrias chicas* of home, family, and friends than with the larger entities of state and nation. Unlike the military of the First French Republic, the Popular Army proved unable to profit from growing unemployment, massive inflation, and general economic disruption to recruit and motivate the jobless (McNeill 1982:192).

# 3
## Cynicism

At the end of 1937, the Republic came to resemble the Confederacy in its final stage. Rojo observed a "defeatism" behind the lines, largely caused by high prices or shortages of food, clothing, and transportation (cited in Salas Larrazábal 1973:1540; see also Cervera 1999:130). The scarcity of fertilizers and means to ship them lowered crop yields. To avoid price controls and their accompanying bureaucracy, those with a salable surplus bartered with each other.[1] The legal measures that the Republic used to halt barter, which had begun to replace purchase, had only a marginal effect. Swapping favored those with access to real goods and dramatically reduced what was available in urban markets. The deepening of the material crisis turned opportunism into cynicism. Personal interests reigned supreme. Shortages divided the Republic into at least three conflicting social groups: peasants who demanded higher prices for their products; urban workers and rural proletarians who needed price controls; and soldiers who, like workers, wanted cheap food and clothing but, unlike the other groups, were more able to take what they coveted.

In February, a seventeen year old from the province of Alicante wrote to his brother who was serving in the army that "in the rearguard hunger is busting our balls [*pica en los cojones*]."[2] Without massive purchases from abroad, he had no faith that civilians could be supplied. The plight of urban residents was most perilous. In the winter of 1937–38, lack of transportation prevented fulfillment of promises to provide Madrid with more meat and bread.[3] Females grumbled their defeatism in food lines (Cervera 1999:195, 208). In larger stores shoplifting became common. A Nationalist physician reported that in Madrid, normal rationing provided civilians with only five hundred calories per day instead of the recommended twenty-three to thirty-three hundred (Carro 1938:6). Defectors from the Republican zone showed significant weight loss. In February a Republican lieutenant colonel reported from Barcelona that workers could not afford to feed or clothe themselves and blamed the situation on the devaluation of Republican money (Martínez Bande 1974a:321). Everyone in Barcelona believed that if hidden wheat, oil, and oranges emerged there would be enough food to go around. Although the costs of rent and electricity were effectively stabilized and, in most cases, reduced, many still could not afford food. Long lines demoralized housewives and the elderly. By dropping loaves of bread from airplanes on the major urban centers, Nationalists added a bit to the diet but more to the despair of residents (Aragón 1940:240).

More sinister strategic bombing disrupted the urban economy and terrorized the population. In January, the Italians acted on their own and launched air raids on Barcelona, killing hundreds (Thomas 1961:513; Jackson 1965:408. Villarroya i Font 1981:118, 158).[4] From 16 to 18 March, Barcelona suffered numerous air assaults that killed nearly one thousand and injured many more. Neither the January nor the March attacks targeted strictly military objectives but rather aimed to intimidate civilians, including women and children. They were only partially successful since they eliminated fewer than expected.[5] Starvation and financial ruin remained greater dangers for urban residents than bombardments (Mira 1939:4093). Furthermore, the destruction enraged large portions of the city's youth who, to retaliate, became perhaps the last enthusiastic recruits of the Popular Army. These early 1938 raids were much more destructive than previous ones on Madrid and Alicante where, as has been mentioned, nearly half the bombs failed to explode. Ciano, the Italian foreign minister and the son-in-law of the Duce, was perversely proud of the devastation and terror that his bombers sowed. Western powers, including the usually cautious Cordell Hull, the U.S. secretary of state, protested what would become the fate of civilian populations in World War II.

The terror bombings revealed cracks in Nationalist unity. Generals Yagüe and Moscardó protested the indiscriminate killing and destruction, thereby reinforcing their reputation for nonconformist courage. Even Franco was unhappy with the attacks and asked Mussolini to suspend them (Coverdale 1975:349). Privately, though, certain Nationalist agents, whose attitudes could clearly be regarded as fascist, had no second thoughts about the activities of their Italian allies. Nationalist emissaries expressed the desire that working-class districts in Barcelona be reduced to rubble.[6] The destruction would serve both social and hygienic needs.[7] They expected that it would eliminate the *gentuza* responsible for the "misfortunes of Spain" and, at the same time, purify "filthy neigh-

borhoods." Franco's agents hoped that bombing would be so accurate and
deadly that the *generalísimo* would find it superfluous to shoot thousands when
he conquered the city. These Nationalists were particularly intent upon the
destruction of part of the Calle Muntaner, the refuge of "hundreds of Jews,
Russians, and others committed to the triumph of the Reds."

Refreshingly, ordinary soldiers displayed less fanaticism. They continued to
be accused of wasting munitions. On the Jarama front well after the famous
battle, both Republicans and Nationalists had ritualized artillery exchanges.
Each side fired twelve thousand rounds at the other without causing a single
injury.[8] To end ritualization, save munitions, and reduce the deterioration of
weapons, the battalion commander made the nonbelligerent but economical rec-
ommendation to ignore enemy fire unless the target was in full view and
within range. Firing weapons to promote the appearance of war was generalized and indicated the unwillingness of many on both sides to engage in truly
aggressive behavior. Discipline was sometimes lax. In December 1937 certain
units stationed in Brihuega disobeyed marching orders.[9] Two companies saun-
tered at a turtle's pace and, after nine kilometers, refused to continue their
efforts. Their disobedience delayed the relief of a battalion, and, more generally, discouraged nearby army units.

At the end of 1937, desertions on quiet fronts—such as the Teruel sector—
were significant in large sectors of the Republican army. The Third Battalion
of the 148th Mixed Brigade stationed near Perales de Alfambra reported that
in spite of its best efforts, many men continued to flee to the enemy. To
decrease the number of desertions, it recommended "constant vigilance" and
the formation of squads of veteran antifascists mixed with inexperienced new
recruits. After the flights of several soldiers and an officer, the captain of the
affected company was ordered to stop desertions using "all the means—even
violent ones—at his disposal."[10] To discourage attempts at flight, captains and
political delegates were commanded not to sleep at night but instead to patrol
the trenches. An "absolute prohibition" on leave was suggested. The commissar recommended deceiving troops by telling them that all deserters had been
captured and shot.[11]

One by one, men attempted to flee to the Nationalists on certain sectors of
the Aragon front.[12] For loyal officers, desertions were especially dangerous
because they could reveal valuable information to the enemy. For instance,
troops on both sides were often poorly armed and wanted to keep information
on their shortages confidential. Both Nationalists and Republicans were careful to note which soldiers fled with their arms. Giving a gun or a rifle to the
adversary was nearly as damaging as offering one's own living and breathing
body. Good soldiers were rewarded with deserters' weapons. In the Twenty-
second Mixed Brigade, the main reason for the "numerous desertions" was that
most soldiers were not "100 percent anti-fascist" and feared real combat.[13]

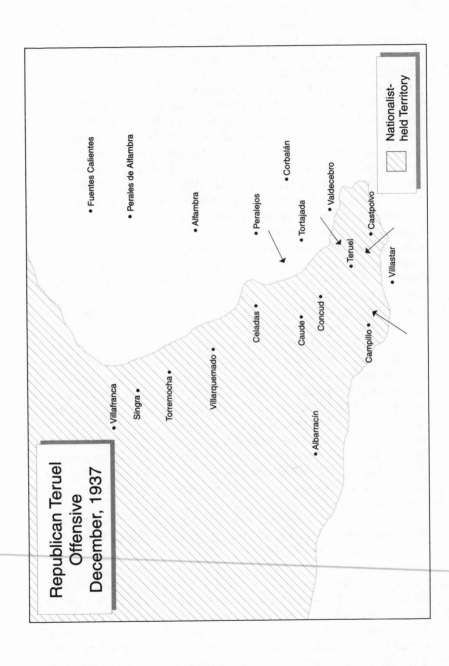

Republican Teruel
Offensive
December, 1937

Nationalist-
held Territory

Villafranca
Singra
Torremocha
Villarquemado
Albarracín
Celadas
Caude
Concud
Campillo
Villastar
Castpolvo
Teruel
Valdecebro
Corbalán
Tortajada
Peralejos
Alfambra
Perales de Alfambra
Fuentes Calientes

Again, the mixing of veterans and recruits was recommended to promote a combative spirit. Although this method could be effective in boosting morale, it ran the inverse risk of contaminating good soldiers who might begin to imitate the unenergetic and selfish ways of the uncommitted. All officers were told to act as "little commissars" and create a totalitarian world in which soldiers would be exposed only to the appropriate line. At the end of 1937 intensive indoctrination and surveillance, especially of "forced recruits," became general in many sectors of the Republican army.[14] Commissars were warned that desertions reflected poorly on their political work and that they would be held responsible for evasions of their men.[15]

Even the strictest surveillance could not always prevent the flight of the alienated, who would take advantage of an unexpected event or an accidental lapse of surveillance to abandon the ranks.[16] For example, sudden after-dinner vomiting by a sentry induced his companion to seek help. In the confusion, the sentry himself and another soldier fled to the enemy. Penalties for dereliction of duty became draconian. In the Popular Army, failure to execute sentry duties could lead to twelve years in a work camp.[17] Falling asleep at one's post was punished by up to six years' imprisonment. It should also be noted that Nationalists had problems that were similar in kind, but probably not in quantity or intensity, to the Republicans (Martínez Bande 1974a:48). In the Seventy-first Division from 1 November 1937 to 1 May 1938, sixty-one deserted to the enemy and six to the rearguard.[18] In relatively small numbers, Nationalist soldiers encircling Madrid fled to the Republic, despite threats to punish their families.[19] When General Yagüe needed more troops, he requested that they send Castilians and Navarrese, not Galicians, whom he continued to believe were inferior soldiers.[20]

After the fall of Gijón in late October, Republican intelligence information revealed that Franco was planning to attack Madrid. The Republican high command proceeded to devise a new offensive that it expected would throw the Nationalists off balance (Jackson 1965:398–400; Thomas 1961:504–16). Republicans chose the Aragon town of Teruel, a minor provincial capital with 13,500 inhabitants and an unenviable reputation for the harshest climate in Spain. The struggle over its possession announced the centrality of the Aragon theater in 1938. The fight to control this region would decide the outcome of the war. The Republican high command gathered seventy-seven thousand troops and over three thousand motor vehicles, an impressive logistical achievement (Martínez Bande 1974a:53). The battle did not initially involve International Brigades, and it was hoped that it would remain a purely Spanish show. According to a PCE Central Committee informer, preparations for the offensive were careful and effective.[21] Líster's Eleventh Division claimed that more than two thousand "apolitical" recruits were purged, trained, and transformed into effective fighters.[22] However, other

troops who were not members of elite or shock units were not so well prepared. Many of them did not know how to handle a rifle.

   Republicans inaugurated the top-secret Teruel offensive on 15 December.
Like the previous surprise attack at Brunete, it achieved immediate success.
Nationalist officers became worried that the enemy had molded an improved
striking force (Kindelán 1945:121). Soon, however, the Popular Army met stiff
resistance from a small (approximately 4,000) Nationalist garrison stationed
in the town of Teruel. Just as significantly (and often ignored), energies devoted
to looting delayed the Republican advance.[23] In the morning of 16 December,
in the village of El Campillo a Republican officer reported "scandalous" and
"horrible plundering" by troops who took whatever they pleased. Popular
Army soldiers confiscated cows, pigs, rabbits, furniture, and even construction materials for personal use. Nor was army property safe from acquisitive
individuals who stole cavalry horses and saddles.[24] In the nearby village of
Villastar, pillaging of a similar nature occurred. When confronted with their
questionable behavior, the looters claimed that the quartermaster—whose office
had gained a deserved reputation throughout the Republic for corruption—had
authorized them to confiscate private property.[25] Plunder had profound consequences. Communists concluded that Teruel could have been conquered
sooner if groups of soldiers who had first entered the city had focused their
energies on eliminating the "rebels [who were] entrenched in the Seminary,
Civil Government building, etc. rather then committing acts of immorality, such
as looting etc."[26]

   The Spanish war was unexceptional. In other civil wars plunder made troops
forsake "the decisive battle." "Some of the Cossack units [of the White armies
during the Russian civil war] were so weighed down with booty that they were
quite unable to fight" (Figes 1996:666). In the French revolutionary wars, "what
made pillage most disastrous . . . was its impact on the combat effectiveness of
the troops. Men did not loot as organized battalions or companies; they searched
for food and booty as individuals or in small groups. When a unit gave itself
over to pillage, it dissolved as a combat unit and could no longer advance, hold,
or retreat in order" (see Lynn 1984:114). Of course, Nationalists often accused
Republican soldiers of looting and pillaging, especially during retreats, but during the battle of Teruel, their accusations were confirmed by Republican officers who feared that the unchecked pillaging gave the fascists a great propaganda
opportunity. The duke of Wellington remarks are apposite: "A starving army is
worse than none" (quoted in Carlton 1992:285). Nationalist forces at Teruel
seemed to have had a disciplinary apparatus that more effectively repressed plundering (Kemp 1957:142). Perhaps pillaging was more significant on the Republican side because of its inability to feed, clothe, and pay its troops. License to
steal may have both motivated Republican forces to stay in the fight and, at the
same time, weakened their battle effectiveness.

Although Republicans were able to achieve their initial objective, the ferocity of a much smaller number of Nationalist defenders once again stymied their strategy. Attackers faced stiff resistance from insurgent troops who held Teruel, which, however, they had not sufficiently fortified (Martínez Bande 1974a:43). The Republican vanguard managed to enter the city on 19 and 20 December.[27] Despite the reversal of roles, the hand-to-hand fighting resembled that of Madrid's University City in November 1936. The Condor Legion supported the defenders from the air. What had previously occurred so often on the Republican side befell the Nationalists at Teruel. Scarce supplies of food and drink led to the latter's demoralization. After four days without supplies, the "reds" lured Nationalist soldiers away from their positions with the bait of bread and water (Martínez Bande 1974a:160–61). Republican offers of sustenance and peace dissolved commitment and induced Nationalist fighters to capitulate (Martínez Bande 1974a:293). On 8 January after a valiant effort, the Nationalist garrison finally surrendered.

Opinion in the Nationalist zone was profoundly shocked and upset by Republican success, the first time the Popular Army had been able to capture an enemy provincial capital. The *generalísimo* felt compelled either to respond to the Republican challenge or to lose both national and international prestige. He decided to forgo his plan for a Madrid offensive and concentrated his efforts on recapturing Teruel. In contrast to the situation at Brunete, Franco no longer had some of his best troops tied down by the campaign in the north. Republicans knew that the enemy would send these reinforcements to relieve the besieged but remained powerless to prevent it.[28] The Nationalist counterattack became increasingly effective. Certain Republican brigades defending Teruel bravely withstood some of the most violent insurgent aviation, artillery, and tank assaults of the war, while others abandoned their lines. Popular Army troops became exhausted, unwilling to fight, and subject to panic. Reserves were either unavailable or inexperienced. The massive draft in the Republican zone remedied the manpower loss of the Army of the North but had filled the ranks with replacements who had little training or will to fight. At the end of December, Rojo warned his men against any retreat (Martínez Bande 1974a:124). Yet in the last days of 1937 and the first of 1938 some abandoned positions "without any justifiable motive."

Teruel was the great winter battle of the war, and neither side was ready to confront the cold. Dozens froze to death due to insufficient clothing or blankets. A Communist informer complained that no one in Líster's Eleventh Division had received winter garments. Many had gone into battle in civilian dress.[29] Frostbite took a toll on countless fingers and toes. Some Nationalist soldiers tried to stay awake by drinking large quantities of coffee but died frozen in their sleep (Bolín 1967:309). Nationalists claimed that Líster's Eleventh Division, which was chosen for the initial attack, suffered 35 percent casualties.[30] Despite detailed instructions designed to overcome "egoism" and ensure efficient truck transportation, traffic jams (and frightened ambulance drivers) obstructed the evacuation of the Republican wounded.[31] All Loyalists were extremely disappointed by the insufficiency of aviation support, and many were critical of their artillery. One analyst attributed artillery ineffectiveness to its "atomization," which was an unfortunate result of the mixed brigade system. Unlike their enemy, the Republicans could not concentrate their guns.

In the second half of January, deteriorating Spanish performance forced Republican authorities to call in International Brigadiers, who would suffer very heavy casualties that Nationalist intelligence estimated—with perhaps some exaggeration—at fifteen thousand.[32] An insurgent physician claimed that Republican health services functioned inefficiently at Teruel (see Marín Corralé 1939:21). Under these circumstances, it was not surprising that significant desertions and disobedience occurred. Nationalist sources reported "many deserters" in the Popular Army's Sixty-eighth Division, and Líster, whose forces were assigned the task of detaining those who attempted to flee, confirmed the battle unworthiness of the Sixty-eighth.[33] Rojo's report of 31 December referred to the execution of six "agitators" after a "disbanding" and demanded that others receive similar punishments "to set an example" (quoted in Alpert 1989:210). Some retreating forces engaged in looting and pillaging, "unworthy of the Soldiers of the People" (quoted in Martínez Bande 1974a:277). When entering and leaving Teruel, they became acquisitive and subversive individualists.

On 20 January, two battalions of the Eighty-fourth Brigade refused orders to occupy positions to relieve exhausted troops.[34] Retribution was swift. On that day, Republican authorities executed forty-six men, almost all of whom were low-ranking soldiers or noncommissioned officers. Eighty more were to be put on trial; others were transferred, and their officers were demoted. Nationalist documents estimated that in this unit one hundred men were shot (Alpert 1989:210). The high command of the Popular Army noted that some units had been heroic (especially Gustavo Durán's 47th division) but that others had "abandoned their positions or had failed to complete their missions."[35] The abandonment of arms was "a shameful sign of fear" that "would be punished most harshly." Demotions of commissioned and noncommissioned officers for incompetence were numerous in one brigade involved in the operation.[36] By the end of January, Nationalists had taken 2,260 prisoners, welcomed 869 deserters, and encountered 1,175 corpses. They estimated that of the fifty-four thousand Republican soldiers who participated in the Teruel offensive, 40 percent or twenty to twenty-five thousand men were casualties.[37] The Popular Army's failure at Teruel destroyed Rojo's plans for an offensive in Estremadura. The Republic had lost many of its best remaining troops and equipment, and it would remain on the defensive until the summer of 1938.

Action around Valdecebro, a small village northeast of Teruel, showed the deficiencies of the Popular Army in February. At the beginning of that month, 600 new recruits were integrated into four battalions, bringing their total strength to 1,831 soldiers.[38] The recruits had not received military training and did not know how to handle weapons. Furthermore, many of their rifles did not work. When Nationalists attacked on 19 February, one battalion retreated. One-third of the unit was composed of new and frightened recruits who were exhausted after an all-night march of twenty kilometers. It seems that motor vehicles were seldom used to transport soldiers. Republican repression was futile: "Even though they had to shoot a few [of those who retreated], officers' attempts to stop them were in vain. The terror of the (Nationalist) machine gun was greater than that of their officers' pistols."[39] Their withdrawal demoralized other battalions. Consequently, Nationalists were able to capture Valdecebro.

By the third week of February, Nationalist counterattacks and the superiority of their artillery and aviation forced the Popular Army to abandon Teruel itself. Republican soldiers surrendered en masse without offering significant resistance. El Campesino and his forces came under intense criticism even from Communist comrades (Cordón 1977:322). According to them, El Campesino "cowardly" abandoned his forces and fled Teruel at the end of February (Líster 1966:182). The Nationalists took 14,500 prisoners and found 10,000 Republican corpses (Thomas 1961:515). Hundreds and perhaps thousands of others abandoned their arms as they escaped the provincial capital. Even though Nationalists suffered losses of nearly 44,000 during the Battle of Teruel, Prieto—the minister of defense, whom French journalists incorrectly labeled "the only great man of the Republic"—became not a Spanish Clemenceau but rather a convinced defeatist (Martínez Bande 1973:222). If ministers like Prieto were permitted a certain amount of pessimism, rank-and-file soldiers were not. Their "defeatism" was immediately and brutally sanctioned.[40] In the second half of 1938 sentences for the crime of pessimism could reach fifteen or even twenty years of confinement. During the final year of war Popular Army policies generally hardened. In 1938 the Republic developed a procedure whereby those soldiers stationed in the rear who exhibited symptoms of psychological disturbance or complained of mental illness were transferred to the front (Mira 1943:74–75).

As had occurred in the early days of militias on quiet fronts, Republicans once again neglected fortification construction during their two-month occupation of Teruel.[41] Despite the difficulties of digging with primitive tools in the hard and rocky Spanish terrain, fortification construction should have been a top priority. As in the First World War, strong entrenchments could have neutralized the heavy artillery and aviation attacks that were employed to soften up the enemy before going over the top. Yet fortification troops had a mixed record. Few volunteered for fortification work, and most battalions were seriously understaffed. The Ministry of Defense therefore prohibited any dismissals or transfers (*bajas*) from fortification battalions. In effect, this order caused a number of old, sick, and physically incapacitated workers—who were sometimes compelled to become sappers—to remain in their units. They labored little, thus demoralizing their healthier and more energetic colleagues.[42] Doctors were often unable to distinguish the truly ill from fakers, and productive workers became embittered by the limits of medical science. Some units of construction workers were able convert from "union" to "military" discipline and become effective trench builders.[43] Other former wage laborers, especially in Aragon and in Castilla–La Mancha, were more reluctant to make the change and toiled at a slower pace. For example, commissars at Puebla de Albortón (Zaragoza) were ordered to make sure that sappers worked hard and did not waste time.[44] The battalions formed by the CNT and UGT in the Levante "worked too slowly, given the [urgent] situation. This [slowness] was caused by bad organization and a lack of discipline."[45]

The fact that normal army rations were insufficient for those engaged in physically taxing labor compounded the Popular Army's perennial problem of food scarcity.[46] For sappers, nutrition was the key to morale and productivity throughout the war. Its dearth increased tensions between soldiers and local residents, especially peasants in Aragon or anyone who might have a surplus.[47] Furthermore, inefficient manpower policies limited or eliminated leave. Near Caspe in March 1938, 225 fortification soldiers were reported to be "completely exhausted."[48] Winter was especially difficult for these units. The lack of clothing—and footwear—demoralized sappers. During the rainy winter of 1937, a commissar in Madrid reported that 25 percent of his soldiers were shoeless.[49] Material deficiencies fomented colds that put "numerous" soldiers near Madrid out of action.[50] So did dirty water, which sometimes threatened epidemics.[51] Even if soap were available, an inadequate water supply often prevented fortification workers from washing their clothes, which suffered more wear and tear than garments of soldiers in other branches of the Popular Army.

Nor was conscription effective. CNT and UGT recruitment in Barcelona of "volunteers" was designed to compensate for desertions. Of the three thousand enrolled, fewer than half were actually incorporated by the end of March. By mid-April, three thousand were reported to have joined, but they did so "with great inertia." Catalans were particularly unenthusiastic. "As an example of the spirit that characterizes this [Catalan] province," 70 percent of those enrolled were refugees from Aragon, who lacked employment opportunities, and only 25 to 30 percent were Catalans or Barcelona residents.[52] Mobilization decrees had the effect of reducing unemployment among the most desperate sectors of the population (on mobilization decrees see Bricall 1978:1:91). Nationalist sources reported that in Alicante, Assault Guards went from house to house to enroll forcibly young draft resisters.[53] The Republic possessed few officers and noncommissioned officers who could control and train draftees. The inadequacy of basic training—except perhaps for the International Brigades—meant that the "we're all in this [mess] together" attitude, so necessary for armies to function well, was missing.[54] The Republic neglected the lessons of most professional armies, which discovered that "long hours of repeated drill made armies more efficient in battle. Drill also imparted a remarkable esprit de corps to the rank and file, even when the soldiers were recruited from the lowest ranks of society. . . . When a group of men move their arm and leg muscles in unison for prolonged periods of time, a primitive and very powerful social bond wells up among them. . . . The artificial community of well-drilled platoons and companies could and did very swiftly replace the customary medieval hierarchies of prowess and status" (McNeill 1982:117, 131; see also 1995).

The avoidance of military service by anyone who was not totally desperate recalls the Russian civil war (Pipes 1994:59). In early 1938 defections on quiet fronts created problems for both armies. Officers of the Nationalist Army of the North reported that "the number of desertions to the enemy and to the rear is considerable . . . but not worrisome" given the large numbers enrolled.[55] Nevertheless, they recommended exhaustive searches and swifter prosecution of deserters and, if implicated, their families. The head of the Nationalist general staff worried about "relatively frequent" flights from the Army of the Center and urged radical measures to stop them.[56] On the Republican side, the lack of food provided the rank and file with convincing excuses to explore no man's land and thus encouraged flight. To supplement an inadequate diet, soldiers would hunt or set traps beyond their lines.[57]

It did not help that officer training was generally deficient in the Popular Army. Candidates lacked both interest and discipline.[58] Proficient officers and sergeants were too few in number. Many candidates in officer training academies used the schools to escape the front lines and hide from danger (Gárate Córdoba 1976b:235). One student estimated that 80 percent of his classmates were employing the academy "as a refuge where they hoped to stay until the war ended" (94). Some spent up to six months in training, a period unheard of in the Nationalist camp. Formal artillery instruction had little connection with real-life situations at the front. On the other hand, there were a number of innovative and serious military instructors on the Republican side (59). In the Catalan War School, soldiers were subjected to war games played with live ammunition. Although this real-life training was unsurprisingly responsible for a number of injuries, the one-month course provided soldiers with useful knowledge. During its brief existence the Asturian Infantry School produced lieutenants at the same rhythm—and perhaps ability—as the Nationalists (165–79).

Whereas insurgents chose their officer candidates from university graduates; Republicans picked militiamen and others who lacked advanced education or even basic literacy. Many of them were unable to finish their courses. Nationalist admission and promotion standards seem to have been much more selective (Gárate Córdoba 1976b:192). Indeed, the Republican rank and file sometimes suspected the educated in their own ranks of being surreptitious "fascists" (Aroca Sardagna 1972:27). The victory of the insurgents was, in many ways, the triumph of counterrevolutionary middle-class males.[59] Franco's provisional lieutenants probably performed more consistently than their Republican counterparts. Nationalists, with considerable German assistance, instituted an effective program to train *alféreces provisionales* (provisional second lieutenants) (Payne 1967:388–89). Twenty-two training schools were eventually established, and from October 1936 to May 1937, the program commissioned over five thousand *alféreces*. By the end of the war the total reached almost twenty-three thousand, most of whom were middle-class university graduates between the ages of eighteen and thirty. Their losses were among the highest of any military category. Like Confederate officers in the U.S. Civil War or British officers of World War I, their generous shedding of blood earned the loyalty of their men (Holmes 1985:349).

In contrast, it does not seem that the Republic produced thousands of newly minted officers prepared to die for it. It had a special need for well-trained cadres since less than 10 percent of the regular officer corps served in the Popular Army (Payne 1967:414). Yet it was never able to create a core of effective lower-ranking officers. Nationalist officers won proportionally many more medals for valor and courage than did comparable Republican cadres. The latter accounted for 10 percent of the total medals awarded; the former earned nearly 30 percent, including many of the most prestigious decorations (Gárate Córdoba 1976b:238, 1976a:333–34). They also died in a much greater proportion—10 percent of the total—in an army seemingly more unified and perhaps more depoliticized than the *Ejército popular* (1976a:42, 85). This figure is nearly double that of the Carlist and Falangist units, which experienced 6 percent killed (Coverdale 1975:398). It is, however, lower than the 15 to 20 percent fatality rate of Moroccan troops (de Madariaga 1992:20).

Franco made junior-officer instruction a top priority, and General Orgaz, who was in charge of their training, praised the *provisionales* for being the first to advance in the face of enemy fire (Gárate Córdoba 1976a:122, 346). Although air force commander Kindelán believed that the quality of the Nationalist officer corps declined as the war continued and that provisional lieutenants "only knew how to die bravely," he nonetheless noted that "this was enough [of a contribution]" (Kindelán 1945:163). The *alféreces* casualty rate may have been surpassed on the Republican side only by the International Brigades, who suffered a 33 percent mortality rate. Soviet advisors were, of course, influential on the planning of operations of the Popular Army, whereas Germans and to a lesser extent Italians set the model for Nationalist training. Russian assistance in officer training seemed to have been less helpful for the Republicans than German support for the Nationalists. The German army had won an international reputation for first-rate military education. The success of the Nationalist *alféreces provisionales* was paralleled by the achievements of their *sargentos provisionales*. The insurgents trained several thousand of the latter whose efficiency matched the provisional lieutenants.[60]

The fortunes of the Republic degenerated militarily and materially after Teruel. Despite the objections of the inspector general of health, domestic scarcities in the Republican zone led the quartermaster to reduce rations: "It is well-known that local output . . . is totally used up, and we have to live exclusively from imports and these . . . do not cover our needs nor even allow us to maintain the present rations."[61] For example, the Ministry of Economy could deliver less than half of the wheat and flour that was needed. At the beginning of 1937 the Republic felt obliged to pay premium prices for foreign wheat, but authorities hoped that a plentiful future harvest would render recourse to the world market unnecessary.[62] Unfortunately, by the end of 1937 the wheat crisis had become severer.[63] The shortage of domestic grain made it necessary to find substitutes, but these worsened the quality and taste of bread. Provisions of feed grains destined for livestock had to be reduced, and hard currencies, which were needed for other purposes, were again channeled into buying foreign grain. Either because of government incompetence or, more likely, deception by farmers, officials were unsure of their own statistics, but they suspected that localities were hiding great quantities of grain and creating much of the deepening deficit.

Concealment (*occultación*) and illegal export of food created other scarcities. Throughout 1938, Tribunales Especiales de Guardia judged the "considerable number of infractions" of price controls on all types of commodities.[64] Special courts were established to defend the "anonymous consumers" of the Republic against "greedy merchants and speculators" who hid necessities, "causing prices to rise and creating discontent among the civilian population." A dozen government decrees were issued to repress black-market sales and establish price controls. For example, wholesalers were limited to a 10 percent profit on most commodities and retailers to a 25 to 40 percent markup.[65] In the Tarragona district "clandestine exporting, hoarding, and speculation" occurred regularly.[66] "Barefaced trading" in rice, oil, wine, and many other goods led the district quartermaster to advocate that soldiers and police control all roads, railroads, and ports in order to confiscate all unauthorized exchanges. Elite and selective battalions of *Etapas* were ordered to patrol communications routes. In principle, *Etapas* units enrolled personnel who were seasoned antifascists who had joined Popular Front organizations before 19 July 1936. Many were wounded veterans that had served in shock units. The indisciplined and uncommitted were usually dismissed from *Etapas,* but even in selected units the temp-

tation of corruption was sometimes too enticing.[67] In one prison camp in
Valdilecha (Madrid) *Etapas* soldiers cooperated with their officers and commissar to trade illegally food, soap, and tobacco originally destined for their
prisoners. They used some of the proceeds to hold a great banquet to celebrate
an officer's birthday. Officers involved in the profiteering were eventually
demoted and punished. Similar cynicism motivated Assault Guards, even though
most of them had been members of antifascist organizations.[68] Security of
employment, not ideological commitment, spurred most to join the elite unit.
Their noncommissioned officers were incompetent and "immoral." Commissars had established schools for noncommissioned officers, but they showed little interest in learning. Officers themselves preferred hunting to "theoretical"
instruction. Material deficiencies of arms, clothes, and beds provided good
excuses for absences. Even unit football matches were poorly attended.

In the winter of 1937–38, honest *Etapas* units arrested small and large black
marketeers in the provinces of Teruel and Lérida.[69] The men of *Etapas* patrolled
the latter province searching for deserters and fugitives, several of whom they
found hiding in isolated farmhouses.[70] "Hoarders and monopolists" controlled
thousands of kilos of corn, oats, beans, and almonds. These well-armed and
well-financed dealers employed trucks to move the large amounts of food at
their disposal. They offered troops bribes of one thousand to fifteen hundred
pesetas.[71] The *Etapas* turned them down and thus smashed a "close-knit network" of prosperous black marketeers in the town of Torrefarrera (Lérida).

Unions (*sindicatos agrícolas*) violated antispeculation measures as much as
merchants and traders did. Organizations and individuals hoarded and illegally
exported great quantities of food supplies that were needed either for the army
or to obtain foreign currency. The inappropriately named 18 July Cooperative
of Tíjola (Almería) took matters into its own hands by confiscating a wagon
of oil owned by the province and distributing its contents to its own members.[72]
Furthermore, the unions—like the collectives—could not or would not provide
reliable production statistics (see de Baráibar 1938:142–57). Spanish republicans learned, as had the Bolsheviks, that "the class war was primarily a war
for information" (quoted in Lih 1990:159). At the beginning of 1938, the CNT
accounting section wrote to its Peasant Regional Federation of the Center complaining that it knew nothing about the numbers, kind, and costs of livestock
that belonged to its members.[73] Even though the accounting office paid the
wages of a number of farmworkers, it was unaware of quantities of available
meat, eggs, milk, and so on. A variety of fears spurred peasant reluctance to
provide information. As has been seen, *campesinos* felt that the products of
their labor might be unduly expropriated; moreover, they wanted to retain their
autonomy. Collectives that had been formed voluntarily resisted the control of
higher-ups. National organizations seemed unwilling or unable to coordinate
*colectividades* (Bernecker 1982:129, 262).

Lack of solidarity was widespread. The collectives blended an ideal utopian future with regression to a medieval autarky. Such was the case in the Chinchón district where "the majority" of collectives had been created when small owners joined the unions.[74] Many who did not have enough land to make a decent living were ready to give collectivization a chance, since working their small and scattered plots was terribly difficult.[75] At the same time, collectives and union locals in La Mancha did not wish to pay taxes, including ones devoted to the war, to either national or local governments.[76] Collectivists and unionists in La Mancha rejected revenue agents' requests for more money. Agents responded by threatening to confiscate a collective's wine, a valuable commodity. During the war, exporting merchant firms continued to control much of the wine trade despite the fact that their directors had either fled or were in hiding. These businesses were more than willing to surpass the officially established price.

The CNT-UGT Collective of Relleu (Alicante) worked out its own special arrangement with the baking industry of Alicante. Without any official authorization, the latter provided extra daily rations of bread to wage-earning woodcutters (and to some of their own family members) in Relleu as compensation for their "hard labor."[77] In other words, those with food, such as the Alicante baking industry, could exchange it for energy supplies, but, as the provincial governor angrily concluded, the practice left without bread "the residents of this capital [Alicante] who suffer from fascist air attacks." Once again, urban residents with nothing to trade went hungry.

Collectivists distrusted changes that full cooperation with higher-ups might bring. The head of the CNT's Agricultural Section of the Center, a veterinarian who wanted to reform Castilian grazing found—like many agricultural reformers before him—that peasants were "supremely ignorant," "stuck in their routines," and resistant to "modern techniques."[78] CNT collectivists in Liria (Valencia) lamented the "ignorance" and "egoism" of their peasants.[79] Antagonisms were mutual. Collectivists in the province of Ciudad Real wanted to lynch the corrupt secretary of the Federación de la Tierra.[80] Solidarity often had to be imposed from above even if it risked alienating collectives and reducing their initiative. Regional and district authorities tried to enforce a standard wage scale. The collective in Carabaña (Madrid) was ordered to reduce its daily wage from fifteen pesetas per day to the local maximum of ten.[81] District and regional CNT officials believed that the higher salaries were "immoral" and risked demoralizing other collectives in the area. They concluded that a collective in Estremera (Madrid) was administered "terribly" and should be investigated.[82]

As Republican military fortunes declined, so did the Loyalist currency.[83] The printing of more bills aggravated the problem. In June 1936 in the then-unified Spanish nation, 5.4 million pesetas were in circulation. At the end of the war in the Republican zone alone more than 12.8 billion pesetas had been disseminated (Banco de España 1979:279). In 1938 for the first time in Spanish history, the Republic was obliged to print a five-thousand-peseta bill. In the Republican zone so many different types of currency were in circulation that in January 1938 the government ordered that all scrip issued by regional and local organizations be withdrawn. Laurie Lee, a British poet who served in the International Brigades, reported that in the winter of 1937–38, recruits were given new one-hundred-peseta notes (Lee 1991:85). Lee, a Hispanophile who had traveled throughout the Iberian Peninsula, recalled that he could have lived for weeks on one such note before the war. By 1938 the Republican currency proved nearly useless since there was little to buy in the barracks town of Tarrazona de la Mancha. Lee and his mates ended up paying over one thousand pesetas for three chickens.

On the Aragon front in the summer of 1938, during a short armistice held to retrieve dead bodies, a Republican soldier recognized a friend in the Nationalist Army and asked his buddy to transmit two thousand Republican pesetas to his girlfriend in Navarra (Colmegna 1941:179). His Nationalist pal replied that the proffered money was worthless in Franco's zone. The disdain for Republican currency paralleled the experience of the Confederacy in the U.S. Civil War, when even Confederate soldiers scorned their own money and were more than happy to receive Federal greenbacks. Loyalist inflation was so destructive that government spending was unable to stimulate the economy. Soldiers' wages and widows' pensions failed to prime the economic pump of the Republic. The Republican hyperinflation must also be compared to the stability of prices in the Nationalist zone in 1936 and 1937. In insurgent-controlled areas most of the rise of the cost of living, which was limited to 50 percent, occurred in 1938. During that year, shortages of raw materials, especially cotton and leather, forced a reduction of worktime and increased the cost of clothing and other commodities.[84]

Peasants with livestock were reluctant to sell to Republican authorities because the official price of meat was too low.[85] Urban "privilege" in the form of price controls backfired. Furthermore, peasants and shepherds would hide information concerning the number of animals and engage in "clandestine speculation" and "passive resistance" to a controlled economy.[86] A colonel in the quartermaster's office concluded that peasants were more concerned with their own personal interest than the general welfare. Authorities therefore could not calculate the number of animals available nor plan for the future. To correct the problem, the Institute of Agrarian Reform and other organizations threatened to confiscate all unreported livestock. In the province of Granada, the civil governor warned that statistics furnished by municipalities would be verified, that all unaccounted livestock would be impounded and their owners prosecuted as enemies of the Republic.[87]

A consequence of peasant egotism was the decline of horse transport, which meant an equivalent lack of mobility for an army that was only very partially motorized. In addition, the lack of fodder translated into hunger for military horses and livestock.[88] Perhaps, as in the Russian civil war, substantial numbers of requisitioned animals perished for lack of feed (Figes 1990:169). Even when, for example, straw was available, it could not be transported. The civil war greatly exacerbated Spain's traditional lack of forage crops, a problem that had produced "a serious disequilibrium" between pasture and arable (Ministerio de Agricultura 1936:16). Authorities feared that peasants had responded to feed shortages and confiscation threats by slaughtering their animals, especially the younger ones. Officials worried that if these practices continued, animals needed for work and for reproduction would quickly become unavailable. Authorities recommended that prices be raised since only higher meat charges could encourage peasants to breed livestock. They were seconded by peasant unions, such as the CNT Peasant Federation.[89] Those who argued that the artificially low price was the obstacle were quickly proven correct when a higher price brought a sudden abundance of slaughtered animals that were beyond working age and whose meat could be sold to the public.[90]

At the same time, consumers could not afford more elevated prices, and the Republic continued to impose controls to protect them. It decreed that sellers declare all merchandise to the proper authorities.[91] In the province of Valencia throughout 1938, police confiscated large and small quantities of every sort of commodity. As one historian of the Russian civil war has indicated, the reliance on coercion was a tribute to the primacy of material incentive. When the latter was absent, only force was effective (Lih 1990:219). At the end of June 1938 the Republican government officially put the military in control of food supplies (Bernecker 1982:156). Edibles traveling without proper documentation became state property. Unfortunate owners, who were sanctioned, claimed—sometimes plausibly but more often not—that they were unaware of the various steps that were needed to obtain suitable documents. *Etapas,* Assault Guards, and other police expropriated not only privately owned goods but also those of unions, cooperatives, and villages. They imposed price and quality controls in towns, such as Requena (Valencia), where they had been previously ignored because "a good number of people did not aid the cause, even if they were not officially fascists."[92] Small traders of watermelons or milk disobeyed the *tasa* or adulterated their goods. The extent of cheating may be gauged from an examination of the Special Tribunal of Alicante. From 18 April 1938 to the end of the year it issued 121 judgments. Seven concerned spying, 17 high treason, 48 "defeatism," and, most significantly, 99 for "illegal pricing" (Sánchez Recio 1991:172).

It is hard to know to what extent the confiscations and price controls protected the consumer, but the legislation and its enforcement undoubtedly diminished production. The political economy of the Republic alienated those who had a surplus to sell on the market. The "farmer who works without stopping," (*el labrador que trabaja sin cesar*), as villagers put it, inevitably came to dislike a regime that discouraged profits and might confiscate rice, wine, or animals. Peasant attitudes during civil wars in Russia and Spain were similar, and farmers concluded that hard work was counterproductive in a period when the state or local bands could expropriate without "fair" compensation (Lih 1990:249). Controls and accompanying bureaucracy encouraged relatively well-off peasants and even collectives to return to subsistence farming.[93] In one Aragon town, Sariñena, merchants simply closed their businesses and lived off their stocks.[94] In the province of Castellón, merchants, restaurant, and bar owners were fined one thousand pesetas for overcharging. Regulations and travel restrictions also discouraged organizations—such as unions, collectives, and cooperatives—from participating in the market economy. So did the inability of the economy to supply basic tools, fertilizers, and energy supplies to farmers. The contraction of available commodities and consumer goods hardly inspired peasants to produce more than they needed.

Peasants in the Republican zone seemed to have had a greater desire to avoid the market and consume their own products than their counterparts in Nationalist territory (Dirección General de Agricultura 1938). In Valencia, farmers discontinued growing oranges and planted only what their own families could consume (Abad 1984:356).[95] The few observers—largely diplomatic personnel—who were able to travel in both zones reported that Nationalist farms were well-tended and Republican ones neglected (Jackson 1965:417). Oddly enough, the relatively uninterrupted agriculture and commerce of the Nationalist zone resembled the victorious North during the U.S. Civil War. The absence of merchandise in the Republic recalled the collapse of Russia during World War I. At that time, Russian peasants—like their Spanish counterparts—found little incentive to market their harvest (McNeill 1982:329). The disappearance of commodities also meant the loss of revenue for a state that could not tax them.

Furthermore, de facto decentralization continued to dominate the Republican zone and rendered it impossible for police and troops to confiscate enough to feed soldiers and urban workers. In response, Spanish Communists urged the adoption of aspects of the centralized Soviet model in which the state could force collectivized peasants to hand over procurements and even to perform labor obligations (Cordón 1977:335). Managers of Soviet collectives were salaried state workers.[96] Yet even the behemoth of the Russian state often found centrifugal forces and peasant opposition too much to resist. In Republican Spain, problems were even more serious. Needy soldiers were not always effective as enforcers. Throughout the war they wasted fuels, such as wood and gasoline (Gárate Córdoba 1976b:90). Greedy disorganization squandered the Republic's considerable financial efforts to acquire petroleum products

(Martínez-Molinos 1990:226–27). To warm themselves, troops illegally chopped down forests, "causing the disappearance of a resource so important for the Republic."[97] Republican soldiers illicitly cut fruit and olive trees to obtain scarce firewood.[98] These "abusive and destructive cuts" endangered the forests of the rear.[99] Even *Etapas* was suspected of illegal destruction of the environment.[100] Rules were imposed to restrict ecologically "disastrous" cutting. Union and Confederate armies caused similar environmental destruction in the agricultural South during the U.S. Civil War (Gallagher 1997:160). So did the armies of the French Revolution.

Soldiers stationed in isolated grazing areas worked out mutually satisfying deals with local peasants and forgot the needs of the rest of the country.[101] Some also engaged in shady transactions to obtain more food for themselves.[102] Others with direct access to the kitchen withheld supplies from the troops or would inflate their numbers. They used surpluses to barter directly with local residents, thereby avoiding the use of devalued Republican currency. The army's olive oil, chick peas, sugar, and rice were exchanged for villagers' meat, coal, and other goods. Authorities calculated that this exchange totally ignored the official price (*tasa*) established by the government in September 1937 and upheld, at least in principle, by the Republican quartermaster (*Servicios de Intendencia* 1938:8). Food in the marketplace was worth two to four times the value of the *tasa*, which had increased for olives and olive oil only 25 to 50 percent from 1937 to 1938 (Ministero de Agricultura 1938?). In Sinarcas (Valencia) the unauthorized dealings of the aviation squadrons involved dozens in the town and nearby villages.[103] The aviators exchanged thousands of liters of oil with village women who supplied them with thousands of eggs, hundreds of kilos of wheat and barley, and assorted animals. Official military vehicles purveyed this trade, which developed into a lucrative commercial affair. Throughout the Republican zone, black marketeering was the only way that women and especially female refugees in war zones found to feed their families (Nash 1995:144; on female Confederates see Faust 1996:240). Women would trade the products that they could raise—such as rabbits, hens, and eggs—for the military staples of lentils, rice, and tobacco.[104]

Soldiers' disregard for the carefully planted crops of peasants and collectives did not help to increase food supply.[105] Nor did their evictions on short notice of collectives' housing and schools.[106] In Barcelona, police and those with access to food supply were tempted to use their position for their own private advantage. Some in the Agrarian Collective of Barcelona, which possessed both irrigated gardens and over one hundred retail stands in markets throughout the city and its suburbs, profited from the high price of food to engage in illegal deal-making. One member had worked out his own private arrangement with a *carabinero,* who would expropriate the vegetables he wanted from the collective's fields.[107] Other members of the collective seemed powerless when they tried to stop what they considered to be theft by police. The forces of order responded to their protests with abuse, insults, and threats.

Collectivists were tempted to sell secretly their produce to individual merchants who ignored the *tasa*.[108] The driver, female sales personnel, and a supervisor involved in the *"straperlo"* that is, illegal trafficking in commodities subject to price controls, were suspended without pay. By August "the fields that were close to the city were constantly assaulted. . . . More than 40,000 kilos of vegetables were lost or damaged. The poor—and perhaps others—continued their old-regime practice of gleaning the fields. These losses were caused not only by direct theft but also because we have to pick them [to avoid pilfering] before they are ripe."[109] The stealing of mature plants made it impossible to obtain seeds for next year's crop.

New problems emerged. Growing and competing bureaucracies that fixed prices—Comité Regulador de Precios, Comisión Nacional de Abastos, Ministerio de Agricultura, and other organizations—compounded material difficulties.[110] The failure to coordinate their actions led to an "economic catastrophe." In Catalonia, the *Generalitat*—realizing the difficulties of enforcing the maximums—wanted to permit greater pricing flexibility for producers, but its liberal policies clashed throughout 1938 with the national government's aim to protect consumers (Bricall 1978:1:113–14). Republican authorities attempted to coordinate military and civilian provisioning by including representatives of the quartermaster and the ministries of agriculture and economy on planning and distribution committees.[111]

Quartermasters reached agreements with local collectives around Madrid and in other regions. These arrangements usually permitted peasants to enroll in units stationed near their villages and thus to continue to work the fields. In return, they would furnish most of their crops to cooperating units.[112] Sometimes soldiers agreed to perform fieldwork, since the draft had created labor shortages throughout the Republican zone.[113] In the spring of 1938, both the CNT and the UGT peasant unions lobbied for the use of soldiers as harvesters and peasant exemptions from military service.[114] For example, in Castile and Estremadura, soldiers worked the fields. Agreements to use army or prison labor were often responsible for satisfactory relations between the military and the local population, but, in certain cases, accords risked ignoring the big picture. Both unions complained that the draft of more than twenty age groups had emptied the countryside of "useful men," especially skilled rural labor, such as shepherds, sheep shearers, and milkers. The lack of hands meant that a large percentage of the harvest went to waste.

In the province of Granada and throughout Castilla–La Mancha, women replaced men in the fields, although a continuing oppressive sexual division of labor made rural women unenthusiastic about taking the place of mobilized males (Puig i Vallas 1991:41–45; Rodrigo González 1985?:78–80; *Las Mujeres*

1991:243–45). In the cities, women replaced wage-earning men who had left for the army, but females did not inherit the respect reserved for their male predecessors. In trams and streetcars, soldiers refused to pay for their tickets and treated female conductors and controllers with discourtesy.[115]

The labor scarcity benefited refugees and prisoners in certain regions by giving them the chance to earn wages. In the summer of 1938, prison labor was also used to harvest in the province of Ciudad Real.[116] The annihilation of ideological enemies was replaced by a desire to put the captured to work. Employment of prison labor by both sides showed that the earlier period of massacres had been partially superseded. As could be expected, many prisoners worked poorly. Lack of transportation, fuel, and other material necessities impeded their productivity. In the fall of 1938 the CNT peasant committee of Catalonia recognized the severe food shortage.[117] It recommended several measures that were designed to avoid raising *tasas:* draft exemptions for peasants, agricultural training for women, and government subsidies to increase the productivity of the land.

On the Andalusian front, at the time of the Teruel engagement, the front lines were porous with dozens of soldiers and civilians from each side deserting to the enemy or to the rear. The motives of deserters from both camps varied.[118] Deserters left the Popular Army because of late pay, devalued paper currency, lack of soap, poor food, and scanty winter clothing. Wage laborers in civilian life, they defected when the other side promised opportunities for better pay or plunder. Nationalists had their own problems with the cynical. Many of their men who defected to the Loyalists were opportunists, believing—wrongly as it turned out—that the Republic would eventually triumph.[119] The general staff of the Popular Army classified these opportunists as "indifferent" since they lacked any real commitment to the Republic. As in other civil wars, they absconded because life became too difficult or, even more frequently, to rejoin their families.

One Nationalist report concluded that on a quiet sector of the Andalusian front "discipline did not exist." Officers were afraid of imposing it "for fear that individuals would revolt."[120] Sentences for those who went AWOL (absent without leave) were lax. On this tranquil section, the overwhelming majority of casualties were caused by sickness, not wounds. Although Nationalist soldiers who were recruited from captured "red zones" were not particularly enthusiastic, they were nonetheless more reluctant to desert to the Republican side than those who had never left the Nationalist zone. Servicemen who had lived in Loyalist areas "were disillusioned and aware of the privations that awaited them."[121] In the Alpujarras, desertions from Franco's forces were attributed primarily to individualism and the lack of patriotism.[122] Like their enemies, Nationalists recommended severe surveillance of potential defectors, especially soldiers with immediate family in the enemy zone. However, unlike

Republican forces in the south, insurgent officers insisted and usually made sure that each soldier had the right to prompt pay, sufficient and well-prepared meals, decent clothing, periodic leave, and prompt medical attention.

In Andalusia at the end of 1937 and the beginning of 1938, artillery engagements were not usually hazardous.[123] On an ordinary day at Baza (Granada), Nationalist artillery fired thirty shells, only five of which exploded and caused no damage. Nor was the malfunctioning entirely accidental. The "fascists" may have made a virtue of the continual duds. For example, in one unexploded shell Republicans found the message: "This is a joke since it is the Day of the Virgin."[124] Soldiers of the Popular Army also possessed undependable munitions. Some of the malfunctions were due to carelessness and incompetence; deliberate sabotage caused others.[125] Eighty-six percent of the injuries of four Nationalist divisions stationed in the province of Badajoz in February 1938 were classified as light or relatively light.[126] Both armies warned against unwise consumption of munitions, especially ritualization of fire. The *generalísimo* himself noted "the huge consumption of munitions by our armies, including those on quiet fronts and sectors where there are no attacks, compels us to remember the great importance of saving ammunition."[127] He fretted that "excessive use" would produce a shortage.

A misunderstanding between the two sides occurred when the Republicans fired on enemy lines to celebrate the capture of Teruel. The Nationalists interpreted this gesture falsely: "Believing that they were being attacked," they retaliated with rifles, machine-guns, mortars, and bombs.[128] The release of aggressive energies could not be sustained, and a more pacific normality quickly returned. Enemy salvos became harmless target practice, neither deadly nor dangerous. Republicans permitted the "fascists" to perform gymnastics openly, a clear violation of the rules of trench warfare where snipers, machine gunners, mortar men, and common soldiers with hand grenades were supposed to open fire on any living and moving target.[129] The 145th Mixed Brigade of the Eastern Army reported that "[exchanges] never were intense. . . . Our [artillery] was totally inactive."[130] In fact, friendly fire seemed as dangerous as enemy artillery and machine guns. Malfunctioning weapons on both sides encouraged tranquility. In one exchange on New Year's Eve, only seven out of twelve enemy shells exploded, and they caused no damage.[131] Except for an occasional raid or aviation attack, in which one-third of the bombs released were duds, little disturbed the calm of the New Year.[132] On 18 January, only fourteen of fifty-six "fascist" artillery shells exploded, and those that did work caused few injuries.[133] Again, on 26 January, half of enemy shells were inoperative. The calm was broken in the middle of February by a series of raids and counterattacks, which provoked angry Nationalist counterattacks.[134] Revenge was one of the strongest motives for fighting.[135] When the tranquility of the front was disturbed, soldiers reacted violently.

The general calm in the south and center permitted Nationalists to transfer the bulk of their forces eastward and to prepare a major post-Teruel offensive toward the Levant and Catalonia (Jackson 1965:519). Between Zaragoza and Teruel, Franco concentrated 100,000 men, approximately 700 Italian and 250 German planes, and 150 to 200 tanks. The knowledge that Republican troops and rearguard were weakened by material shortages, especially the lack of food, bolstered Nationalist morale.[136] The offensive began on 9 March with a devastating artillery and aerial barrage (Thomas 1961:519). The dominance of Nationalist aviation, estimated at four to one, demoralized even the best Republican troops (Salas Larrazábal 1973:1763; Bolloten 1991:570). Aviation attacks alarmed the men, but, according to senior officials, were never sufficiently intense to justify a massive disengagement. Republican artillery was especially deficient, and it "fled shamefully."[137] These "disorganized flights" discouraged an infantry that quickly broke and ran. Thousands of Loyalist troops and hundreds of officers abandoned their weapons as they fled from the front. So faint was resistance—with the exception of Líster's division—that by 19 March the main Nationalist assault forces suffered only 1 percent casualties (Payne 1967:401; on Líster see Coverdale 1975:350). Even though he never gave up hope for a turnaround, Rojo believed the overwhelming majority of the troops were "good for nothing." Men violently attacked loyal officials who tried to stop their unauthorized retreats. Military and civilian leaders, like Rojo, Pozas, Prieto, and Líster, described soldiers from diverse and physically separated units as filled with "panic," "fear," "demoralization," and "madness," which spread like an epidemic (Líster 1966:190). Prieto lamented that troops did not understand how their lack of resistance would create "disaster."

Belchite and Quinto (Zaragoza) fell quickly. Tank formations using German panzer tactics encircled entrenched Loyalist troops, while planes bombed them when they retreated. Nationalist forces advanced quickly and encountered little opposition even from well-fortified Republican positions. Senior Republican officers wrote that their troops were seized by a "collective panic" and "fled dishonorably" (Rojo and Pozas quoted in Salas Larrazábal 1973:1812). Negrín concluded that the defeat of his army was caused more by "moral collapse than technical deficiencies."[138] Foreign volunteers reported that young Spanish conscripts shamelessly abandoned their positions (Bessie and Prago 1987:228). Rank-and-file legionnaires confirmed that Republicans showed themselves to be second-class troops (Kemp 1957:161). In his report, General Carlos Masquelet attributed the collapse of his forces on the eastern front primarily to the lack of bravery of the Twenty-fourth Division, which fled "without order or discipline."[139] In some units, officers died fighting, but many others rapidly abandoned their positions with their men. For example, the Eleventh Brigade of the Thirty-fifth Division was "an example of demoralization."

Republicans were unnerved by shortages of food, transportation, and munitions (Martínez Bande 1975: 45–62, 208–21, 264–67). A deficit of trucks prevented the transport of reserves for counterattacks. Given Nationalist air superiority, Republican services had difficulty operating during the day, but had little excuse for not functioning during the night. From the very first day of operations, the quartermaster completely failed to provide supplies. Material shortages—lack of small arms, artillery, aviation support, and "all kinds of equipment"—caused flights and unauthorized retreats. Differences between the quantity and quality of small arms seemed to have been minimal in the early years of the war, but by 1938 the Nationalists had a clear advantage (see Kemp 1957:44, 155, 177). The poor training and superficial commitment of both commissioned and noncommissioned officials, a perennial problem in the Popular Army, also contributed to the collapse. The inability to produce competent low-ranking and noncommissioned officers weakened the small group cohesion that was so necessary for success in combat. Revolution and terror in the Republican zone had eliminated many potentially useful military officials, preventing the Popular Army from following the Bolshevik example of employing large numbers of old-regime officers. Furthermore, commanders were unwilling to send their best officers and men to training centers and believed that formal instruction did more harm than good (Cordón 1977:239). In their "shameful and dishonorable flight," "many officers" ripped insignias off their uniforms and blended into the fugitive crowd. Soldiers, seized "by collective panic," followed their officers' example of every man for himself. By the end of May, the Nationalist conquest had finished off what remained of revolutionary Aragon. The *alféreces provisionales* demonstrated their bravery during the Aragon campaign by falling in such large numbers that the *generalísimo* himself had to order that they stop taking unnecessary risks (Gárate Córdoba 1976a:187). The Republican defeat was mainly military and should not be attributed, as Noam Chomsky (1969:111–15) and Burnett Bolloten (1991:531) have done, to the political alienation of revolutionary anarchists who were frustrated by the destruction of the collectives.

Under the shock of debacle on the eastern front, which opened the prospect of imminent Nationalist victory, the major trade-union federations signed a program for unity:

The CNT and the UGT will cooperate in the rapid constitution of a potent war industry. It is the unions' urgent and indispensable task to establish a strict spirit of vigilance against any kind of sabotage and passivity in work. Production must be improved and increased.

The CNT and the UGT believe that a salary that is tied to the cost of living and that takes into account professional categories and productivity must be instituted. In this sense the industries will defend the principle of 'the more and better the production, the greater the pay.'

The two organizations yearn for the recovery of national wealth and to coordinate the economy legally so that the independence of the country is assured to its fullest extent. (Peirats 1971:3:37–39)

The Communists termed the program "a great victory for the Popular Front and democracy" (quoted in Bernecker 1982:136). Many in both unions considered this pact a synthesis of Marxism and anarchosyndicalism, a fraternal embrace of Marx and Bakunin. If so, this joining of hands and spirits aimed to make the workers and peasants labor harder and produce more for the unions and the nation.

The Nationalists profited from Republican weakness to pursue their offensive. The Republican Maginot line—the supposedly impregnable fortifications of the Cinca, which had been given top priority as early as August 1936—was easily overrun at the end of March (Salas Larrazábal 1973:1755). As the Nationalists advanced, only one or two battalions remained in place, and an "infinity of soldiers retreated without orders or coordination."[140] Artillery was again abandoned. "Panic" or, in more neutral terms, instinctual individualism affected various units. In one case, retreating officers were forced at gunpoint to return to the front to lead their troops.[141] Fleeing soldiers might also be viewed as subversive individualists who rationally concluded that they must save their own skins, not the Republic. "Panic" and flight were merely manifestations of the end of group solidarity. Collapse of group cohesion makes the battlefield, as S. L. A. Marshall put it, "the lonesomest place which men share together" (quoted in Holmes 1985:66). Official military manuals—and those of the Republic were no exception—always argue that flight is many times more dangerous than facing the enemy (Mira 1943:153). Battle observers of all persuasions have almost universally been hostile to running away. Officers, from Lord Moran to General Trochu, and sociologists, such as Gustave Le Bon, have disdainfully labeled panicky men as a mob, animals, a herd, or a flock. A contemporary military historian has written that panickers "seem to lose many of their human characteristics, and become animals, given over to the hysteria of the herd" (Holmes 1985:228; see also Vallejo Nágera 1939:82). More analytically but nearly as negatively, Freud has argued "a panic arises if a group [of soldiers] become disintegrated. . . . The mutual ties [of the group] cease to exist, and a gigantic and senseless fear is set free" (Freud 1959:28).

Perhaps, though, the "panicky" soldier was more rational than observers are willing to admit. He quickly calculated that he stood a better chance of surviving if he acted individualistically rather than collectively. Most writers on military affairs ignore that there are various types of sudden flight. A high-ranking commissar who observed the "panic" in March concluded that it was different from previous ones he had witnessed (quoted in Martínez Bande

1975:219). In contrast to earlier waves, soldiers were not "bewildered" nor "exhausted." "The soldiers who fled . . . did not lose their judgment this time. They preserved their reason and were able to respond clearly to questions. They did not exhibit deep demoralization nor show signs of panic. . . . Almost all had abandoned their weapons but not their own suitcases or personal possessions, which they took treated with perfect reason [*con perfecto raciocinio*]." Furthermore, they found support on the home front even though mayors and other local officials were warned that if they hid or cooperated with hometown deserters they too would be shot. The countless decisions of Republican soldiers to leave military service and become subversive individualists resulted in the collapse of the Aragon front and the division of the Republican zone into two parts.

The inhabitants of threatened areas literally bet their money on a Nationalist future. They did not wish to sell to Republican troops and impatiently awaited the insurgent arrival. In early April, Franco's forces captured Tremp and Lérida, whose Popular Front could raise only a few dozen men for a last-ditch defense (commissar cited in Martínez Bande 1975:281). The capitulation of these towns was a severe blow to the Republican effort. Lérida's fate showed that the Loyalists had lost still another provincial capital. In addition, the fall of Tremp, which supplied Barcelona with much of its electricity, forced Spain's greatest industrial city to depend upon outdated steam-generating plants (Thomas 1961:530). Industrial production was adversely affected, and the entire region was in danger of collapse. Alarmist rumors, which are as destructive of morale as poor food or heavy casualties, destroyed any will to fight (Dollard 1943:53). The quick fall of both towns displayed once again the weakness of the Popular Army. The lack of courage was linked to indiscipline, and soldiers in certain units did not bother to salute their officers and mocked those who did. Improvised supply trucks could not provide sufficient water and food to Republican troops, who sometimes relied upon pillage.[142] Dearth was generalized, and delivery trucks had to be accompanied by armed guards to reach their destination and avoid being hijacked by other hungry and dehydrated troops.

Lack of reserves rather than sporadic enemy resistance delayed Nationalist advance. Republican fortifications were either poorly organized or nonexistent.[143] Fortification battalions remained seriously undermanned. "Most gave orders; few carried them out." Workers continued to lack everyday necessities such as shoes, blankets and mess kits. Precipitous retreats, which caused the abandonment of many items, intensified these shortages.[144] Given the lack of footwear, leg injuries downed "a considerable number." Local unions, mayors, and military commanders gave a low priority to recruitment of construction personnel. In Building Battalion Eleven, composed of 467 men stationed in Cortes de Arenoso (Castellón), 8 soldiers were killed, 72 had deserted, and 178 had "disappeared," that is, either had deserted or had surrendered to the enemy.[145] Responding to the high level of desertions and disappearances, commissars increased the number of their lectures and began literacy classes. On 15 April, Nationalist units—demonstrating overwhelming superiority in morale, material, and mobility—reached the coast at Vinaroz. Its capture cut the eastern Republican zone into two parts and, for all intents and purposes, divided Catalonia from the Republican Levante, Castile, and Andalusia. The separation of the Republic into various zones hindered its war effort and also increased the Nationalist advantage in food supply and population. The geographical fracturing of the Republic obstructed transportation and communication between its zones. The splintering of the Loyalist zone forced the transfer of major institutions. Evacuations, as was evident in Madrid in 1936, sparked tensions between workers and managers. The former continued to be more concerned with their personal and familial problems than with workplace responsibilities. Management of the Republican Mint (Factoría de Moneda) complained that a group of its employees frequently missed work during April and May during preparations to transfer the mint from Castellón to a safer location in Aspe (Alicante).[146] During the move, certain union militants neglected wage labor and instead devoted their energies to providing their families with food. The shift to the village of Aspe produced friction between relatively privileged mint employees and everyday townspeople. The latter resented the former because they "had food that was much superior in quantity and quality." Furthermore, the mint personnel retained a special status, conferred during the dictatorship of Primo de Rivera, that gave employment preference to the sons of salaried personnel. The evacuation of civilians from areas about to fall into Nationalist hands provided the strong with additional opportunities to take advantage of the weak. For example, a union member was accused of selling the mules and carts used to move female evacuees and keeping much of the proceeds for himself.[147]

The geographical division of the Republic inspired crackdowns. In Almería, to discourage desertions and repel an influx of refugees from newly conquered or endangered areas, the joint committee of the CNT-UGT refused union membership to anyone between fifteen and sixty years old (Quirosa-Cheyrouze y Muñoz 1986:239). In Ciudad Real, dozens of persons who were suspected of revolting against the Republic were arrested.[148] In addition, "five thousand men," presumably draft-dodgers and deserters, were "recuperated," that is, captured. In April, the Republic called up all workers for fortification duty, and massive desertions were reported (Salas Larrazábal 1973:1887, 2028 on mobilizations). Laborers abandoned the Popular Army before the socialization of basic training. On many fronts, the lack of trained and committed personnel prevented the organization of effective diversionary attacks and raids.[149]

The Army of Estremadura provided a good example of the problems of the Ejército Popular. In March 1938, it launched an offensive designed to take pressure off retreating Republican forces in the east.[150] The operation aimed to capture Talavera del Tajo, as it was called during the war. The March offensive was quickly aborted after initial difficulties. Both troops and especially officers were responsible for failure. According to the chief commissar, the latter had been promoted because "they worked hard for the interests of their [Communist] party." Their morale was "very bad," and they lacked "faith and enthusiasm." "Poor attitude, indiscipline, and political struggles in the army" were the rule. The defeat revealed the ineffectiveness of the Army of Estremadura and showed the difficulties of usefully employing Loyalist soldiers on a quiet front.

In April, the Republican high command again pushed for an operation to take pressures off the eastern front, which, as has been seen, Nationalists were cutting into two. The Army of Estremadura was ordered to occupy Navatrassiera, La Calera, and Carrascalejo. Nationalists accused the Republican forces in Estremadura of committing atrocities and provided a detailed report on the alleged massacre that had taken place in the village of Carrascalejo (Cáceres) in April 1938.[151] According to the Nationalists, the Republican forces trying to capture the town had encountered resistance. On 9 April, the "reds" finally seized and occupied it for ten hours. Most residents had already fled, but a few managed to hide and claimed to be eyewitnesses to the bloodletting and pillaging of the Popular Army. Republican soldiers from the *pueblo* itself brutally slaughtered the mayor, his wife, and their four children, who ranged from seven months to fourteen years old, and then mutilated their bodies with machetes. A Falangist corporal had his eyes gouged out and his tongue burned. They tortured and killed a half dozen other Falangists. The church, where a number of women and children had taken refuge, was destroyed in the battle, and a number of persons inside perished. Houses were looted and livestock annihilated.

The truth of these accounts is unfortunately impossible to disprove or verify; yet the indiscipline of the Estremadura army and similar atrocities of retreating Republican soldiers lends some plausibility to the Nationalist report. Adding further credibility to the charges, the president of the Popular Army's Permanent Tribunal of the Army of Estremadura accused specific units of engaging in rape and murder.[152] Rape, though, seemed relatively rare in the Spanish conflict. In civil wars, rape is usually a crime not of sexual passion but—like shaving heads—of hatred employed to humiliate the female enemy (see Carlton 1992:259).

Republican diversionary efforts in Estremadura had little consequence. To distract the Nationalists from completing their conquest of Levante, in May officers ordered their forces to frontally attack well-defended and fortified Nationalist positions.[153] Although Republicans lost the element of surprise and the enemy effectively resisted, the attack nonetheless persisted. By the beginning of June it was clear that the offensive had failed, but it was not canceled. Despite a report of 4 June, which covered up the mistakes and errors of the operation and even praised the officers responsible, it became evident that the Popular Army in Estremadura did not have the training, will, or means to undertake a May offensive. Furthermore, the Army of the Center, a zone where tranquility prevailed, made no contribution to diversionary efforts.

In their romp through a number of conquered Aragon villages, some Nationalist troops engaged in looting of household goods.[154] The Moors, in particular, gained reputations for sacking, massacre, and raping of civilian populations (de Madariaga 1992:87).[155] In Andalusia in July, Nationalist officials reported looting and pillaging in "liberated" areas, and they threatened to shoot any of their own soldiers who engaged in "actions typical of the Red Army."[156] It does, however, seem that instances of pillaging were more controlled and less frequent among Nationalist forces than Republicans. This may be attributed to insurgent military discipline. Perhaps plunder was less of a problem for Nationalists since they—unlike their enemies—were able to pay their troops regularly with sound currency. They could also feed hungry populations in southeastern Aragon and elsewhere.[157]

Nationalists inherited the successes and failures of Republican efforts in olive-producing areas. Before the arrival of Franco's forces, villages in lower Aragon had encountered serious difficulties gathering the olive harvest, their main crop. According to one Nationalist expert, the "reds" had managed the largest olive oil mills with skill and competence.[158] In fact, the informant confirmed that rumormongers in the Republican zone had been correct and that there was enough oil for the military and civilian populations of Catalonia and Aragon. The expert confirmed the cynical view that a surplus of oil existed but that it did not reach those who needed it. The lack of transport and, just as importantly, labor hindered distribution. Hands were in short supply and unable or unwilling to gather the bountiful harvest of the early months of 1938. The peasants, in particular, showed "resistance and disinterest" during the collection. They continued the refusal of work that they had engaged in during the Second Republic (Collectif Equipo 1997:41). In this case, they did not want to pick olives in return for "red money," which they realized to be devalued and perhaps totally worthless in the near future. They knew that in Nationalist zones, even recently liberated ones, Republican money was not accepted.[159] However, the arrival of the Nationalist army and its currency did not entirely solve the problems. Transportation, containers, and especially labor were still needed for harvesting, since many peasants had fled to regions that remained in "red" hands. To save the crop, Nationalists opted to employ cheaply paid (four pesetas per day) prisoners of war.

The success of the Nationalist spring offensive and their advance to the sea raised the prospect of immediate Loyalist defeat. Franco believed that he could

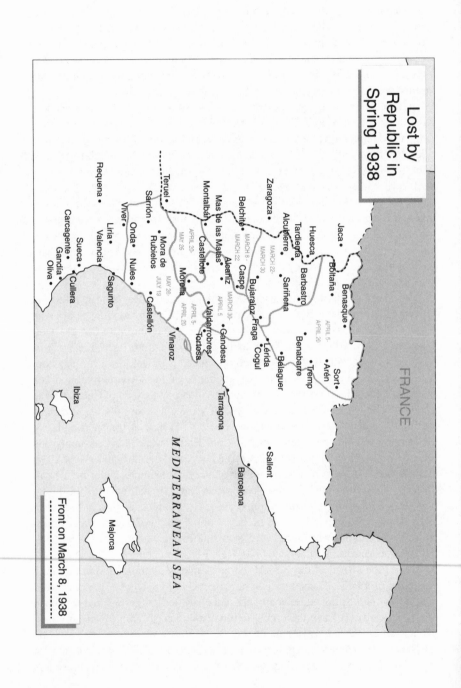

Lost by
Republic in
Spring 1938

Front on March 8, 1938

FRANCE

MEDITERRANEAN SEA

Ibiza

Majorca

Barcelona

Sallent

Tarragona

Tortosa

Vinaroz

Benabarre
Tremp
Balaguer
Lérida

Sort
APRIL 5,
APRIL 20
Arén

Benasque
APRIL 5,
APRIL 20

Boltaña

Jaca

Huesca

Barbastro

Sariñena

Tardienta

Alcubierre

MARCH 22
MARCH 30

Zaragoza

Belchite
MARCH 8

Caspe
MARCH 22

Alcañiz

Bujaraloz·
Fraga
APRIL 5
Cogul

Gandesa
APRIL 5

Valderrobres
MARCH 30

Mas de las Matas

Montalbán

Castellote
APRIL 20
MAY 26

Morella
JULY 19
APRIL 20

Teruel

Sarrión

Mora de
Rubielos

Viver

Onda

Nules

Castellón

Requena

Liria

Valencia

Sagunto

Sueca

Carcagente

Gandia

Cullera

Oliva

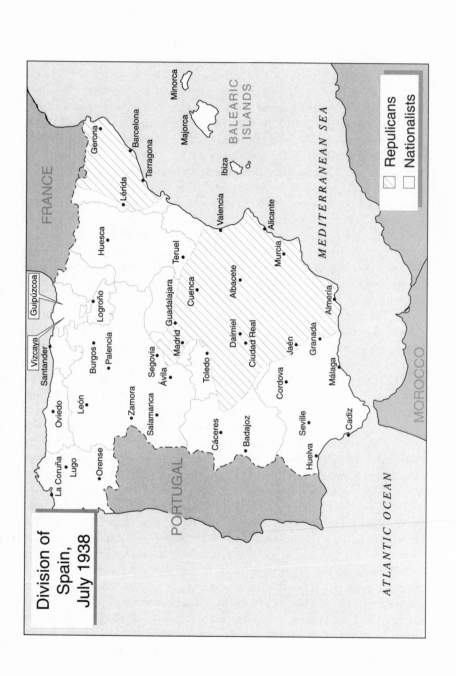

Division of
Spain,
July 1938

FRANCE

PORTUGAL

MOROCCO

ATLANTIC OCEAN

MEDITERRANEAN SEA

BALEARIC
ISLANDS

Minorca

Majorca

Ibiza

Vizcaya
Guipúzcoa

La Coruña
Lugo
Orense
Oviedo
León
Zamora
Santander
Burgos
Palencia
Salamanca
Segovia
Ávila
Logroño
Huesca
Lérida
Gerona
Barcelona
Tarragona
Valencia
Alicante
Murcia
Almería
Granada
Málaga
Jaén
Cordova
Seville
Huelva
Cadiz
Badajoz
Cáceres
Toledo
Madrid
Guadalajara
Cuenca
Teruel
Albacete
Ciudad Real
Daimiel

Repulicans
Nationalists

quickly capture Valencia and the rest of Catalonia (Martínez Bande 1977:15–24). The Republic seemed lost but was able to survive for several reasons. The persistent fear of French intervention, which aimed to prevent a German ally on its southern border, may have convinced the *generalísmo* to slow the offensive (Salas Larrazábal and Salas Larrazábal 1986:330; Howson 1999:234–35). Nationalists were alarmed that the conquest of Catalonia might provoke direct French assistance to the Republic, and they switched their objective to Valencia. From 17 March until 13 June, the French Republic allowed a new flow of arms and supplies, not all of Soviet origin (Czech shipments were significant), to its Spanish counterpart. The border opening was particularly important since Nationalist and Italian control of the Mediterranean made it very perilous for the USSR to ship its aid by sea. Plentiful equipment (including 300 Soviet airplanes and 25,000 tons of material) and fresh troops enabled Republicans to defend the Valencian region and thus to halt the Nationalist advance (Coverdale 1975:351). Despite the reclosing of the French border on 13 June, Russian supplies, purchased in part on credit, continued to flow to the Republic (Viñas 1979:414). Yet this dependence on outside help showed that the Second Spanish Republic could not equal the revolutionary First French Republic, which had built an arms industry capable of supplying its troops.

The Popular Army's defense of the Valencian region was one of its greatest military achievements. As the Battle of Madrid had already illustrated, the Republic's foremost victories were defensive. The successful Valencian effort was, in part, obtained by strict discipline, which Nationalist historians have labeled "terror" (see Salas Larrazábal 1973:1956; Martínez Bande 1977:126). New recruits were carefully watched and quickly shot if caught deserting. Topdown discipline replaced the self-imposed variety. Nonetheless, reinforced discipline or "terror" cannot entirely explain the Republican triumph. Junior officers in particular displayed heroism and willingness to sacrifice that inspired their men.[160] In sharp contrast to the Nationalists whose services functioned effectively, Republicans lacked transport, medical care, and even shoes or blankets but nevertheless fought admirably.[161] They killed or wounded thousands of Nationalist troops. The Republican leadership gave the Valencian defense top priority since the region was the source of the little food that (barely) sustained Republican Castile (Modesto 1969:180). More than one hundred thousand from some of the best units stationed on quiet fronts in Estremadura and the center were transferred to the east. Franco did not have the reserves to match this effort and was often reluctant to use ordinary conscripts in major battle (Payne 1967:389). The achievement of Valencia showed the ability of the Popular Army, despite material disadvantages, to inspire a strong defense at certain times. Reserve units that had not been destroyed during the Aragon clashes fought particularly well (Payne 1970:351). By July 1938, the Army of Levante had two hundred thousand soldiers, including twenty-four fortifications battalions (Martínez Bande 1981:304). Authorities mobilized the civilian population, including middle-aged men, for construction. All building workers were assigned to fortifications, and the rear guard was scoured for shirkers. Mobilization efforts surpassed the precedent of Madrid (Martínez Bande 1977:29). In the first half of May an effective and highly professional crash program was undertaken. Sappers built upon the strong defensive structures erected in the aftermath of the Battle of Teruel. Three shifts per day were organized, and work was so intense that sometimes labor shortages developed.

The solid defenses of Valencia redeemed the Republican reputation damaged by the easy conquest of the Bilbao belt (*cinturón*). In addition, geography and climate helped the Loyalists. The mountainous terrain created numerous obstacles to the Nationalist advance. "The solid mass of the Maestrazgo resembled a giant castle that [Nationalists] had to storm stone by stone" (Martínez Bande 1977:70). It was "a geographic maze well suited for defense" (Payne 1967:401). Republicans were also assisted by bad weather, which made offensive movements much more difficult. Fortifications around the small town of Viver (Castellón) were particularly well-constructed and capable of resisting five-hundred-pound bombs (Thomas 1976:2:894). Nationalist attacks were futile against abundant and profound fortifications around Valencia itself. Republican aviation may have equaled Nationalist air power. Between 18 and 23 July, Franco's forces suffered thousands of casualties, and they also worried about guerrilla infiltration into their territory (Pons Prades 1977:25–26; Martínez Bande 1978:23). General García Valiño fretted about several companies of Republican commandos engaging in sabotage missions behind his lines.

The shielding of Valencia also can be seen as a positive response by soldiers to the Popular Army's efforts to improve their culture, especially the ability to read and write. The programs of the Republican armed forces taught literacy to tens of thousands and inspired pride in those involved (Prats 1938:31).[162] Commissars were rightly satisfied with the libraries and newspapers that they had created from scratch. A crash officer-training program discovered some real talent among former illiterates, who composed almost a quarter of males (and 40 percent of females) (figures from Nash 1995:19). In this case the Popular Army's training academies demonstrated that they could form competent officers quickly. A combination of a new esprit de corps, gratitude to the Republic, camaraderie, and self-preservation converted unlikely recruits into formidable soldiers.[163] It was at these moments, which were too rare for the success of the Republic, that it succeeded in creating citizen-soldiers.

At the same time, the morale of libertarian troops defending the Levante was shaky.[164] They showed a mixture of sacrifice and selfishness.[165] Suffering hundreds of casualties, they held off the better-armed enemy. Nonetheless, by the middle of May, small groups of between ten and twenty well-armed deserters were daily demanding food and assistance from CNT collectives and isolated farms in the district of Liria (Valencia).[166] The Liria collectives and in general those in the Valencian region had had a history of tension with regular army troops who requisitioned food and shelter without proper authorization.[167] Armed and hungry deserters, even if not ostensibly "fascist," represented a serious challenge to order in the Republican zone. They also reinforced fears among owners that the Republic was unable to secure their property. To halt the flux from the front, CNT officials recommended intensive patrolling of the countryside. Civilians complained about the conduct of certain units who embarked on drunken sprees in Valencia.[168] They kidnapped officials who attempted to discipline them and made civilians dig fortifications. Nationalist authorities accused retreating Republican forces of looting, pillaging, and assassinating near Bielsa (Huesca) and in Castellón.[169]

Insurgents probed weaknesses and initiated night raids against poorly armed units of the Popular Army protecting Valencia. Some of the latter retreated despite the orders and insults of a commander who called them cowards and opportunists (*chaqueteros*). They were exhausted, subject to "collective panic" and desertion (Martínez Bande 1977:53–54, 127). The failure of revolution and low pay demoralized others.[170] Many tried to better their lot by claiming disability and applying for reduced service. By the fall of 1938 in the Army of Levante, authorities reacted to suspicions of malingering by reviewing and questioning every soldier with a partial or full disability.[171] Health problems also lowered morale. In one battalion stationed near Soneja (Castellón), 35 percent of soldiers had scabies.[172] Rotten food gave others stomach disorders.[173] Officers had plenty of reason to worry that *franquista* propaganda that dwelled on Republican food shortages would continue to find a receptive audience among Popular Army soldiers.[174] The 101st Division reported that the calorie content of rations was too low to support basic activities.[175] Troops stationed at headquarters ate only one meal per day, usually beans with rice or potatoes. The latter had replaced other crops and had quickly become a key staple in the Republican zone (Ministerio de Agricultura 1938?). Many men could not acquire tobacco. Long lines in front of shops located in the rear also gave ample opportunity for grumbling against the Republican leadership.[176]

Civilian authorities accused commanders, especially General Miaja, of failing to coordinate military and civilian fortification efforts.[177] Many materials and hours of labor, including that of convicts, were poorly employed. According to a military intelligence report on fortifications protecting Valencia, security forces had organized three building battalions of prisoners and guards in the proportion of one guard for every six prisoners.[178] When the Subdirección General de Seguridad commanded the battalions, they were productive. In fact, they outperformed the Popular Army's own fortification brigades. However, after the Justice Ministry took charge, output declined drastically. One of the major reasons for the descent was the insufficiency of surveillance. For example, at Serra (Valencia) only two guards surveyed four hundred workers. An inspection in the sector of Albuixech revealed that none of the 180 men were working. Lack of food and tools also reduced output. Authorities planned to set output minimums and to requisition tools from storeowners and peasants.

On 1 May, Negrín profited from the defense of Valencia and the survival of the Republic in order to publish his Thirteen Points. The prime minister wished to solicit support from moderate public opinion both at home and abroad. He wanted to persuade property owners in the Republican zone and in the Western democracies that the Republic was, as Communists and others insisted, both democratic and bourgeois. In this context, among the most important of the Thirteen Points was protection of private property and guarantees of religious freedom. Most Catholics and property owners in the Republican zone probably remained skeptical. Owners persisted in hiding their possessions, whether food or vehicles, from Republican authorities.[179] Foreigners whose property had been collectivized seldom saw it returned (Bolloten 1991:636). Western democracies that Negrín was trying to persuade remained doubtful that Spain was a bourgeois republic. The United States maintained its neutrality, and although France was tempted to intervene militarily in favor of the Republic, Great Britain made sure that it would not.

Catholics, especially priests, continued to be persecuted for conspiring against the Republic. In one Catalan district (Solsona in the province of Lérida), the clergy organized deserters.[180] The impoverished inhabitants of Torres del Obispo (near Jaca) remained both very devout and extremely reactionary (Gabriel 1938:99). Mass was celebrated surreptitiously. In Republican eyes, the church and its servants remained key elements of Spanish "fascism." Religion indicated political affiliation (Lannon 1987:207). Other distrusted elements were property owners and white-collar professionals (doctors, lawyers, and military men). Hundreds of Catalan deserters, some religiously indifferent and others profoundly Catholic, remained hidden in the mountains (Martínez Bande 1975:86–87). The geography of Spain permitted a variety of dissidents to conceal themselves in the highlands.[181] Resistance to the Republic was not always based on political or religious motives. One small town, Montán (Lérida), was so united against the state, which was Republican in this instance, that all of its drafted young men had successfully avoided serving.[182] They continued to work the fields as if the war never existed. Draft-dodgers in the Republican zone usually adopted individual strategies to avoid conscription. Neither they nor their supporters rioted en masse in major cities as the Irish had in New York City during the U.S. Civil War or Londoners did during the English conflict (Carlton 1992:68).

Negrín and his closest advisors decided that only a spectacular military action could alter the declining fortunes of the Republic. They especially wanted to relieve pressure on the Valencian and Estremaduran fronts where Nationalists were making some progress. As the site of a new offensive, they chose a bend of the Ebro River, between Fayón (Zaragoza) and Benifallet (Tarragona). The Battle of the Ebro, as it became known, would develop into the longest and bloodiest struggle of the entire conflict (Martínez Bande 1978:62). After July, it may have been the Ebro offensive—not Republican fortifications—that was ultimately responsible for Loyalist control of Valencia. The Republican goal was to confuse communications between the Nationalists in the Levante and Catalonia and to restore, if possible, direct links between Catalonia and the rest of Republican Spain (Thomas 1961:544). The Popular Army concentrated one hundred thousand men, one hundred planes, and one hundred heavy guns (Jackson 1965:454). Recent recruits, who were not the optimum fighting age, formed the overwhelming majority of many divisions. They were either very young, eighteen or nineteen years old, or past the age of military prowess, thirty to forty (Tagüeña Lacorte 1978:130). In addition, divisions that fought the battle were far from complete. For example, the elite Thirty-fifth had three brigades that each held over three thousand men. The division totaled nearly twelve thousand men, of whom about forty-five hundred men were not armed. Many of the Popular Army's best troops were under Communist leadership. Others, draftees from Barcelona, were angered by the terror bombings of their city and proved eager to fight (Pons Prades 1974:26). Republicans crossed the river in the night of 24 July, achieving complete surprise on this front that, according to a high-ranking Nationalist officer, was characterized by *far niente* (Kindelán 1945:140–47). Like its forerunners, the greatest confrontation of the war ruptured the live-and-let-live laziness on both sides. At the beginning of the battle, Republicans did not experience the fierce resistance to their initial thrusts that had characterized Nationalist defenses at Belchite, Teruel, and Brunete. Nationalist troops, who had neglected to construct fortifications, fled during the attack. The insurgent Fiftieth Division did not offer even token resistance. Republican troops were able to hold former Nationalist territory for a week, despite powerful enemy artillery and air attacks. They captured thousands of prisoners while suffering only hundreds of casualties.

But soon the familiar pattern asserted itself: the Nationalists were able to call up reinforcements to stem the Republican offensive and ultimately to push it back. The lack of Republican aggressiveness in Estremadura and on other fronts allowed Nationalists to move the Seventy-fourth Division from Villanueva de la Serena (Cáceres) to reinforce the Ebro line. From the first day Nationalist domination of the air restricted Loyalist mobility (Kindelán 1945:140; Howson 1999:241). The entire Condor Legion and heavy artillery were thrown into battle and devastated Republican troops. Kindelán could not comprehend how the "reds" allowed logistic incompetence to interfere with their air force in a battle of their own making. The Popular Army lacked trucks to move men and materiel. It was especially difficult to transfer heavy artillery across the river. Transport was never effectively rationalized. Like food supplies, trucks were hoarded by the units that possessed them. These deficiencies, especially the shortage of trains, led to the suspension of planned offensives (Rojo 1974:85).

The Nationalist counteroffensive was relentless but extremely slow since it lacked sufficient reserves. On the Ebro, as around Valencia, Republicans offered fierce resistance that won the respect of elite Nationalist forces.[183] However, by early August Franco had put the Loyalists on the defensive. The insurgents demonstrated once again their logistic superiority. According to a pro-Nationalist historian, Franco's support services functioned "nearly perfectly" (Martínez Bande 1978:314). Líster (1966:173) admitted that the enemy constructed formidable fortifications, organized artillery effectively, and fought methodically. Lincoln volunteers reported poor performances by some Spanish troops (Rosenstone 1969:326–27). Draconian discipline was imposed, and officers were authorized to execute deserters and self-injurers on the spot (Martínez Bande 1978:160). In early August, commissars tried to create an atmosphere of hatred for the former, but by the end of the month, desertions had intensified, especially among the youngest soldiers (Tagüeña Lacorte 1978:155). The sporadic lack of supplies and clothing induced even some of the most dedicated and politically aware soldiers to abandon their positions. Republican combatants were well paid (20 pesetas per day) but poorly shod with only sandals (Martínez Bande 1978:100). Republican reserves also suffered demoralization. Many were over thirty and had previously tried to avoid military service but had been rounded up in a desperate attempt to fill vacant units. By 10 September, the Popular Army had lost twenty-five thousand soldiers, many of them through voluntary flight (225). Republican patrols recaptured and shot a few of the unlucky (Pons Prades 1974:276). Nationalist intelligence realized that Republican reserves were inadequate and often unarmed. An important exception was the police, usually Guardias de Asalto or Carabineros (Negrín's favorites) who had limited military experience but were needed to repress potential individualist rebellions and anarchist riots.[184] Even with logistical and aerial dominance, it took until November to oust the Republicans from the salient they had won in July. By that time, both armies were exhausted and had depleted whatever modern weapons they possessed.

Republican casualties exceeded Nationalist ones. Loyalists suffered seventy thousand casualties during the four-month battle.[185] Tagüeña estimated total losses of the Popular Army at the end of November at sixty thousand men. Líster agreed that the Popular Army sacrificed many of its best remaining troops. For example, the Thirty-fifth Division, which was assigned some of the toughest tasks, suffered four thousand casualties. "When the Internationals left, we lost more than three thousand excellent veterans, most of them officers." To replace them, the division received thirty-five hundred men, "in majority deserters, amnestied ex-prisoners, and older draftees" (Tagüeña Lacorte quoted in Martínez Bande 1978:239).[186] In the Forty-fifth Division, another three thousand Internationals left the front, and the Army of the Ebro lost a total of six thousand first-rate soldiers. The lack of success at the Ebro broke the spirit of many of the Lincolns, who became war-weary and home-sick (Rosenstone 1969:319). Some International battalions suffered casualty rates of 80 percent. The withdrawal of the remaining Internationals, who were eventually sent home in November, further damaged the quality of Republican forces. In December, Nationalists would take advantage of greater Republican losses in quantity and quality to launch a major offensive against Catalonia.

The Battle of the Ebro resembled in many ways that of Brunete. The Popular Army won an initial advantage by using a large force to initiate a surprise attack on a summer night. Nocturnal assaults were recognition that Nationalists had superior means and methods. They revealed Republican dependence on surprise, which compensated for troops of "little combativity" (Martínez Bande 1981:94). Night attack—the military strategy of the poor—was the Republican response to obvious inferiority. Most military experts, including Clausewitz, have regarded night offensives ambivalently at best (Holmes 1985:123). It is a form of warfare in which even the best troops get lost and confused (Wintringham 1939:287). Soldiers—like most people—are least effective between midnight and 6:00 A.M. Furthermore, less aggressive troops may have experienced a sense of shame during night attacks and wished to see the faces of their enemy (Pons Prades 1974:262).

The insurgents would gradually prevail in a war of attrition. In the closing months of 1938, they received dramatically increased aid from the Germans (Coverdale 1975:374). In the middle of November, Germany and Nationalist Spain signed a new agreement in which the continuing need for supplies induced Franco to make major concessions to his Nazi ally, which gained favorable mining rights and a Nationalist promise to pay the entire expenses of the Condor Legion (Jackson 1965:463). In greater quantities than ever before, German arms and materiel flowed rapidly to Franco's forces. On the other side, despite bureaucratic obstacles and the exhaustion of the gold deposited in Moscow, the Soviets continued to ship supplies to the Republic; nevertheless, the badly needed *matériel* did not reach Catalonia until February 1939, when it was nearly too late to help Popular Army forces (Viñas 1979:420; Howson 1999:242–43).

During the Ebro battle, conditions degenerated further in what remained of the Republican zone. On the Estremadura front, Nationalist troops made gains in August, and Miaja had to send some of his better units from Levante to stop them (Martínez Bande 1978; Rojo 1974:49). The leadership of the Popular

Army had a difficult time allocating soldiers to avoid inordinately weakening its numerous fragile fronts. They therefore found it difficult to initiate successful diversionary actions. Indeed, Communists have attributed the ultimate failure of the Ebro offensive and the eventual Republican defeat to the passivity of Popular Army forces in the south and in the center that did not launch attacks to support the Ebro offensive (Modesto 1969:246). Their Leninist perspective has attributed the blame to high-ranking officers and important politicians.[187] However, the Communist "top-down" history ignores popular cynicism. Like soldiers, civilians struggled for their own rights and neglected the collective good. Workers only marginally associated with war industries fought to get higher rations reserved for defense personnel.[188] Civilian and military authorities had to institute strict control of roads and inspection of merchandise in Catalonia and Levante to counter rampant hoarding and black marketeering.[189] All food, energy, and soap products needed a circulation voucher, and hundreds of armed soldiers scrutinized everything that moved on highways. They confiscated vehicles and imprisoned any soldier without proper travel authorization. At Requena (Valencia), *Etapas* devoted more men (14) to controlling the Madrid-Valencia highway than to any other task, including guarding prisoners of war (5) or patrolling the town and its outskirts (4).[190] All commodities circulating in the Republican zone that were not accompanied by an official voucher—including those that belonged to unions and Popular Front organizations—were to be impounded. Nonprecious metals, junked cars, hides, paper, and rags could be expropriated if their owners—whether individuals or organizations—did not register them.[191] The army controlled prices and regulated food distribution to avoid riots by women, which did occur both in Madrid and Barcelona.[192] Soldiers detained those who sold at above official prices or who butchered animals without permission. In the province of Almería alone, hundreds if not thousands of individuals were involved in hiding or adulterating food and—most frequently—violating price controls.[193] A forty-six-year-old man was fined one thousand pesetas for transporting forty-nine kilos of flour without proper documentation.[194] A miller was caught with 32,500 eggs and was fined fifty thousand pesetas and sentenced to two years in a work camp.[195] A small shopkeeper, whose house was located on the highway, engaged in the black marketeering of hundreds of kilos of soap.[196] He was fined one thousand pesetas and sentenced to two months imprisonment. Corruption touched even the smallest of villages. In Sufli (Almería), the supply delegate who sold the oil earmarked for his town to a neighbor was caught and fined three thousand pesetas.[197] Another mayor provided local *labradores* with illegal travel documents that allowed them to ship pigs outside the province.[198]

Mayors and town councils attempted—probably successfully—to ignore price controls, but they risked provoking formal complaints from their own citizens. In one case, the JSU (Juventudes Socialistas Unificades) of Félix (Almería) denounced the entire town council to authorities.[199] Soldiers themselves would constantly steal from fields and gardens, even if the produce was destined for "the collective good of our army."[200] The head of the General Staff of the Army of the Center, José López Otero, was forced to admonish his troops that the "continual requisitions of horses and mules that our units have wrongfully committed are causing grave harm to the national economy and agriculture in particular."[201] He reminded them of the official order of 6 July 1937 that prohibited any requisitions of livestock for any length of time. On behalf of the Republican forces in the Center and the South, Vicente Rojo complained directly to Negrín concerning food shortages, vitamin deficiencies, and the inability to obtain dependable production figures.[202] The general recommended centralization of distribution and purchase of imports that could provide greater nutritional value for civilian and military populations.

Products that should have been abundant, such as orange juice, never reached the front in sufficient quantities. Chemicals and materials, which could have been produced in Spain, had to be imported. For example, waterproofing materials, such as tallow, usually came from abroad.[203] Even when imports arrived at the port of Barcelona, they could not be transported.[204] Sixty tons of coal and fourteen hundred tons of cotton stagnated on the docks. There was no means to move raw materials to factories in Vich, Ripoll, Manresa, and Mataró where they could be processed into shirts, socks, gloves, and footwear for Republican soldiers. These bottlenecks idled workers, who may have thought that military contracts would at least provide them with some employment. Concealment aggravated shortages of other raw materials, such as non-precious metals, rags, paper, hides, cloth.[205] National authorities suspected local officials of inadequate zeal and made them bear responsibility for hoarding in their jurisdictions.

Lack of food and consequent poor health undermined discipline (Puig Casas 1999:207). Protein and perhaps carbohydrate consumption was adequate, but the soldiers' diet lacked vitamins, especially D and B.[206] Nor was hygiene adequate. More than a thousand cases of scabies were reported for August alone. In the Castellón sector near Artana, what senior officers considered cowardice undermined the Republican war effort.[207] The enemy was able to occupy positions "without resistance" and Republican soldiers retreated in disorder while abandoning munitions to the enemy. Among the many reasons for the lack of combative spirit were a "false notion of friendship" that led to the decline of officers' authority, poorly maintained weapons, disinterest in building fortifications, and a complacency—promoted by live and let live—that the enemy would not attack. High command attributed "inefficiency" to the "cowardice of low-ranking officers" who neglected labor on fortifications in spite of repeated orders.[208] Construction inadequacies were potentially mortal because the Republic had placed its hopes in gaining time. "To fortify is to win" was its slogan in August. Battalion officers often turned in "totally false reports" that hid their "cowardice and incompetence." In the fall of 1938, the same army corps continued to be wracked by desertions.[209]

Fleas, of course, were even more numerous than defectors. Malaria was rampant (539 cases), and was by far the most important infectious disease. In the Army of the Center eleven to twelve thousand cases were reported between 1937 and 1938 (Estellés Salarich 1986:52). In the Levante, a shortage of personnel inhibited a prevention program. There were even a few cases of typhoid fever. In general, although hospital care for the most seriously ill or injured was satisfactory, healthcare personnel were insufficiently numerous and inadequately instructed to treat the ill. Many had been assigned to Sanidad because they were too weak physically to serve in other branches.[210] This sort of selection, which was common in many wars, was counterproductive since soldiers had little confidence that the wounded would be evacuated quickly or treated effectively (for U.S. Civil War see McPherson 1988:484). Stretcher-bearers needed strength and endurance.

A physician who practiced in both zones reported that the major reason for the better recovery rate of Nationalist soldiers was the ability of Franco's forces to transport the wounded quickly to hospitals (Zúmel 1986:85). The Republican forces permitted too much time to elapse. Polluted water and infected food service personnel caused seventeen cases of typhoid fever in September.[211] In contrast, at least some Nationalist troops were vaccinated against typhoid (Colmegna 1941:206). Scabies had spread "alarmingly" among Republican troops. The skin disease was so widespread that health officials recommended that special treatment centers be established.[212] Therapeutic centers were instituted, and soldiers were forced to follow strictly a regulated personal hygiene program. Most of those treated were cured in less than a week. However, the quartermaster did not supply the centers with enough food, and the sick went hungry. "Conditions in the hospital were no better than those elsewhere. There was no heating, the food was meager, and amenities generally were, if anything, less than at home" (Mira 1939:1217). The pilfering of hospital food may have also depressed patients.[213] Nor were clean clothing and soap sufficient. Furthermore, a number of infected soldiers had to remain on the front. To these health problems was added venereal disease.[214]

In August, the sick outnumbered the wounded by nearly two to one, a proportion that resembled Nationalist figures on quiet fronts and also the British and U.S. armies in World War II.[215] But by September, the Republican ratio rose to five to one.[216] During that month, accidents put almost as many soldiers out of action as enemy fire. Soldiers stationed in the same sector near Chóvar (Castellón) suffered from ill health, caused in large part by lack of food: "The official ration does not supply even half of the needed proteins. Nor are fats adequate. Calories never surpass 2,400. Vitamins are always insufficient."[217] Scanty food and deficiencies of vitamin A delayed or prevented recovery of those wounded by enemy artillery. The most powerful propaganda weapon in the Nationalist arsenal was broadcasting on loudspeakers their daily menu to Republican troops stationed in opposing trenches.[218] Insurgents proved their claims of good eating by emerging from the trenches and showing the incredulous and envious "reds" samples of their meals, including sherry and tobacco. When Nationalists asked for a taste of Republican food, the *"rojos"* politely declined.

On other fronts, nutritional deficiencies generated small and large protests.[219] Many soldiers had a more ample supply of munitions than food, clothing, or water.[220] Veterans of the Abraham Lincoln Brigade overwhelmingly agreed that the key to leadership was making sure that men were fed and clothed (Dollard 1943:58). Commissars realized this and sought their own sources of food to win over minds by ministering to bodies.[221] Servicemen became depressed when they learned that their families in the rear also lacked a proper diet. Soldiers stationed at Alturas or Locau, many of whom were recruits who had replaced the killed or injured at Teruel, needed water for washing. They committed unspecified outrages (*desmanes*) in villages.

Carlos de Baráibar, a Socialist close to Largo Caballero, was one of the few to examine the failure of the food processing industry and transportation in the Republican zone.[222] In the fall of 1938, he noted that the most consequential problem that the Republic faced was provisioning itself. City dwellers regarded peasants as fascists who hid their produce or charged outrageous prices for it. Yet, according to de Baráibar, peasants were profoundly committed to a new, revolutionary Spain; however, they were victims of unwise policies pushed by Communists and others who ignored the just needs of the countryside. The maximums set by the government were especially unfair. He asserted that agricultural *tasas* had risen only 30 to 40 percent since July 1936. In contrast, the price of clothing had jumped 600 to 850 percent. Maximums only intensified the food supply problem by encouraging the peasantry to restrict production, thus dividing the urban proletariat from the Spanish peasantry, which was still demographically dominant. De Baráibar argued that the Republic could not win without a complete economic reorganization, but, understandably given the complexity of the problem, he neglected to provide a clear outline of the necessary changes.

Throughout the war, complaints about leave were almost as frequent as those about food. Both lowered the morale of Republican forces.[223] Some took off for a short period, and a few had the good fortune to be posted close to the Mediterranean coast, where they spent much of the day on the beach (Gárate Córdoba 1976b:99). During a quiet spell in the Huesca sector on the Aragon front, soldiers would go AWOL and then return to their posts a few days tardy.[224] In defiance of draconian penalties, many reentered late from authorized leave.[225] In certain units, latecomers composed the majority of those arrested.[226] The Popular Army could not punish all offenders since to do so might have dangerously reduced manpower. Whether on quiet or active fronts, the rank and file griped constantly concerning favoritism. Officers defended leave policy by arguing that they awarded it on the basis of a soldier's "meritorious actions" and his replaceability.[227] Ideology, even if dispensed by the most articulate commissars, could not overcome homesickness and hunger. Desires to go home increased when Nationalists conquered villages where Republican soldiers had been raised.[228] Geography proved more powerful than politics.

There were enough abuses and arrests to lend credence to the popular assumption that everyone with official access to food and supplies was corrupt.[229] Commissars were posted to watch and control quartermasters, but the situation of dual power increased tensions and consequently lessened the efficiency of the latter. Employees of the quartermaster aroused jealousies and continued to be suspected, often with reason, of taking advantage of their position for personal gain.[230] Shortsighted regional quartermasters made exaggerated requests during periods of generalized shortage and thus rendered impossible the task of civilian officials in charge of distribution and allocation.[231] For example, while the populations of certain high-priority cities—such as the port and arsenal town of Cartagena—were nearly starving, quartermasters of the nearby Army of Levante asked for twice as much olive oil and soap than their real needs dictated.[232] CNT members reported "misbehavior" and "irregularities" in the Communist-dominated quartermaster's service of the XIX Corps of the Army of Levante.[233] "Certain elements . . . without scruples" took advantage of their positions for "their own personal benefit." To avoid provoking jealousies and resentments, officers were ordered not to eat or drink their special rations in front of their men.[234] They were also told to keep their women out of sight. Powerful currents of corruption overwhelmed nominal political commitment and showed the tendentiousness of CNT partisans who blamed problems on Communists or other political parties. Throughout revolutionary history, chauffeurs and dockers have achieved notoriety for misappropriation (Cobb 1987:260, 282). Truck drivers quite plausibly claimed that they should not be sanctioned for goods missing from their vehicles, since armed hitchhikers were able to stop them and steal whatever they wanted.[235] By the summer of 1938, it was hard to know the identity of these myriad thieves.

Both camps continued to ignore prohibitions on fraternization, including a September 1938 order from the *generalísimo* himself.[236] Nationalist and Republican soldiers and officers met in the fields of Aragon to gather melons and tomatoes and voiced similar complaints concerning the exploitation of workers.[237] They exchanged tobacco, rolling paper, and propaganda. On the Catalan front, a Nationalist chaplain, who had defied an order not to exchange words or goods with the enemy, was placed under arrest for two weeks.[238] Spurred by the British and French press, which reported that on diverse fronts soldiers were exchanging newspapers and even playing ball together, the Nationalist high command reiterated a total prohibition on all contact with the enemy.[239] Nationalists supposedly initiated fraternization, but Republican troops were receptive to their overtures.[240] Officers of the Popular Army ended budding friendships by shooting and injuring several insurgent soldiers.

The Army of Estremadura provides the best (or the worst, from a militant perspective) example of fraternization. Both sides regarded the Estremadura theater as "nondecisive" (Martínez Bande 1981:15). This "nondecisiveness" is accurate only in the narrowest military terms. After the lines were stabilized in the summer of 1936, aggressive war in this part of the peninsula became a distant memory until 1938. No major battles occurred during that period in Estremadura. However, if the war is analyzed from the standpoints of both experience and outcome, then this front was crucial. Líster (1966:223–35) has attributed to Republican inaction on the Estremadura front major responsibility for the failures in 1938 of the Ebro offensive and the subsequent collapse of Catalonia. From February to July 1938, Nationalist attacks had gradually moved the front from the province of Cordova into Badajoz.[241] The insurgents were determined to eliminate what was called the Mérida pocket, which some of the Republican leadership—especially Largo Caballero—had wanted to use as a stepping stone to divide the Nationalist zone and hinder enemy communications with Portugal. In April and May, Nationalists occupied Valsequillo (Cordova) and Blázquez and forced Republicans to abandon the Sierra del Torozo and the Sierra Trapera.

Near Castuera in the rich Serena Valley, fraternization was common and even "habitual."[242] What was unusual in this case was that fraternizers were from supposedly elite forces. Republican Assault Guards of the Twelfth Brigade, which totaled fourteen hundred men, made frequent contact with Falangists and a requeté, who sported a beret. Requetés had earned a reputation as one of the fiercest components of the Nationalist armies, and Assault Guards were frequently called upon to round up deserters in the Republican zone (Blinkhorn 1975:261; Martínez Bande 1975:53). Nonetheless, the usual trading of tobacco and newspapers occurred among small groups of a dozen soldiers.[243] They called each other "comrades," embraced, and consumed alcoholic beverages together. They gave each other affectionate nicknames (rojillos, el Madrileño, and Gil el Espartero), revealing the formation of a community that recognized individual differences (see Pitt-Rivers 1954:168). A Falangist alférez (provisional lieutenant) proposed a group photo, but prudent Assault Guards politely declined. Officers wanted to end fraternization because it demonstrated insufficient antifascism. They feared it would encourage desertions and reveal significant information to the enemy.

The Assault Guards had been used as a shock brigade, but apparently a long stay in the trenches had dwindled their fighting spirit. The Twelfth contained "many alienated men."[244] Other units that were near the Twelfth lost their will to fight.[245] Their neighbors' habits of trading and conversing with the enemy, consorting with females and taking unauthorized leave set an example that other companies followed. "Prolonged inactivity" in "a majority of sectors" produced immobility.[246] This passive attitude earned the condemnation of those investigating the collapse of the Popular Army on this front. Soldiers charged repeatedly that the Twelfth had become a Communist fiefdom where the uncommitted and even known rightists found a safe haven.[247] Favoritism and *caciqueo* were rampant, and troops tried their best to avoid activity. In March, thirty-two Assault Guards went over to the Nationalists.[248] The Twelfth, despite its supposed elite status, had more desertions in March than any other unit.[249] At the beginning of April, sixty Assault Guards fled to the enemy, and others followed.

In his report on the collapse of the Army of Estremadura, General Asensio confirmed assertions that Socialists made in early June. He implied that the fraternization of the Twelfth Brigade revealed enough information to the enemy to allow a successful attack.[250] Nationalists had profited by advancing through the Twelfth's sector, which quickly collapsed in "disorderly retreat." The Twelfth lacked cohesion, had no commissar and had acted with great independence and "political partiality." In Estremadura, live and let live did not signify an informal agreement that recognized an equal balance of force or a basic commitment to one's country or cause as it had in World War I. During that conflict, nonaggressive soldiers refused to permit the enemy to occupy their trenches. In contrast, the Estremaduran variety of live and let live allowed individuals or small groups of Republican soldiers to avoid danger and save their own skins. Informal agreements to prevent casualties marked a fervently individualistic desire to preserve one's own body and failed to preserve a basic patriotic or ideological commitment.

In June, Nationalists captured strategic positions on the left bank of the Zújar River, sometimes without facing Republican resistance. Once again, the Twelfth Brigade, whose penchant for live and let live was well-known, abandoned defensible positions. Attempts to retake them failed, in part because of the lack of artillery support. In addition, health officials could not evacuate the wounded.[251] Spoiled food put others out of action.[252] Some units fought surprisingly well, whereas others—especially those with large numbers of recruits—lacked "speed and mobility." Desertions were numerous. During combat between 20 and 24 June, the 109th Mixed Brigade reported only 11 killed and 26 injured but 659 "disappeared."[253] An enemy who knew where to attack, how to soften up the adversary with artillery and aviation, and when to follow up with effective cavalry charges outclassed Republican forces.

Inexperienced Popular Army troops had little "combative spirit" and became demoralized.[254] Some important villages were abandoned "without any resistance" to divisions of Galicians who, as we have seen, were not usually known for their ferocity.[255] The enemy captured at least two thousand Republican soldiers.[256] Nationalist successes encouraged fifth columnists to attack the Republican army in Castuera and surrounding towns.[257] The Republican counterattack between 21 June and 1 July was ineffective (cf. Vila Izquierdo 1984:138).

By the end of July 1938, the Republic had lost the Mérida pocket and the fertile Serena Valley (Badajoz) (Martínez Bande 1981:213). Strategically, the loss meant the end of any hope of separating the Nationalist armies in the north from those in the south. The defeat was also significant since only the rich lowland areas of Valencia matched the Serena Valley in agricultural wealth (Pons Prades 1977:318). If some units defended their positions with great valor or fought their way out of encirclement with knives and bayonets, others fled without a fight.[258] Many soldiers had neglected to fire their arms to obstruct the enemy advance. The 103rd Brigade, which had a record of abandoning positions since the year's beginning, was especially disappointing. It "unjustifiably" retreated twice and proved incapable of defending a twenty-kilometer front. A lack of manpower, transportation, and weapons propelled its collapse.[259] Forty percent of its troops needed firearms. Perhaps because they did not possess any weapons, most of the Republican deserters stationed in Estremadura defected unarmed.[260] The noncommissioned officers of the 103rd were untrained and inexperienced.[261] Many of their men lacked shoes. Most of the brigade's best veterans had been transferred to the eastern front. Authorities decided to disarm the 103rd, distribute its weapons to other troops, and assign a large number of its men to fortification brigades. Inadequate leave policy, which left troops in the trenches for months and even years, nonexistent or poorly situated fortifications, fraternization with the enemy, and poor leadership convinced numerous servicemen in the Army of Estremadura not to fight.

The deficiencies of what a chief commissar believed to be an egotistical and unqualified officer corps contributed to the defeat of the Army of Estremadura. Officers defied regulations by locating their command posts too far from the front and by permitting their relatives easy access to them. Officers ignored the most elementary lessons of military science. Lectures offered by experts on fortifications, weapons, topography, and tactics had little impact. Those who had graduated from Escuelas Populares were often incompetent. Upon completing an intensive course that lasted only ten days, the schools had promoted soldiers to sergeant. Repeating charges leveled against the Twelfth, a number of observers accused the entire Army of Estremadura of Communist favoritism and corruption.[262] The accusations of anti-Communists were reminiscent of the charges leveled by antilibertarians against the militias at the war's outbreak.

According to anti-Communist officers, the Army of Estremadura had become "the private hunting ground" of the Party. More ominously, they asserted that Communists shot their enemies and justified this by claiming that they were trying to escape. The PCE had allowed Colonel Juan Bautista Gómez, a Mexican, to run the 115 Brigada Mixta during seven months. "An adventurer without conscience," Gómez desired only "a continuous orgy." He permitted subordinates to loot the quartermaster's stocks. It was said that Communist officers offered themselves big banquets at public expense.

The July defeat was the culmination of all these real or imagined inadequacies. The 148th Mixed Brigade also fought poorly or not at all. Guerrilla units attached to the Army of Estremadura "dedicated themselves exclusively to the task of pillaging villages abandoned by civilians."[263] The continual failures of these units showed the persistent cynicism that dominated the Army of Estremadura. In July, the Twelfth Brigade again failed to hold the line.[264] In fact, at least forty-six men, including two officers and four sergeants, deserted to the enemy. Defections from the Twelfth were so numerous that when that unit was withdrawn, Nationalist soldiers joked that they were surprised that any of its men remained.[265] The losses of the Twelfth during the campaign to eliminate the pocket at the end of July were reported to be 1,134 men (Martínez Bande 1981:242). Its mishaps were blamed on Ricardo Burillo, an Assault Guard and a member of the PCE who had participated in the unsuccessful defense of Toledo and who had led the Estremadura army since November 1937. Burillo had acquired a checkered war record. Although he had commanded the unsuccessful siege of the Toledo Alcázar, General Asensio praised his role in the defense of the Sierra de Guadarrama in the late summer of 1936 (Asensio 1938:20–21). In Estremadura, Burillo was more efficient eliminating his party's political opponents than in conducting warfare (Martínez Bande 1976:11).[266] He refused to put miners on the front lines while young Assault Guards remained in the rear. He therefore created the Twelfth Assault Brigade to fight on the front. This caused "considerable bewilderment" among the guards who resented front-line duty, particularly when most of their fellow guards stationed outside of Estremadura remained in the rear. Burillo heightened the hostility by his reluctance to promote officers of the Twelfth. A "nonintervention agreement" with the enemy encouraged rampant desertions.[267] In addition to the 12th, other brigades—such as the 86th and 104th— were highly affected by defections.[268] The 114th Mixed Brigade was so wracked by flights that fascist cells and organizations were suspected of organizing them.[269] From its very beginning, the 113th Brigade had also suffered "a high percentage of desertions toward Nationalist lines."[270] Its soldiers' main goal was "tranquility and harmony with the enemy," and they conversed constantly with fascists: "They remained inactive, unaggressive, and unwilling to follow orders. They spent entire months without firing a shot when we had a ten to one advantage in troops. They were completely apathetic."[271] Some members of the 114th who had fraternized with the enemy were imprisoned.[272] The number of self-inflicted wounds was high enough to make any injury suspect, and as a result, soldiers were occasionally thrown into military prisons without proof of deliberate self-mutilation. In fortification brigades, the situation was even worse. Authorities suggested that one hundred local and devoted antifascists who had belonged to Popular Front organizations before 19 July 1936 be dispersed as undercover agents among laborers. Their mission was to gather information that could help smash an alleged fascist ring. The desertions that accompanied live and let live caused much valuable time and resources to be diverted from fighting Nationalists to conducting investigations.

Many defections were consequences of the rampant corruption in recruiting centers in Ciudad Real and Orgaz, where the bribing of doctors and other officials was thought to be widespread. Despite legislation that threatened severe punishment, corrupt and politically unreliable physicians and officers exempted thousands of perfectly healthy soldiers from front-line duty. Those with influence and the correct (Communist) political connections found cushy jobs far from the front.[273] Others received "disabilities out of favoritism" from recruitment officers and doctors. The unprivileged and even fervent antifascists became discouraged, and some tried to flee.[274] In the early spring, street demonstrators in Almadén protested directly to the head of the Army of Estremadura, and a Ciudad Real newspaper demanded the repeal of decisions of the military Medical Tribunals. Popular pressures forced a review of all their judgments, and 77 percent of the "disabled" were declared fit for normal service.

Many of the deserters were from towns and villages of Castilla–La Mancha. Approximately one thousand took to the hills and, with the proper assistance, might have been prepared to act as Nationalist guerrillas (Salas Larrazábal 1973:2060). In April 1938, in the provinces of Toledo, Ciudad Real, and Badajoz, Republican forces undertook "an extensive operation to clean out armed groups of refugees, deserters, and enemies of the [Republican] regime . . . that lived off the land . . . with the complicity of the civilian population."[275] These groups were the closest equivalent in the Spanish civil war to the Greens, the bands of irregulars who sprang up during the Russian civil conflict to fight Reds and Whites alike. Throughout the summer of 1938, mopping up operations, which bagged more than several hundred deserters, continued in the Sierra de Alcaraz (Albacete) and the Toledo hills.[276] One immodest officer claimed to have smashed the local fifth column that had organized the flights of "hundreds" of defectors to the Montes de Toledo.[277] Elite units were ordered to patrol strategic points in the Montes.[278] Using armed force, they apprehended "personnel who had deserted, draft dodgers, and the fascists who had infiltrated among them." Republican officials feared that the fugitives might link up with advancing Nationalist forces.[279] Intelligence agents estimated that "three thousand individuals—deserters and refugees"—were hiding from the Army in the Sierra de Porzuna and in the Campo de Montiel.[280] Chances of capturing them were slim. The massive nature of desertions and draft dodging implied a significant degree of popular support for those who took to the hills: "There are villages where local authorities aid and abet those avoiding military service." The *pueblo* protected its own, not the Republic. In these towns young men lacked what one military historian has called "initial motivation" or the willingness to join or be drafted into an army (see Lynn 1984:35). Nor was avoidance of military service limited to the anonymous. Well-known ministers and other prominent officials engineered exemptions for family members and close friends (Rojo 1974:33).

Commissars suspected that those joining an antifascist organization after 19 July who had families in the fascist zone might desert.[281] Recent recruits, several of whom were shot and killed in June 1938 when they tried to flee to the enemy, seemed to have been less reliable than veterans.[282] For example, the Army of Estremadura quickly drafted union workers from the province of Ciudad Real to construct fortifications. Building on the front had been nearly entirely neglected even though soldiers had been inactive for months and had had plenty of time on their hands.[283] The conscripted laborers assumed that they would be working in the rear and were dismayed to find themselves on the frontlines. They objected to working at the front, claiming that the unions, not the government, had mobilized them. Therefore, they believed that they were not obligated to put their lives on the line. Encouraged by the long and loosely guarded front, nearly seven hundred of these largely illiterate and "politically uneducated" union workers deserted to the rear in the summer of 1938. The number of defectors overwhelmed the resources of local authorities and permitted deserters to abandon the lines with impunity. The military consequence of this alienation was inadequate fortifications. Construction was so neglected that even after two years on a relatively stable front, no adequate defense system had been built. Especially needed was a second line of trenches. These deficiencies facilitated the Nationalist offensive and made it surprisingly rapid and effective.[284]

The demoralization of the Army of Estremadura seemed even greater than the feckless Army of Andalusia.[285] Soldiers' pay never arrived, and men were not provided with uniforms or shoes, let alone tobacco.[286] Lack of transport lowered output. So did in certain cases the shortage of tools, especially the unavailability of dynamite to mine the rocky terrain.[287] Even with supplies, many units "worked badly" and were "depressed."[288] Their officers had acquired poor reputations. Commissars charged that the commander of the Fifty-second Battalion of Fortifications was not a true antifascist and was more interested in his pay than anything else. Some of his men, who were spread out in the fields gathering the harvest, had "returned discreetly to their homes." Many deserters counseled others to do the same. They were discouraged for several reasons. They were not paid regularly and were conscious of the steady remuneration in the Nationalist Army.[289] Defectors charged that certain officers abused and threatened them. The transfer of one especially abusive captain to a new company provoked the desertions of most (172) of its soldiers. Attempts to limit flight by posting guards sometimes failed since the guards themselves would also defect. Few sergeants and corporals could control their men.

In June and early July, the General Staff permitted some of the best troops that it possessed—including several divisions, an antitank group, and heavy artillery—to be transferred to the Levante, where they were needed to save Valencia.[290] Reassignments had removed approximately half (25,000–30,000) of the troops of the Army of Estremadura, including its most experienced veterans.[291] Burillo reported that Negrín and his generals had concluded that "an inch of ground in Levante was worth miles in Extremadura" (Burillo quoted in Martínez Bande 1981:243). Even though the Popular Army outnumbered the enemy in Estremadura, remaining Republican soldiers were "nearly worthless." They had spent too much time in the trenches without being relieved or granted leave. The Republic did not take advantage of the Estremaduran calm to improve or to train its troops. Investigators of the SIM (Servicio de Investigación Militar), an agency that the Republic created in August 1937 to fight against subversive activities, confirmed the pernicious effect of the transfer of good soldiers from certain Loyalist positions.[292] The intelligence service charged that the reassignment left an entire area—Villanueva de la Serena—vulnerable, even though it was likely that Nationalists might attack there.[293] The initial objective of the well-coordinated Nationalist offensive in Estremadura was to prevent more Republican troops from leaving for the east. However, on 2 July, Franco—realizing the transfers had weakened his enemy—ordered the "elimination of the Mérida pocket" (Vila Izquierdo 1984:138). The prospects of capturing the Serena Valley, one of the wealthiest cereal and livestock areas that remained in the Republican zone, and of controlling a new railroad line to Andalusia convinced the *generalísimo* to alter his objectives.[294] From 20 to 24 July, Nationalists would take advantage of the "low morale" of Republican forces to conquer an unexpectedly large sector of the front. Insurgents were superior in communications, vehicles, and arms. For example, on a one-hundred-kilometer front, Republican forces had only thirteen hundred rifles. Loyalist cavalry, infantry, and artillery all functioned poorly and without coordination. Aviation was nonexistent. The lack of railroad track in the region inhibited transportation. Nor had officers stopped the frivolous use of automobiles, whose careless circulation continued to produce an inordinate number of accidents. Republican hospitals maintained their reputation for being poorly equipped and distinctly inferior to their Nationalist counterparts (Gómez-Trigo Ochoa 1986:35; Zúmel 1986:88).

The food and labor problems of the Republic directly affected the outcome of the battle. During the offensive approximately sixty-five hundred men were engaged in collecting the harvest instead of digging fortifications. Even when qualified personnel were in uniform, lack of transportation prevented them from inspecting construction and fortification sites. As before, requests by certain brigades for more victuals than they really needed exacerbated scarcities of food.[295] The quartermaster had warned that the food reserves of certain units stationed in wealthy agricultural areas were unnecessarily large (*Servicios de Intendencia* 1938:22). Five days after the attack began, thousands were still working in remote *pueblos* far from the control of their officers. "Massive desertions" demonstrated that Republican military cadres had never militarized these peasants.[296]

Measures taken to stop unsuitable practices were largely ignored. Officers continued to inflate the numbers of their troops so that they could get more supplies, even though they risked arrest if caught. Hoarding by some units was spectacularly revealed when they received transfer orders and requested an unusually high number of trucks and vans to move their illicitly accumulated goods. Others just took what they needed from peasants.[297] The rapidity of enemy progress prevented the evacuation of thousands of tons of supplies.[298] The Nationalist advance finally forced one of the "municipalities and collectives [that] had always resisted a full accounting of their stocks . . . to offer (the quartermaster) 10,000 kg. of cheese a few hours before it would fall into the hands of the enemy." Civilians were as mendacious as the military. The *Etapas* Battalion uncovered the extent of peasant and merchant deception in Estremadura.[299] From February to August 1938, *Etapas* impounded nearly 54,000 eggs, 5,055 liters of oil, 42,900 liters of wine, 21,378 kg. of potatoes, 7,128 kg. of wheat, and tons of other food products all of which lacked proper documentation for sale or travel. In addition, they seized an "infinity of things" including "a great quantity of bills, silver, cloth," rare books, furniture, and so on. Other units reported "price gouging."[300]

Solidarity of the *pueblo* proved once again much stronger than Popular Front or Republican ideology. The deficit of containers and shortages of raw materials, uniforms, and shoes made the quartermaster's task still more difficult. The conscription policies of the government deepened shortages. When skilled shoemakers were drafted, soldiers had to make do with crude sandals cobbled from recycled tires. After the division of the Republic in April, Catalan raw materials and finished goods could not find their way into Estremadura. In addition, scarcity of transportation hampered the evacuation. The lack of auto parts from Catalonia lengthened already long repair times for trucks and other vehicles.[301] The mechanics felt pressured and exhausted. They had to cannibalize old vehicles, and metal workers were forced to produce parts from scratch.

Juan Negrín appointed General José Asensio Torrado to investigate the collapse of the Estremaduran army. Asensio had been one of Largo Caballero's
favorite generals and had won the respect of Basque Nationalists and other non-
Communist republicans. However, the PCE had blamed him for the loss of
Málaga. In May 1937 the general was indicted for neglecting to supply the
Málaga front with arms and munitions and imprisoned pending trial (Bolloten
1991:359). That Negrín decided to appoint Asensio to conduct the investigation was therefore a sign of his rehabilitation.[302] The prime minister, who is
often simplistically accused of being a crypto-Communist, must have had his
suspicions concerning the Army of Estremadura (cf. Martínez Bande 1977:194;
Asensio 1938).[303] While not directly condemning the Communists, Asensio
noted "personal and party interests" that posed obstacles to the investigation.[304] Socialist militants of Estremadura who cited PCE favoritism in certain brigades and in the Milicias de la Cultura seconded his accusations.[305]
These socialists named names and identified acts of corruption that recalled
"old times of *caciquismo.*" For example, the possession of a PCE card became
a passport to safety and comfort. As he gravitated towards anti-Communism,
eventually joining the Casado conspiracy, Burillo himself agreed that Communist influence had been sectarian and excessive (Martínez Bande
1981:244).[306] Other reports from lower-ranking officials verified charges of
incompetence and disorganization.[307] For example, cavalry officers complained
that their men and horses were used solely to contain "disorderly retreats."[308]
The cavalry became overly involved in policing operations in the rear, thus
ignoring the front and wasting valuable livestock. The SIM itself, supposedly
dominated by the PCE, accused Burillo of incompetence, egotism, and
favoritism.[309] It was widely believed that in the Army of Estremadura only
Communists, Masons, and Assault Guards were promoted.

In his investigation, General Asensio found no criminal offenses but rather
numerous professional errors. Officers of different units were often incompetent, did not communicate with each other, and left their troops demoralized.
The latter lived near their families and often had "a comfortable and soft existence." The Army of Estremadura "still conserved many habits of the heroic
popular militias," from which it had originated.[310] It "had not been sufficiently
purged and disciplined." Spies remained within its ranks, and they were able
to provide the enemy with valuable information on a loosely guarded and
extensive front. Deserters and shirkers flourished in the rear.

In early August, another enemy attack produced near total collapse.[311] The
enemy advanced rapidly, but Popular Army authorities feared that an evacuation would further demoralize the troops and delayed the removal of civilians. Poor communication (many villages lacked telephones) and nonexistent
transportation made flight even more difficult. Nevertheless, thousands of
civilians, many of them refugees from the Nationalist zone in 1936 or 1937,

followed retreating Republican soldiers. They assumed correctly that if they remained in insurgent areas they might experience a fate similar to the massacred of Badajoz or Almendralejo. Insurgents did execute hundreds of Republican supporters who stayed in their villages (Solé i Sabaté and Villarroya 1999:194). The panicked flight and unplanned evacuation resulted in the loss of thousands of heads of livestock.[312] The defeat cost the Republic over 6,300 troops, 3,588 rifles, 6,900 kgs. of coal, 3,000 kgs. of wool, and other supplies. Burillo was expelled from the PCE and replaced by Colonel Adolfo Prada Vaquero.[313] According to Prada, neither senior nor junior officers "knew how to do their duty." Only by sacking senior officers of all major units and by imposing "severe punishments" was the "disorderly retreat of the troops" halted. In early August, as the enemy continued to advance, most of the high command of the Estremadura Army was relieved of its posts. *Etapas* picked up eight thousand soldiers who had fled to the rear.[314] Soldiers were warned that if they withdrew without permission they would lose not only their "honor" (which did not seem to count for much even in this part of the Mediterranean where anthropologists have usually asserted its importance) but also their lives.[315] They were reminded that during the failed Asturian campaign at least thirty brigade commanders were executed. Prada's efforts were rewarded in the second half of August when the Popular Army finally began to resist effectively the Nationalist advance (Martínez Bande 1981:254–55).

By the end of August, Republican forces in Estremadura were able to launch a counterattack that revealed the thinning of Nationalist reserves, many of whom had been transferred to the Ebro and Valencia fronts. Nationalists lacked the manpower to end the conflict quickly. For insurgent troops stationed in Estremadura, "two years of stabilization [of the front] resulted in an erosion of morale and combat inexperience. This is shown by the great number of sick soldiers" (Martínez Bande 1981:261–72). Nationalist troops proved little better than their Republican counterparts who were supported this time by battle-hardened reinforcements from four divisions that had participated in the successful defense of Valencia.

As in Estremadura, the troops that remained on the Andalusian front were not particularly aggressive. On 6 November a Nationalist officer reported on his inspection tour of the Guadalquivir: "There is absolute tranquility all down the line. Not a rifle shot, not a shell, nor a round from a machine gun" (quoted in Martínez Bande 1981:285). Disregarding repeated orders, threats of punishment, and actual arrests, these men frequently fraternized with the enemy.[316] Low-ranking soldiers arranged truces in which each side agreed not to fire on the other. Soldiers who broke the peace would be penalized by having to drink wine in no man's land in full view and close range of both sides. To cement the unwritten accord, soldiers would embrace and exchange newspapers, cigarettes, and coins. One unit got on fabulously with its "neighbors," who occasionally supplied it with ample quantities of tobacco. Indeed, a soldier was tempted to mail a cigarette to a friend but feared that "lazy censors" would steal it.[317] Conversing with "fascists" broke up the awful monotony of trench existence and was the principal amusement of the day. On at least one occasion, the reputed enemies even hunted partridges together since "the meals were too light." Most officers seemed to be unaware of the arrangements, but some, especially lieutenants, were complicit.

In Andalusia desertions on both sides encouraged calm and sapped the aggressive urge. The overwhelming majority of the nearly forty-two thousand Republican troops of the Army of Andalusia seemed at least nominally committed to the Popular Front since most were peasants who had joined either the UGT or CNT.[318] By May 1938, Republicans were deserting twice as much as their Nationalist counterparts. During that month, 57 Republican soldiers fled to the Nationalists, whereas 20 Nationalists escaped to the Republicans. In June, 56 ran to the Nationalists, and 32 Nationalists journeyed to the other side. Sometimes, though, the flux was reversed. The IX Corps of the Army of Andalusia reported losing 290 to the Nationalists and gaining 375 Nationalist deserters in turn.[319] According to one report, the IX captured fewer than a half dozen prisoners during the entire year, indicating that live and let live characterized its front. The above figures show the difficulty of making broad statistical comparisons of Nationalist and Republican desertions. The Nationalist officer and historian, Ramón Salas, gives global figures of five Republican desertions for each Nationalist in his monumental and admirable *Ejército popular,* but it is not clear how, where, and when this ratio has been calculated (cf. Salas Larrazábal 1973:1580).[320] It is nevertheless probable that the Popular Army suffered greater desertions than the Nationalists. Perhaps in a civil war of attrition, the side that can retain even the nominal loyalty of most of its troops will emerge victorious.

The high command responded by issuing harsh regulations concerning desertions.[321] It condemned the "excessive generosity of Republican sentiment" that had led to "impunity" for deserters. The "Fascists," they claimed, tortured and shot their deserters. This "regime of terror" effectively prevented the "immense majority of their soldiers" from abandoning Nationalist lines. The Republican general staff decided to compel the deserter's brother or father to take his place. The remaining immediate male family members would be employed in fortification work. In addition, female family members would be interrogated to see if they were convinced antifascists. Only relatives who had joined Popular Front organizations before 19 July 1936 would be exempt from punitive measures.

Even on the quiet front of Andalusia, desertion was risky. In July, forty-four soldiers deserted from the Republican camp, and twelve were shot while trying. Nevertheless, Republican soldiers continued to test their luck. In August, eighty-nine deserted, and ten died in the attempt. At the beginning of that month, a general order was issued that punished self-mutilation by death (Salas Larrazábal 1973:2026). In September, seventy-seven abandoned the Republic, while twelve paid for their failures with their lives. At the same, thirty-four Nationalist soldiers defected to the other side.[322] Desertions were usually individual acts of rebellion, but sometimes they occurred in tiny groups. One lieutenant, accompanied by two of his men, carefully and shrewdly arranged their escape by assigning several deaf men to sentry duty.[323] Military historians have seldom acknowledged that the buddy relationship could encourage desertions as well as sacrifices in battle.

On other fronts, long prison sentences for unsuccessful desertions replaced capital punishment. In a mountainous area near Jaca (Huesca), several dozen deserters were condemned to prisons or work camps for twelve to twenty-five years.[324] In the International Brigades, desertions among foreign volunteers were infrequent but did occur.[325] Nationalist sources claimed that "many . . . refused to go to the front . . . 500 were imprisoned in the Hostalets de Bas concentration camp."[326] In April 1938, three German soldiers were shot for desertion and disobedience in the Vilaseca sector.[327] Desertions were said to affect only 1 percent of the Lincolns and usually occurred after major battles (Rosenstone 1969:311).[328] British volunteers cheered the pep talk in early 1938 of Communist leader Harry Pollitt, but immediately after his speech they surrounded him and requested that they be sent home (Lee 1991:94). Disillusioned international volunteers, usually Polish and French, would not defect but would drown their disillusionment in drink (see Lee 1991:27).[329]

To overcome inertia and acquire information on the enemy, both sides encouraged raiding. The command's kinetics confronted rank-and-file passivity. Raiding showed the high brass's disdain for quiet fronts. Soldiers, they believed, should almost always be in motion. Rest and recreation were for restorative purposes only. Thus raids—to capture enemy soldiers, to obtain information, and to keep soldiers in an aggressive state—were essential. Yet commanders' plans were stymied by many soldiers' desires to avoid risks, and only an elite or a minority of troops carried out raiding missions.[330] Soldiers stationed in Torrelodones (Madrid) needed to be "inculcated with an offensive spirit."[331] Their raids to capture prisoners continued to be fruitless.[332] Yet, perhaps because of hunger, Republicans unsuccessfully attempted to raid Nationalist supplies and to rustle livestock.[333] Divisional leaders were ordered to study and propose "raids in all directions" with the goals of trying to scout enemy lines, capture prisoners, and "maintain the offensive spirit of the troops."[334] On the Guadalajara front, Republican troops would raid supply and communications lines.[335] In Colmenar del Arroyo (Madrid), Nationalist officials were more easily able to form small but elite raiding parties.[336] One sergeant, two corporals, and five soldiers were to be selected according to the "most rigid" criteria. They needed to be in excellent physical and mental condition, have "no interests [i.e., family] in the enemy zone," and be "solidly Nationalist." In the Sierra north of Madrid in the fall of 1938, the Popular Army feared Nationalist raids.[337]

The reigning vagrancy in certain units provoked an understandable reaction of commissars who attempted to get their men to perform. Their activist inclinations made commissars highly unpopular. The soldiers regarded them as spoilsports, killjoys, and "naggers." In certain units, they were responsible for seeing that those on sick leave returned on time.[338] Commissars shot the disobedient and the cowardly on the spot.[339] The rank and file considered them accountable for most wartime difficulties, especially the lack of food and clothing. Throughout the war in various units, officers and men would gang up against conscientious commissars to render them ineffective.[340] In turn, commissars complained about "bourgeois" and corrupt officers.[341] Near Arganda (Madrid) they referred disparagingly to the officers as the "Junta de Burgos."[342] Professional military men, who seemed to be incompetent and lazy, especially frustrated commissars. According to them, officers "with only very few exceptions" were geographically loyal to the Republic and indifferent to its fate. They permitted their troops, the majority of whom "lacked [class] consciousness and combative spirit," to do nothing.[343] Officers neglected to support the efforts of commissars to impose discipline. The strains between commissars and officers weakened the Republican Army. To get what they wanted, crafty soldiers learned how to pit the two groups against each other. The rank and file exploited the gray area of overlapping authority to pursue its own interests.

Colonel Segismundo Casado of the Army of the Center, who would later lead a rebellion against the Negrín government, complained that troops walked around "dressed incorrectly, not saluting, without military order or discipline."[344] Soldiers were overly friendly with superiors instead of respecting them.[345] Near Jaca, saluting was also forgotten.[346] Officers and men roamed Madrid poorly attired, without headgear, and with no concern for military decorum. Senior officers complained "of the spectacle that innumerable officers and troops offered to the heroic civilian population of Madrid."[347] To maintain discipline, the Vigilance Service was ordered to arrest all offenders and send them to the front.

Increasing desertions pushed headquarters to apply the tough measures approved in June.[348] The need for continual reminders of elementary military discipline demonstrated that the behavior of many Popular Army soldiers did not meet basic standards. As winter approached, the lack of shoes, clothes, and food once again inspired many flights to the rear or to the enemy.[349] Abandonment of the front was encouraged by what some commissars termed the permissive attitudes of authorities toward "professional deserters" who successfully avoided combat.[350] These "professionals" preferred a short stay in jail or in a disciplinary brigade to front-line duty. They were immune to the commissar's pep talks. Their success in finding a relatively safe niche disheartened active combatants. Arrests fostered discipline, but even a more effective punishment was to put deserters' families in the hands of the SIM. The decision to institute the practice of collective responsibility by holding families liable for the actions of their relatives may have been inspired by parallel *franquista* practices or the Bolshevik model during the Russian civil war. The SIM, originally created by Indalecio Prieto in August 1937, has received deserved opprobrium for its nefarious, Soviet-inspired activities against the POUM and CNT (Thomas 1961:492; Martínez Bande 1974a:32; Pons Prades 1974:304; Bolloten 1991:606). But beyond these political tasks it had its hands full with the never-ending job of preventing desertions. Since its resources were insufficient for this job, it needed the help of commissars and their political delegates.[351] As we have seen, authorities were empowered to draft a male relative (father or brother) to take the absent soldier's place or to assign the relative to a fortification brigade. In fact, information sheets on deserters listed ages, names, and addresses of brothers.[352] In the winter of 1938–39 in the XIII Army Corps of the Levant, the "major problem" was the increasing number of desertions.[353] Troops simply did not wish to fight and hoped that the war would end as quickly as possible. Soldiers lost all confidence in their officers who had concluded that certain divisions would be totally useless in the event of an enemy attack.

The high command kept finding serious deficiencies in fortification construction and maintenance.[354] A CNT inspection team lamented the failure to build proper defenses in the Levante.[355] According to CNT inspectors, troops possessed too much alcohol and pornography.[356] Despite intensive propaganda against drink, a Republican physician commented that it was impossible to stop this "vice" that was "too deeply rooted in the average man" (Mira 1943:77–78, 148). He unsuccessfully urged psychiatrists to suppress "nasty, degrading literature in the army." Republican troops ignored calls in the official mental-hygiene booklet not "to squander your life in sexual excitement" and took pleasures whenever they could (154). They neglected warnings from health officials to use free condoms to avoid venereal disease. Until the end of the war, VD remained a problem that officials feared could damage the "race." Both troops and officers were reminded that they would be prosecuted for desertion if VD led to their discharge from the military.

The Republic's evident physical and moral decline did not reconcile all Nationalist soldiers with their army. On 31 October 1938, Franco imitated recent Republican repression and strengthened penalties for self-mutilation.[357] Courts-martial for treason were established to judge without delay the self-injured. Those convicted would receive dangerous assignments. The Republic continued to welcome a steady stream of deserters. In December 1938 and January 1939, in the midst of the successful Nationalist campaign in Catalonia, sixty-one Nationalist soldiers stationed in Andalusia defected to the Republic. Those artillerymen with "extremist" (i.e., leftist) backgrounds were repeatedly guilty of "indiscipline."[358] Some were jailed for persistent absenteeism. A stay in disciplinary brigades was recommended for the many who possessed "little military spirit." This punishment would have "a healthy effect" on remaining soldiers. Ultimately, though, the Nationalist problem with deserters was more limited. The steady stream of desertion from the Nationalist zone dwindled throughout 1938 and early 1939. The decline reflected the opportunism, not ideology, that motivated many potential runaways.

During the Christmas season homesickness overtook many soldiers in both camps.[359] In November, the Army of the Center reported "systematic [Republican] desertions to the enemy."[360] The history of one brigade showed that the number of deserters to the enemy (152) plus the number shot for trying to desert (12) almost equaled those killed (35) and wounded (165).[361] In December, a commissar in the Levant reported that eight soldiers of the Popular Army had gone over to the enemy and twelve had deserted to the rear; whereas, five Nationalists came over to the Republic.[362] Near Mérida, deserters from the Nationalists were—not surprisingly—militants of Popular Front organizations whom Nationalists had drafted or captured.[363] Republican authorities drew a characteristic profile of defectors to the other side: he was a soldier who had never joined a Popular Front organization or had affiliated only after July 1936. He had not integrated himself into his unit, was a loner, and had few army buddies.[364] His family often remained in the "fascist" zone. Usually apolitical, he was suspected of practicing Catholicism. He wanted to go home not only to mother but also to Mother Church (e.g., see Puig Casas 1999). Those prosperous prior to the conflict were as likely to flee the Republic as devout Catholics.

By 1938 cynicism was so mighty that individuals frequently defied the sociological profile. Soldiers with good political and union credentials, who had volunteered for military service, and who had many friends in the army and families in the Republican zone betrayed the Republic.[365] Battle-hardened veterans, proven militants of antifascist organizations, and their sons went over to the enemy.[366] Nationalists were just as surprised as Republican authorities by defections of Loyalist war heroes and men with impeccable records.[367] Persuasion and propaganda produced little effect upon the increasingly skeptical majority. Of sixty-two men deserting or missing in action during retreats in July 1938, almost 10 percent or six had joined antifascist organizations before 19 July 1936.[368] The overwhelming majority were workers from Alicante drafted in 1938 who were between the ages of seventeen and twenty-one. At least forty-eight of the sixty-two were bachelors. Thus, returning to wife and kids was not the primarily reason for their defections. Considerable resentment against those who spent their time in the rear—especially soldiers in the quartermaster and health service—inspired men to sneak over the top. The Health Service had acquired a partially deserved reputation for being sympathetic to "fascists."[369] In a few battalions, deserters were mainly from the middle classes—lawyers, doctors, and white-collar workers; in others, they were raw recruits who had to be monitored very closely.[370] Upon arrival at the front, novices tended to defect to the enemy; later, they were more likely to desert to the rear. Paradoxically, in certain brigades new recruits seemed to have labored more efficiently than cynical veterans who were accustomed to a unionized work rhythm.[371] Their slackening discouraged sincere antifascists who wanted to contribute to the war effort. To increase productivity, entire companies that had a reputation for low output might be transferred.[372]

Some deserters engaged in what could be called Stirnerian individualism, in which personal desires took precedence over all social institutions. Love promoted subversion (Freud 1959:73). Using an army vehicle and expense account, one *Etapas* commissar abandoned his troops, wife, and children to court his mistress.[373] A few other commissars were equally egotistical and corrupt.[374] The only official response to the problem was greater control and repression—more barbed wire between the trenches, more patrols, and more complete files on personnel.

In the Sierra north of Madrid where the front was "excessively tranquil" from October to December 1938, twenty-seven soldiers of the Twenty-sixth Mixed Brigade tried to desert. Eight of them were shot fleeing to the enemy.[375] In December, "severe measures" were taken to avoid more attempts. Troops' desire for combat was nonexistent. Recent draftees—especially the more mature (33–35 years old) who had wives and children—were "cautious, timid, and don't wish to fight."[376] Wisdom (or at least self-interest), it is said, grows with age (Collier 1987:122). By 1938, the Popular Army enrolled men much older than those in the enemy's ranks (Payne 1967:407). The maturer had many reasons to dislike military service, but one of them was the pay cut they were forced to accept when drafted.[377] More than younger soldiers, older men refused to take any risks and were solely motivated by highly contagious fears. The total inactivity on this front, where "the war went unnoticed," reinforced desires to avoid combat. The few soldiers who did wish to fight wanted to participate in the battle of Catalonia; 235 men, many of whom were Catalan, volunteered for the eastern front.[378] The "immense majority," however, had absolutely no combat experience and did not wish to acquire any. They were content just to have cleverly engineered their way to a tranquil front.

Soldiers of the Fourteenth Division seemed to have behaved in a similar fashion. They belonged to a distinguished unit that originally had been led by Cipriano Mera, one of the outstanding commanders of the libertarian movement.[379] The division's brigades had seen action at the battles of Guadalajara and Brunete. However, by the fall of 1938 they were physically sick of the war.[380] On this front in the province of Guadalajara, the ratio of the ill to wounded or killed in action was forty to one. When defending the approaches to Madrid during the month of October, 404 were evacuated because of sickness compared to 9 who were killed or wounded. The Fourteenth Division received only 4 Nationalist defectors, whereas 77 of its soldiers deserted to the enemy, usually bringing their weapons with them. In fact, it was more dangerous for Republican soldiers to desert than to remain in their trenches. Three were shot trying to desert, but 2 were killed by enemy fire. Informal agreements endorsing live and let live were customary on this front. Republicans fired thousands of bullets and shells daily at Nationalists, but the enemy response was not menacing. During the entire month, Nationalists wounded only 7 and killed 2. Despite nearly constant lessons on the need to be offensive, Republican raids were ineffective and captured only 2 Nationalists.

Commissars were "embarrassed" because, despite their best efforts, all anti-desertion measures had failed. Defections resulted from three major sources. First, veteran units, which had been ordered to send personnel to newly formed units, selected the least reliable and doubtful men.[381] Once again, the egotism of the small group, which wanted to keep the best for itself, took precedence over the "general good." Second, competent and respected commissioned and noncommissioned officers were scarce. Third, material shortages persisted. Lack of tobacco, meat, and what soldiers considered to be the unfair assignment of leave persistently disheartened men.[382]

Food had been relatively abundant in the summer, but victuals, uniforms, soap, and especially blankets and shoes were lacking at the onset of the Castilian winter.[383] Commissars discouraged drawing lots to distribute clothes and shoes, supplies of which barely sufficed to cover one-fifth of the men. Authorities feared that the unlucky who lost and thus remained ragged and unshod might riot.[384] In other units, coats were available for less than half of the personnel as the Castilian cold approached.[385] These deficiencies were aggravated by the unavailability of transportation, a problem caused in part by the selfish practices of certain chauffeurs and repairmen who were "apathetic" or "lazy" and worked "without enthusiasm" or even "with repugnance."[386] Nationalists experienced similar problems with chauffeurs, some of whom were punished by being sent to the front (Colmegna 1941:182). Transport difficulties were intensified by officers who overused private vehicles, a practice banned in the Tenth Corps in October when, to save gasoline, only train and bus travel were authorized.[387]

Authorities worried that Madrid would go hungry.[388] To overcome food shortages, units were encouraged to dig gardens.[389] The quartermaster in the

Sierra around Madrid established chicken farms to supply eggs to mitigate the high cost of living.[390] The Republic tried to compensate for its inability to furnish meaningful pensions to widows and orphans by employing them in these poultry farms, but the unions strongly objected to proposed employment policies that would have displaced their members.

Repressive Nationalist practices around Seville might have given rise to a more potent Loyalist guerrilla movement in Andalusia. The Nationalist military admitted that it had jailed so many Sevillian militants and workers, a large number for burning churches and public buildings, that the economy suffered from a deficiency of hands.[391] The prisons of the other major cities of the region—Cadiz, Cordova, Málaga, Seville, and Granada—overflowed with a penal population often double capacity. By May 1938, fourteen thousand Andalusia prisoners overwhelmed the jails and labor camps of the region.[392] The flight of many other workers heightened the labor shortage. Both sides' need for laborers may have eventually restrained their initial propensities to execute the captured.

Despite arrests in 1938, the guerrilla movement continued.[393] *Guerrilleros* aided regular Republican troops by supplying them with information or helping civilians cross enemy lines. Republican soldiers would, in turn, assault prison camps, liberate prisoners, and kill their guards.[394] In June 1938, a regular guerrilla unit of one hundred soldiers, which was attached to the Army of Estremadura, raided Nationalist-controlled territory around Badajoz and blew up a bridge and four cars.[395] This limited success came at a high price. Of one hundred *guerrilleros* sent on a raiding- and information-gathering mission, only nineteen returned. Most of the survivors were either sick or injured.[396] The head of the information section of the Estremadura Army came to question the effectiveness of guerrilla operations.[397] He believed that raids did little damage to the enemy and that raiders falsified their reports. Nor did they coordinate their actions with other Republican forces. In February 1938 the general staff reorganized guerrilla forces in part to prevent "illegal" guerrillas from acting in the name of the Popular Army.[398]

In other regions, the guerrilla presence was less notable than in Andalusia or Estremadura. In the north, "extensive interrogation" of prisoners allowed Nationalists to smash one network.[399] In Aragon and Catalonia, captured spies revealed information that led to the seizure of dozens of alleged Republican agents and guerrillas.[400] The detentions were said to have been responsible for preventing the assassination of General Moscardó, the hero of the Toledo Alcázar in 1936 and the head of the Army of Aragon in 1938. The arrests hindered the assignment of a division of approximately twelve hundred *guerrilleros* to the mountains.[401]

Republican and Nationalist spies did not act solely for ideological motives but were enticed to perform dangerous tasks for thousands of (usually Nationalist) pesetas.[402] In the territory they controlled near Madrid, Nationalists imposed a "reign of terror" by ordering the execution of two civilians for every soldier injured by enemy guerrillas and by threatening to turn villages into ghost towns if guerrilla activity continued.[403] The order to shoot civilians in retaliation for military casualties was later amended in favor of granting monetary compensation in hard coin to those who helped capture Republican fighters. Repressive incentives worked. Republican agents could not move behind the Nationalist lines as fishes in water. For the proper rewards, large numbers of citizens were prepared to denounce them to insurgent authorities.[404] In Palmaces de Jadraque (Guadalajara), a Republican spy paid his former neighbors in the Nationalist zone for information, but he garnered little sensitive intelligence from these small-town residents and was captured. They did, however, inform him that the Nationalist rearguard was not demoralized since it possessed basic necessities.[405]

Insurgent authorities employed informers throughout their labor camps, making escapes quite difficult.[406] Unsuccessful attempts cost the lives of prisoners fleeing Nationalist concentration camps.[407] In Villamayor (Salamanca) an informer reported that several prisoners were plotting a breakout, and this tip allowed officials to catch them in the act. Pious Nationalists generously offered the betrayed the services of a chaplain to administer to their final "spiritual" needs and then, after an invocation of the divine, quickly shot them. Evasion from camps in Basque Country or the north, where the population was either hostile or indifferent to the Nationalists, proved as difficult as in other regions, such as Andalusia.[408] Two who escaped from the Santona (Cantabria) concentration camp on New Year's Eve, 1937, were quickly recaptured. They had gone to the village of Ancillo, where they found a boatman who was willing to take them to France. However, he wanted to charge them the enormous sum of twenty thousand pesetas.[409] Not surprisingly, the destitute fugitives could not raise the money and were quickly seized. In 1938, the last full year of the conflict, cynicism eclipsed idealism.

# 4

# Survival

At the beginning of 1939, Republicans wanted to divert Nationalists from an imminent conquest of Catalonia with audacious offensives in Andalusia, Estremadura, and Madrid (cf. Rojo 1974:80–84). Republican leaders were on the verge of enacting a plan to land a brigade at Motril (Granada) that would rupture the passivity of this front, march to Malaga, and raise all Andalusia. However, coordination of the various Republican armies had broken down. In particular, Miaja came under harsh Communist criticism for his failure to launch a diversionary attack during the battle of Catalonia (Cordón 1977:351).[1] Despite the optimism of Rojo and some other Republican—especially Communist—leaders, letters from the soldiers reveal a demoralization of Republican forces that confirm the judgment that it would have been quite difficult to launch a potent offensive in Andalusia. These epistles are rarer in Spain than, for example, in the U.S. Civil War or even in the seventeenth-century civil wars in the British Isles, perhaps because of high rates of illiteracy in a Catholic country that had not created a broad system of mass education. Yet they are priceless since they reveal the hidden "backstage," which often can only be captured by overhearing conversations among faithful friends or family (Scott 1985:27).

The letters disclose, above all, the desire for the war to end immediately and unconditionally. Individual soldiers wanted to avoid danger and to return home. As in the Russian Army in 1917, fraternization and desires for an immediate peace regardless of the consequences were widespread (Wildman 1987:1:26–30). "Sleeping dogs" continued to "lie" on the Andalusian front.[2] Exchanges between Republican and Nationalist troops involved more than trading goods and constituted peace offerings that discouraged hostilities. Soldiers stationed in the province of Jaén had good reason not to fear the "fascists," with whom they conversed frequently. Republican servicemen exchanged rolling paper made in their zone for tobacco grown in Nationalist areas. One wrote home to ask for goods that he could trade with his buddies "in the fascist zone."[3] When newly arrived Republican soldiers, who had been sent to relieve front-liners, began to fire at the enemy, the Nationalists responded by telling them: "Reds, don't shoot. It's not our fault." This pacific initiative led to affectionate embraces between adversaries, with men promising each other that the front would remain calm and that they would warn the other side if officers ordered an attack. Every morning, enemies shared cigarettes and news. As a result, a soldier from a local village was thrilled to learn how his friends and acquaintances in the Nationalist zone were faring. Partying and singing transpired at night.

Overworked and understaffed censors, whose job it was to read tens of thousands of letters, deplored the "poor combative spirit" of the men, most of whom were conscripts from Catalonia and Valencia.[4] Hundreds tried to deceive the censors—who discouraged telling relatives bad news—by writing on the inside of envelopes or below the stamp.[5] The best way to avoid unwanted official interference was to have buddies on leave distribute letters directly to friends and families. A soldier confessed that although he hated fascism, "because it reeked of militarism," he hated war even more. *Milicianos* of the first hour admitted their disillusionment and wished only that the war would end immediately. The well-known defeatism of Azaña found more favor among the troops than the resistance of Negrín. One opined that those, such as the Communists and specifically Negrín, who called for continued struggle "with or without bread," had never been hungry. His comrade thought that Negrín's plea hid the profiteering of many. Negrín's famous girth did not lend credibility to his calls for sacrifice, and he became known as "Mr. Lentils" (Pons Prades 1974:351; Peers 1943:82). The lentils themselves were called "Dr. Negrín's Resistance Pills." A self-admitted cynic from Murcia, where draftees were hiding from the enemy with the complicity of the population, believed that volunteering to fight was the stupidest possible action. An unknown prophet made the nearly correct prediction that it would be over by March. Selfishness dominated the Republican zone, as it often did in the Confederacy during the final years of the U.S. Civil War.[6] In addition, in the Baena area, homesick Catalans felt a special antipathy for the Andalusians who in turn resented what they considered Catalan arrogance and superior airs. The negative image of their region and a widespread perception that they contributed relatively little to the Republican effort upset Catalans (Pons Prades 1974:175, 185).

A general defeatism or indifference to the fate of the Republic pervaded the soldiers' letters. They were sick of life in the trenches. Complaints denounced the unvarying meals of rice, olive oil, and bread every day for breakfast, lunch, and even for Christmas dinner.[7] Others lamented receiving only bread for breakfast, no oil for months, and dried peas or inescapable lentils instead of rice. There was no dessert worthy of the name. Censors found that gripes about food were the most common of all complaints. The lack of culinary variety has always annoyed soldiers. It is said that the "dreary predictability" of the diet of the Russian soldiers in World War I—when they consumed only bread for breakfast, cabbage soup with meat for lunch, and porridge for dinner—contributed to the collapse of morale of the Imperial Army in 1917 (Holmes 1985:126). To protest an inadequate diet, some refused to pick olives. Others consoled themselves and their families that they were better nourished and clothed than the civilians of the *pueblo* where they were posted. Letters conveyed the sad spectacle of barefooted women and children who regularly begged for the scanty leftovers of the Popular Army.

Whether civilian or military, the unprivileged agreed that they all might perish from hunger and cold. The "rags" that they wore did not alleviate their feelings of nakedness. Two hundred men, it was claimed, had died of cold in the Sierra Nevada. In other regions, soldiers learned of deaths from hunger. They were informed that the local mayor had labeled as "fascists" women in Crevillente (Alicante), who had asked for bread.[8] Rumors circulated of female food riots in Madrid. In that city, in December 1938 average calorie consumption reached its nadir of 770 per day (Grande Covián 1986:63). In February hundreds of *madrileños* were dying of hunger (Cleugh 1963:198). The civilian population was subject to all sorts of vitamin deficiencies (*pelagra*), and accompanying symptoms of skin disease, diarrhea, and dementia. In many villages the social divisions were simplified into two categories: those who had food and those who did not. Black marketing demoralized the front and the rear. People with access to a black market were fortunate. In certain villages, profiteering had disappeared since there was nothing to buy. Money was sometimes unable to purchase food. Efforts by the Republic to use its last available foreign currencies to purchase supplies that would guarantee the survival of the population were fruitless (cf. Viñas 1979:429). In November the director of food supplies (director general de Abastecimientos) reported a "catastrophic situation" (quoted in Martínez Bande 1979:19). He was ignorant of the fate of the wheat harvest.

Soldiers wondered why in Andalusia so little olive oil reached the front. If they suspected that peasants were hiding their stashes or exporting them clandestinely to other provinces, they would have been correct.[9] Horse, car, truck, and train moved small and large quantities of oil secretly from the province of Jaén, the most important zone of olive production, to other areas where they were traded for desired commodities. As in the French Revolution and the Russian civil war, officials found it nearly impossible to monitor numerous individuals, called sackmen or bagmen in the Russian case, who trafficked in relatively small quantities of goods. Authorities were unable to calculate precisely the amounts concealed but were certain that it was considerable. Officials recognized "the mania of hiding." Olive growers and olive oil producers—like others who sold on the market—hid their stocks and refused to report quantities to authorities. The lack of hands caused by conscription further intensified the shortage of oil. Labor shortages and an inability to feed available workers halved the normal harvesting output. Disorganization of distribution exacerbated scarcities. Quartermasters did not recycle containers quickly enough for oil to be allocated efficiently. Road transportation, especially trucks, was overemployed, whereas more efficient and cheaper railroads were underemployed. The result of all this was that the civilian and military population of the Republic did not have enough oil, a staple of the Spanish diet. In contrast, the Nationalist-controlled parts of Andalusia helped to feed Morocco, the Balearic Islands, and even Castile without rationing or major price increases until the middle of 1938 (Jackson 1965:414).

Retarded paydays and purported unfairness of leave added to the grievances. Pay was as much as four months late, preventing soldiers from sending money to their families to purchase food or clothing. Late salaries also angered hospitalized soldiers.[10] On many fronts, paymasters and quartermasters continued to be suspected of corruption.[11] Delayed paydays and the decreasing value of Republican currency made desertions increasingly attractive. For example, the low value of Republican money disgusted a disillusioned Moor who had deserted from the Nationalists and joined the Popular Army. He demanded his wages in silver.[12]

Some wanted leave so badly that they took it without authorization, defying the risk of getting shot for desertion. Others searched desperately for a doctor's excuse. A few soldiers begged friends and family to get medical certificates, falsely claiming that their mothers were sick. But even a certified sick mother or many months in the trenches were no guarantees that a soldier would receive a *permiso*. Leave was reserved for men that had rendered special services, such as turning in their comrades who were planning to desert to the Nationalists.[13] Nonetheless, many journeyed to the city to spend the night, thus repeating the experience of the militias in the early days. Soldiers could often go AWOL with impunity since tensions between commissars and officers continued to offer them leeway.

The vocabulary of "us" (low-ranking soldiers) versus "them" (officers) conveyed resentment. The "sick," the exempt, and just about anyone who managed to avoid the front lines aroused envy among the less fortunate. Censors reported that, after food, shirkers (*emboscados*) generated the largest number of complaints. *Enchufados*—those with cushy jobs in the rear or those who had access to better food or clothing—reminded front-line soldiers of privileged *señoritos* (upper-class playboys) and were accordingly labeled "fascists."[14] One soldier wrote to a family member that he had learned that *enchufados* in Murcia were able to sabotage a truck that was about to take them to the front.[15] Another working in the quartermaster's office revealed that his colleagues were warm and well-fed and concluded that war affected above all "poor workers who [were the only ones] to die on the battlefield." One savvy CNT militant experienced a disagreeable surprise when he returned to his union headquarters in 1938 only to find its leadership engaged in hoarding and speculating with foreign and domestic cigarettes, which—along with food coupons—had become valuable assets (Pons Prades 1974:248). Popular cynicism, which was summarized by the feeling that only the well connected and privileged would survive and prosper, pervaded the front and the rear. Some of the disgruntled referred to deserters not as *desertores,* as official terminology labeled them, but rather as *escapados.* This sympathetic attitude to draft dodgers is in stark contrast to the hatred that soldiers in other wars felt toward skulkers, but it did not stop Republican soldiers in Catalonia from shooting the *emboscados* that they discovered during their retreats (see Linderman 1987:221; Solé i Sabaté and Villarroya 1999:260). The committed noted that those drafted in 1938 were much more likely to desert than draftees of 1937. Militants conceded that they could not understand that the 1938 class of conscripts—workers who had suffered exploitation "all their lives"—would nonetheless take the first available opportunity to flee to the Nationalists. When devoted Republican soldiers questioned potential deserters why they "wanted to continue to be exploited," they replied cynically that the "fascists" were going to win.

To prevent desertions, Republican authorities circulated letters showing that Nationalists had confiscated the property of the families of "reds." This had little effect. By February, desertions had "increased substantially."[16] Commissars, seeking the reasons behind the wave, rejected the idea that enemy propaganda or a secret organization had influenced or organized defectors. Instead, they blamed the problem on leave. Many on leave never returned to their posts, and *permisos* lowered morale of even the best soldiers who returned to the front as convinced defeatists.[17] Libertarians in uniform registered additional complaints about repression of militants of the CNT and those of Juventudes Libertarias enrolled in the military.

Soldiers continued to steal. The Civil Governor of the province of Madrid reported "in the fields thefts (*desmanes*) by uncaring individuals (*individuos desaprensivos*) that harm production and reduce the legitimate profit of growers."[18] Since villages lacked the necessary police to stop the pilfering, the governor asked military commanders to put an end to it. Puebla de la Mujer

Muerta reported that a squadron of cavalrymen had behaved "worse than militiamen of the early days of war. They took anything they liked."[19] They had
stolen, eaten, or destroyed dozens of cabbages, goats, lambs, sheep, and beehives since mid-January.

Nationalist offers of rewards for the capture of *guerrilleros* reduced the effectiveness of irregular warfare and prefigured the regime's postwar elimination
of partisans.[20] *Franquistas* found it easy to entice volunteers into serving in
counter-insurgency operations.[21] All of the thirty-two men of a Republican
guerrilla unit that infiltrated into the Nationalist zone around Montefrío
(Granada) in the last days of 1938 were quickly captured. Other Republican
*guerrilleros* were also unsuccessful in this sector. Military police, Nationalist
sympathizers, and local Falangists sufficed to counter the threat.[22] On the Catalan front, Nationalist authorities seemed to have easily identified and nabbed
Republican guerrillas and spies who attempted sabotage behind their lines.[23]
Guerrilla activity revived only in the decades following the defeat of the Popular Army.[24] In the immediate aftermath of the war, it remained an essentially
police—not military—problem.[25] Resistance of small groups persisted in
Asturias and in the Sierra de Aracena.

Despite their previous repressive measures, Republicans continued to confront a high level of desertions.[26] In this context, commissars concluded that
the apolitical were most likely to abandon the cause.[27] Patrols were alert for
individuals traveling without authorized leave, and authorities issued a warning to officers that they would be sanctioned if their men deserted. Soldiers of
the Army of Levante were given notice that all deserters to the enemy would
be shot if captured. Runaways to the rear were to be imprisoned or forced to
serve in a disciplinary brigade, which CNT militants likened to an Inquisitional
torture.[28] Prisoners who were forced to work were sometimes placed on half
rations.[29]

Numerous desertions from the Ninety-sixth Mixed Brigade, stationed in Levante, hindered its fighting ability.[30] Commissars tried to reduce the number of
defectors through persuasion and propaganda, but flights, especially among
new draftees, increased daily. The high number of soldiers shot for desertion
(65) aroused suspicion among the brigade's anti-Communists. They claimed
that a large percentage of those executed were, in reality, murdered because
they were not in the PCE but instead belonged to the UGT or CNT. Some of
the deceased bequeathed written testimony that they had feared execution by
the Communist "reign of terror." Republicans, Socialists, anarchosyndicalists,
and foreign observers—such as George Orwell, Franz Borkenau, and Laurie
Lee—have accused the PCE of initiating or encouraging "Checkas" that assassinated loyal antifascists. These dedicated writer-volunteers spent a good deal
of time avoiding police or trying to get out of jail.[31] Yet the attention devoted
to political repression has resulted in the ignorance of its nonpolitical forms.

It may have been the climate of mass desertions and corruption that allowed the most unscrupulous to settle accounts with their political or personal adversaries. For the Nationalists, the problem of desertions remained more circumscribed.[32] Defectors from Nationalist ranks were often former left activists. Mayors and other town officials in Andalusia and Estremadura had ignored the military's desire to forgive and forget the leftist backgrounds of soldiers enrolled in the Nationalist army. Local authorities continued to harass family members of these men and deny them the combatants' subsidy. Despite decent material conditions in the military, disappointed soldiers refused to return from leave.

In December, insurgents stepped up pressure on a variety of fronts. In the Sierra surrounding Madrid, a series of Nationalist raids and Republican counterattacks kept soldiers on edge.[33] More significant was a major offensive against the Republican army along the Segre-Ebro front on 23 December when approximately three hundred thousand men attacked from Lérida to Tortosa. During this confrontation, which became known as the Battle of Catalonia, Nationalists proved superior to Republican forces in every type of weapon.[34] Nationalist aviation, which included the Condor Legion, far outclassed the Republican force and bombed the Catalan capital at will. The formidable CTV also participated in the campaign (Coverdale 1975:381). Against them were arrayed three hundred thousand Republican soldiers, many of them recent draftees who possessed malfunctioning weapons, lacked clothes and food, and had lost fighting spirit (see Rojo 1974:24, 268–69; Tagüeña Lacorte 1978:180). The recently concluded Battle of the Ebro had eliminated the best officers, and Republican military schools were unable to produce a competent new batch (Rojo 1974:51, 110). Many took the first opportunity to desert. A few may have ironically alerted the enemy that they were "going to tie up their sandals and get ready to run" (quoted in Martínez Bande 1979:60). Rojo (1974:74) admitted that he had come to regard panic as "a natural phenomenon." Nor was he surprised when even light artillery fire caused a *desbandada* or when exhausted troops, who had previously fought admirably, fled in fear. Rumors—which help to explain and relieve powerful emotions—provoked massive defections and increased exponentially whenever disaster or major defeat loomed. Entire towns emptied when it was learned that the "fascists" were advancing.

The collapse of Republican authority produced a spirit of every person for himself. Repeating the errors of the summer of 1936, Republican soldiers—who were hungry and ill clad in the cold Catalan winter—once again abandoned whatever arms and materiel they possessed (Tagüeña Lacorte 1978:180). Azaña reasoned that the collapse in Catalonia was worse than that of April 1938 when the Republican zone was cut into two parts. The enemy destroyed Modesto's forces, who had constituted some of the most valuable units of the

Popular Army (Salas Larrazábal 1973:2202). As in Estremadura, specialized elite units of the *carabineros* and Assault Guards did not provide a heroic example (Rojo 1974:134). Only the militant and mainly Communist units of Líster, Galán, and Tagüeña sporadically offered serious resistance. The Catalan Maginot Line, built by thousands of workers, showed once again that troops with little will to fight rendered even the best fortifications useless (Salas Larrazábal 1973:2213; Martínez Bande 1979: 57). As in the past, secondary or tertiary defensive lines were not constructed. Resistance to fortification work, which had existed throughout the conflict, was openly displayed as mayors used their influence to help their citizens avoid labor (Rojo 1974:119; Martínez Bande 1979:142). High-ranking officials and ministers "offered a terrible example" by employing their pull to protect friends and family from the fighting (Rojo 1974:33). Although parts of Catalonia offered excellent terrain for guerrilla activity, none developed. The rear had no desire to continue the war (Rojo 1974:100). Hungry civilians welcomed Nationalist forces as long as they distributed food (Cleugh 1963:188). This explains why many nonmilitant workers did not know or care in April 1939 whether they "won" or "lost" the war (Vilanova 1995:28). To stop the frequent flights, which dissolved the Popular Army into a civilian mass, more mobile guards units were recommended (Tagüeña Lacorte 1978:185). On 24 January the catastrophes moved Negrín and Azaña, to declare a "state of war," and thus change the policies of the Republican leadership whose entrenched antimilitarism and fear of Bonapartism had previously avoided this measure.

The division of the Republic made it difficult for the high command of the Popular Army to send fresh troops to the Catalan front. XVI Cuerpo conscripts, drafted in January 1939, could not be supplied and were told to bring their own clothes, blankets, and shoes with them (Martínez Bande 1979:99). Many deserted at this time of "numbing cold."[35] Even if soldiers from other fronts had been available, they might not have been prepared to turn the tide. Troops transferred from other regions to Catalonia were often volunteers who were "poor fighters since they were largely Catalans . . . motivated more by the thought of rejoining their families than by a desire to fight" (Rojo 1974:99)[36]

Diversionary attacks to relieve Catalonia were failures. On the southern front in Cordova province, Republicans continued to prove incapable of mounting an offensive that could distract or delay the Nationalist effort in the northeast.[37] The Popular Army had amassed more than one hundred thousand men at Peñarroya-Valsequillo (Cordova) and in early January 1939 launched an attack on a fifteen-kilometer front; however, once again, relatively small numbers of Nationalist reserves proved able to stem the Loyalist advance. The insurgent counterattack produced panic and flight of the Popular Army. Six hundred "reds" were killed, many of them recruits from Valencia who had not yet been issued uniforms. These unfortunate draftees—who had the look and dress of peasants—were often old, physically unfit, and too weak to serve in any military capacity. They were so starved for food that after the first days of combat an enormous number had unwisely eaten uncooked pork and had fallen severely ill. "This is the reason why the offensive failed. A mass of men cannot fight when they are hungry." Calls by Communists and others for early and total militarization of all able-bodied men did not take into account the inability of the Republic to sustain its forces (cf. Cordón 1977:330).[38] The Republic came to resemble the dying Confederacy (Linderman 1987:220). As the Estremadura offensive collapsed, "fascist" radio gained an audience among the soldiers of the Army of the Center.[39] In that zone, Castilian peasants were abandoning the villages controlled by the Republic. Troops forced those caught fleeing to work a double shift.

On 26 January, General Yagüe's troops entered Barcelona and encountered virtually no resistance. The Catalan capital, which doubled as the capital of Euskadi in exile, did not repeat the heroic defenses of Madrid and Valencia. It should be recalled that the defense of Madrid occurred before the conflict turned into a war of attrition during which urban populations persistently suffered from hunger. One contemporary wrote, "the prime reason for the almost light-hearted surrender of Barcelona was sheer starvation" (Peers 1943:73). The "lowest morale" characterized "80 percent" of reinforcements (Rojo 1974:115). Some of them were given arms but not food (Cleugh 1963:190). "With a few honorable exceptions, all those who gave encouragement to the troops had disappeared" (Rojo 1974:126). Not many were interested in either defending or fortifying the city. As was often the case throughout the war, the quartermaster service, which had stockpiled food in anticipation of a siege, was unable to get available supplies to the troops, and crowds of women assaulted its stores. Female protesters tried to lynch those who attempted to stop them (Rojo 1974:34; Pons Prades 1974:327; Martínez Bande 1979:159).[40]

At the end of 1938, Catalan workers had lost any remaining desire to sacrifice for the Republic.[41] Hyperinflation boosted the cost of oil to 150 pesetas per liter, a dozen eggs sold for 200, and a chicken was offered at 400 to 500 (Pedro y Pons 1940:9). Republican money was so worthless that often only barter could acquire foodstuffs. Soup kitchens offered little but lentils, beans, and—less frequently—bread. Tagüeña noted "the complete failure to nourish the cities, where those not directly connected to the army or the parties and unions went hungry" (quoted in Martínez Bande 1979:36). In other words, in urban areas nonmilitants—unless they had friends or family in the countryside—suffered more than militants. The inability to feed major urban populations severely damaged a republic that had initially won their loyalty. The autarkic village—whatever its ostensible ideologies—contributed to urban hunger but could feed its own (Simoni and Simoni 1984:133). Madrid likewise suffered from a dearth of gas, coal, wood, and almost no electric heating

(Peers 1943:68, 80). Normal rations were reduced from eight ounces of food per day to two. Milk was available only for babies. At the end of 1938, Madrid suffered thirty-five thousand cases of pellagra, and official rations provided each person only twelve hundred calories per day (Mira 1939:1217). In February 1939, hundreds of people per week were dying of starvation.

By the fall and winter of 1938, Barcelona was almost totally dependent upon thermal power plants since in May the Nationalists had captured the major hydroelectric centers. The thermal plants were capable of producing enough electricity to maintain the war effort, but they required much maintenance and thus a competent and devoted workforce. The anarchosyndicalist leader, Juan Peiró, concluded that effort was absent. Peiró, who was in charge of the electricity sector, complained directly to Negrín about the desperate situation: factory committees neglected or disobeyed almost all orders from the government. Government officials were even refused admittance into certain plants. Tools needed for essential repairs disappeared and were presumably stolen; thus machinery could not be repaired. Many workers reported sick, but the government's request that medical personnel verify their illnesses—as occurred in the military after March 1938—was refused. At the San Adrián de Besos plant, which was reportedly one of the most modern, three eight-hour shifts operated around the clock, but rampant tardiness among the workers caused periodic blackouts. Even political commissars in the plants had high rates of absenteeism, and days passed without their presence on the job. Ultimately, the problem was blamed on the "little desire to work" and "the laziness" of the workers. Part of the explanation was that food shortages forced workers to spend much time in search of sustenance. Wage earners devoted a good portion of their day to tending their own gardens. As one Voltairean domestic put it, "I am for that party who lets me cultivate my cabbages" (quoted in Woolsey 1998:140). Peiró and others concluded that without strengthening the government's authority in the plants, the city would soon be without power. Nationalist bombing raids, shortage of transport, and lack of fuel slowed the Catalan economy. Public transportation—metro, trams, and trains—were adversely affected. More workers were forced to expend precious calories walking to work, and absenteeism may have risen in response (Pedro y Pons 1940:8). A Nationalist physician observed that prisoners survived dearth better than workers since the former did not have to commute to their jobs.

The fall of Barcelona speeded up the final collapse of the Popular Army. Panicky troops fled north of the city: "We saw many retreats (*desbandadas*) in this war but nothing compared with this. Even some commanders abandoned their posts and tried to flee to France" (Tagüeña Lacorte 1978:191). As at the beginning of the conflict, gender segregation diminished, and women—usually officers' wives—returned to their spouse's headquarters for protection. "Defeatist crimes" increased significantly. Even battle-hardened veterans could no longer be trusted. In February 1939, Republican soldiers in the Sierra surrounding Madrid risked and sometimes lost their lives in attempts to desert to the enemy.[42] In the Twenty-sixth Mixed Brigade, desertions—and those shot trying—doubled.[43] Republican forces in Catalonia dissolved, and Franco conquered the region with unexpected rapidity. On 4 February the Nationalists occupied Gerona, and two days later Azaña, Negrín, Companys, Aguirre, and Martínez Barrio crossed over to France. In the first two weeks of February approximately half a million Spaniards, including thousands who were wounded, sought refuge in France. The Nationalists may have encouraged this mass exodus by allowing the enemy an escape route that avoided a last-ditch defense. This was the greatest flight of the entire conflict and reminded observers of the massive exodus from Málaga two years earlier. Fortifications were abandoned, and many soldiers near Valencia deserted to the rear, even though they were warned that "anyone who turns his back to the enemy out of cowardice will be shot as a warning to the rest."[44] Soldiers on both sides seemed to have made a concerted effort not to get killed or injured in what they believed were the final weeks of the conflict.[45] Warfare was ritualized with customary and predictable artillery exchanges that caused few injuries.

The end of the war revealed that the diminutive scale of metallurgical factories diminished overall productive capacity and showed that CNT plans to centralize and rationalize the industry were only partially achieved. Some in small workshops in Valencia and Murcia labored in defense industries with enthusiasm and devotion.[46] Yet the Confederation argued that "the absurd respect for private property" had delayed centralization and therefore lessened production. The petty bourgeoisie had successfully maintained possession of its workshops. Even when the shop floor had been rationalized, the lack of raw materials hindered production.

In large factories in the Levant and in Andalusia, tensions remained between major trade unions. When the War Ministry created or controlled plants, which it often did in Valencia, UGT and/or PCE members were given employment preference. The dynamism and momentum of the UGT discouraged CNT militants who resented their second-class status. Workers would opportunistically join the UGT, which many CNT members considered no better than a company union. To the great disappointment of the anarchosyndicalists, former CNT adherents would quickly switch to the rival organization if they thought it to be personally advantageous.

The UGT and CNT fought over limited resources, especially machinery, in the factories they dominated. The CNT maintained a strong presence in many smaller workshops. It had over half the members in one atelier in Gandía (Valencia), which employed fewer than 70 members. It dominated a cooperative of 350 workers in Denia (Alicante). The CNT position in larger factories under more direct state control grew progressively weaker. The UGT came to outnumber the CNT in major state-controlled arms factories by a margin of three or four to one (Santacreu Soler 1992:141). In Novelda (Alicante) of 1,500 (mostly female) munitions workers, only 200 joined the libertarian organization. In a second plant of 1,250 workers in Alicante, the CNT achieved parity with the UGT, but in a third large factory in the same region, only 400 of 1,300 workers were in the CNT. In a fourth, 1,280 were in the CNT and 800 in the UGT. This plant, the Fábrica Siderúrgica del Mediterráneo, had technical personnel that had joined the either the UGT or CNT but "who tomorrow would work for fascism."[47]

In larger plants that built and repaired planes known as "Moscas," CNT workers complained of harsh discipline imposed by Communist management. Their "reign of terror" was worse than that implanted by the "most monstrous bosses" during "the ominous dictatorship [of Primo de Rivera]." The disgruntled libertarians claimed that if a worker arrived ten minutes late, he would lose 50 percent of a day's pay. They refused to accept "this robbery" and asserted that they would fight it "with violence," if necessary. Commissars in the factory denied that discipline was unjust and draconian. Nevertheless CNT officials asserted that their members were threatened with sentences in fortifications brigades.

The imminent defeat of the Republic did not pull the CNT and UGT together but further apart.[48] As the Republic sank, libertarians continued to protest Communist domination of military transport and their "persecution" of CNT members. The Confederation even threatened to withdraw its formal cooperation. Although in certain villages, both unions collaborated in the work of collectives; in others conflict resumed. In Torrenueva (Ciudad Real), the CNT had a constituency of female refugees from Cordova, whereas natives who controlled the town council belonged to the UGT. The Confederation claimed that the UGT had persecuted and jailed five libertarian militants. In Casas Altas (Valencia) a fight broke out between male Communists and stone-throwing female collectivists.[49] In Chinchón, a prosperous village near Madrid, the CNT and Communists fought over control of land in the spring of 1938.[50] In the center, CNT officials claimed that the UGT dominated the Institute for Agrarian Reform, whose mechanics refused to fix machines belonging to the Confederation or to its collectives.[51] CNT repairmen had to be especially proficient at cannibalizing machines since they could not ask for help from "official bodies."[52] These mechanics met the challenge so well that even the UGT was persuaded to request their assistance. At the end of the year, in the province of Madrid, the Communists claimed that the CNT collectives and cooperatives were hoarding food and refusing to supply the quartermaster.[53] This may have been true, but the Communist solution of turning the collectives' land over to individual peasants was unlikely to resolve supply problems.

Employers in the Republican zone, as well as in the Nationalist one, maintained significant wage differences between men and women. By November

1938, the majority of wage earners in Republican defense industries were female. They usually labored in shifts from eight to ten hours per day. Like many of their male colleagues, their commitment to a trade union seemed marginal. The male monopoly on almost all union leadership positions might have rendered them inactive. Female wage laborers were nonetheless capable of defending their interests. The high priority given to arms production resulted in relatively good salaries, although, like soldiers, they too suffered from food shortages. In a small workshop in Villena (Alicante) women workers threatened to strike over food scarcities.[54] In other factories, female wage earners rejected and resented the discourse of union leaders who told members that they must literally "tighten their belts". At the same time, gender tensions divided workers. Certain managers purchased sex by promising their female workers salary raises. Others awarded their mistresses cushy jobs and extra food rations. Less privileged male workers resented the growing biological bargaining power of women.

An inspection tour of collectives by union officials in the province of Ciudad Real showed the complex record of agrarian collectivization in a region where small owners continued to dominate politically and economically.[55] Even after the experience of nearly two and a half years of collectivization, most villagers were ignorant of its meaning and purpose. In one village, Pueblo de Alhambra, the collective functioned well, but in most of the sixteen villages inspected, collectives either did not exist or were controlled by a minority of small proprietors whom, many thought, profited unduly from them. They ran collectives as a kind of private enterprise and would not admit new members who had a perfect right to join. This de facto managerial elite also refused to share the fruits of its labor with the rest of the CNT and was reluctant to accept the libertarian organization's vision of solidarity. Even CNT members, many of whom had joined after 18 July, were unaware of their organization's guidelines. In Daimiel, where seventeen hundred were members of the Confederation and over one thousand were collectivists, only a few dozen showed up for a lecture and discussion on the theme of collectivization. In the district of Infantes, which contained seven hundred CNT members and one thousand collectivists, only one hundred attended a similar talk. Villagers were disgusted by oligarchic domination of both the collective and union local. In this district, where the CNT local controlled nearly all expropriated lands and claimed to have over twenty-seven hundred members, workers' attitudes toward wage labor remained unchanged: "They still felt that they were working for the bourgeois in the same conditions as before." Regional CNT officials recommended that if resistance to work endured, malingerers should be expelled from the union and declared enemies of the Republic, thereby enabling the state to take punitive measures against them.

The opportunist will to survive was not limited to the Republican zone. A labor shortage forced employers in Nationalist territory to hire workers who had been committed leftists. For example, after the Nationalist conquest of Asturias, "75 percent" of the approximately 180 male and female workers in a ceramics factory in Lugones "remained contaminated by the Marxist virus." These wage laborers quickly adapted to the new political situation and in some cases became model workers.[56] Prudence and fear limited their ability to protest or sabotage the Nationalist war effort. At the same time, the stability of wages and prices in the Nationalist zone, at least until 1938, diminished resistance to the regime among wage earners who were offered ample opportunities for overtime. In an explosives factory in the same town, the paternalistic tradition helped to create a pliable work force. The company provided its workers with housing, electricity, heat, health insurance, schools, and a church.

Nationalist prison camps overflowed with captured soldiers. From 5 to 28 February in Barcelona, Tarragona, Ruis, Lérida, Barbastro, and Gerona, authorities processed 21,018 prisoners. *Franquista* officials continued to add tens of thousands during the first weeks of March, making a total of nearly forty-two thousand in less than two months.[57] Toward the end of the war, Nationalist policing of ports hindered the escape of hundreds of *guerrilleros* in Asturias (Pons Prades 1977:181). In Nationalist disciplinary brigades and concentration camps, political prisoners and common criminals were supposed to be segregated, and the former subjected to intensive political and religious propaganda.[58] Carlist chaplains tended to the "spiritual" and "moral" needs of prisoners who were forced to attend mass.[59] To discourage attempts at flight, political and military inmates were to be interned in camps far from their homes.[60] The confined were constantly warned that they would be shot if caught trying to escape. Nonetheless, desperate and starving men risked their lives for freedom.[61] The prisons' lack of resources encouraged flight.[62] The shortage of guards fostered prisoners' evasion attempts. In some camps guards were unwilling or unable to impose discipline. Nor were they sufficiently armed. As late as September 1938 there were incidents in which sentries fled with their deserting prisoners. Perhaps everyday cold and hunger—for they shared the awful food and shelter of the inmates—made them identify with their wards and rendered their desire to defect stronger than the prospect of being on the victorious side. Informers among the inmates or civilians betrayed the unfortunate.

Nationalist prisoners were supposed to be engaged in public works projects or in assisting the military. The presence of mini-Gulags on both sides showed their common emphasis on labor. The productivist ideologies of the left are well known and require no further elaboration. The Nationalists too wanted prisoners to "redeem themselves through labor" (Richards 1998:80). The iron mines of Vizcaya were compelled to establish production quotas. A stay in an even harsher concentration camp would punish a worker who did not meet them.[63] Important enterprises, such as Babcock and Wilcox, were able to hire all the prison labor that they wanted.[64] Private firms ignored the supposed restrictions on the use of forced labor, which mandated that capitalists could employ prisoners only during periods of full employment.[65] Their exploitation of the interned continued into 1940. They paid the wives of their prisoners two pesetas per day and an extra peseta for each child under fifteen years old (Richards 1998:80; Moreno Gómez 1986:337).

Although free, the mobile—whether shepherds, gypsies, drivers, chauffeurs, and sometimes women—were universally distrusted figures during the war. The lack of trust in the mobile contrasted sharply with the confidence placed in large numbers of fixed doormen and maids who willingly denounced their residents and bosses. The ability of the itinerant to profit from transport shortages and the difficulties of travel fueled popular resentment and official suspicion.[66] Shepherds—along with gypsies—could guide defectors to the other side (Pitt-Rivers 1954:183). They exchanged useful news about the enemy or conveyed important information to the people that had bribed them. Nationalist authorities placed shepherds under house arrest and ordered soldiers to make sure that herders could not obtain information on troop movements.[67] Sometimes, itinerants facilitated exchanges of food and other commodities between zones (Pons Prades 1974:238). The imposition of the *tasa* disrupted the commercial activities of gypsies who had engaged in traditional trading of livestock.[68] In the fall of 1938, Republican authorities arrested four married gypsy men who were buying and selling dozens of animals without authorization in the province of Valencia. In a dispute over grazing, soldiers of the Popular Army shot dead two gypsies near Fuente-Alamo (Albacete).[69] Women earned—and suffered for—their reputation as gossips. One of the leading psychiatrists of the Republican Army observed that females near the front had to be closely controlled since they conveyed "private, uncensored news to both sides" (Mira 1943:125).

As has been seen, chauffeurs and mechanics profited throughout the war from their easy mobility and relative liberty.[70] Some chauffeurs came to prefer speculative or even criminal activities to regular wage labor, confirming anthropologists' argument that wage labor in many areas of the Mediterranean was regarded as a humiliating violation of masculine and family honor (Collier 1987:16). Pilfering was dramatic in the transportation sector. According to one CNT militant, transportation workers acted "shamefully, worse than when the bourgeoisie ran things. They stole tools, blankets, and jackets. We should send an inspector into [their] homes. [I ordered] fifty or sixty comrades who were not doing anything back to work . . . [I even] fired a pervert [i.e., a gay worker]."[71] Activists were reluctant to discuss the situation in public but said in private that the only way to correct problems in garages and repair shops was to empower a "slave driver" (*negrero*) to stop theft, disobedience, drunkenness, and even sabotage. This "slave driver" must have been somewhat ineffective since "immorality" continued to flourish among teamsters.[72]

In 1938 the pilfering of auto parts led to the expulsion of two apprentices from a Madrid workshop.[73] Using deceitful documentation, a driver stole potatoes, was caught, and assigned to a fortification brigade.[74] With the complicity of most of their colleagues, chauffeurs lent vehicles and services in exchange for food, and mechanics made repairs on private cars in public garages in return for favors.[75] These abuses led activists to conclude that workers had no "class consciousness." Commissars also noted lax discipline and low productivity in garages and repair shops.[76] Fights that had led to serious injuries had erupted on the shop floor, but those responsible managed to avoid sanctions. Absenteeism and lateness also went unpunished. Unauthorized repairs were performed on a car, which was used for the private enjoyment of the personnel. Managers and CNT rank-and-file committees usually protected the guilty.

Drivers who were supposed to transport mail, as well as mailmen themselves, would give priority to those who bribed them with food and money.[77] Postal workers were tempted to convert for their own personal use what they were conveying, and by the spring of 1937 the service had won a "public and notorious reputation for disorder" (*Claridad,* 15 March 1937). In the fall of 1937 a mailman was convicted of stealing.[78] Throughout the war, drivers were reputed for their selfishness.[79] The "dirty business" (*negocio sucio*) of chauffeurs and their agents created "scandals worthy of fascists."[80] The offenders were totally indifferent to the needs of the collectivity. Chauffeurs refused to permit accompanying postmen to take a change of clothes or even stamped packages. Instead, they filled the available space with their own highly priced merchandise.

Soldiers with access to automobiles might imitate their civilian counterparts. A military driver loved to go joy riding in his Cadillac in the company of known prostitutes who, according to one CNT militant, "were morally unhealthy for those of us who really believe in the cause for which we are fighting."[81] The driver's taste for expensive cigarettes led others to suspect him of pimping and perhaps of black marketeering. For the good of the "social cause," a libertarian activist demanded that he be disciplined. Militants kept insisting upon a tough policy, including dismissal of those who accepted or tolerated bribes. Yet the activists themselves sometimes set a poor example for the rank and file. A union official engaged in what others considered shady dealings in supply contracts and was publicly drummed out of the organization.[82] It may have provided some consolation when Madrid investigators concluded that the situation in Cuenca was even worse than in their own city. In Cuenca workshops, "a spirit of banditry" existed: "When a car is left on the street all of its parts are stolen." A militant concluded that problems in the provincial city, like those of Madrid, could only be resolved with a "hard hand" (*mano dura*).[83]

Even after the fall of Barcelona at the end of January, the Republic still held Madrid and controlled one-third of Spain. Negrín and especially the Communists wished to carry on resistance. If Madrid remained unvanquished, the Republic, they hoped, might be saved by a new European war in which it would be transformed into the antifascist ally of Great Britain and France. However, popular demoralization—as much or more than the "betrayal" of the democracies or the machinations of anti-Communist plotters—dashed these prospects. Prominent Republican politicians and non-Communist officers—Casado, Julián Besteiro, and Cipriano Mera—opposed Negrín and the Communists.[84] They believed, not unreasonably, that it was impossible to carry on resistance given the lack of food, clothing, and arms for both civilians and the military. The problem of supplies was "extremely grave and without hope of relief" (Casado quoted in Bolloten 1991:696). No transportation was available to bring food from the Levante. Spare parts and tires were lacking.

Some also harbored illusions that without the Communists, they could negotiate with Franco a more favorable surrender. Colonel Casado—supported by Anarchists, Republicans and Socialists—led the non-Communist officers who sought peace. They established the Junta of Madrid, which gathered those who opposed Negrín's declared policies of last-ditch resistance. The Junta seized power on 5 March and a few days later a civil war within a civil war erupted between Communist forces and those of the Junta. "Not the least of the ironies of the Spanish Civil War was that it ended the same way that it began: with a revolt by a large minority of the Republican Army against the current Republican government on the grounds that the latter was dominated by the Communists and about to give way to a Communist dictatorship" (Payne 1970:364).[85] On 10 March a cease-fire was declared, and the Junta tried to reach a peace without reprisals with Burgos. The Junta was as unsuccessful as Prieto and other Republicans who had futilely tried for a year to conclude a compromise with the Nationalists. The latter continued to insist that their adversary surrender unconditionally. During the last days of March, Republican soldiers fraternized openly with their Nationalist counterparts and abandoned the front for their homes (Thomas 1961:600; Alpert 1989:297). In this context, fraternization and desertion reached their zenith. Burgos radio broadcasted the serial numbers of bills that Nationalist authorities would honor, and Madrid merchants refused to accept others (Jackson 1965:469). Nationalist soldiers were all-powerful and could—and sometimes did, at least in the south—take whatever they wanted.[86] On 1 April, the war was over. Madrid residents had more to eat during the first week of "liberation" than they had in any week for over two years (Peers 1943:85).

*Franquistas* stinted neither with food nor repression. The military dictatorship shot tens of thousands and imprisoned immediately perhaps 250,000 (Payne 1970:368).[87] To avoid punishment, some members of the defeated army took to the same Sierra where deserters and fugitives had hidden during the civil war. Others perished in failed attempts to leave the country. The conflict killed and injured an estimated 350,000 to 500,000, a decline of approximately 2 percent of the population.[88] During the Thirty Years' War in Germany, the fall of population was between 20 to 25 percent, and the British Isles suffered an 11.6 percent decline in their seventeenth-century civil wars. The U.S. Civil War caused about a 3 percent diminution, and the Russian civil war saw a fall of perhaps 9 percent. During World War II the population of the USSR declined by 15 percent (figures in Carlton 1992:214; Pipes 1994:508–9). The Spanish civil war has retained its symbolic charge and political significance, but it was less bloody than other conflicts.

# Conclusion

The Republic proved incapable of fighting an industrial war, particularly a trench war, which required massive supplies of food, clothing, materials, and weapons. Although Loyalists inherited initial advantages in resources and industry, their enemies proved logistically superior. The ephemeral Republican victories at Teruel and Ebro and even the defense of Madrid may have boosted morale, but they could not resolve its problems of political economy. Privation caused growing alienation. The Republic was unable to retain the commitment and devotion of the urban dwellers who initially sustained it. Nor did it arouse the enthusiasm of rural populations, including collectivists, who resented its price controls. Historians have often attributed the difficulties of collectives to outside forces, that is, the pressures of the war and the attacks of the Confederation's political enemies (see Bernecker 1982:130).[1] Certainly, without the support of an efficient and united government, it is difficult to see how either agrarian or industrial collectives could have prospered. However, internal divisions among workers themselves compounded political tensions and economic deficiencies. Many, if not most, gave priority to their own needs first and then considered those of communities larger than themselves and their families. Activists devoted to a cause had to confront a relatively selfish rank and file. Village requirements provoked more solidarity than region, republic, or revolution. The degree of commitment declined as the group became bigger or the cause more abstract.

In striking ways, productivist militants and managers in Spanish collectives came to resemble their Soviet counterparts who, despite the assistance of a powerful and centralized state, also reported problems of motivation and discipline. As in the USSR, many collectivists expressed a strong distrust of all those—in the Spanish case, women, elderly, gypsies, and sometimes even soldiers—who were not considered full-fledged producers. Hoarding goods and information showed that agrarian collectives were not the beehives of solidarity that their apologists have argued. Bartering and black marketeering abandoned many urban residents and much of the Popular Army to hungry fates. The Republic proved incapable of sufficiently mobilizing peasant energies to win its life and death struggle. Its wage and price controls and the indiscipline of its troops backfired by reinforcing agrarian egotisms. A social-historical approach from below shows that the conflict between rural and urban was as consequential for the Republic's decline as the political disputes, class divisions, and international rivalries, which have been the traditional focus of much Spanish civil war historiography.

Some historians have charged that the Western democracies were guilty of appeasement and insufficient antifascism. Thus, they have logically taken the spotlight off internal factors. In their eyes, the Spanish war was a prelude to the Second World War. Their approach has provided insights into the politics and diplomacy of the period. Yet perhaps now it would be more fruitful to see the Spanish war not only in its contemporary international context but also as an example of a civil war in a developing Western nation. Therefore, I have made constant references to and comparisons with the English, French, U.S., and Russian civil wars.

My perspective has begun from the foundation block of the individual. Both Marxists and bourgeois have dismissed individualisms as false forms of resistance and have contrasted them with conscious revolutionary activity or conventional political activism.[2] The recent emphasis on gender assumes, like class perspectives, an identity that neglects individual dissidence. But this feminist and Marxist dismissal of individualisms ignores fundamental material needs of workers and peasants who, "on the basis of their daily material experience," were able "to penetrate and demystify the prevailing ideology." A perceptive Republican soldier concluded from his own war experience, "the most common gauge of collective adventure was personal vicissitudes. In spite of all the messages of massive propaganda—whether written, broadcasted, or painted—that insisted on the common interest, people displayed their sharp individualist edge as though trying to save themselves from the misfortunes of the rest" (Pons Prades 1974:280). No system, whether libertarian communism, socialism, capitalism, or feudalism, has been fully successful in making the subordinate classes, whether male or female, internalize the dominant ideology.

Self-indulgence and self-interest of the anonymous had major consequences. Flights and retreats of subversive individuals decided battles. As General Rojo pointed out, the indifferent rear triumphed over a supposedly courageous vanguard (Rojo 1974:43).[3] Individualisms weakened the infrastructure of trench warfare. The reluctance to build fortifications, resistance to labor, and the acquisitive or entrepreneurial hoarding of food debilitated the Republican war effort. Perhaps these weaknesses were more important in the defeat of the Republic than any of the supposedly "decisive battles" in the north, at Teruel, or on the Ebro. The Republic—like the U.S. South in its war for independence—had only to endure to triumph. The proponents of the holding strategy believed that the Republic might have been saved if it lasted until a European-wide struggle erupted, when the Western democracies would have made it a partner in the antifascist struggle. Yet as we know, its military and civilian populations collapsed six months before the outbreak of the Second World War.

A materialist approach from the bottom up shows that the Republic could not satisfy basic physical needs of its troops. Soldiers' experiences of hunger, cold, and disease on tranquil fronts undermined their desire to continue the war, and protecting their own bodies came to have the highest priority. The inability of the Popular Army to fulfill material necessities also deepened skepticism about Republican ideology. Opportunism and cynicism flourished in the Republican zone, and these attitudes made it difficult for commanders to use soldiers to attack or to put pressure on the enemy. Nor could they easily withdraw their best reserves from quiet fronts for fear of collapse. Self-preservation helped to generate a national war of attrition. As the conflict continued, soldiers of the Popular Army lost any remaining desire to sacrifice for the Republic or, for that matter, any abstract political or revolutionary cause. They would not, as Republican leaders hoped, make a contribution to a decisive battle or battles which could turn the tide.

Soldiers found that many of the enemy shared their dislike of war and would cooperate in arranging informal and unwritten truces. Yet Nationalists were more consistently able to overcome rank-and-file passivity and create a better fighting force. *Franquistas* fed, clothed, and paid their troops much more regularly than Republicans. Nationalists persistently demonstrated the effectiveness of professional soldiers and mercenaries. The insurgents earned respect because of the fortitude and tenacity of the small garrisons of Moors and Falangists who were stationed in villages and towns. Their tough defense against Republican attacks gave officers enough time to call up reinforcements who were able to stymie the enemy. This pattern repeated itself throughout the conflict. It showed the inability of the Popular Army to match the feats of the New Model Army of the seventeenth century. No Republican Cromwell emerged to halt plundering by hanging offenders on the spot (Kenyon

238 Conclusion

1988:138, 202). Nor did the civilian authority imitate the English parliamentary model by efficiently taxing the population and by regularly supplying and paying its military forces.

The Popular Army failed to equal the successes of French revolutionary armies of the late eighteenth and early nineteenth centuries that—despite shortages of food, equipment, and arms—were able to defeat professional and mercenary soldiers. In fact, in contrast to the soldiers of the French Republic, who also experienced great material shortages but remained loyal, those of the Spanish Republic frequently mutinied.[4] Perhaps part of the explanation may be that the Spanish revolution, unlike its French counterpart, never had the support of most of the bourgeoisie or property owners. The middle classes, let alone the upper classes, were skeptical about the Republic's ability to protect their possessions. In fact, in their desire to secure property, Nationalist forces more closely resembled the National Guard of the early years of the French Revolution than Spanish Republican soldiers whose looting and expropriations increased the skepticism of both big and small bourgeois about the Republic's ability to safeguard property. More peasants might have been persuaded to aid the Popular Army if it could have kept its pillaging under control. Oddly enough, despite its progressive intentions, the Spanish Republic in wartime paralleled in important ways the slaveowning South in the U.S. Civil War or the Napoleonic regime after the disastrous Russian campaign. Massive foot dragging on the home front and desertions on the war front contributed greatly to the downfall of all three. At any rate, too much stress should not be put on outcome. In other words, the issue of why and how the Nationalists won (or the Republic lost) should not preclude a profound investigation of the experience of the anonymous during the civil war.

Perhaps all controlled economies during wartime necessitate coercion. As Richard Cobb (1987:288) has pointed out, "no one could claim that the peasantry might be brought round by persuasion or by appeals to a revolutionary patriotism of which they were totally devoid." However, the expropriations of food and supplies by Republican forces seemed less efficient and less planned than those of the French revolutionary armies or those of the Bolsheviks. The French organized groups of urban dwellers, the *armées révolutionnaires,* who requisitioned grain for their towns. They fulfilled their main goal of providing the capital with bread. The *sans-culottes* soldiers were able to guarantee grain circulation and distribution and to enforce the maximum. The *armées révolutionnaires* proved much more efficient in mobilizing the resources of an entire nation than the *Etapas* or other Spanish Republican forces. The Parisian reign of terror achieved its aims; its less fearsome and more haphazard Madrid/Valencian successor did not. The economy of the Spanish Republican zone could not support its *levée en masse.*

Maybe to their credit, Spanish Republicans did not possess the implacability of their French or Russian predecessors. They never executed generals held responsible for military failures. In contrast, seventeen French generals in 1793 and sixty-seven in 1794 were put to death for their defeats (Best 1986:88). Nor did Spanish Republicans imitate Lenin, who waged a "merciless and terroristic struggle and war with the peasant bourgeoisie and [any] other that retains grain surpluses" (quoted in Lih 1990:152). The Bolshevik leader, using words of "astounding violence," in the summer of 1918 called for "ruthless war on the kulaks. Death to all of them" (quoted in Figes 1996:618). Grain was brutally collected in kind. Communist terror helped prioritize food distribution and nourish the Red Army (Lih 1990:152; Pipes 1994:13). At the same time, the Bolsheviks proved more capable than the Whites by mobilizing five million peasants (Figes 1990:169). Perhaps, despite the Red Army's frequent looting and confiscations, peasants trusted that the Bolsheviks would divide up the land.

Ironically, after its victory, the Franco regime copied the Republican regime's policies of imposing unreasonable and unworkable price controls on wheat. The Nationalist *tasas* discouraged production for the official tariff, created a black market, and promoted hoarding (Barciela López 1986:393). Quickly, many low-income Spaniards experienced hunger. Once again, the Nationalist regime—like its Republican predecessor—was unable to bridge the gap between urban and rural. Several months after Franco's victory, starvation resumed in the cities, and hoarding and misreporting of information continued in the countryside. Both regimes erected an inefficient, incompetent, and corrupt bureaucracy to control transportation and prices. Both suffered from the solidarity of the *pueblo* that often refused to cooperate with central authority (Pitt-Rivers 1954:207–8). A recent history has demonstrated the corruption and incompetence of postwar agriculture policies but—in line with the political perspectives of most historians of Spain—has ignored the continuities between the Republican and Franco eras (Richards 1998:137–41). These continuities were apparent not only in the poor productivity of agriculture but also in the lack of enthusiasm of workers for work.[5] The Franco regime eventually was converted to freer market policies. Perhaps the Spanish Republic would have done better by permitting free trade and then taxing heavily its beneficiaries.

Unlike the Russian Whites in their civil war, who confronted an enemy with similar political and social demands, the Spanish counterrevolutionaries could rely upon a competent officer class that, in contrast to its Russian counterpart, had not been decimated and destroyed by the world war.[6] The neutrality of Spain during World War I was one of the most astute policies ever undertaken by Spain's governing elites and may have prevented that nation from following the Soviet example. Furthermore, neither propertied nor clerical elites had suffered the disruptions of the Great War. In 1936, church, state, army, and industry were largely intact. Like the Russian Whites, the Nationalists made few concessions to national minorities and even fewer to the impoverished peasantry. Yet the Spanish counterrevolution nevertheless triumphed. The bourgeoisie has often been seen as the class that fostered individualism and made egoism into social policy. In contrast, the working class has been identified with doctrines of solidarity. However, if the Spanish civil war is seen as a class war, the bourgeoisie may have displayed more cohesion than the working class. Its doctrines of nation, religion, and property rights provoked greater loyalties than the competing ones of internationalism, rationalism, revolution, and collectivism. Examination of anonymous individuals in the Republican zone renews questioning of the interpretation of the Spanish civil war and revolution as the struggle of the oligarchy against the people.

Notes
Bibliography
Index

# Notes

## Introduction

1. Leninists, such as Enrique Líster, modify the classic Marxist view and believe that the actions of leaders and high-ranking officers—not the "masses" or common soldiers—are decisive. See Líster 1966:99, 117, 280. A similar perspective is found in Modesto 1969:286.

2. The truism, a paraphrase of Heidegger, is found in Morris 1991:384.

3. This includes the valuable work of Goldstone 1991.

4. Fraser (1986) is one of the few who explores the "lived experiences" (29) of Spaniards, but he focuses primarily on militants. So do most accounts by International Brigades' veterans. See Herrick 1998:220: "I lived in Spain some nine months, and had not made friends with one Spaniard. I hardly knew what a Spanish man or women thought, except what I read in the papers."

5. An anthropologist who studied the town of Aracena (Huelva) in the twentieth century has pointed out, "Above all else, men and women had the strongest material and moral obligations with respect to immediate family members, and only after these obligations were fulfilled could practical aid be given and moral commitments made to other members of the community." See Maddox 1993:138.

6. On this subject in eighteenth-century England, see Thompson 1975:255–308.

7. This sentiment is echoed in many other monographs of the same author. Unless otherwise indicated, all translations are my own.

8. Again, for examples of this approach see the monographs of José Manuel Martínez Bande and others published by the Servicio Histórico Militar.

9. For a similar problem concerning financial and commercial documents, see Viñas 1979:15.

10. Communists share this analysis. See Martín-Blázquez 1938:203; Líster 1966:9, 73.

11. Quoted in Scott 1985:11; see also 286: "Power-laden situations are nearly always inauthentic; the exercise of power nearly always drives a portion of the full transcript underground."

## 1. Militancy

1. Much of the following information is from Simpson 1995.

2. In some towns, the elimination was formal, and Catholic teachers retained their jobs and salaries. See Collier 1987:92.

3. Azaña had published *Estudios de política francesa contemporánea: La política militar* in 1919.

4. Leftist historiography usually minimizes this disorder. Cf. Fraser 1986:90; Preston 1986:44.

5. General Motors, 2 July 1936, Barcelona 1329, Archivo Histórico Nacional-Sección Guerra Civil (hereafter AHN-SGC).

6. On its ability to create confusion even among the most committed Republicans, see Semprún 1993:103.

7. Cf. Thomas 1961:157: "In the streets [of Madrid] the people ruled. . . . Syndicalism had thus come to Madrid as a result of the great anti-popular rising. For the workers July 20 was a day of triumph." Preston (1986:88–89) attributes the victory over "fascism" in Madrid in November 1936 to the "people" and the "whole population." "The one great and unique weapon the Republic possessed was popular enthusiasm" (115). On the right, Salas Larrazábal (1973:203) has argued that "the Spanish people, and this made the civil war possible, if not unavoidable, were split into two groups, which were irreconcilable and numerically equivalent."

8. One contemporary of the English civil war wrote, "There were very few of the common people that cared much for either of the causes but they would have taken any side for pay and plunder." Quoted in Ashley 1990:2; see also Underdown 1985:3–4.

9. For this position, see Leval 1975:80. Even Leval realized that the anarchist emphasis on work and production would diminish personal freedom.

10. This conception of counterrevolution, like much of the rest of the literature, assumes mass politicization.

11. Colmegna (1941:32) blames these acts on "modern Jews," i.e., the left.

12. The Spanish masses were violently anticlerical in a way that, for example, the Russian peasants were not. The former identified the church with the ruling elites; the latter used religion as a way to resist an atheistic state. See Fitzpatrick 1994:61.

13. Narración, 21 December 1936, Extremadura 24, AHN-SGC.

14. In one Aragon town, an assassin went from bar to bar with the priest's testicles wrapped in paper, see Casanova 1999:140.

15. For an anthropological interpretation of this phenomenon that emphasizes its millenarian aspects, see Lincoln 1985:241–60. Along similar lines, see de la Cueva 1998: 364–68.

16. D. Rafael, Médico-Director del Hospital, 29 January 1937, Extremadura 24, AHN-SGC.

17. Milicias, nd., Zona Republicana (hereafter ZR), a. 94, l. 1334, c. 10, Archivo General Militar de Avila (hereafter AGM).

18. Albuquerque, 1 January 1937, Extremadura 24, AHN-SGC.

19. Albuquerque, 1 January 1937, Extremadura 24, AHN-SGC; Rosique Navarro 1988:130, 240. In Badajoz, violent and destructive acts of anticlericalism had been rare during the early years of the Republic.

20. D. Rafael, Médico-Director del Hospital, 29 January 1937, Extremadura 24, AHN-SGC. For a discussion of the numbers killed in Ronda, see Corbin 1995: 609–25.

21. José Gutierrez, 28 January 1937, Extremadura 24, AHN-SGC.

22. D. Rafael, 29 January 1937, Extremadura 24, AHN-SGC; cf. Richards 1998:31: "The terror in the Republican zone . . . was less selective, relatively without direction and performed no particular social function."

23. Los compañeros, November 1936, Barcelona 839, AHN-SGC.

24. Casanova (1999) finds this social mixture of victims common in Aragon.

25. Informe, 2 February 1938, Barcelona 811, AHN-SGC.

26. Informe, 15 August 1937, PS Madrid 542, AHN-SGC; a more glowing version of mountain people is found in Martínez Bande 1984.

27. Al juzgado, 25 December 1937, Aragon R 136, AHN-SGC.

28. Tercio, nd., Aragon R 136, AHN-SGC.

29. Declaración, 7 September 1937, Aragon R 136, AHN-SGC. On Falangist responsibility for many assassinations, see Chaves Palacios 1996:101.

30. Bautista Vilar (1990:176) claims that Nationalists killed proportionally more Protestant clergy than Republicans eliminated Catholic priests.

31. Segunda, 18 October 1936, ZR, a. 94, 1. 1334, c. 10, AGM.

32. Ministerio, 14 January 1937, ZR, a. 54, 1. 474, c. 7, AGM.

33. For example, the militias of the JSU were always well supplied. See Tagüeña Lacorte 1978:91.

34. Ilustrísimo, 11 August 1938, ZR, a. 54, 1. 473, c. 4, AGM.

35. Ironically, Martín-Blázquez himself was accused of embezzlement when he abandoned the Republic and remained in Paris after an official mission. See Cordón 1977:201.

36. Cf. the one-year experiment of price controls during the French Revolution. See Cobb 1987.

37. Informe, nd., Madrid 542, AHN-SGC.

38. Milicias, nd., ZR a. 94, 1. 1334, c.10, AGM, p. 12; Líster (1966:156) tendentiously attributes the practice only to anarchists.

39. For a similar situation in the French Revolution, see Cobb 1987:254.

40. A los camaradas, 6 December 1936, Gijón F 89, AHN-SGC.

41. A similar situation troubled Confederate troops during the U.S. Civil War. See Linderman 1987:184.

42. The Carlist areas of Alava also provided a significant number of volunteers. See Ugarte 1990:2:60.

43. Declaración, 4 August 1936, Causa General, Archivo Histórico Nacional (hereafter AHN).

44. Análisis, nd., ZR, a. 63, 1. 853, c. 18, AGM.

45. Pipes (1994:23) asserts that one volunteer in the Russian civil war was worth twelve conscripts. Cf. Esdaile 1990:1:151.

46. Alpert (1984:218) gives a figure of 1,025,500 for the Nationalists; Payne (1970:343), using Soviet sources, offers figures of a similar magnitude.

47. For example, during the Albarracín offensive in July–August 1937, see Martínez Bande 1973:62.

48. Declaración, 3 September 1936, CGG reel 159, AGM.

49. Información, 9 January 1938, Zova Nacional (hereafter ZN), a. 42, 1. 2, c. 2, AGM. Loyal Civil Guards would soon be allowed to join the Guardia Nacional Republicana.

50. Thus, at the end of July, General Miaja was able to establish his headquarters at Montoro, which was only a few miles from Cordova. Martínez Bande 1969:56.

51. Antecedentes, nd., Cuartel General del Generalísimo (hereafter CGG) a. 4, l. 273, c. 1, AGM; Relato, 6 December 1937, CGG, a. 4, l. 273, c. 1, AGM.

52. Salas Larrazábal and Salas Larrazábal 1986:51; Martínez Bande 1976:27: "The militiamen, except for rare cases that confirmed the rule, were unable to achieve any success in the war against 'fascism.' They scattered or fled quickly when faced with enemy aviation or with some well-commanded soldiers." Martínez Bande repeats this judgment in his many other works. See also Asensio 1938:14.

53. Fourteen to twenty-three thousand were airlifted in August and September.

54. Usually at any one time, over thirty thousand Italians were stationed in the Iberian Peninsula.

55. Conclusiones, 20 October 1936, Barcelona 496, AHN-SGC.

56. In an odd way, they prefigured the massive African immigration of *harkis* and guest workers to France, Spain, and other European countries that would occur after the Second World War.

57. Burgos, 21 January 1937, ZN, a. 31, l. 9, c. 23, AGM.

58. Tió (1982:68) claims that olive oil was divided equally between the enemies.

59. General Motors delivered thousands of trucks.

60. Columna de Madrid, 2 September 1936, CGG, reel 159, AGM; Declaración de Agustín Tello, CGG, reel 159, AGM.

61. According to the U.S. journalist, Jay Allen, in Vila Izquierdo 1984:89.

62. Cf. Thomas (1961:247), who doubts reports of the "massacre"; Vila Izquierdo (1984:58) relates four thousand executions. Coverdale (1975:192) reports that Italian government sources confirm massive bloodletting.

63. Population and voting information is found in Rosique Navarro 1988:37, 235, 304; Jackson (1965:268) reports that the Nationalists executed forty-one armed resisters. See also Bolloten 1991:5.

64. Declaración(es), September 1936, CGG, reel 159, AGM; Pons Prades 1977:341.

65. Resumen del Señor Juez, November 1936, CGG, reel 159, AGM; Informe, 8 June 1938, reel 45, AGM; Villa de Olleria, 10 October 1936, Madrid, 524, AHN-SGC.

66. Informe, 1 February 1937, ZN, a. 44, l. 4, c. 2, AGM.

67. Valencia, 7 August 1937, ZR, a. 54, l. 473, c. 2, AGM.

68. Reservado, 2 September 1936, ZR, a. 93, l. 1280, c. 1, AGM.

69. Espinosa, 18 September 1936, ZR, a. 97, l. 966, c. 14, AGM.

70. Teniente, 30 September 1936, ZR, a. 97, l. 966, c. 7, AGM.

71. Auditoria, 20 January 1938, ZN, 107 División, a. 37, l. 1, c. 13, AGM.

72. Higher ranking and more accomplished officers usually sided with the Nationalists.

73. Declaración, 15 June 1937, Causa General, AHN.

74. Diligencia, 30 December 1936, Causa General 380, AHN.

75. Declaración, 14 August 1936, Causa General 379, AHN.

76. For more details see Gabriel 1938:26–27; Borkenau 1963:100–101. Some prostitutes proved to be good fighters and nurses. See Aroca Sardagna 1972:104. Nationalists, of course, equated committed Republican women with either nymphomaniacs or lesbians. See Vallejo Nágera 1939:225.

77. Columna, 24 December 1936, ZR, a. 75, l. 1200, c. 20, AGM.

78. Grupo, 24 November 1936, ZR, a. 75, l. 1200, c. 21, AGM; Directivas, 17 October 1936, ZR, a. 75, l. 1200, c. 22, AGM; Martín-Blázquez 1938:129; Bray 1937:87. See also the Nationalist report from the Aragon front cited in Martínez Bande 1970:257.

79. Adicción, 9 December 1938, ZR, a. 75, l. 1200, c. 11, AGM.

80. Woolsey 1998:94: "This extreme federalism was more important to most of the country people than the class-war aspects of the struggle."

81. Informe, 27 January 1937, ZR, a. 72, l. 1129, c. 2, AGM; Payne 1967:355.

82. Columna, 27 November 1936, ZR, a. 75, l. 1200, c. 17, AGM.

83. Tengo, 22 October 1936, ZR, a. 97, l. 955, c. 1, AGM.

84. Primera, 19 January 1937, ZR, a. 58, l. 627 bis, c. 1, AGM.

85. Comandancia, 23 October 1936, ZR, a. 94, l. 1334, c. 16, AGM.

86. Segunda, 18 October 1936, ZR, a. 94, l. 1334, c. 10, AGM.

87. Adicción, 9 December 1938, ZR, a. 75, l. 1200, c. 11, AGM.

88. Circular, 13 September 1936, ZR, a. 94, l. 1334, c. 1, AGM.

89. See list of workers in Sindicato de comunicaciones, Madrid 159, AHN-SGC.

90. Cotizantes, militantes, revolucionarios, 9 May 1938, Madrid 159, AHN-SGC.

91. Resumen, nd., Madrid 159, AHN-SGC.

92. Comité provincial de enlace, CNT-UGT, 30 July 1938, Madrid 1619, AHN-SGC.

93. Communists, for example, have accused General Asensio of thinking that it was impossible to defend Madrid. See Cordón 1977:232. Asensio refutes this. See also Asensio 1938; Líster (1966:54, 88) repeats the accusation and also accuses him of poor generalship.

94. Miaja was the only undefeated leader of the Popular Army. See Salas Larrazábal 1973:3618.

95. Columna, 13 November 1936, ZR, a. 75, l. 1200, c. 16, AGM.

96. Getafe, 30 December 1936, ZN, a. 22, l. 1, c. 1, AHN-SGC.

97. Other estimates are much lower. Martínez Bande (1976:176) cites only nine dead and 191 injured on 17 November.

98. Martínez Bande (1976:178) states that he died on 19 November.

99. Durruti had called on workers to sacrifice for the revolution and not to ask for more pay and less work.

100. Ejército del Centro, Estado Mayor, 3 December 1936, ZR reel 45, AGM.

101. General Motors, 20 November 1936, Barcelona 1329, AHN-SGC; Consell d'empresa CNT-UGT Elizalde, 11 December 1936, Arxiu nacional de Catalunya (hereafter ANC).

102. Nota, 25 December 1936, CGG, a. 5, l. 282, c. 4, AGM.

103. Informe, nd., Madrid 542, AHN-SGC.

104. CLUEF reports, April–May 1937, Madrid 2157, AHN-SGC.

105. On Castilian peasants joining the UGT's FETT [sic] because of its lower dues, see actas, 26 December 1937, PS Madrid 2467, AGM.

106. CNT, 5 April 1937, Barcelona 839, AHN-SGC.

107. Acta de la Junta, 7 September 1936, and 3 January 1937, Madrid 2448, AHN-SGC; Sindicato Postal Rural, 8 September 1936, Madrid 2625, AHN-SGC.

108. CNT carteros, 2 September 1937, Madrid 2321, AHN-SGC.

109. Acta de la Junta, 1 May 1937, Madrid 2448, AHN-SGC.

110. Comité de control, 17 January 1937, Madrid 1008, AHN-SGC.

111. Asamblea, 14 March 1937, Madrid 1008, AHN-SGC.

112. Sociedad de obreros de linoleum, 17 March 1937, Madrid 708, AHN-SGC; Asamblea, Sindicato único de transporte, 10 June 1937, Madrid 991, AHN-SGC, Reunión de comités, 19 February 1938, Madrid 991, AHN-SGC; Asambleas, 6 September 1936 and 7 February 1937, Madrid 858, AHN-SGC; *Claridad,* 4 March 1937. *CNT,* 21 December 1937, implied that Communists wanted to bend the rules for newcomers.

113. Reunión, 10 July 1937, Madrid 991, AHN-SGC.

114. Reunión de comités, 26 April 1938, Madrid 991, AHN-SGC.

115. Reunión de comités, 3 May 1938, Madrid 991, AHN-SGC.

116. Acta, 10 September 1936, Madrid 1008, AHN-SGC.

117. A todos los obreros, nd., Madrid 1008, AHN-SGC; Acta, 18 October 1936, Madrid 1008, AHN-SGC.

118. Acta, 1 November 1936, Madrid 1008, AHN-SGC.

119. Informe, 20 January 1937, reel 45, AGM.

120. Informe, ? January 1937, ZR, a. 47, l. 72, c. 1, AGM.

121. Borkenau adds "there was a dead silence when these words were uttered, and it is difficult to say whether this silence indicated support or opposition."

122. Acta, 7 September 1936, Madrid 2448, AHN-SGC.

123. Acta de la junta general, 18 November 1936, Madrid 3686, AHN-SGC.

124. For absenteeism in Russia, where the rate in metal factories could be as high as 80 percent, see Figes 1996:611.

125. Acta del comité de control, 13 October 1936, Madrid 3638, AHN-SGC.

126. Acta, 6 October 1936, and 31 January 1937, Madrid 1008, AHN-SGC.

127. Bosch Sánchez 1983:23; Unión, 13 October 1936, Barcelona 1329, AHN-SGC.

128. Primera, 24 November 1936, Barcelona 1329, AHN-SGC.

129. Acta, 4 December 1936, Barcelona 1329, AHN-SGC.

130. Comité de fábrica, actas UGT y CNT, September 1936, ANC.

131. Comité de fábrica, actas UGT y CNT, 7 October 1936, ANC.

132. Comité de fábrica, actas UGT y CNT, 19 October 1936, ANC.

133. Junta general, Sociedad de obreros de linoleum, 3 October 1936, Madrid 3686, AHN-SGC.

134. Sociedad, 22 September 1936, Madrid 708, AHN-SGC.

135. This paragraph is based on a letter, Talleres E. Grasset, 28 December 1936, Madrid 445, AHN-SGC.

136. Sesión, Boetticher y Navarro, 13 November 1936, Madrid 858, AHN-SGC.

137. Sesión del pleno, 13 December 1936, Madrid 858, AHN-SGC.

138. Acta de la reunión, 7 January 1937, Madrid 991, AHN-SGC.

139. Acta, Boetticher y Navarro, UGT-CNT, 8 October 1936, Madrid 858, AHN-SGC.

140. Acta, Unión Bolsera Madrileña, 3 December 1936, Madrid 858, AHN-SGC.

141. Acta, Unión Bolsera Madrileña, 20 December 1936, Madrid 1008, AHN-SGC.

142. Similar expropriations of Republicans' possessions also occurred in the Nationalist zone. See Collier 1987:162.

143. Malefakis (1970:386 n.75) indicates a more massive collectivization. Anarchist sources claimed that nearly half of the peasants in the Republican zone were "collectivists." See Bernecker 1982:111. In Levant, the collectivization of 20 percent of the land affected 40 percent of the population or 130,000 people.

144. Figures in Fraser 1986:348; Mintz 1977:199; Simoni and Simoni 1984:122. For much larger estimates of collectivists and collectives see Bernecker 1982:196–250. He states that there were 300,000 collectivists in Aragon composing 70 to 75 percent of the population. Prats (1938:81) and Peirats (1971:1:286) provide even higher figures of 450 collectives and 433,000 collectivists in Aragon. Thomas (1971:242) and Bolloten (1991:74) follow Prats's (a Socialist) and Peirats's (an anarchist) figures for Aragon.

145. Los compañeros, 24 November 1936, Barcelona 839, AHN-SGC.

146. Informe, 4 January and 19 April 1937, Barcelona 839, AHN-SGC.

147. Libertarian historians, of course, emphasize spontaneous collectivization. See Leval 1975:91, 160; Prats 1938.

148. The story and its accompanying complexities are ably treated by Viñas 1979.

149. The authors incorrectly blame hoarding on "wealthy Fifth columnists."

150. See Simmel 1991:29: "The fact that people carry around small denominations of money in their pockets, with which they can immediately purchase all sorts of small articles, often on a whim, must encourage industries that thrive from this possibility. This and in general the divisibility of money into the tiniest sums certainly contributes to the frivolous style of the external, and particularly the aesthetic areas of modern life, as well as to the growing number of trivialities with which we furnish our life."

151. 23 División, 3 January 1937, ZN, a. 42, l. 2, c. 2, AGM.

152. Orden, 9 December 1936, ZR, a. 75, l. 1200, c. 11, AGM.

## 2. Opportunism

1. Comandancia, 24 December 1936 and 12 January 1937, ZR, a. 94, l. 1334, c. 1, AGM.

2. Milicias, 17 January 1937, ZR, a. 94, l. 1334, c. 1, AGM.

3. Al Estado, 22 January 1937, ZR, a. 97, l. 971, c. 2, AGM.

4. Much of the following information closely follows Claridad, 4 March 1937.

5. Información, 20 January 1937, ZN, a. 31, l. 9, c. 4, AGM.

6. See telegrams, 22 to 31 December 1936, ZR, a. 67, l. 840, c. 1, AGM; Martínez Bande 1969:119–23; Wintringham 1939:85–87.

7. A minority of Republican military men felt that the offensive strategy was flawed and that the Republic should rely on a defensive strategy. See Martín Blázquez 1938:162.

8. Cf. Wintringham (1939:85–88), who ignores this and other incidents and attributes Republican failure to the betrayal of a major.

9. Ultimas horas, 10 February 1937, ZR, a. 54, l. 473, c. 2, AGM.

10. There is general agreement with this assessment, see Kindelán 1945:64.

11. Similar criticism is found in Solé i Sabater and Villarroya 1999:188. Cf. also Serrano 1986:128–34.

12. Fuerzas, 19 December 1936, ZR, a. 98, l. 968, c. 21, AGM.

13. Gobierno Militar, 8 January 1937, CGG, reel 159, AGM; Pons Prades (1977:314) reports that the number of attackers was twenty-one.

14. Copia, 14 January 1937, CGG, reel 159, AGM.

15. Telegrama, 12 July 1937, CGG, reel 159, AGM.

16. Telegrama, 11 November 1937, CGG, a. 5, l. 285, c. 25, AGM.

17. Ejército, 22 April 1938, CGG, a. 5, l. 285, c. 25, AGM; Martínez Bande 1981: 200–201.

18. Informe, nd., ZR, a. 54, l. 474, c. 4, AGM.

19. T.P., 18 August 1937, ZN, a. 32, l. 9. c. 23, AGM.

20. Informe, 3 January 1938, ZN, a. 36, l. 1, c. 3, AGM; Solé i Sabater and Villar-roya (1999:190–93) provides the most complete account. For yet another version of this plot based on oral history, see Pons Prades 1977:341.

21. Consejos de Guerra, ZN, a. 36, l. 1, c. 30, AGM.

22. 21 División, 31 December 1938, ZR, a. 71, l. 1090, c. 10, AGM.

23. Información, 17 August 1937, ZR, a. 71, l. 1092, c. 11, AGM.

24. Informe, 11 September 1938, ZR, a. 71, r. 166, l. 1091, c. 13, AGM.

25. For a pathbreaking treatment of quiet fronts, which has greatly influenced this study, see Ashworth 1980. On the U.S. Civil War, see Linderman 1987:67–68; Grossman 1996:34.

26. S. L. A. Marshall concluded that only 15 percent of U.S. infantrymen fired their weapons during World War II. His estimate has recently been challenged.

27. Parte, 29 June 1937, ZR, a. 65, l. 984, c. 1, AGM.

28. On the popular fear they provoked, see Woolsey 1998:39.

29. Informe, 25 February 1937, ZR, a. 59, l. 669, c. 6, AGM.

30. Valencia, 10 February 1937, ZR, reel 45, AGM.

31. Sardá 1970:445. The author estimates that of 500 million marks spent in Spain, over 300 million were budgeted to the Condor Legion.

32. Informe, 25 February 1937, ZR, a. 59, l. 669, c. 6, AGM.

33. Informe, nd., ZR, reel 45, AGM.

34. Informe, 25 February 1937, ZR, a. 59, l. 669, c. 6, AGM.

35. Valencia, 10 February 1937, ZR, reel 45, AGM; Wintringham 1939:152; Kemp 1957:72–80.

36. Cf. Thomas (1961:380), who claims that the Republican forces suffered twenty-five thousand casualties and the Nationalists twenty thousand. See Coverdale 1975:219.

37. Informe, 19 March 1937, ZR, reel 45, AGM; see also Mira 1943:81.

38. The same wound was rumored to have occurred in the Nationalist Army.

39. II Cuerpo, 21 November 1937, ZR, a. 72, l. 1114, c. 11, AGM.

40. On the Lincoln's reputation, see Colmegna 1941:138.

41. On the composition of the Junta, see Bolloten 1991:295–96.

42. 8 and 15 January 1937, Consell d'empresa CNT-UGT Elizalde, Arxiu nacional de Catalunya.

43. Cf. Coverdale (1975:233, 252–53), who argues that the Nationalist offensive on the Jarama did not take place. Even more importantly, he notes "the failure of Franco's troops on the Jarama to mount an offensive that would have busied the Republican units in that sector and prevented the reserves around Madrid from being concentrated to the north of the capital." Coverdale attributes this "failure" to Franco's desire for political reasons not to win the war too quickly and his reluctance to see the Italians triumph in a major battle.

44. Informe, 19 March 1937, ZR, reel 45, AGM.

45. Acta, 20 March 1937; Comandancia, 27 March 1937, ZR, reel 45, AGM.
46. Batallones, 27 July 1937, ZR, a. 56, l. 550, c. 2, AGM.
47. Batallones, 30 November 1937, ZR, a. 56, l. 550, c. 2, AGM.
48. See Al Coronel, 14 April 1937, ZR, reel 45, AGM.
49. Comisario, June–July 1937, ZR, a. 56, l. 550, c. 2, AGM.
50. Comandancia, 29 May 1937, ZR, a. 57, l. 606, c. 21, AGM.
51. Cf. Martínez Bande 1980:145: "In Asturias, there were no cases of passivity."
52. Análisis, nd., ZR, a. 63, l. 853, c. 18, AGM.
53. Lt. Col. Buzón, Información, 21 November 1937, ZR, a. 63, l. 853, c. 7, AGM.
54. Cuartel, 22 January 1937, CGG, a. 2, l. 145, c. 74, AGM.
55. Carreras Panchón 1986:10; Mira 1943:73, 114: "The total percentage of men temporarily discharged because of war neurosis was not more than 1.5 percent." "The number of mental casualties in the Spanish Republican Army was surprisingly low."
56. Telegrama, 18 February 1937, ZN, a. 15, l. 4, c. 43, AGM.
57. Gobernador, 10 November 1936, ZN, a. 15, l. 1, c. 88, AGM.
58. Sexta, 23 December 1936, ZN, a. 32, l. 9, c. 4, AGM.
59. Copia, 21 December 1936, ZN, a. 15, l. 1, c. 88, AGM.
60. Normas, 6 March 1937, ZR, reel 93, AGM.
61. Sexta, nd., ZN, a. 39, l. 9, c. 6, AGM.
62. 5[0] C.E., February–August 1937, ZN, a. 31, l. 1, c. 1, AGM.
63. At times, it showered bombs on its own troops. Colmegna 1941:78, 141.
64. This is one of the most important conclusions of the report by Lt. Col. Buzón, Información, 21 November 1937, ZR, a. 63, l. 853, c. 7, AGM.
65. Souchy Bauer 1982:56; Lt. Col. Buzón, Información, 2 June 1937, ZR, a. 63, l. 853, c. 7, AGM.
66. Lt. Col. Buzón, Información, 2 June 1937, ZR, a. 63, l. 853, c. 7, AGM.
67. Lt. Col. Buzón, Información, 2 June 1937, ZR, a. 63, l. 853, c. 7, AGM.
68. Ejército, 22 May 1937, ZR, a. 63, l. 854, c. 8, AGM.
69. Ejército, 31 May 1937, ZR, a. 63, l. 854, c. 8, AGM.
70. Lt. Col. Buzón, Información, 2 June 1937, ZR, a. 63, l. 853, c. 7, AGM.
71. Análisis, nd., ZR, a. 63, l. 853, c. 18, AGM.
72. Lt. Col. Buzón, Información, 21 November 1937, ZR, a. 63, l. 853, c. 7, AGM; Jackson (1965:379) reports that the raid occurred on 26 September.
73. Lt. Col. Buzón, Información, 21 November 1937, ZR, a. 63, l. 853, c. 7, AGM.
74. Jefatura, 2 July 1937, CGG, a. 5, l. 279, c. 21, AGM.
75. Declaración, 12 September 1937, Causa General 382, AHN, Aroca Sardagna 1972:47.
76. Informe, 21 May 1937, Barcelona 1568, AHN-SGC.
77. Sexto, 17 May 1937, ZN, a. 15, l. 32, c. 8, AGM.
78. Comisión de Transportes, 21 January 1937, ZN, a. 40, l. 4, c. 35, AGM; Ejército del Norte, 18 August 1937, ZN, a. 16, l. 38, c. 18, AGM; Viñas et al. 1975:1:188.
79. Payne (1967:380) mentions that Quiepo levied fines against merchants who raised prices.
80. See also "Impressions of a recent visitor of Franco's Army," Public Record Office, W 8166/1/41, 21 April 1937, in which a British observer stated "the soldiers

were well fed, and food was well cooked." I thank Prof. Judith Keene of the University of Sydney for this document.

81. Orden, 17 November 1937, ZR, a. 74, l. 1180, c. 22, AGM; Wintringham 1939:94–95; these are generalizations. Certain Republican units in particular regions and in different periods ate better than others. For example, in Estremadura, no hunger was reported throughout 1937, but by 1938 the situation had changed dramatically.

82. Ración normal, nd., ZN, a. 41, l. 3, c. 23, AGM.

83. Mando, 1 September 1938 and 15 October 1938, ZN, a. 43, l. 11, c. 93 and c. 101, AGM; Minuta, nd., ZN, a. 41, l. 3, c. 23, AGM; Aragón 1940:310–13; Colmegna 1941:54–58, 108, 206.

84. En Zaragoza, 18 May 1938, ZN, a. 15, l. 1, c. 104, AGM.

85. Regimiento, 8 January 1938, CGG, a. 2, l. 145, c. 80, AGM.

86. For example, the Communist viewpoint is expressed in Cordón 1977:335. Especially in Catalonia, food shortages have been blamed on politics. The PSUC-CNT struggle was said to be responsible for the disorganization of Barcelona food supplies. Borkenau 1963:183.

87. Al V Cuerpo, 21 and 24 April 1937, a. 60, l. 697, c. 23, AGM.

88. Informe, 8 May 1937, a. 58, l. 627 bis, c. 1, reel 45, AGM; Líster 1966:123.

89. Informe, 7 November 1937, ZR, reel 45, AGM.

90. Segundo, 15 February 1938, ZR, a. 90, l. 761, c. 6, AGM.

91. Al Señor Jefe, 22 April 1938, ZR, a. 90, l. 761, c. 6, AGM.

92. XIX Cuerpo, 16 August 1937, ZR, a. 72, l. 1106, c. 13, AGM.

93. Cf. Graham (1999:485–542), who repeatedly argues that the "liberal Republic" engaged upon "liberal normalization" and "the restitution of the liberal economic order." Graham states "the lack of wheat and other basic foodstuffs in Catalonia was, then, the result of an absolute shortfall." This is only part of the story.

94. Acta, 16 April 1937, ZR, a. 90, l. 761, c. 1, AGM.

95. Instrucciones, ZR, a. 90, l. 760, c. 12, AGM.

96. Conforme, 18 February 1937, ZR, a. 90, l. 760, c. 12, AGM.

97. Queso, 28 January 1937, ZR, a. 90, l. 760, c. 12, AGM.

98. Primer Cuerpo, 14 March 1937, ZR, a. 90, l. 760, c. 12, AGM.

99. Sr. Capitán, 22 February 1937, ZR, a. 90, l. 760, c. 12, AGM.

100. Causa General 1291, AHN.

101. Nota, 5 April 1937, ZR, a. 90, l. 760, c. 12, AGM. Orwell (1980:190) reported that hospital food was too rich and abundant. This was certainly preferable both physiologically and psychologically to malnutrition.

102. Conforme, 18 February 1937, ZR, a. 90, l. 760, c. 12, AGM.

103. Cf. Eguidazu (1978:171), who finds the collapse of the Republican peseta on foreign exchange markets insignificant since it was not used for foreign trade, which the Republic conducted exclusively in foreign currencies backed by its precious metals reserves. Viñas (1979:197) also emphasizes the inconvertibility of the Republican peseta on international markets.

104. Figure from *Rapport de la mission* 1937?:28.

105. Informe, 30 May 1937, ZR, reel 45, AGM.

106. Informe, 30 May-4 June 1937, ZR, a. 59, l. 664, c. 3, AGM.

107. Informe, 30 May-4 June 1937, ZR, a. 59, l. 664, c. 3, AGM.

108. Informe, 6 June 1937, ZR, a. 59, l. 664, c. 3, AGM.

109. Informe, 30 May-4 June 1937, ZR, a. 59, l. 664, c. 3, AGM.

110. Informe, 30 May-4 June 1937, ZR, a. 59, l. 664, c. 3, AGM.

111. Informe, 23 May 1937, ZR, a. 73, l. 1154, c. 22, AGM.

112. Acta, 30 June 1937, PS Madrid 2467, AHN-SGC.

113. Federación, 25 September 1937, PS Madrid 2467, AHN-SGC.

114. See Instrucciones, 27 March 1937, ZR, a. 90, l. 760, c. 12, AGM; on similar bloated numbers see Figes 1990:191.

115. Acta, 22 May 1937, PS Madrid 2467, AHN-SGC.

116. Boletín, nd., ZN, a. 38, l. 14, c. 1, AGM; Nota, 10 October 1937, CGG, a. 5, l. 28, c. 4, AGM.

117. *Solidaridad Obrera*, 7 May 1937; Juzgado general de contrabando, 1336 AHN-SGC. On women's demonstrations, see Ucelay Da Cal 1982:309–23; Kaplan 1982: 548–65.

118. 5 División, 21 May 1937, a. 69, l. 1045, c. 16, AGM.

119. Informe, 15 May 1937, ZR, a. 62, l. 768, c. 1, AGM; for a critical assessment of this document, see Casanova 1985:254–59.

120. Informe, Graus, 15 August 1937, PS Madrid 542, AHN-SGC.

121. SIFNE, 27 May 1937, CGG, a. 5, l. 282, c. 4, AGM.

122. This information is based on Brigada Mixta 24, 1 August 1937, ZR, a. 73, l. 1153, c. 1, AGM.

123. Informe, 3 June 1937, ZR, a. 70, l. 1074, c. 12, AGM.

124. Parte, 1 July 1937, ZR, a. 69, l. 1045, c. 1, AGM.

125. Instrucciones, 13 August 1937, ZR, a. 69, l. 1045, c. 3, AGM.

126. Instrucciones, 13 August 1937, ZR, a. 69, l. 1045, c. 3, AGM.

127. Personado, 12 September 1937, ZR, a. 69, l. 1045, c. 17, AGM.

128. On the weakness of nationalist sentiment among Moroccans recruited by Nationalists, see Madariaga 1992:67–97.

129. Grupo, January 1939, ZN, a. 43, l. 1, c. 32, AGM.

130. Nevertheless, discontent arose among the families, see Madariaga 1992:82.

131. Intendencia, 19 May 1939, ZN, a. 31, l. 6, c. 25, AGM; Aragón 1940:310–13; Kemp 1957:45.

132. Informe, nd., ZR, reel 45, AGM.

133. Camarada, nd., ZR, reel 45, AGM.

134. Parte, 13 September 1937, ZR, a. 69, l. 1045, c. 17, AGM.

135. Exco. 1 June 1937, ZN, a. 19, l. 4, c. 17, AGM; similar policies would be adopted by Mussolini's Salò Republic. See Eatwell 1996:110. During the Russian civil war, Trotsky had reinstituted the medieval practice of collective responsibility by holding families of officers (including wives and children) personally liable for the misdeeds of their husbands, sons, or brothers. See Pipes 1994:52.

136. V Cuerpo, 9–10 June 1937, ZN, a. 41, l. 1, c. 4, AGM.

137. Cuerpo, 3 June 1937, CGG, a. 2, l. 145, c. 76, AGM.

138. See reports from El Escorial, 1 March 1937 to 9 July 1937, ZR, a. 69, l. 1034, c. 12, 13, AGM.

139. Informe, 4 June 1937, and Información, 5 June 1937, Resumen, 9 June 1937, ZR, a. 69, l. 1035, c. 13, AGM.

140. Del jefe, 29 April 1937, ZR, a. 70, l. 1075, c. 10, AGM.

141. Brigada, May 1937, ZR, a. 76, l. 1238, c. 6, AGM.

142. Pons Prades 1974:211–19; Tagüeña Lacorte 1978:108. See also "Impressions of a recent visitor of Franco's Army," Public Record Office, W 8166/1/41, 21 April 1937, who reported that on certain days on the Guadarrama front he "hardly heard a shot fired."

143. 43 Brigada Mixta, September 1937, ZR, a. 75, l. 1196, c. 10, AGM.

144. Estado, May 1938?, ZN, a. 27, l. 23 bis, c. 13, AGM.

145. Información, 9 January 1938, ZN, a. 42, l. 2, c. 2, AGM.

146. Estadística, 12 October 1937, ZR, a. 73, l. 1154, c. 22, AGM.

147. Comisariado, 29 September 1937, Vinaroz 5/15, AHN-SGC; Linderman (1987:56) argues that the employment of military justice should be the last resort of an effective armed force. The fear of personal dishonor should be a sufficient guarantee of good soldierly behavior.

148. Informe, 3 June to 11 June 1937, ZR, a. 70, l. 1074, c. 12, AGM.

149. Actividades, 4 June 1937, ZR, a. 70, l. 1074, c. 12, AGM.

150. Antonio Rodes, September 1937, ZR, a. 77, l. 1253, c. 25, AGM. Cf. Alvarez 1989:104.

151. On the absolute necessity of care packages from home, see Puig Casas 1999:115.

152. Informe, 13 November 1937, ZR, a. 69, l. 1044, c. 11, AGM; cf. the more triumphalist account in Estellés Salarich 1986:51.

153. Carlton (1992:95) states that the official daily ration of the Cavalier army was forty-five hundred calories.

154. II Cuerpo, ZR, a. 69, l. 1044, c. 11, AGM.

155. Informe, 11 October 1937, ZR, a. 64, l. 935, c. 3, AGM.

156. Informe, 31 May 1938, ZR, a. 64, l. 935, c. 3, AGM.

157. Intendencia, 19 May 1939, ZN, a. 31, l. 6, c. 25, AGM; Aragón 1940:112–15.

158. Informe, 7 November 1937, ZR, reel 45, AGM.

159. Prieto's reform of the commissariat eliminated Alvarez's position. See Cordón 1977:312 and Bolloten 1991:542.

160. 40 Brigada Mixta, ZR, a. 74, l. 1185, c. 17, AGM.

161. In the U.S. Civil War, venereal disease also seemed widespread. See McPherson 1988:488.

162. 42 Brigada Mixta, September 1937, ZR, a. 75, l. 1196, c. 10, AGM.

163. II Cuerpo, 1 March 1938, ZN, a. 18, l. 2, c. 21, AGM.

164. Orden, 2 November 1937, ZR, a. 74, l. 1180, c. 22, AGM.

165. Normas, 11 June 1937, ZR, a. 69, l. 1035, c. 13, AGM.

166. Telegrama, 19 May 1937, ZN, a. 15, l. 11, c. 46, AGM. Literate nonsmokers could easily trade their ration of cigarettes for enemy papers.

167. Copia, 13 May 1937, ZN, a. 15, l. 11, c. 46, AGM.

168. Cuarta Brigada, ZR, a. 72, l. 1128, c. 4, AGM.

169. Ejército del Centro, 18 June 1937, ZR, a. 69, l. 1046, c. 4, AGM.

170. See also Bolloten 1991:469. Cervera (1999:117) believes that the offensive in Estremadura would have been successful.

171. Colonel Rudolf von Cilander, "La primera batalla sobre Brunete," ZR, a. 69, l. 1035, c. 13, AGM.

172. Ejército, 8 November 1937, ZR, a. 64, l. 943, c. 4, AGM.

173. Colonel Rudolf von Cilander, "La primera batalla sobre Brunete," ZR, a. 69, l. 1035, c. 13, AGM.

174. Informes, 13 July 1937, ZR, a. 75, l. 1197, c. 6, AGM.

175. "A counterattack by fresh troops can have an effect completely out of proportion to the number of troops attacking. It is basically for this reason that the maintenance of fresh reserves has always been essential in combat, with battles often revolving around which side can hold out and deploy their reserves last." Grossman 1996:71.

176. XVIII Cuerpo, Enrique Jurado, 11 August 1937, ZR, a. 68, l. 995, c. 8, AGM.

177. Salas Larrazábal 1973:1257; Macho 1952:27–28; Casas de la Vega (1977: 326–28) on mutiny of the XIII International; Murillo Pérez (1990:219) on the decline of fighting spirit in the north.

178. Informes, 13 July 1937, ZR, a. 75, l. 1197, c. 6, AGM.

179. Informes, 13 July 1937, ZR, a. 75, l. 1197, c. 6, AGM.

180. Jefe XVIII Cuerpo de Ejército, 24 July 1937, ZR, a. 68, l. 995, c. 8, AGM.

181. Parte, 22 July 1937, ZR, a. 68, l. 995, c. 8, AGM.

182. Trabajos, 8 July 1937, ZR, reel 45, AGM.

183. Líster (1966:144, 281) claims that his quartermaster provided his men with cold water and hot meals.

184. Blood banks did not exist until the end of the war.

185. Ejército, 1 August 1937, ZR, a. 59, l. 664, c. 3, AGM.

186. Seleccionar, 28 July 1937, ZR, a. 69, l. 1038, c. 11, d. 4, AGM.

187. At Teruel, Antón's unit suffered serious reverses, and he was demoted.

188. Informe, 28 July 1937, CGG, a. 5, l. 279, c. 25, AGM.

189. A los compañeros, 26 October 1937, Madrid 542, AHN-SGC.

190. On arms in the rear, see Batallones, 15 November 1937, ZR, a. 56, l. 550, c. 2, AGM.

191. Reunión, 6 June 1937, Barcelona 1329, AHN-SGC.

192. Informe, 17 July 1937, ZR, a. 71, l. 1103, c. 10, AGM.

193. Comisariado, 11 August 1937, ZR, a. 71, l. 1103, c. 10, AGM.

194. Acta, 23 July 1937, Madrid 542, AHN-SGC.

195. Informe, 10 August 1937, CGG, a. 5, l. 279, c. 28, AGM.

196. Informe, 22 August 1937, CGG, a. 5, l. 279, c. 28, AGM.

197. See Fraser (1986:393) for anarchist charges that Communist troops had much better armaments.

198. 5 Cuerpo, February-September 1937, ZN, a. 19, l. 1, c. 29, AGM.

199. Estado, 29 December 1937, CGG, a. 5, l. 285, c. 30, AGM.

200. Doy, 5 May 1937, ZR, a. 55, l. 540, c. 5, AGM.

201. División 28, nd.; Ejército, nd.; Informe, nd., ZR, a. 65, l. 987, c. 7, AGM.

202. Nota, 10 October 1937, CGG, a. 5, l. 282, c. 4, AGM.

203. Instrucciones generales, 21 September 1937, ZR, a. 65, l. 787, c. 3, AGM; Instrucciones, 21 September 1937, ZR, a. 74, l. 1172, c. 2, AGM.

204. Instrucciones, 21 September 1937, ZR, a. 74, l. 1172, c. 2, AGM, p. 53.

205. For these earlier reproaches, see Normas, 3 April 1937, ZR, a. 70, l. 1075, c. 9, AGM.

206. Ejército, 16 September 1937, Aragon R 1, AHN-SGC; on the difficulties of finding enemy lines when deserting, see Fraser 1986:466.

207. 11 June 1937, Consell d'empresa CNT-UGT Elizalde, Arxiu Nacional de Catalunya.

208. Acta, 9 October 1937, Aragon R 1, AHN-SGC; Commissars knew that it was difficult but necessary to distinguish *agents provocateurs* from mere complainers.

209. Circular, 7 October 1937, Vinaroz 5/15, AHN-SGC. See also Puig Casas 1999:121.

210. Resuelto, 22 September 1937, ZN, a. 37, l. 1, c. 11, AGM.

211. El Teniente-Coronel, 14 November 1937, ZN, a. 37, l. 1, c. 1, AGM.

212. Primera, 17 February 1938, ZN, a. 37, l. 1, c. 3, AGM; cf. Martínez Bande (1980:116), who reports the "rush of volunteers" in La Coruña at the end of July 1936.

213. General, 27 February 1938, ZN, a. 37, l. 1, c. 3, AGM. In April, three soldiers were severely disciplined.

214. S.E., 23 October 1937, ZN, a. 37, l. 1, c.1, AGM.

215. 4 División, 29 August 1937, ZR, a. 69, l. 1040, c. 13, AGM.

216. "Sorpresa. Compañeros de los proyectiles que saldrán de este canon, no temais que no explotarán ninguno, soy de los vuestros, UHP"; En la información, CGG, 15 January 1937, a. 5, l. 285, c. 26, AGM.

217. Estado, 13 October 1937, CGG, a. 5, l. 285, c. 26, AGM.

218. República, 10 November 1937, ZR, a. 60, l. 705, c. 9, AGM.

219. Estado, 6 December 1937, CGG, a. 5, l. 285, c. 26, AGM. See also "Impressions of a recent visitor of Franco's Army," Public Record Office, W 8166/1/41, 21 April 1937, where the British observer reported the failure of the Republican bombing of Valladolid.

220. SIFNE, 17 September 1937, CGG, a. 5, l. 285, c. 26, AGM.

221. El Jefe, 4 September 1937, ZR, a. 60, l. 705, c. 9, AGM.

222. Comentarios, 18 January 1938, ZR, a. 57, l. 606, c. 10, AGM; Salas Larrazábal 1973:2522.

223. Ejército, 4 October 1937, ZR, a. 76, l. 1233, c. 6, AGM.

224. Al Comisario, 30 August 1937, ZR, a. 69, l. 1038, c. 11, AGM.

225. Ejército, 8 November 1937, ZR, a. 64, l. 943, c. 4, AGM.

226. Cf. the "psychiatric" explanation of Mira 1943:134: "This fugue [to home] is to be considered a reinsertion into the core of family life, because the subject has regressed to his infantile level of behavior and wants to be cheered and protected, instead of himself to be the protector."

227. Acta, 9 October 1937, Aragon R 1, AHN-SGC.

228. Sanidad, 22 November 1937, Aragon R 1, AHN-SGC.

229. Informe, 23 November 1937, Aragon R 1, AHN-SGC; Vila Izquierdo 1984:133; Líster (1966:283) notes that even many competent physicians who were loyal to the Republic had right-wing ideas.

230. Acta, 18 December 1937, Aragon 1 R, AHN-SGC; for the shedding of overcoats, see Herrick 1998:156.

231. Similar problems occurred in the Red Army in the Russian civil war. See Figes 1990:193.

232. Estado, 23 December 1937, Aragon R 1, AHN-SGC.

233. Copia, 14 November 1937, Aragon R 1, AHN-SGC.

234. Ejército, 28 November 1937, Aragón R 1, AHN-SGC.

235. Comisario, 15 June 1937, ZR, a. 56, l. 550, c. 2, AGM.

236. Acta, 18 December 1937, Aragon 1 R, AGM.

237. Batallón, 1 September 1937, ZR, reel 45, AGM.

238. Comisario, 14 August 1937, ZR, a. 56, l. 550, c. 2, AGM.

239. Vestuario, 28 November 1937, Aragon 32, AHN-SGC; Comisario, 11 June 1937, ZR, a. 56, l. 550, c. 2, AGM.

240. Comisario, June-July 1937, ZR, a. 56, l. 550, c. 2, AGM.

241. Batallones, 30 November 1937, ZR, a. 56, l. 550, c. 2, AGM.

242. Al comisario, 13 November 1937, ZR, reel 45, AGM.

243. Informe semanal, 28 August 1937, ZR, a. 65, l. 987, c. 7, AGM.

244. Actas, 26 December 1937, PS Madrid 2467, AHN-SGC; Bernecker 1982:128.

245. Prats (1938:48) notes that the soldiers stationed in Aragon spoke Catalan.

246. En el departamento, 5 August 1937, AASM-512–42, Fundación Pablo Iglesias (Madrid).

247. Informe fiscal, February 1937, Barcelona 839, AHN-SGC.

248. Informe, nd., Madrid 542, AHN-SGC; Mintz 1977:176; Casanova 1985:22; Souchy Bauer (1982:77) reports that the Albalate de Cinca collective had 113 families and a total of 450 people.

249. Indeed, secret police did intercept the letters.

250. Personado, 27 April 1937, Barcelona 839, AHN-SGC.

251. Sr. Delegado, 18 January 1938, AASM-514–10, Fundación Pablo Iglesias.

252. Los agentes, 26 July 1937, Barcelona 839, AHN-SGC.

253. Actas, 26 December 1937, PS Madrid 2467, AHN-SGC.

254. Informe, 24 March 1938, ZR, reel 93, AGM.

255. Desde, nd., AASM-510–40, Fundación Pablo Iglesias.

256. Frente de Aragón, nd., CGG, a. 4. l. 279, c. 25, AGM.

257. Informe, nd., ZR, a. 47, l. 71, c. 6, AGM.

258. El Departamento, 5 August 1937, ZR, a. 47, l. 71, c. 3, AGM.

259. Informe, 16 June 1937, Barcelona 839, AHN-SGC; Con fecha, 27 November 1937, Barcelona 1329, AHN-SGC. On Soviet collectives, see Fitzpatrick 1994:64. Mintz (1977:219) and Peirats (1971:1:281) report that individuals had perfect freedom to enter and leave certain collectives; Leval (1975) shows that rules on returning property varied from one collective to another.

260. CNT-UGT, 20 April 1937, Aragon R 51, AHN-SGC.

261. Caspe, 2 July 1937, Aragon R 51, AHN-SGC.

262. Informe, José Carrasquer, 3 November 1937, AASM-514–21, Fundación Pablo Iglesias. The informant was a member of a family of CNT activists.

263. CNT, 5 July 1937, Barcelona 624, AHN-SGC.

264. Informe, José Carrasquer, 3 November 1937, AASM-514–21, Fundación Pablo Iglesias.

265. Sr. Gobernador, nd., ZR, a. 47, l. 71, c. 6, AGM.

266. CNT, 5 April 1937, Barcelona 839, AHN-SGC.

267. Acta, 28 November 1937, Madrid 542, AHN-SGC.

268. CNT, 18 January 1938, AASM-514–10, Fundación Pablo Iglesias.

269. Informe, nd., Madrid 542, AHN-SGC.

270. Acta, 12 June 1937, PS Madrid 2467, AHN-SGC; Acta, 6 June 1937, PS Madrid, 2467, AHN-SGC; Mintz 1977:189 claims that there were ten collectives with a total of 224 members in the Priego district.

271. Mintz (1977:195) reports that there were over three hundred collectivists or approximately 20 percent of the village.

272. Informe, July 1937, Madrid 542, AHN-SGC; see also Casanova 1985:186–92.

273. Informe, 31 July 1937, Madrid 542, AHN-SGC.

274. For a critique of "neo-capitalism" see Bernecker 1982:133. "Neo-autarky" might be a more appropriate description.

275. Para el Comité Regional, Caspe, March 1937, AASM-512–48, Fundación Pablo Iglesias.

276. Consejo Regional de Defensa Aragón, nd., ASSM-512–49, Fundación Pablo Iglesias; Informe, September 1937, ZR, a. 47, l. 71, c. 3, AGM.

277. Para el Comité Regional, Caspe, March 1937, AASM-512–48, Fundación Pablo Iglesias. Cf. Prats 1938:95.

278. La Cooperativa Obrera, nd., AASM-514–14, Fundación Pablo Iglesias.

279. Reunión, 5 October 1937, PS Madrid 2467, AHN-SGC; cf. the idealist picture presented in Suero Serrano 1982:100.

280. Federación, 3 November 1937, PS Madrid 2467, AHN-SGC.

281. Circular, nd., January? 1938?, PS Madrid 2467, AHN-SGC.

282. Ministerio de Agricultura 1936:4: "Se ha considerado como zona leal la formada por las provincias cuya capital está al lado del Gobierno legítimamente constituído, pero hay extensas comarcas de las provincias de Granada, Córdoba, Badajoz, Toledo, León, Burgos, Huesca, Zaragoza y Teruel . . . que no han podido recogerse en la presente Estadística."

283. Para el Comité Regional, Caspe, March 1937, AASM-512-48, Fundación Pablo Iglesias; cf. Leval 1975:143; see Carrión 1973:135–37.

284. Informe, Barbastro, 24 August 1937, AASM-510–41, Fundación Pablo Iglesias; Leval 1975:221. According to Souchy Bauer (1982) Barbastro was the headquarters of one of the largest regional federations. Of seventy villages in the district, forty-seven were collectivized.

285. Some collectives, however, contributed a voluntary war tax. The Calanda collective claimed that it was never taxed. See Collectif Equipo 1997:77.

286. Cf. Leval (1975) for a view that emphasized solidarity and efficiency of collectives.

287. Acta, 2 July 1937, PS Madrid 2467, AHN-SGC.

288. A la federación, 20 June 1938, PS Madrid, 2467, AHN-SGC.

289. Acta, 22 August 1937, PS Madrid 2467, AHN-SGC.

290. Sometimes even anarchosyndicalist sources admitted this. See Souchy and Folgare 1977:178. On Republican law, see Cervera 1999:136, 146.

291. Federación, 1 May 1937, Barcelona 624, AHN-SGC.

292. Causa General 1491, AHN.

293. Auto, 15 October 1938, Causa General 1636, AHN.

294. Comisaria, 26 July 1937, Barcelona 839, AHN-SGC.

295. A la presidencia, 4 May 1937, Barcelona 839, AHN-SGC.

296. Informe, 26 February 1938, Barcelona 839, AHN-SGC.

297. Copia, 26 July 1937, Barcelona 839, AHN-SGC; Copia, 26 July 1937, Barcelona 839, AHN-SGC.

298. Consejo, 7 June 1937, Barcelona 839, AHN-SGC.

299. Informe, 20-23 October 1937, AASM-512–25, Fundación Pablo Iglesias; Simoni and Simoni 1984:155.

300. En Caspe, 9 January 1937, Barcelona 839, AHN-SGC.

301. A la Consejería, 27 May 1937, Barcelona 839, AHN-SGC.

302. Informe, nd., Barcelona 839, AHN-SGC.

303. Reunidos, 29 March 1937, Barcelona 839, AHN-SGC; Mintz 1977:100; Borkenau 1963:108; Casanova 1985:24.

304. Exc., 29 November 1937, Barcelona 1329, AHN-SGC.

305. IV Cuerpo, 26 June 1937, ZR, a. 70, l. 1075, c. 5, AGM.

306. Informe, 27 October 1937, ZR, a. 70, l. 1074, c. 10, AGM.

307. Casanova 1985:174; Colectividad, 5 April 1937, Castellón 254, AHN-SGC.

308. Caspe, 25 July 1937, Barcelona 839, AHN-SGC.

309. Consejo, 1 January 1938, ZR, a. 60, l. 714, c. 5, AGM.

310. Consejo, 18 January 1938, ZR, a. 60, l. 714, c. 5, AGM. A corps had between 20,000 and 35,000 men. In August 1937 the VI had 20,500.

311. Ejército, 31 May 1938, Causa General 577, AHN.

312. El Exco., 20 March 1938, ZR, a. 60, l. 714, c. 5, AGM.

313. Informe, 20-23 October 1937, ZR, a. 47, l. 71, c. 4, AGM.

314. Acta, 9 October 1937, Aragon R, AHN-SGC.

315. See Casanova (1985:269–71) for a critique of the literature.

316. See Leval (1975:315) who described the Valencian millers, organized by the CNT and UGT, and their demands for requisitions and price controls.

317. El Sr., 23 September 1937, Vinaroz 5/12, AHN-SGC. On Mantecón's political history, see Casanova 1985:223; Bolloten 1991:244, 529; see Líster (1966:160) for praise of Mantecón.

318. Acta, 22 November 1937, Madrid 542, AHN-SGC.

319. Actas, 26 December 1937, PS Madrid 2467, AHN-SGC.

320. Actas, 26 December 1937, PS Madrid 2467, AHN-SGC. For figures, see Mintz 1977:190.

321. Informe, 15 August 1937, PS Madrid 542, AHN-SGC; problems of discipline and subsequent sanctions resembled contemporary Soviet collectives. Cf. the idealistic picture of Graus presented in Prats 1938:89.

322. Acta, 9 September 1937, PS Madrid 2467, AHN-SGC.

323. Acta, 15 December 1937, PS Madrid 2467, AHN-SGC; Informe, 22 October 1937, PS Madrid 2467, AHN-SGC.

324. Acta, 11 October 1937, PS Madrid 2467, AHN-SGC.

325. Acta, 11 October 1937, PS Madrid 2467, AHN-SGC.

326. Acta, 28 November 1937, AHN-SGC, PS Madrid 2467, AHN-SGC.

327. Informe, 11 October 1937, ZR, a. 64, l. 935, c. 3, AGM.

328. Al camarada, 20 September 1937, Barcelona 624, AHN-SGC.

329. Abad 1988:85; see CLUEF reports, April–May 1937, Madrid 2157, AHN-SGC.

330. See Leval (1975) for a description from the libertarian perspective.

331. Llosa de Ranes, 17 April 1937, Madrid 2157, AHN-SGC.

332. CLUEF de Oliva, 21 April 1937, Madrid 2157, AHN-SGC.

333. Informe, 6 July 1938, Barcelona 624, AHN-SGC; on persons belonging to the collective, see Mintz 1977:165.

334. CNT, 7 September 1937, Barcelona 1329, AHN-SGC.

335. A raíz, 11 September 1937, Barcelona 1329, AHN-SGC.

336. Acta, 13 September 1937, PS Madrid 2467, AHN-SGC; Martín-Blázquez 1938:121. Chauffeurs and drivers were also a highly privileged group during Soviet collectivization. See Fitzpatrick 1994:141.

337. Informe, nd., Madrid 2467, AHN-SGC.

338. Informe, nd., AASM-512–34, Fundación Pablo Iglesias.

339. Consejo Regional, January 1938?, AASM-515–7, Fundación Pablo Iglesias.

340. Sr. Gobernador, 20 January 1938, AASM-514–10, Fundación Pablo Iglesias.

341. It has been argued that the larger the town the less collectivization of land. See Souchy Bauer 1982:88.

342. The following is from the libro de actas, 1936–1937, PS Lérida, AHN-SGC.

343. However, both refused at times to cooperate with *rabassaires*.

344. See Martínez Bande (1975:114), which puts the April 1936 population of Lérida at more than thirty-eight thousand.

345. For the problem in Valencia, see Bosch Sánchez 1983:203.

346. Cf. the picture of collectivist singing and laughing during work in Simoni and Simoni 1984:112.

347. The sociological origins of Lérida managers are unknown, but in an Aragon collective, they were overwhelmingly former day laborers. See Simoni amd Simoni 1984:112.

348. Actas, 26 December 1937, PS Madrid 2467, AHN-SGC.

349. A gypsy woman later accused this militant's daughter of being a thief.

350. Compañeros, nd., PS Madrid 2467, AHN-SGC; cf. the happier picture of women in the Cretas collective. See Simoni and Simoni 1984:113.

351. Colectividad, 11 November 1937, Barcelona 1329, AHN-SGC.

352. Actas, 15 August 1937, Barcelona 496, AHN-SGC.

353. Sindicato, 25 September 1937, Castellón 139, AHN-SGC.

354. Al ecmo., 27 July 1937, Castellón 156, AHN-SGC.

355. Colectividad, 9 October 1937, Barcelona 1329, AHN-SGC; Federación, 21 September 1937, Barcelona 1329, AHN-SGC.

356. Informe, 18 March 1937, Vinaroz, 3/5, AHN-SGC.

357. Denuncia, 18 January 1937, Vinaroz 3/5, AHN-SGC. A Socialist leader had been assassinated in December 1936.

358. Normas, 1 October 1937, Barcelona 1329, AHN-SGC.

359. Actas, July-December, 1937, Castellón 230, AHN-SGC; *Rapport de la mission* 1937?:29.

360. Cf. Montseny (1986:97), where the former minister of health claims that there was no *tifus exantemático* in the Republican zone and that the health standards were

satisfactory on the fronts and in major cities.

361. Cf. the elitist views of Mira 1943:126: "Never in history did the best brains of a nation come into such close contact with the population and the army as in the recent Spanish War. They succeeded in explaining to the dullest soldiers and civilians what was going on in the world and why they were called upon to fight."

362. El Frente, 29 September 1937, AASM-512–19, Fundación Pablo Iglesias.

363. Informe, 25 October 1937, AASM-514–21, Fundación Pablo Iglesias; cf. Casanova 1985:127; Simoni and Simoni 1984:119; Mintz 1977:176; Souchy Bauer (1982:44) states that Mas de las Matas had thirty-two hundred residents of whom two thousand were in the CNT. The same number belonged to the collective.

364. Informe, 20-23 October 1937, AASM-512–25, Fundación Pablo Iglesias.

365. Segunda Sesión, 11 December 1937, AASM-510–38, Fundación Pablo Iglesias.

366. Acta, 5-6 December 1937, AASM-510–37, Fundación Pablo Iglesias.

367. Acta, 5-6 December 1937, AASM-510–37, Fundación Pablo Iglesias.

368. Informe, nd., ZR, reel 45, AGM.

369. Catalan Communists reportedly objected to price controls. See Fraser 1986:326.

370. Acta, 2 February 1937, Barcelona 1329, AHN-SGC. See also Seidman 1991.

371. Hispano-Suiza, 28 July 1937, Barcelona 1329, AHN-SGC.

372. Relativo, 21 November 1937, ZR, a. 46, l. 69, c. 8, AGM.

373. Actas, 2 June–5 July 1937, Madrid 524, AHN-SGC.

374. Lt. Col. Buzón, Información, 21 November 1937, ZR, a. 63, l. 853, c. 7, AGM.

375. Desde, 8 May 1937, ZR, a. 63, l. 855, c. 1, AGM.

376. II Cuerpo, 23 June 1937, ZR, a. 63, l. 855, c. 1, AGM.

377. Telegramas, 28-29 June 1937, ZR, a. 54, l. 473, c. 1, AGM; Informe, 4 November 1937, ZR, a. 54, l. 473, c. 2, AGM.

378. Informe, nd., ZR, a. 47, l. 71, c. 7, AGM; Viñas 1979:240. Howson 1999:100.

379. Análisis, nd., ZR, a. 63, l. 853, c. 18, AGM.

380. Informe, 5 August 1937, ZR, a. 63, l. 854, c. 6, AGM.

381. Propuesta, nd., Madrid 542, AHN-SGC.

382. Gobierno, 4 September 1937, CGG, a. 2, l. 191, c. 2, AGM.

383. Lt. Col. Buzón, Información, 21 November 1937, ZR, a. 63, l. 853, c. 7, AGM.

384. Análisis, nd., ZR, a. 63, l. 853, c. 18, AGM.

385. Informe, 30 July 1937, CGG, a. 5, l. 279, c. 25, AGM.

386. Hospital, 21 November 1937, Madrid 1568, AHN-SGC.

387. Informe, 6 January 1938, Barcelona 2048, AHN-SGC.

388. Flechas Negras, 19 August 1937, ZN, a. 15, l. 4, c. 43, AGM.

389. Cf. the psychological explanation of the Nationalist physician, Vallejo Nágera (1939:137) who attributes desertions to mental confusion.

390. Juzgado, 10 June 1937, ZN, a. 27, l. 25, c. 4, AGM.

391. See Copia, 21 December 1936, ZN, a. 15, l. 1, c. 88, AGM.

392. Lt. Col. Buzón, Información, 21 November 1937, ZR, a. 63, l. 853, c. 7, AGM.

393. Acta, 9 October 1937, Aragon R 1, AHN-SGC; Lt. Col. Buzón, Información, 21 November 1937, ZR, a. 63, l. 853, c. 7, AGM.

394. Lt. Col. Buzón, Información, 21 November 1937, ZR, a. 63, l. 853, c. 7, AGM.

395. 5 Cuerpo, October 1937, ZN, 51 División, a. 41, l. 1, c. 3, AGM.

396. Relación, 20 October 1937, ZN, 51 División, a. 41, l. 1, c. 3, AGM.

397. Informe, July-August 1937, Gijón F 89, AHN-SGC; Al señor, 24 January 1937, Gijón F 89, AHN-SGC.

398. Propuesta, nd., Madrid 542, AHN-SGC.

399. Análisis, nd., ZR, a. 63, l. 853, c. 18, AGM.

400. Lt. Col. Buzón, Información, 21 November 1937, ZR, a. 63, l. 853, c. 7, AGM.

401. On the "broken contract," see Holmes 1985:321. In this sense, most soldiers—except the most fanatical or devoted—are mercenaries.

402. Análisis, nd., ZR, a. 63, l. 853, c. 18, AGM.

403. Análisis, nd., ZR, a. 63, l. 853, c. 18, AGM; Orwell (1980:34) reported Spanish-made cartridges would jam even the best guns.

404. Lt. Col. Buzón, Información, 21 November 1937, ZR, a. 63, l. 853, c. 7, AGM.

405. Análisis, nd., ZR, a. 63, l. 853, c. 18, AGM.

406. Lt. Col. Buzón, Información, 21 November 1937, ZR, a. 63, l. 853, c. 7, AGM.

407. Lt. Col. Buzón, Información, 21 November 1937, ZR, a. 63, l. 853, c. 7, AGM.

408. Propuesta, nd., Madrid 542, AHN-SGC.

409. Análisis, nd., ZR, a. 63, l. 853, c. 18, AGM.

410. Análisis, nd., ZR, a. 63, l. 853, c. 18, AGM.

411. Thomas (1961:480) estimates eighteen thousand; Fraser 1986:427.

412. Estado, 24 October 1937, CGG, a. 5, l. 282, c. 4, AGM.

413. 25 November 1937, Causa General 1637, AHN.

414. For example, the General Motors factory in Barcelona had suppliers that were located in Bilbao.

## 3. Cynicism

1. Sentencia, 9 February 1938, Causa General 1179, AHN; Bricall 1978:1:141.

2. Auto, 23 November 1938, Causa General 718, AHN.

3. Ampliación, 16 January 1938, ZN, a. 38, l. 2, c. 7, AGM.

4. Villarroya i Font states that nearly five hundred were killed in January 1938.

5. Carreras Panchón (1986:21) claims that the total dead and wounded did not surpass the number injured in traffic accidents.

6. Informe, 16 July 1938, ZR, a. 46, l. 69, c. 20, AGM.

7. Richards (1998:44) has aptly discussed the biological metaphors employed by Nationalists. Anarchism and separatism in Barcelona had to be destroyed like "cancers."

8. El Jefe, 13 and 14 December 1937, ZR, a. 73, l. 1154, c. 21, AGM.

9. Informe, 7 December 1937, ZR, a. 70, l. 1074, c. 10, AGM.

10. 22 Brigada, 1 November 1937, ZR, a. 73, l. 1151, c. 15, AGM.

11. Confidencial, nd., CGG, reel 204, AGM.

12. 153 Brigada, December 1937, Aragon R 4, AHN-SGC.

13. Orden, December 1937, CGG, reel 204, AGM.

14. Al membrete, 19 Brigada Mixta, 15 January 1938, CGG, reel 204, AGM.

15. El Comisario, 14 January 1938, ZR, a. 69, l. 1038, c. 11, AGM.

16. Informe, 30 March 1938, Causa General 577, AHN.

17. Sentencia, 11 November 1938, Causa General 577, AHN.

18. División, 9 May 1938, ZN, a. 39, l. 3, c. 4, AGM.

19. Grupo, 30 January 1938, ZN, a. 38, l. 2, c. 7, AGM.

20. Cuartel, 26 January 1938, CGG, reel 128, AGM.

21. Las operaciones de Teruel, 25 February 1938, ZR, reel 93, AGM.

22. Informe al Comité Central del Partido Comunista, 3 January 1937, ZR, reel 93, AGM; Conclusiones Batalla de Teruel, nd., ZR, reel 93, AGM.

23. Informe detallado, 29 December 1937, ZR, reel 93, AGM.

24. Líster (1966:174–75, 185) does not mention this pillaging in his account of the capture of Campillo.

25. Bolloten (1991:369) implies that Communist influence was responsible for this corruption. This ignores the political economy of the Republican zone. As Bolloten himself points out (589), Communists themselves accused Negrín of tolerating "thieves, speculators, and saboteurs."

26. Informe al comité central, 3 January 1938, ZR, reel 93, AGM; see also the brief mention of looting in Salas Larrazábal 1973:1670.

27. Informe, 20 December 1937, ZR, reel 93, AGM.

28. Sub-Sección Información, 10–31 December 1937, ZR, reel 93, AGM.

29. Conclusiones, Batalla de Teruel, nd., ZR, reel 93, AGM.

30. CGG, 29 January 1938, CGG, a. 5, l. 285, c. 29, AGM.

31. Informe detallado, 29 December 1937, ZR, reel 93, AGM; Instrucciones, 20 December 1937, ZR, a. 72, l. 1106, c. 15, AGM.

32. Estado, 25 January 1938, CGG, a. 5, l. 285, c. 29, AGM; a member of the Lincoln Brigade disputed Nationalist claims that the XV Brigade had been wiped out. See Rosenstone 1969:250.

33. CGG, 29 January 1938, ZN, reel 30, AGM; Líster 1966:179.

34. 40 División, 20 January 1938, ZR, a. 65, l. 781, c. 2, AGM.

35. Ejército, 27 February 1938, ZR, a. 73, l. 1135, c. 8, d. 2, AGM; see also Landis 1989:116.

36. Ejército, 30 January 1938, ZR, a. 77, l. 1248, c. 26, AGM.

37. Keegan (1976:276) suggests that a high ratio of total casualties to the number of fighting troops will cause an army to collapse.

38. XXII Cuerpo, 22 February 1938, ZR, a. 77, l. 1248, c. 26, AGM. A full battalion contained approximately one thousand men.

39. XXII Cuerpo, 22 February 1938, ZR, a. 77, l. 1248, c. 26, AGM.

40. Informe, 28 March 1938, ZR, reel 45, AGM; Acta, 24 July 1938, ZR, reel 45, AGM.

41. Martínez Bande 1974a:316; Las operaciones de Teruel, 25 February 1938, ZR, reel 93, AGM; Informe, 25 December 1937, Aragón 32, AHN-SGC; Batallones, 7 April 1938, ZR, a. 56, l. 550, c. 2, AGM.

42. Informe, 15 December 1937, ZR, reel 45, AGM; Secreto, 18 June 1938, ZN, a. 31, l. 10, c. 5, AGM.

43. Informe, 2 December 1937, ZR, reel 45, AGM; II Cuerpo, 5 July 1938, ZR, a. 70, l. 1051, c. 16, AGM.

44. Sexta Brigada, 11 November 1937, Vinaroz 5/15, AHN-SGC.

45. Informe, 8 August 1938, ZR, a. 65, l. 785, c. 10; ZR, reel 93, AGM; for another report that praises the output of fortification workers in Levante, see Batallones, 17 April 1938, ZR, a. 56, l. 550, c. 2, AGM.

46. Informe, 15 December 1937, ZR, reel 45, AGM; Acta, 26 October 1938, ZR,

reel 45, AGM.
47. Acta, 26 January 1938, ZR, reel 45, AGM.
48. Batallones, 28 March 1938, ZR, a. 56, l. 550, c. 2, AGM.
49. Informe, 15 December 1937, ZR, reel 45, AGM.
50. Informe, 15 December 1937, ZR, reel 45, AGM.
51. Acta, 16 January 1938, ZR, reel 45, AGM.
52. Batallones, 17 April 1938, ZR, a. 56, l. 550, c. 2, AGM.
53. Sigüenza, 30 June 1938, ZN, a. 31, l. 10, c. 5, AGM.
54. On the training of the Internationals, see Wintringham 1939:111.
55. Ejército, 16 February 1938, CGG, a. 2, l. 145, c. 79, AGM.
56. General Jefe, 9 March 1938, CGG, a. 2, l. 145, c. 82, AGM.
57. Pliego, 2 April 1938, ZR, a. 75, l. 1218, c. 7, AGM.
58. Gárate Córdoba 1976b:61–65. On Republican inability to forge competent officers, see Rojo 1974:47.
59. Cf. the Russian civil war, where the bourgeoisie generally was unwilling to sacrifice. See Figes 1996:556.
60. Líster 1966:90 admits Nationalist superiority in training.
61. Inspección general, 20 January 1938, CGG, reel 204, AGM.
62. Evening Standard, 12 February 1937 in CGG, a. 5, l. 279, c. 21, AGM.
63. El Inspector, 18 November 1937, CGG, reel 204, AGM.
64. Gaceta de la República, 31 August 1938. On decrees, see Cervera 1999:146.
65. Ordenes, 10 June 1938, Causa General 1291, AHN.
66. Jefatura, nd., CGG, reel 204, AGM.
67. Destacamento, 25 January 1938, 10; Secretario, 26 January 1939, Causa General 467, AHN.
68. Acta, 22 December 1938, ZR, a. 72, l. 1127, c. 19, AGM.
69. Batallón, 14 December 1937, ZR, a. 65, l. 793, c. 2, AGM.
70. Batallón, 21 January 1938, ZR, a. 65, l. 793, c. 2, AGM.
71. Batallón, 23 January 1938, ZR, a. 65, l. 793, c. 1, AGM.
72. Sentencia, 19 August 1938, Causa General 1179, AHN.
73. Al comité, 28 January 1938, PS Madrid 2467, AHN-SGC.
74. CNT, 31 March 1938, PS Madrid 2467, AHN-SGC.
75. El caso, nd., PS Madrid 2467, AHN-SGC.
76. Alcázar de Cervantes, 31 October 1938, PS Madrid 2467, AHN-SGC. According to Mintz (1977:188) nine collectives in the district of Alcázar de Cervantes contained over twenty-six hundred members. For a similar problem in Badajoz, see Gallardo Moreno 1994:88.
77. Fiscalía, 13 September 1938, and Declaración, 21 September 1938, Causa General 718, AHN.
78. Informe, fall? 1938, PS Madrid 2467, AHN-SGC. On peasant resistance to reform in the countryside, see Blum 1978:chapter 13.
79. Federación, 25 May 1938, Barcelona 811, AHN-SGC.
80. Ilustrísimo, 11 August 1938, ZR, a. 54, l. 473, c. 4, AGM.
81. Federación, 17 August 1938, PS Madrid 2467, AHN-SGC; Mintz (1977:197) reports that 375 persons or nearly 20 percent of the population were collectivists in Carabaña.

82. Federación, 18 May 1938, PS Madrid 2467, AHN-SGC.

83. Las operaciones de Teruel, 25 February 1938, ZR, reel 93, AGM; Azaña 1990: 3:520; Líster 1966:243; Sardá 1970:448.

84. Relación de las materias primas, October 1937, CGG, a. 5, l. 279, c. 21, AGM.

85. Propuesta, 10 January 1938, ZR, a. 67, l. 850, c. 6, AGM.

86. Explotación local, 22 April 1938, ZR, a. 67, l. 850, c. 9, AGM.

87. Gobierno civil, 17 January 1938, ZR, a. 67, l. 850, c. 9, AGM.

88. Explotación local, 22 April 1938, ZR, a. 67, l. 850, c. 9, AGM.

89. Informe, 20–23 October 1937, ZR, a. 47, l. 71, c. 4, AGM.

90. Información, 9 January 1938, ZN, a. 42, l. 2, c. 2, AGM.

91. See files in PS Madrid, 1945 and Castellón 25, AHN-SGC.

92. Informe, 30 August 1938, ZR, a. 65, l. 793, c. 6, AGM.

93. On the collectives' tendency toward self-sufficiency see Maurice 1978:53–85.

94. Informe, nd., Madrid 542, AHN-SGC.

95. Cf. Santacreu Soler (1992), which emphasizes economic dynamism.

96. State control in Russia has provided historians with sources, such as official inspection reports and letters of protest, which historians of Spain lack.

97. Ejército, 7 March 1938, ZR, a. 90, l. 761, c. 6, AGM.

98. Orden circular, 31 January 1939, ZR, a. 68, l. 1010, c. 2, AGM; see also Lee 1991:119.

99. Orden, 31 October 1938, ZR, a. 65, l. 986, c. 1, AGM.

100. Jefatura, 19 September 1938, ZR, a. 65, l. 793, c. 6, AGM.

101. Informe, 10 October 1938, ZR, reel 45, AGM.

102. Primer, February-March 1938, ZR, a. 90, l. 761, c. 6, AGM.

103. Informe, 14 March 1938, ZR, a. 65, l. 793, c. 6, AGM.

104. Secretario, 26 January 1939, Causa General 467, AHN.

105. Informe, 5 October 1938, Barcelona 624, AHN-SGC.

106. Informe, 4 July 1938, Barcelona 811, AHN-SGC; Informe, 9 July 1938, Barcelona 811, AHN-SGC.

107. El Consejo, 11 July 1938, PS Madrid 2436, AHN-SGC.

108. Colectividad, 19 October 1938, PS Madrid 2436, AHN-SGC.

109. Informe, 15 August 1938, PS Madrid 2436, AHN-SGC. On the "failure" of the CNT agrarian collective in Badalona, see Fraser 1986:449.

110. Company, 15 August 1938, Madrid 542, AHN-SGC.

111. Ministerio, 31 August 1938, CGG, a. 5, l. 279, c. 21, AGM.

112. República, 4 June 1938, ZR, a. 74, l. 1185, c. 10, AGM.

113. Orden, 19 August 1937, ZR, a. 77, l. 1266, c. 4, AGM; Bosch Sánchez 1983:181.

114. Informe, 2 June 1938, PS Madrid 2467, AHN-SGC; Ejército, 12 October 1938, ZR a. 89, l. 743, c. 6, AGM; Secreto, 18 June 1938, ZN, a. 31, l. 10, c. 5, AGM.

115. Ejército, 13 July 1938, Causa General 577, AHN.

116. Informe, 19 August 1938, PS Madrid 2467, AHN-SGC.

117. Acta, 30 September 1938, Barcelona 624, AHN-SGC.

118. Ejército del Sur, December 1937, ZN, a. 18, l. 9, c. 21, AGM; cf. Salas Larrazábal (1973:1580), which emphasizes ideological reasons.

119. Ejército del Centro, 26 December 1937, ZR, reel 45, AGM.

120. Información, 9 January 1938, ZN, a. 42, l. 2, c. 2, AGM.

121. Ejército del Sur, 23 December 1937, ZN, a. 18, l. 9, c. 21, AGM.

122. III Cuerpo, 9 February 1938, ZN, a. 18, l. 10, c. 1, AGM.

123. Ejército de Andalucía, 8 December 1937, ZR, reel 76, AGM.

124. Telegrama, 11 December 1937, ZR, reel 76, AGM.

125. Jefe, 16 March 1937, and Informe, 24 March 1937, ZR, a. 69, l. 1045, c. 16, AGM.

126. II Cuerpo, 1 March 1938, ZN, a. 18, l. 2, c. 21, AGM.

127. Telegrama, 26 December 1937, ZN, a. 16, l. 33, c. 45, AGM.

128. Telegramas, December 1937-February 1938, ZR, reel 76, AGM; Orwell (1980:44) reported a similar misunderstanding among Republican troops when Nationalists fired their weapons to celebrate the fall of Málaga in February 1937.

129. Telegrama, 24 December 1937, ZR, reel 76, AGM.

130. Resumen, 12–19 February 1938, Aragón R 1, AHN-SGC.

131. Telegrama, 1 January 1938, ZR, reel 76, AGM.

132. Telegrama, 7 January 1938, ZR, reel 76, AGM.

133. Telegrama, 18 January 1938, ZR, reel 76, AGM; Telegrama, 23 January 1938, ZR, reel 76, AGM.

134. Sección, 18 February 1938, ZR, reel 76, AGM.

135. Dollard 1943:63.

136. Ejército, 3 March 1938, ZN, a. 15, l. 13, c. 59, AGM.

137. Conclusiones, March 1938, ZR, a. 64, l. 796, c. 16, AGM.

138. Telegram of 16 March 1938 quoted in Viñas 1979:372.

139. El derrumbamiento, 2 April 1938, ZR, a. 62, l. 768, c. 1, AGM.

140. Informe, 4 April 1938, Barcelona 811, AHN-SGC.

141. Batallones, 7 April 1938, ZR, a. 56, l. 550, c. 2, AGM.

142. Numero 8, 9 April 1938, ZR, a. 77, l. 1250, c. 12, AGM; Ejército, nd., a. 77, l. 1249, c. 6, AGM. See also Puig Casas 1999:175.

143. Informe, 4 April 1938, Barcelona 811, AHN-SGC.

144. Batallones, 17 April 1938, ZR, a. 56, l. 550, c. 2, AGM.

145. Batallones, 7 April 1938, ZR, a. 56, l. 550, c. 2, AGM. Other battalions showed a better spirit.

146. Escrito, November 1938, ZR, a. 47, l. 71, c. 5, AGM.

147. Federación, 19 May 1938, Barcelona 623, AHN-SGC.

148. Ilustrísimo, 11 August 1938, ZR, a. 54, l. 474, c. 4, AGM.

149. Informe, 5 April 1938, ZR, a. 71, r. 166, l. 1089, c. 5, AGM.

150. Ordenes, 4 August 1938, ZR, a. 54, l. 474–1, c. 2, AGM; Vila Izquierdo 1984:135.

151. Resumen, 24 April 1938, CGG, a. 5, l. 278, c. 24, AGM.

152. Informe, 20 August 1938, ZR, a. 54, l. 473, c. 8, AGM. This information questions the assertion that "violent revolutionary justice" was gradually brought under control by the Republic. Cf. Richards 1998:13.

153. Ordenes, 4 August 1938, ZR, a. 54, l. 474–1, c. 2, AGM.

154. Ejército, 29 March 1938, ZN, a. 16, l. 34, c. 44, AGM; Colmegna 1941:157.

155. For a similar reputation in Badajoz villages, see Gallardo Moreno 1994:116.

156. See Telegrama, 25 July 1938, ZN, 112 División, a. 37, l. 1, c. 10, AGM.

157. Cuerpo, 10 May 1939, CGG, a. 2, l. 191, c. 2, AGM.

158. Aceite, 22 May 1938, CGG, reel 128, l. 57, c. 44, AGM.

159. Instrucciones, nd., CGG, a. 4, l. 655, c. 84, AGM.

160. Informe, 83 Brigada Mixta, ZR, reel 93, AGM; Memoria, 10 May 1938, ZR, a. 70, l. 1075, c. 1, AGM.

161. Memoria, 10 May 1938, ZR, a. 70, l. 1075, c. 1, AGM; Martínez Bande 1977:98.

162. For a similar phenomenon in the Red Army in the Russian civil war, see Figes 1996:601.

163. For a general discussion, see Best 1986:32–33. Fitzpatrick (1994:232) emphasizes that many peasants who were indifferent or hostile to the regime enthusiastically accepted its avenues for social mobility. A sociology of the armies defending Valencia is needed to provide a fuller explanation for Republican success.

164. Comité Regional, 18 May 1938, ZR, a. 70, l. 1074, c. 10, AGM.

165. Informe, 16 May 1938, ZR, reel 93, AGM.

166. Informe, 6 June 1938, Barcelona 811, AHN-SGC.

167. Federación, 25 May 1938, Barcelona 811, AHN-SGC; Bosch Sánchez 1983:312–27.

168. Informe, 20 May 1938, Barcelona 811, AHN-SGC.

169. Cuenta, 21 July 1938, CGG, a. 5, l. 278, c. 23, AGM.

170. Informe, 16 May 1938, ZR, reel 93, AGM.

171. Orden, 20 September 1938 and 4 October 1938, ZR, a. 68, l. 1012, c. 10, AGM.

172. 15 División, 22 August 1938, ZR, a. 75, l. 1201, c. 17, AGM.

173. Informe, 16 July 1938, Barcelona 811, AHN-SGC.

174. II Cuerpo, 5 July 1938, ZR, a. 70, l. 1051, c. 16, AGM.

175. 101 División, 7 August 1938, ZR, a. 72, l. 1127, c. 20, AGM.

176. Sigüenza, 24 July 1938, ZN, a. 31, l. 10, c. 5, AGM.

177. Informe, 12 July 1938, Barcelona 821, AHN-SGC.

178. El general, 2 August 1938, ZR, a. 56, l. 550, c. 2, AGM.

179. Informe, 1 August 1938, Barcelona 811, AHN-SGC.

180. Informe, 7 May 1938, ZR, a. 46, l. 69, c. 20, AGM.

181. Sentencia, 8 July 1938, Causa General 1017, AHN.

182. Informe, 8 July 1938, ZR, a. 46, l. 69, c. 20, AGM.

183. Relación, 28 April 1939, ZN, a. 35, l. 7, c. 10, AGM.

184. Punto, nd., CGG, a. 4, l. 246, c. 3, AGM.

185. Punto, nd., CGG, a. 4, l. 246, c. 3, AGM; Líster (1966:214) put Republican losses at fifty thousand of which "only" fifteen thousand were lost definitively. Tagüeña Lacorte 1978:174.

186. Tagüeña was twenty-three when he was given command of a division. His memoirs are a respected source even for *franquista* historians. See Martínez Bande 1979:104, 115.

187. Cf. Líster 1966:223: "The soldiers and almost all the officers of Center-Southern zone shook with enthusiasm [vibraban de entusiasmo] when they learned of the Ebro offensive and demanded to fight."

188. Ministerio, 14 July 1938, CGG, reel 204, AGM.

189. Circular, Barcelona, 25 July 1938, CGG, reel 204, AGM; Compañía, August 1938, ZR, reel 45, AGM.

190. Informe, 30 August 1938, ZR, a. 65, l. 793, c. 6, AGM.

191. Ejército, 2 September 1938, ZN, reel 30, AGM.

192. On a protest in Badalona, see Fraser 1986:452.

193. See files in Causa General 1179, AHN.

194. Alfredo, 27 May 1938, Causa General 1179, AHN.

195. Alfredo, 2 June 1938, Causa General 1179, AHN.

196. Sentencia, 6 April 1938, Causa General 1179, AHN.

197. Certifico, 21 June 1938, Causa General 1179, AHN.

198. Don, 21 June 1938, Causa General 1179, AHN.

199. Sentencia, 1 July 1938, Causa General 1179, AHN.

200. El Comisario, 15 August 1938, ZR, a. 69, l. 1038, c. 11, AGM.

201. Ejército, 31 May 1938, Causa General 577, AHN.

202. Señor Presidente, 14 August 1938, CGG, a. 5, l. 279, c. 21, AGM.

203. Ministerio, 4 October 1938, CGG, a. 5, l. 279, c. 21, AGM.

204. Ministerio, 3 October 1938, CGG, a. 5, l. 279, c. 21, AGM.

205. Ministerio, 2 September 1938, CGG, a. 5, l. 279, c. 22, AGM.

206. Notas, 31 August 1938, ZR, a. 68, l. 1012, c. 6, AGM; Copia, 1 September 1938, ZR, a. 68, l. 1012, c. 6, AGM.

207. Circular, 3 September 1938, ZR, a. 68, l. 1010, c. 2, AGM.

208. Orden, XXI Cuerpo, 3 September 1938, ZR, a. 68, l. 1012, c. 1, AGM.

209. XXI Cuerpo, 7 October 1938, ZR, a. 68, l. 1010, c. 2, AGM.

210. XXI Cuerpo, September 1938, ZR, a. 68, l. 1012, c. 6, AGM.

211. See Wintringham (1939:249) for his own experience of the disease.

212. A los jefes, 18 September 1938, ZR, a. 68, l. 1012, c. 10, AGM.

213. Informe, 8 September 1938, ZR, a. 22, l. 1000, c. 13, AGM.

214. XXI Cuerpo, 4 February 1939, ZR, a. 68, l. 1012, c. 10, AGM.

215. II Cuerpo, 1 March 1938, ZR, a. 18, l. 2, c. 21, AGM; Holmes 1985:191.

216. Cf. the somewhat suspect figures of Mira (1943:113), who states without citing references that in 1938 the quiet Madrid front suffered "600,000 casualties [sic]," 52 percent of whom were wounded, 40 percent sick, 6 percent killed, and 1 percent undiagnosed. Mental casualties were less than .5 percent of the sick.

217. Informe, 1 October 1938, ZR, a. 68, l. 1012, c. 6, AGM.

218. Ejército, [fall?] 1938, ZN, a. 5, l. 278, c. 19, AGM.

219. Acta, 20 September 1938, ZR, reel 45, AGM.

220. Informe, 5 October 1938, ZR, a. 22, l. 1000, c. 13, AGM; Acta, 6 October 1938?, ZR, a. 77, l. 1248, c. 29, AGM.

221. Actividades, 4 June 1937, ZR, a. 70, l. 1074, c. 12, AGM.

222. "Los campesinos, las subsistencias y la guerra," Timón, October 1938, pp. 142–57. See also Problemas nacionales, nd., ZR, a. 47, l. 72, c. 10, AGM.

223. Informe, 28 May 1937 and 3 June 1937, ZR, a. 70, l. 1074, c. 12, AGM.

224. Comisario, 30 December 1937, ZR, a. 77, l. 1253, c. 11, AGM.

225. III Bon. September 1938, ZR, reel 45, AGM.

226. Convocada, 18 November 1938, ZR, a. 77, l. 1248, c. 29, AGM.

227. Orden, 5 August 1938, ZR, a. 72, l. 1109, c. 3, AGM.

228. II Cuerpo, 20 October 1938, ZR, a. 76, l. 1243, c. 13, AGM.

229. Parte, 17 November 1938, ZR, reel 93, AGM; X Cuerpo, 20 October 1938, ZR, a. 65, l. 986, c. 1, AGM.

230. Informe, 6 January 1939, ZR, a. 22, l. 1000, c. 13, AGM; Intendencia, nd., ZR, a. 22, l. 1000, c. 13, AGM.

231. Ministerio, 26 October 1938, CGG, a. 5, l. 279, c. 21, AGM.

232. Estado, 22 October 1938, ZN, a. 31, l. 10, c. 5, AGM.

233. Informe, July 1938, ZR, a. 68, l. 1000, c. 14, AGM.

234. República, 23 July 1938, ZR, a. 76, l. 1241, c. 2, AGM.

235. De la reunión, 20 August 1938, ZR, reel 45, AGM.

236. Ejército de Levante, 13 December 1938, CGG, a. 5, l. 278, c. 19, AGM.

237. VII Cuerpo, 1 September 1938, ZR, a. 71, l. 1103, c. 10, AGM.

238. 152 División, 29 July 1938, ZN, a. 35, l. 1, c. 23, AGM.

239. Telegrama, 18 September 1938, ZN, a. 42, l. 2, c. 18, AGM.

240. Informe, 3 January 1939, ZR, a. 68, l. 1011, c. 9, AGM.

241. Informe, 23 August 1938, ZR, a. 45, l. 474, c. 7, AGM.

242. Ejército de Extremadura, 22 August 1938, ZR, a. 54, l. 473, c. 7, AGM; Informe, 10 July 1938, ZR, a. 54, l. 474, c. 5, AGM.

243. As early as November 1936, Franco had banned trading between Nationalists and Republicans. See Whealey 1977:144.

244. Informe, 19 August 1938, ZR, a. 54, l. 473, c. 8, AGM.

245. Reconocimientos, 2–7 July 1938, ZR, a. 54, l. 473, c. 8, AGM.

246. Informe, 19 August 1938, ZR, a. 54, l. 473, c. 8, AGM.

247. PSOE, 9 June 1938, ZR, a. 54, l. 474–1, c. 2, AGM.

248. Cuartel, 1 April 1938, ZN, a. 18, l. 2, c. 21, AGM.

249. Cuartel, 1 April 1938, ZN, a. 18, l. 2, c. 21, AGM.

250. Consideraciones, 4 August 1938, ZR, a. 54, l. 474–1, c. 2, AGM.

251. Informe, 1 July 1938, ZR, a. 54, l. 474, c. 4, AGM.

252. Informe, 4 June 1938, ZR, a. 54, l. 474, c. 5, AGM.

253. 109 B.M., 20–24 June 1938, ZR, a. 54, l. 474, c. 6, AGM.

254. Informe, 17 June 1938, ZR, a. 54, l. 473, c. 8, AGM.

255. Informe, 29 July 1938, ZR, a. 54, l. 473, c. 8, AGM.

256. SIM, 21 September 1938, ZR, a. 54, l. 473, c. 8, AGM.

257. Informe, 29 July 1938, ZR, a. 54, l. 473, c. 8, AGM.

258. Informe, 23 August 1938, ZR, a. 54, l. 473, c. 7, AGM.

259. Informe-Propuesta, 4 July 1938, ZR, a. 54, l. 474, c. 7, AGM.

260. Cuartel, 1 April 1938, ZN, a. 18, l. 2, c. 21, AGM.

261. Informe, 27 August 1938, ZR, a. 54, l. 474, c. 7, AGM.

262. Al hacerse, 25 August 1938, ZR, a. 54, l. 474, c. 7, AGM.

263. VII Cuerpo, 29 July 1938, ZR, a. 54, l. 474, c. 5, AGM; cf. Vila Izquierdo 1984:110, 128.

264. VII Cuerpo, 29 July 1938, ZR, a. 54, l. 474, c. 5, AGM.

265. Informe, 27 August 1938, ZR, a. 54, l. 474, c. 6, AGM.

266. The head of the information section of the General Staff of the Army of Estremadura contested this version. He argued that Burillo was tougher on his own Assault Guards than his other troops. See Informe, 19 August 1938, ZR, a. 54, l. 473,

c. 8, AGM. Despite its dismal military record, Servicio de Investigación Militar (SIM) investigators charged that the Twelfth was Burillo's most favored unit and was personally devoted to him. Informe, 29 July 1938, ZR, a. 54, l. 473, c. 8, AGM. Burillo was deeply implicated both in the assassination of Calvo Sotelo and in the repression of the POUM after May 1937. For details, see Romero 1982. On his role against the POUM, see Bolloten 1991:500, 508, 686.

267. Ordenes, 4 August 1938, ZR, a. 54, l. 474–1, c. 2, AGM; VII Cuerpos, 12 December 1937, ZR, a. 76, l. 1235, c. 1, AGM.

268. Informe, 19 August 1938, ZR, a. 54, l. 473, c. 8, AGM.

269. Asunto, 19 August 1938, ZR, a. 54, l. 473, c. 8, AGM.

270. Asunto, 19 August 1938, ZR, a. 54, l. 473, c. 8, AGM; VII Cuerpos, 12 December 1937, ZR, a. 76, l. 1235, c. 1, AGM.

271. Informe, Tribunal Permanente, 20 August 1938, ZR, a. 54, l. 473, c. 8, AGM.

272. Informe, 19 August 1938, ZR, a. 54, l. 473, c. 8, AGM.

273. Ordenes, 4 August 1938, ZR, a. 54, l. 474–1, c. 2, AGM.

274. Informe, 19 August 1938, ZR, a. 54, l. 473, c. 8, AGM.

275. Salas Larrazábal and Salas Larrazábal 1986:358; Ordenes, 4 August 1938, ZR, a. 54, l. 474–1, c. 2, AGM.

276. Informe, 23 August 1938, ZR, a. 54, l. 473, c. 7, AGM.

277. Ilustrísimo, 11 August 1938, ZR, a. 54, l. 473, c. 4, AGM.

278. Informe, 25 August 1938, ZR, a. 54, l. 474, c. 4, AGM.

279. Informe, 29 July 1938, ZR, a. 54, l. 473, c. 8, AGM.

280. Informe, 29 June 1938, ZR, a. 54, l. 473, c. 8, AGM.

281. Copia, 6 April 1938, ZR, a. 54, l. 473, c. 7, AGM.

282. Información, 5 June 1938, ZR, a. 76, l. 1225, c. 1, AGM.

283. Documento 117, 17 August 1938, ZR, a. 54, l. 473, c. 7, AGM; Copia, nd. [April?] 1938, ZR, a. 54, l. 473, c. 7, AGM. Comisario, 10 July 1938, ZR, a. 54, l. 473, c. 8, AGM.

284. Ordenes, 4 August 1938, ZR, a. 54, l. 474–1, c. 2, AGM.

285. Copia, 29 March 1938, ZR, a. 54, l. 473, c. 7, AGM.

286. Fortificación, 18 August 1938, ZR, a. 54, l. 474, c. 2, AGM.

287. Reconocimientos, 2–7 July 1938, ZR, a. 54, l. 473, c. 8, AGM.

288. Comisario, 10 July 1938, ZR, a. 54, l. 473, c. 8, AGM; El Jefe, 20 August 1938, ZR, a. 54, l. 474, c. 2, AGM.

289. See Declaración prestada por el prisonero, 26 August 1938, ZR, a. 54, l. 473, c. 8, AGM.

290. Informe, 26 August 1938, ZR, a. 54, l. 474, c. 3, AGM; Informe, 23 August 1938, ZR, a. 54, l. 474, c. 7, AGM; Vila Izquierdo 1984:138; Martínez Bande 1981:222.

291. Informe, August 1938, ZR, a. 54, l. 473, c. 8, AGM.

292. Informe, 29 July 1938, ZR, a. 54, l. 473, c. 8, AGM.

293. SIM, 21 September 1938, ZR, a. 54, l. 473, c. 8, AGM.

294. Ministerio, 28 July 1938, ZR, a. 54, l. 473, c. 7, AGM.

295. Informe, 20 August 1938, ZR, a. 54, l. 474, c. 3, AGM.

296. El Jefe, 20 August 1938, ZR, a. 54, l. 474, c. 2, AGM.

297. Informe, 19 August 1938, ZR, a. 54, l. 473, c. 8, AGM.

298. For example, nearly four thousand wagons of wheat. See Informe, 20 August 1938, ZR, a. 54, l. 474, c. 3, AGM.

299. Informe, 25 August 1938, ZR, a. 54, l. 474, c. 4, AGM.

300. Informe, 25 August 1938, ZR, a. 54, l. 474, c. 4, AGM. For municipal sources on hoarding and the refusal of individuals to provide information, see Gallardo Moreno 1994:79–81.

301. Ejército, 16 July 1938, ZR, a. 54, l. 474, c. 4, AGM.

302. A rehabilitation which continues today. See Cervera 1999:186.

303. The general finished his career as the Republican military attaché in Washington. On Negrín's image in Spanish historiography, see Viñas 1979:79.

304. Ordenes, 4 August 1938, ZR, a. 54, l. 474–1, c. 2, AGM.

305. Federación socialista, 3 July 1938, ZR, a. 54, l. 474–1, c. 1, AGM.

306. Bolloten (1991:686) reports that Burillo came to hate the party. Cordón (1977:406) called him a "rabid anti-Communist." See also Salas Larrazábal 1973:3653.

307. See files in ZR, a. 54, l. 473, and l. 474, AGM.

308. Informe, 26 August 1938, ZR, a. 54, l. 474, c. 4, AGM.

309. Informe, 29 July 1938, ZR, a. 54, l. 473, c. 8, AGM.

310. Vila Izquierdo 1984:127; Ordenes, 4 August 1938, ZR, a. 54, l. 474-1, c. 2, AGM.

311. Ejército, 30 August 1938, ZR, a. 54, l. 474, c. 4, AGM.

312. Informe, 3 August 1938, ZR, a. 54, l. 474–1, c. 1, AGM.

313. Bolloten 1991:686; Jefetura, 30 August 1938, ZR, a. 54, l. 474, c. 4, AGM.

314. Informe, 25 August 1938, ZR, a. 54, l. 474, c. 4, AGM.

315. Orden, 16 August 1938, ZR, a. 54, l. 474, c. 6, AGM.

316. The hapless Republican Army in Estremadura also arrested and fined eight soldiers for fraternizing with the enemy. See Vistos, 1 November 1938, ZR, a. 66, l. 798, c. 1, AGM; Fichas de censura, September–October 1938, ZR, a. 66, l. 798, c. 1, AGM.

317. Postal workers usually intercepted tobacco. See Fraser 1986:445.

318. Comisariado, nd., ZR, reel 76, AGM.

319. IX Cuerpo, December 1938, ZR, a. 65, l. 975, c. 1, AGM.

320. Salas encountered similar problems when counting assassinations of political opponents. See Serrano 1986:107.

321. Estado Mayor, 14 June 1938, ZR, reel 45, AGM.

322. Gráfico, August-September 1938, ZR, reel 76, AGM.

323. Informe, 27 September 1938, ZR, a. 68, l. 1011, c. 9, AGM.

324. Tribunal, 29 October 1938, 8 December 1938, 7 January 1939, ZR, a. 65, l. 986, c. 1, AGM.

325. 14 Brigada, 30 July 1938, 22 August 1938, ZR, a. 77, l. 1269, c. 19, AGM.

326. Burgos, 12 June 1938, ZN, a. 31, l. 10, c. 3, AGM; Nationalist authorities estimated that of eighty-five thousand volunteer militiamen, forty thousand were foreigners. CGG, 12 April 1937, CGG, a. 5, l. 282, c. 4, AGM.

327. Ejército, 21 April 1938, ZR, a. 77, l. 1267, c. 2, AGM.

328. Herrick (1998:209) estimates that at least twenty U.S. citizens were shot for desertion.

329. Wintringham (1939:100) states that heavy drinkers were a small percentage of the volunteers. Eby (1974:383) reports that those who frequented bordellos near the

Tarragona beach were tempted to desert.

330. Orden, 23 July 1938, ZR, a. 73, l. 1149, c. 7, AGM.

331. Ejército, 16 July 1938, ZR, a. 73, l. 1135, c. 6, AGM.

332. Reservado, 3 August 1938, ZR, a. 73, l. 1162, c. 4, AGM.

333. Informe, 16 October 1938, ZR, a. 69, l. 1025, c. 4, AGM.

334. Orden, 15 July 1937, ZR, a. 70, l. 1063, c. 6, AGM.

335. Telegrama, 31 December 1938, ZN, a. 38, l. 14, c. 1, AGM.

336. Secreto, 4 April 1938, ZN, a. 39, l. 6, c. 3, AGM.

337. Informe, 18 September 1938, ZR, a. 69, l. 1025, c. 4, AGM.

338. Informe, 23 May 1937, ZR, a. 73, l. 1154, c. 22, AGM.

339. Informe, 4 April 1938, ZR, a. 70. l. 1074, c. 10, AGM.

340. Acta, 18 August 1938, reel 45, AGM.

341. Camarada, 27 January 1938, ZR, reel 45, AGM; Pons Prades 1974:334.

342. Director, 2 May 1938, ZR, reel 45, AGM.

343. Informe, 8 June 1938, ZR, reel 45, AGM.

344. Instrucción, 1 June 1938, ZR, a. 77, l. 1255, c. 1, AGM.

345. Convocada, 18 November 1938, ZR, a. 77, l. 1248, c. 29, AGM.

346. Ejército, 12 November 1938, ZR, a. 65, l. 986, c. 1, AGM.

347. Estado Mayor, 5 June 1938, ZR, a. 75, l. 1208, c. 1, AGM.

348. Orden, 9 November 1938, ZR, reel 76, AGM.

349. Ministerio, 6 September 1938, ZR, reel 45, AGM.

350. Convocada, 18 November 1938, ZR, a. 77, l. 1248, c. 29, AGM.

351. Sección, 6 September 1938, ZR, a. 58, l. 627 bis, c. 3, AGM; Ministerio, 6 September 1938, ZR, reel 45, AGM; Operaciones, 15 September 1938, ZR, reel 93, AGM.

352. See Comisariado, 22 September 1938, ZR, a. 65, l. 986, c. 2, AGM.

353. Informe, 11 December 1938, ZR, a. 65, l. 785, c. 10, AGM.

354. XXI Cuerpo, 5 December 1938, ZR, a. 68, l. 1010, c. 2, AGM.

355. Informe, 29 November–1 December 1938, ZR, reel 93, AGM.

356. Secretariado, nd., ZR, reel 93, AGM.

357. T.P., 8 November 1938, ZN, a. 19, l. 2, c. 27, AGM. Nationalist physicians rarely discussed this issue in order not to challenge the "heroic" image of their army. See Carreras Panchón 1986:19–20.

358. Cuartel, 29 December 1938, CGG, a. 2, l. 145, c. 70, AGM.

359. Teletipo, 28 December 1938, ZR, reel 76, AGM.

360. Acta, 11 November 1938, ZR, a. 18, l. 627 bis, c. 4, AGM.

361. Número, nd?, ZR, a. 73, l. 1155, c. 13, AGM.

362. Información, 11 December 1938, ZR, reel 93, AGM.

363. Ejército, 6 December 1938, ZR, reel 76, AGM.

364. A similar picture of British civil war deserters is found in Carlton 1992:196.

365. Ficha, 17 June 1938, ZR, reel 93, AGM.

366. Fichas, nd., ZR, a. 76, l. 1226, c. 2, AGM; Pliego, 2 April 1938, ZR, a. 75, l. 1218, c. 7, AGM.

367. Información, nd., ZN, a. 44, l. 4, c. 16, AGM.

368. Relación, 29 July 1938, ZR, a. 57, l. 606, c. 18, AGM.

369. Informe, 16 July 1938, ZR, a. 46, l. 69, c. 20, AGM.

370. Convocada, 18 November 1938, ZR, a. 77, l. 1248, c. 29, AGM.

371. Extracto, 18 July 1938, ZR, reel 45, AGM.

372. Acta, 17 September 1938, ZR, reel 45, AGM.

373. Información, 9 September 1938, ZR, reel 45, AGM.

374. Copia, 2 September 1938, ZR, a. 70, l. 1051, c. 16, AGM.

375. See Informes, ZR, a. 73, l. 1155, c. 13, AGM.

376. Informe, 3 December 1938, ZR, a. 73, l. 1155, c. 13, AGM; Antonio Cordón, the Communist undersecretary of defense believed in last-ditch resistance but nonetheless admitted the demoralization of older soldiers at the beginning of 1939. See Cordón 1977:375.

377. Sindicato, 25 September 1937, Castellón 139, AHN-SGC.

378. Informe, 3 January 1939, ZR, a. 73, l. 1155, c. 13, AGM.

379. 14 División, February 1937-December 1938, ZR, a. 70, l. 1075, c. 1, AGM.

380. IV Cuerpo, October 1938, ZR, a. 70, l. 1075, c. 1, AGM.

381. Comisariado, 16 November 1938, ZR, reel 45, AGM.

382. Información, 1 January 1939, ZR, a. 68, l. 1010, c. 2, AGM.

383. Acta, 6 November 1938, ZR, reel 45, AGM; Acta, 8 December 1938, ZR, reel 45, AGM.

384. Acta, 5 November [?], 3[?] December 1938, ZR, reel 45, AGM.

385. Acta, September-October 1938, ZR, reel 45, AGM. The Nationalists also had a shortage of warm boots and had to rotate them among those on guard duty. See Mando, 13 October 1938, ZN, a. 43, l. 11, c. 103, AGM.

386. Acta, 6 November 1938, ZR, reel 45, AGM.

387. X Cuerpo, 20 October 1938, ZR, a. 65, l. 986, c. 1, AGM.

388. Ministerio, 6 September 1938, ZR, reel 45, AGM.

389. Acta, 14 November 1938, ZR, reel 45, AGM.

390. Primer, 24 October 1938, ZR, a. 90, l. 761, c. 4, AGM.

391. Informe, Sevilla, 8 April 1938, CGG, reel 128, AGM.

392. Cuartel, 3 May 1938, CGG, reel 128, AGM.

393. Telegrama, 3 August 1938, CGG, reel 204, AGM.

394. Regimiento, 23 June 1938, CGG, reel 159, AGM.

395. Informe, nd., ZR, a. 54, l. 474, c. 4, AGM.

396. Copia, nd., ZR, a. 54, l. 473, c. 8, AGM.

397. Informe, 19 August 1938, ZR, a. 54, l. 473, c. 8, AGM.

398. Estado, 3 February 1938, ZR, a. 66, l. 800, c. 2, AGM.

399. Estado Español, 30 July 1938, CGG, reel 204, AGM.

400. Cuerpo, 12 November 1938, CGG, reel 204, AGM.

401. Cuerpo, 18 November 1938, CGG, reel 204, AGM.

402. Copia, 9 November 1938, CGG, a. 5, l. 280, c. 7, AGM.

403. Ejército, 28 October 1938, ZN, a. 38, l. 14, c. 1, AGM.

404. Copia, 9 November 1938, CGG, a. 5, l. 280, c. 7, AGM. On betrayal of guerrillas by shepherds, see also Pitt-Rivers 1954:183.

405. Copia, 11 August 1938, ZN, a. 31, l. 10, c. 2, AGM.

406. Copia, 17 March 1938, CGG, a. 2, l. 145, c. 85, AGM.

407. Copia, 27 February 1938, CGG, a. 2, l. 145, c. 82, AGM.

408. Informe, 8 April 1938, CGG, reel 128, AGM; Copia, 1 February 1938, CGG, a. 1, l. 56, c. 17, AGM.

409. Primera, 18 February 1938, CGG, a. 1, l. 56, c. 17, AGM.

## 4. Survival

1. See also Modesto (1969:260–61), who thinks that Andalusian peasants would have assisted the Popular Army in order to reintroduce land reform.

2. Ficha de censura, December? 1938, ZR, a. 66, l. 803, c. 5, AGM.

3. This letter was forwarded to the head of the Andalusian Army.

4. Ministerio, 7 January 1939, ZR, a. 66, l. 803, c. 5, AGM. In the Nationalist zone, all correspondence was also subject to censorship.

5. For Republican censors' propagandistic recommendations, see Mira 1943:126.

6. See Faust (1996:240) on the "new selfishness" of Southern women.

7. Holiday meals had been special occasions when blond tobacco and even cognac could be consumed.

8. A copy of the letter was forwarded to the civil governor of Alicante. It is an open question—given the lack of epistolary sources—whether women in the Republican zone, like women in the South during the final years of the Confederacy, were encouraging their men to desert. See Faust 1996:243.

9. Informe, Delegación de Jaén, 31 August 1938, ZR, a. 67, l. 850, c. 6, AGM. For a general account, which emphasizes that hunger was caused by a massive influx of refugees and stagnation of production, see Cobo Romero 1993:443–69.

10. Orden, 3 November 1938, ZR, a. 72, l. 1108, c. 21, AGM.

11. Acta de acusación, 24 July 1938, ZR, reel 45, AGM.

12. Nota, 11 October 1938, ZN, a. 43, l. 1, c. 17, AGM.

13. SIPM, 26 September 1938, ZN, a. 31, l. 6, c. 2, AGM.

14. This letter writer called the censor an *"hijo de puta."*

15. A copy of the letter was sent to the SIM.

16. Ministerio, 10 February 1939, ZR, a. 66, l. 803, c. 17, AGM.

17. This was true on other fronts as well. See Juicio, 7 December 1938, ZR, a. 77, l. 1248, c. 29, AGM.

18. Ejército, 12 January 1939, ZR, a. 57, l. 606, c. 21, AGM.

19. Copia, 5 March 1939, ZR, a. 68, l. 1021, c. 10, AGM.

20. Telegrama, 30 December 1938, ZN, a. 41, l. 2, c. 12, AGM; Moreno Gómez 1999:372.

21. Rgto., 31 December 1938, ZN, a. 41, l. 2, c. 12, AGM.

22. Comandancia, 13 January 1939, ZN, a. 11, l. 1, c. 28, AGM.

23. Espías, 8 December 1938, ZN, a. 15, l. 13, c. 20, AGM.

24. See Pons Prades (1977) who indicates that guerrilla bands were more active after than during the civil war.

25. Alcaldía, 25 May 1939, ZN, a. 38, l. 1, c. 22, AGM.

26. Orden, 16 December 1938, ZR, a. 68, l. 991, c. 23, AGM.

27. Reservado, 22 December 1938, ZR, a. 65, l. 785, c. 11, AGM. The political problem remained "most serious."

28. De las gestiones, 6 October 1938, ZR, a. 22, l. 1000, c. 13, AGM.

29. Informe, 8 August 1938, ZR, a. 65, l. 785, c. 10, AGM.

30. Informe, 10 December 1938, ZR, a. 68, l. 991, c. 24, AGM.

31. For more allegations of Communist crimes, see Bolloten 1991:276, 595, 633.
32. Copia, 4 January 1939, CGG, a. 2, l. 145, c. 95, AGM.
33. Informes, 6–7 December 1938, ZR, a. 69, l. 1030, c. 8, AGM.
34. Salas Larrazábal contests this superiority and argues that Yagüe's troops were not particularly well equipped. Modesto, on the other hand, asserts that from December 1938 to February 1939 Republican troops fought virtually disarmed since Soviet weapons were not allowed over the French border.
35. XVI Cuerpo, 13 January 1939, ZR, reel 93, AGM.
36. Bolloten (1991:667) attributes the lack of Catalan resistance to the centralization and anti-Catalanism of the Republican government. Material shortages may have been more important.
37. La situación, nd. [February 1939?], ZN, a. 18, l. 10, c. 8, AGM.
38. Cf. the Leninist perspective of Modesto (1969:263), who once again blames the failure of the offensive on poor leadership.
39. Acta, 17 January 1939, ZR, reel 45, AGM.
40. On the quartermaster's inability to distribute food, see Cordón 1977:376; Tagüeña Lacorte 1978:188. If women were concerned with obtaining food, their men demanded tobacco.
41. Letter from J. Peiró to Negrín and annex, 6 January 1939, CGG, reel 204, AGM; Consideraciones, May 1938, CGG, a. 5, l. 280, c. 1, AGM.
42. 29 Brigada, 2 February 1939, ZR, a. 73, l. 1160, c. 6, AGM.
43. Informe, 1 March 1939, ZR, a. 73, l. 1160, c. 6, AGM.
44. Instrucción, 21 February 1939, ZR, a. 68, l. 991, c. 23, AGM; XVI Cuerpo, 3 February 1939, ZR, a. 68, l. 991, c. 23, AGM; Informe, 4 February 1939, ZR, a. 68, l. 1000, c. 13, AGM. Republican officers had been ordered not to appoint to sensitive posts soldiers with relatives in the "fascist" zone. Ejército, 17 February 1939, ZN, a. 22, r. 89, l. 31, c. 17, AGM.
45. Resumen, 1–15 February 1939, ZR, reel 93, AGM.
46. Informe, November 1938, ZR, a. 47, l. 71, c. 5, AGM.
47. Interesa, nd., ZR, a. 47, l. 71. c. 6, AGM.
48. Informe, Transportes, 2 January 1939, ZR, reel 93, AGM.
49. Colectividad, 14 May 1938.
50. CNT, 21 April 1938, PS Madrid 2467, AHN-SGC.
51. Comité, 6 July 1938, PS Madrid 2467, AHN-SGC.
52. Informe, fall? 1938, PS Madrid 2467, AHN-SGC.
53. Estimados, 12 December 1938, PS Madrid 2467, AHN-SGC.
54. Nash (1995:138) stresses the unpaid and unremunerated female labor "which explains how the economy was sustained through such adverse circumstances."
55. The following relies closely on Informes, December 1938, PS Madrid 2467, AHN-SGC. For statistics on numbers of collectivists and union members, see Mintz 1977:188–94.
56. Estado, nd., ZN, a. 31, l. 9, c. 3, AGM.
57. Copia, nd., CGG, reel 162, AGM.
58. Copia, 27 August 1938, CGG, reel 162, AGM. Copia, 5 August 1938, CGG, reel 162, AGM; Cuenta, 1 September 1938, CGG, reel 162, AGM.
59. Tengo, 26 September 1938, CGG, reel 162, AGM; Copia, 25 June 1938, CGG,

reel 162, AGM.

60. Cuartel, 14 December 1938, CGG, reel 162, AGM.

61. Copia, 8 July 1938, CGG, reel 162, AGM.

62. Información, 21 September 1938, CGG, reel 162, AGM.

63. Nota, 8 October 1937, CGG, reel 162, AGM; Explotación, 8 October 1938, CGG, reel 162, AGM.

64. Babcock and Wilcox, 14 January 1939, CGG, a. 1, l. 57, c. 38, AGM.

65. Dirección, 1 June 1937, CGG, reel 159, AGM; Normas, 13 August 1938, CGG, a. 1, l. 57, c. 38, AGM.

66. See, for example, Normas, 12 August 1937, ZR, a. 73, l. 1135, c. 8, AGM; Rojo, 1974:39.

67. Cuerpo, 12 December 1937, ZN, a. 44, l. 2, c. 6, AGM.

68. Sexto, 16 October 1938, ZR, a. 65, l. 793, c. 2, AGM.

69. Fuerzas, 3 March 1939, ZR, a. 56, l. 562, c. 10, AGM.

70. Acta de la reunión, Sindicato único de transporte, 22 May 1937, Madrid 991, AHN-SGC.

71. Acta de la reunión, Sindicato único de transporte, 23 August 1936?, Madrid 991, AHN-SGC.

72. Acta de la reunión, 14 March 1938, Madrid 991, AHN-SGC.

73. Acta de la reunión, 3 May 1938, Madrid 991, AHN-SGC.

74. Acta de la reunión, 7 June 1938, Madrid 991, AHN-SGC.

75. Acta de comités, 8 July 1938, Madrid 991, AHN-SGC.

76. Comisariado, 27 October 1937, ZR, reel 45, AGM.

77. CNT carteros, 26 February 1938, Madrid 2321, AHN-SGC.

78. CNT carteros, 4 January 1938, Madrid 2321, AHN-SGC.

79. Acta, Comités de control de *El Liberal y Heraldo de Madrid,* 16 August 1937, Madrid 834, AHN-SGC.

80. CNT carteros, 29 April 1938, Madrid 2321, AHN-SGC.

81. Informe, CNT, Sección defensa, 28 November 1938, Madrid 3432, AHN-SGC.

82. Acta de la reunión, 25 April 1938, Madrid 991, AHN-SGC.

83. See Reunión, 9 January 1937, Madrid 991, AHN-SGC, and Informe de la comisión que fue a Cuenca, 7 February [1937?], 991, AHN-SGC.

84. Líster (1966:253) sees Negrín in opposition to policies of last-ditch resistance.

85. For a thorough and recent account, see Cervera 1999:378–422.

86. T.P. nd., 32 División, ZN, a. 41, l. 3, c. 43, AGM.

87. For the latest figures, Juliá 1999:407–12.

88. Discussions of deaths and casualties are to be found in Jackson (1965:526–40) and Diez Nicolas (1985:41–55); Kindelán (1945:103) puts "normal" casualties at 7 percent of combat troops.

## Conclusion

1. The argument is repeated by Graham 1999:504.

2. For a critical examination of this position see Scott 1985:292, 317.

3. Of course, it was in Rojo's interest to blame civilians for the defeat.

4. On the loyalty of French soldiers, see van Creveld 1993:24.

5. Cf. Richards 1998:168: "There was [in the postwar period] a profound lack of enthusiasm for work itself. Part of what was destroyed in the Civil War and in the 1940s was pride in a consciousness of being a class with collective aspirations."

6. "There were very few commanders of any caliber to be found in Kolchak's army. Only 5 percent of the seventeen thousand officers had been trained before the war." See Figes 1996:654. See also Holmes 1985:44; Skocpol 1979:136.

# Bibliography

## Archives and Abbreviations

Archivo General Militar (AGM), Avila
  Zona Republicana (ZR)
  Zona Nacional (ZN)
  Cuartel General del Generalísimo (CGG)
Archivo Histórico Nacional (AHN), Madrid
  Causa General
Archivo Histórico Nacional–Sección Guerra Civil (AHN-SGC), Salamanca
Arxiu nacional de Catalunya (ANC), Barcelona
Fundación Pablo Iglesias, Madrid

## Periodicals

*Claridad*
*CNT*
*Gaceta de la República*
*El Liberal*
*Solidaridad Obrera*

## Other Sources

Abad de Santillán, Diego. 1977. *Por qué perdimos la guerra*. Barcelona.
Abad, Vicente. 1984. *Historia de la naranja, 1781–1939*. Valencia.
———. 1988. Ideología y praxis de un fenómeno revolucionario. In *El sueño igualitario: Campesinado y colectivización en la España republicana*, edited by Julián Casanova. Zaragoza.
Almendral Parra, Cristina, Teresa Flores Velasco, and David Valle Sánchez. 1990. Auditoría de guerra de Gijón. In *Justicia en guerra: Jornadas sobre la administración de justicia durante la guerra civil española*. Madrid.
Alpert, Michael. 1984. Soldiers, politics, and war. In *Revolution and war in Spain, 1931–1939*, edited by Paul Preston. London.

————. 1989. *El ejército republicano en la guerra civil.* Madrid.

Alvarez, Santiago. 1989. *Los comisarios políticos en el Ejército popular de la República: Aportaciones a la Guerra Civil española (1936–39).* La Coruña.

Aragón, Bartolomé. 1940. *Con Intendencia militar de las Gloriosas Brigadas Navarras.* Madrid.

Aroca Sardagna, José María. 1972. *Las Tribus.* Barcelona.

Aróstegui, Julio, ed. 1988. *Historia y memoria de la guerra civil: Encuentro en Castilla y León.* Salamanca.

Aróstegui, Julio, and Jesús A. Martínez. 1984. *La junta de defensa de Madrid.* Madrid.

Arranz Bullido, María Angeles. 1990. La política de abastecimientos en la zona nacional. In *Los nuevos historiadores ante la Guerra Civil española,* edited by Octavio Ruiz Manjón Cabeza and Miguel Gómez Oliver. Granada.

Asensio, José. 1938. *El General Asensio: Su lealtad a la República.* Barcelona.

Ashley, Maurice. 1990. *The English civil war.* New York.

Ashworth, Tony. 1980. *Trench warfare, 1914–18: The live and let live system.* London.

Azaña, Manuel. 1982. *La velada de Benicarló.* Translated by Josephine Stewart and Paul Stewart. Rutherford, N.J.

————. 1990. *Obras completas.* 4 vols. Madrid.

Balcells, Albert. 1968. *El problema agrari a Catalunya, 1890–1936.* Barcelona.

————. 1974. *Cataluña contemporánea,* 2 vols. Madrid.

*El Banco de España: Una historia económica.* 1970. Madrid.

Banco de España. 1979. *Los billetes del Banco de España, (1782–1979).* Madrid.

Bar Cendón, Antonio. 1975. La Confederación Nacional del Trabajo frente a la II República. In *Estudios sobre la II República Española,* edited by Manuel Ramírez. Madrid.

Barciela López, Carlos. 1983. Producción y política cerealista durante la guerra civil española (1936–39). In *Historia económica y pensamiento social: Estudios en homenaje a Diego Mateo del Peral.* Madrid.

————. 1986. Introduction to *Historia agraria de España contemporánea,* edited by Angel García Sanz, Ramón Garrabou, and Jesús Sanz Fernández. Barcelona.

Baráibar, Carlos de. 1938. Los campesinos, las subsistencias y la guerra. *Timón* (October), pp. 142–57.

Bautista Vilar, Juan. 1990. La persecución religiosa en la zona nacionalista: El caso de los protestantes españoles. In *Los nuevos historiadores ante la Guerra Civil española,* 2 vols. edited by Octavio Ruiz Manjón Cabeza and Miguel Gómez Oliver. Granada.

Berdugo, Ignacio, Josefina Cuesta, María Dolores de la Calle, and Mónica Lanero. 1990. El Ministerio de Justicia en la España 'Nacional.' In *Justicia en guerra: Jornadas sobre la administración de justicia durante la guerra civil española.* Madrid.

Bernanos, Georges. 1971. *Les grandes cimetières sous la lune.* Paris.

Bernecker, Walther L. 1982. *Colectividades y revolución social: El anarquismo en la guerra civil española, 1936–39.* Translated by Gustau Muñoz. Barcelona.

Bessie, Alvah. 1975. *Men in battle.* San Francisco.

Bessie, Alvah, and Albert Prago, eds. 1987. *Our fight: Writings by veterans of the Abraham Lincoln Brigade, Spain 1936–39.* New York.

Best, Geoffrey. 1986. *War and society in revolutionary Europe, 1770–1870.* New York.

Bezucha, Robert, ed. 1972. *Modern European social history.* Lexington, Mass.

Blanco Rodríguez, Juan A. 1993. *El Quinto Regimiento en la política militar del PCE en la guerra civil.* Madrid.

Blinkhorn, Martin. 1975. *Carlism and crisis in Spain.* Cambridge.

Blum, Jerome. 1978. *The end of the old order in rural Europe.* Princeton.

Bolín, Luis Antonio. 1967. *España: Los años vitales.* Madrid.

Bolloten, Burnett. 1991. *The Spanish civil war: Revolution and counter-revolution.* Chapel Hill, N.C.

Bookchin, Murray. 1978. *The Spanish anarchists: The heroic years, 1868–1936.* New York.

Borkenau, Franz. 1963. *The Spanish cockpit.* Ann Arbor, Mich.

Bosch Sánchez, Aurora. 1983. *Ugetistas y Libertarios: Guerra civil y revolución en el país valenciano, 1936–39.* Valencia.

————. 1988. La colectivización en una zona no latifundista: El caso valenciano. In *El sueño igualitario: Campesinado y colectivización en la España republicana,* by Julián Casanova. Zaragoza

Brademas, John. 1974. *Anarcosindicalismo y revolución en España (1930–1937).* Translated by Joaquín Romero Maura. Barcelona.

Brandes, Stanley. 1980. *Metaphors of masculinity: Sex and status in Andalusian folklore.* Philadelphia.

Bray, Norman. 1937. *Mallorca salvada.* Palma de Mallorca.

Bricall, Josep Maria. 1978. *Política econòmica de la Generalitat 1936–1939,* 2 vols. Barcelona.

Broggi i Vallès, Moisès. 1986. Progressos effectuats per la sanitat militar en el curs de la guerra civil espanyola (1936–39). In *Cinquantenari de la guerra civil espanyola, 1936–1986,* by Moisès Broggi i Vallès, Josep Termes i Ardevol, and Pierre Vilar. Barcelona.

Broggi i Vallès, Moisès, Josep Termes i Ardevol, and Pierre Vilar. 1986. *Cinquantenari de la guerra civil espanyola, 1936–1986.* Barcelona.

Broué, Pierre, and Emile Témine. 1970. *The revolution and the civil war in Spain.* Translated by Tony White. Cambridge, Mass.

Bruneteaux, Patrick. 1996. *Maintenir l'ordre.* Paris.

Calleja Martín, Rosario. 1991. Mujeres de la industria de espectáculos: Madrid (1936–39). In *Las mujeres y la guerra civil: III jornadas de estudios monográficos, Salamanca, Octubre, 1989.* Madrid.

Cantalupo, Roberto. 1951. *Embajada en España.* Barcelona.

Carlton, Charles. 1992. *Going to the wars: The experience of the British civil wars, 1638–1651.* London.

Carr, Raymond. 1980. *Modern Spain: 1875–1980.* Oxford.

————. 1982. *Spain 1808–1975.* Oxford.

Carr, Raymond, ed. 1971. *The republic and the civil war in Spain.* London.

Carreras Panchón, Antonio. 1986. Los psiquiatras españoles y la guerra civil. *Medicina y historia* no. 13.

Carrión, Pascual. 1973. *La reforma agraria de la Segunda República y la situación actual.* Barcelona.

Carro, [Dr.] Santiago. 1938. *Observaciones médicas sobre el hambre en la España roja.* Santander.

Casanova, Julián. 1988. Campesinado y colectivización en Aragón. In *El sueño igualitario: Campesinado y colectivización en la España republicana,* edited by Julián

282                                                          Bibliography

Casanova. Zaragoza.
———. 1999. *Rebelión y revolución.* In *Víctimas de la guerra civil,* edited by Santos Juliá. Madrid.
Casanova, Julián, 1985. *Anarquismo y revolución en la sociedad rural aragonesa, 1936–1938.* Madrid.
Casanova, Julián, ed. *El sueño igualitario: Campesinado y colectivización en la España republicana.* Zaragoza.
Casas de la Vega, Rafael. 1977. *Las milicias nacionales,* 2 vols. Madrid.
Castro Delgado, Enrique. 1963. *Hombres made in Moscú.* Barcelona.
Cervera, Javier. 1999. *Madrid en guerra: La ciudad clandestina 1936–39.* Madrid.
Chaves Palacios, Julián. 1996. *La represión en la provincia de Cáceres durante la guerra civil.* Cáceres.
Chomsky, Noam. 1969. *American power and the new Mandarins.* New York.
Cifuentes Chueca, Julia, and Pilar Maluenda Pons. 1995. *El asalto a la República: Los orígenes del franquismo en Zaragoza (1936–39).* Zaragoza.
Cleugh, James. 1963. *Furia española.* Barcelona.
Cobb, Richard. 1987. *The people's armies.* Translated by Marianne Elliott. New Haven, Conn.
Cobo Romero, Francisco. 1990. La justicia republicana en la provincia de Jaén durante la guerra civil. In *Justicia en guerra: Jornadas sobre la administración de justicia durante la guerra civil.* Madrid.
———. 1993. *La guerra civil y la represión franquista en la provincia de Jaén (1936–1950).* Jaén.
Collectif Equipo Juvenil Conféderal. 1997. *La collectivité de Calanda, 1936–1938.* Paris.
Collier, George A. 1987. *Socialists of rural Andalusia.* Stanford, Calif.
Colmegna, Hector. 1941. *Diario de un médico argentino en la guerra de España, 1936–1939.* Buenos Aires.
Corbin, John. 1995. Truth and myth in history: An example from the Spanish civil war. *Journal of Interdisciplinary History* 25:4 (spring), pp. 609–25.
Cordón, Antonio. 1977. *Trayectoria: Memorias de un militar republicano.* Barcelona.
Coverdale, John F. 1975. *Italian intervention in the Spanish civil war.* Princeton.
Cuesta Monereo, J. 1961. La guerra en los frentes del sur. In *La guerra de liberación nacional.* Zaragoza.
Cueva, Julio, de la. 1998. Religious persecution, anticlerical tradition, and revolution. *Journal of Contemporary History* 33:3, pp. 355–69.
Dallet, Joe. 1938. *Letters from Spain.* New York.
Delgado, Manuel. 1993. *Las palabras de otro hombre.* Barcelona.
Diez Nicolas, Juan. 1985. La mortalidad en la guerra civil española. In *Jornades de Població.* Barcelona.
Dirección General de Agricultura. 1938. *Estadística de la producción de cereales y leguminosas: Años 1936, 1937 y 1938.* Madrid.
Dollard, John. 1943. *Fear in battle.* New Haven, Conn.
Duby, Georges. 1990. *The legend of Bouvines.* Translated by Catherine Tihanyi. Berkeley, Calif.
Durán, Gustavo. 1979. *Una enseñanza de la guerra española.* Madrid.
Eatwell, Roger. 1996. *Fascism.* New York.

Eby, Cecil. 1974. *Voluntarios norteamericanos en la guerra civil española.* Barcelona.

Eguidazu, Fernando. 1978. *Intervención monetaria y control de cambios en España, 1900–1977.* Madrid.

Esdaile, Charles. 1990. Hombres y armas: La ayuda extranjera. In *Los nuevos historiadores ante la Guerra Civil española,* 2 vols., edited by Octavio Ruiz Manjón Cabeza and Miguel Gómez Oliver. Granada.

Estellés Salarich, José. 1986. La sanidaden el Ejército Republicano del Centro. In *Los médicos y la medicina en la guerra civil española.* Madrid.

Faust, Drew Gilpin. 1996. *Mothers of invention: Women of the slaveholding South in the American Civil War.* Chapel Hill, N.C.

Fergusson, Bernard. 1946. *The wild green earth.* London.

Ferrer Córdoba, Pedro. 1986. La Sanidad en la Marina republicana. In *Los médicos y la medicina en la guerra civil española.* Madrid.

Figes, Orlando. 1990. The Red Army and mass mobilization during the Russian civil war, 1918–1920. *Past and Present* no. 129 (November), pp. 168–211.

———. 1996. *A people's tragedy: A history of the Russian revolution.* New York.

Fitzpatrick, Sheila. 1994. *Stalin's peasants: Resistance and survival in the Russian village after collectivization.* New York.

Fraser, Ronald. 1986. *Blood of Spain: An oral history of the Spanish civil war.* New York.

Freud, Sigmund. 1959. *Group psychology and the analysis of the ego.* Translated by James Strachey. New York.

Gabriel, José. 1938. *La vida y la muerte en Aragón.* Buenos Aires.

Gallagher, Gary W. 1997. *The Confederate war.* Cambridge.

Gallardo Moreno, Jacinta. 1994. *La Guerra Civil en La Serena.* Badajoz.

Gárate Córdoba, José María. 1976a. *Alféreces provisionales.* Madrid.

———. 1976b. *Tenientes en Campaña.* Madrid.

García Lorca, Federico. 1967. *Obras completas.* Madrid.

García Sanz, Angel, Ramón Garrabou, and Jesús Sanz Fernández, eds. 1986. *Historia agraria de la España contemporánea.* Barcelona.

Garrido González, Luis. 1979. *Colectividades agrarias en Andalucía: Jaén (1931–39).* Madrid.

———. 1988. Producción agraria y guerra civil. In *El sueño igualitario: Campesinado y colectivización en la España republicana,* edited by Julián Casanova. Zaragoza.

Getman Eraso, Jordi. 1999. The constituency crisis of the Catalan Regional Confederation. Paper presented to the Society for Spanish and Portuguese Historical Studies, University of California, San Diego (April).

Gibson, Ian. 1973. *The death of Lorca.* Chicago.

Gilmore, David E. 1990. *Manhood in the making: Cultural concepts of masculinity.* New Haven, Conn.

Goldstone, Jack A. 1991. *Revolution and rebellion in the early modern world.* Berkeley, Calif.

Goldstone, Jack A., ed. 1986. *Revolutions: Theoretical, comparative, and historical studies.* San Diego, Calif.

Gómez Casas, Juan. 1973. *Historia del anarcosindicalismo español.* Madrid.

Gómez-Trigo Ochoa, Gerardo. 1986. Los médicos y la medicina de la Cruz Roja Española en la guerra civil (1936–39). In *Los médicos y la medicina en la guerra civil española.* Madrid.

González Portilla, Manuel, and José María Garmendia. 1988. *La guerra civil en el País Vasco.* Madrid.

Gracía Rivas, Manuel. 1986. La Sanidad de la Armada en la zona nacional durante la guerra de 1936–39. In *Los médicos y la medicina en la guerra civil española.* Madrid.

Graham, Helen. 1999. Against the state: A genealogy of the Barcelona May Days (1937). *European History Quarterly* 24, pp. 485–542.

Grande Covián, [Dr.] F. 1986. Deficiencias vitamínicas en Madrid durante la guerra civil: Una reminiscencia. In *Los médicos y la medicina en la guerra civil española.* Madrid.

Grossman, Dave [Lt. Col.]. 1996. *On killing: The psychological cost of learning to kill in war and society.* Boston, Mass.

Hay, Douglas, Peter Linebaugh, John G. Rule, E. P. Thompson, and Cal Winslow, eds. 1975. *Albion's fatal tree.* New York.

Hermet, Guy. 1989. *La guerre d'Espagne.* Paris.

Herrick, William. 1998. *Jumping the line: The adventures and misadventures of an American radical.* Madison, Wisc.

Holmes, Richard. 1985. *Acts of war: The behaviour of men in battle.* New York.

Howson, Gerald. 1999. *Arms for Spain: The untold story of the Spanish civil war.* New York.

Jackson, Gabriel. 1965. *The Spanish Republic and the civil war, 1931–1939.* Princeton.

Juliá, Santos. 1979. *Orígines del frente popular en España, 1934–1936.* Madrid.

Juliá, Santos, ed. 1999. *Víctimas de la guerra civil.* Madrid.

*Justicia en guerra: Jornadas sobre la administración de justicia durante la guerra civil española.* 1990. Madrid.

Kaplan, Temma. 1982. Female consciousness and collective action: The case of Barcelona, 1910–1918. *Signs* 7, no. 3 (spring).

Keegan, John. 1976. *The face of battle.* New York.

Kemp, Peter. 1957. *Mine were of trouble.* London

Kenyon, J. P. 1988. *The civil wars of England.* New York.

Kindelán, Alfredo. 1945. *Mis cuadernos de guerra.* Madrid.

Knoblaugh, H. Edward. 1937. *Correspondent in Spain.* London.

Lamas Arroyo, Angel. 1972. *Unos y Otros.* Barcelona.

Landis, Arthur H. 1989. *Death in the olive groves: American volunteers in the Spanish civil war, 1936–1939.* New York.

Lannon, Frances. 1987. *Privilege, persecution, and prophecy: The Catholic Church in Spain, 1875–1975.* Oxford.

Laqueur, Walter. 1996. *Fascism: Past, present, future.* New York.

Lee, Laurie. 1991. *A moment of war.* New York.

Leval, Gaston. 1975. *Collectives in the Spanish revolution.* Translated by Vernon Richards. London.

Lih, Lars. 1990. *Bread and authority in Russia, 1914–1921.* Berkeley, Calif.

Lincoln, Bruce. 1985. Revolutionary exhumations in Spain. *Comparative Studies in Society and History* 27, pp. 241–60.

Linderman, Gerald F. 1987. *Embattled courage: The experience of combat in the American Civil War.* New York.

Linz, Juan J. 1978. *The breakdown of democratic regimes: Crisis, breakdown, and equilibrium.* Baltimore.

Líster, Enrique. 1966. *Nuestra guerra.* Paris.

Lorenzo, César M. 1972. *Los anarquistas españoles y el poder, 1868–1969.* Paris.

Lukes, Steven. 1977. *Essays in social theory.* New York.

Lynn, John A. 1984. *The bayonets of the Republic: Motivation and tactics in the army of the French Revolution, 1791–94.* Urbana, Ill.

Macho, Luis Antonio. 1952. *La batalla de Brunete.* Madrid.

Madariaga, María Rosa, de. 1992. The intervention of Moroccan troops in the Spanish civil war. *European History Quarterly* 22, pp. 67–97.

Maddox, Richard. 1993. *El castillo: The politics of tradition in an Andalusian town.* Urbana, Ill.

Malefakis, Edward E. 1970. *Agrarian reform and peasant revolution in Spain.* New Haven, Conn.

——. 1972. Peasants, politics, and civil war in Spain, 1931–1939. In *Modern European social history,* edited by Robert J. Bezucha. Lexington, Mass.

Malraux, André. 1937. *L'Espoir.* Paris.

Marín Corralé, [Dr.] Angel. 1939. *La fiebre quintana de his en la guerra de España.* Zaragoza.

Martel, Carmen. 1938. *La guerra a través de las tocas.* Cádiz.

Martín-Blázquez, José. 1938. *Guerre civile totale.* Paris.

Martínez Bande, José Manuel. 1969. *La campaña de Andalucía.* Madrid.

——. 1970. *La invasión de Aragón y el desembarco en Mallorca.* Madrid.

——. 1973. *La gran ofensiva sobre Zaragoza.* Madrid.

——. 1974a. *La batalla de Teruel.* Madrid.

——. 1974b. *Por qué fuimos vencidos.* Madrid.

——. 1975. *La llegada al mar.* Madrid.

——. 1976. *Frente de Madrid.* Barcelona.

——. 1977. *La ofensiva sobre Valencia.* Madrid.

——. 1978. *La batalla del Ebro.* Madrid.

——. 1979. *La campaña de Cataluña.* Madrid.

——. 1980. *Nueve meses de guerra en el Norte.* Madrid.

——. 1981. *La batalla de Pozoblanco y el cierre de la bolsa de Mérida.* Madrid.

——. 1984. *La lucha en torno a Madrid en el invierno de 1936–1937.* Madrid.

——. 1990–91. *La lucha por la victoria.* Madrid.

Martínez-Molinos, Guillermo. 1990. El suministro de carburantes. In *Los nuevos historiadores ante la Guerra Civil española,* edited by Octavio Ruiz Manjón Cabeza and Miguel Gómez Oliver. Granada.

Mateo del Peral, Diego, Nicolás Sánchez-Albornoz, Gonzalo Anes Alvarez, Luis Angel Rojo, and Pedro Tedde. 1983. *Historia económica y pensamiento social: Estudios en homenaje a Diego Mateo del Peral.* Madrid.

Maurice, Jacques. 1975. *La reforma agraria en España en el siglo XX (1900–1936).* Madrid.

——. 1978. Problemática de las colectividades agrarias en la guerra civil. *Agricultura y Sociedad* (April–June).

Mayer, Arno J. 1971. *Dynamics of counterrevolution in Europe, 1870–1956.* New York.

McNeill, William H. 1982. *The pursuit of power: Technology, armed force, and society since A.D. 1000.* Chicago.
———. 1995. *Keeping together in time: Dance and drill in human history.* Cambridge, Mass.
McPherson, James M. 1988. *Battle cry of freedom: The civil war era.* New York.
*Los médicos y la medicina en la guerra civil española.* 1986. Madrid.
Ministerio de Agricultura. 1936. *Estadística.* Valencia.
———. 1938? *Estadística de cereales y leguminosas.* Barcelona.
Mintz, Frank. 1977. *La autogestión en la España revolucionaria.* Madrid.
Mira, Emilio. 1939. Psychiatric experience in the Spanish civil war. *British Medical Journal,* 17 June, pp. 1217–20.
———. 1943. *Psychiatry in war.* New York.
Modesto, Juan. 1969. *Soy del Quinto Regimiento.* Paris.
Montseny, Federica. 1986. La Sanidad y la asistencia social durante la guerra civil. In *Los médicos y la medicina en la guerra civil española.* Madrid.
Moreno Gómez, Francisco. 1986. *La guerra civil en Córdoba (1936–1939).* Madrid.
———. 1999. La represión en la posguerra. In *Víctimas de la guerra civil,* edited by Santos Juliá. Madrid.
Morris, Brian. 1991. *Western conceptions of the individual.* New York.
Moulinié, Henri. 1979. *De Bonald.* New York.
*Las mujeres y la guerra civil: III jornadas de estudios monográficos, Salamanca, octubre, 1989.* 1991. Madrid.
Murillo Pérez, María Guadalupe. 1990. Auditoría de Guerra de Gijón: Causas tramitadas por los Tribunales Populares Especiales de Guerra de Avilés, Mieres y Trubia. In *Justicia en guerra: Jornadas sobre la administración de justicia durante la guerra civil española.* Madrid.
Nash, Mary. 1995. *Defying male civilization: Women in the Spanish civil war.* Denver, Colo.
Noja Ruiz, Higinio. nd. *Control y colectivización.* Valencia.
———. 1937. *La obra constructiva en la revolución.* Valencia.
Orwell, George. 1980. *Homage to Catalonia.* New York.
Oudard, Georges. 1938. *Chemises noires, brunes, vertes en Espagne.* Paris.
Parker, Geoffrey. 1973. Mutiny in the Spanish Army of Flanders. *Past and Present* 58, pp. 38–52.
Payne, Stanley G. 1967. *Politics and the military in modern Spain.* Stanford, Calif.
———. 1970. *The Spanish revolution.* New York.
———. 1980. *Fascism: Comparison and definition.* Madison, Wisc.
———. 1993. *Spain's first democracy: The Second Republic, 1931–1936.* Madison, Wisc.
Pedraz Penalva, Ernesto. 1990. La administración de Justicia durante la guerra civil en la España Nacional. In *Justicia en guerra: Jornadas sobre la administración de justicia durante la guerra civil española.* Madrid.
Pedro y Pons, A. 1940. *Enfermedades por insuficiencia alimenticia observadas en Barcelona durante la guerra 1936–1939.* Barcelona.
Peers, E. Allison. 1943. *Spain in eclipse.* London.
Peirats, José. 1971. *La CNT en la revolución española,* 3 vols. Paris.
Picardo Castellón, Manuel. 1986. Experiencia personal en un hospital quirúrgico de

primera linea durante nuestra guerra civil. In *Los médicos y la medicina en la guerra civil española*. Madrid.

Pipes, Richard. 1994. *Russia under the Bolshevik Regime, 1919–1924*. New York.

Pitt-Rivers, J. A. 1954. *The people of the Sierra*. New York.

Poggi, Gianfranco. 1993. *Money and the modern mind: George Simmel's philosophy of money*. Berkeley, Calif.

Pons Prades, Eduardo. 1974. *Un soldado de la República*. Madrid.

———. 1977. *Guerrillas españolas, 1936–1950*. Barcelona.

Prats, Alardo. 1938. *Vanguardia y retaguardia de Aragón*. Buenos Aires.

Preston, Paul. 1986. *The Spanish civil war 1936–39*. Chicago.

Preston, Paul, ed. 1984. *Revolution and war in Spain, 1931–1939*. London.

Puig Casas, Lluís. 1999. *Personal memories of the days of the Spanish civil war in Catalan and English*. Translated by Idoya Puig. Lewiston, N.Y.

Puig i Vallas, Angelina. 1991. Mujeres de Pedro Martínez durante la guerra civil. In *Las mujeres y la guerra civil: III jornadas de estudios monográficos, Salamanca, octubre, 1989*. Madrid.

Quirosa-Cheyrouze y Muñoz, Rafael. 1986. *Política y guerra civil en Almería*. Almería.

Ramírez Jiménez, Manuel, ed. 1975. *Estudios sobre la Segunda República española*. Madrid.

*Rapport de la mission sanitaire de la Société des Nations en Espagne*. 1937? Paris.

*Los regulares de Larache en la Guerra civil de España*. 1940. Madrid.

Richards, Michael. 1998. *A time of silence: Civil war and the culture of repression in Franco's Spain, 1936–1945*. Cambridge.

Rodrigo González, Natividad. 1985? *Las colectividades agrarias en Castilla-La Mancha*. Toledo.

Rodríguez García, Yolanda. 1990. Procesados en la Audiencia Provincial de Burgos (1936–1940). In *Justicia en guerra: Jornadas sobre la administración de justicia durante la guerra civil española*. Madrid.

Rojo, Vicente. 1974. *Alerta los pueblos*. Barcelona.

Romero, Luis. 1982. *Por qué y cómo mataron a Calvo Sotelo*. Barcelona.

Rosenstone, Robert A. 1969. *Crusade of the left: The Lincoln Battalion in the Spanish civil war*. New York.

Rosique Navarro, Francisca. 1988. *La reforma agraria en Badajoz durante la IIa República*. Badajoz.

Ruiz Manjón Cabeza, Octavio, and Miguel Gómez Oliver, eds. 1990. *Los nuevos historiadores ante la Guerra Civil española*, 2 vols. Granada.

Salas, Delfín. 1989. *Tropas regulares indígenas*. Madrid.

Salas Larrazábal, Ramón. 1973. *Historia del Ejército popular de la República*. Madrid.

Salas Larrazábal, Ramón, and Jesús María Salas Larrazábal. 1986. *Historia general de la guerra de España*. Madrid.

Sánchez Recio, Glicerio. 1990. Justicia ordinaria y justicia popular durante la guerra civil. In *Justicia en guerra: Jornadas sobre la administración de justicia durante la guerra civil española*. Madrid.

———. 1991. *Justicia y guerra en España, 1936–39*. Alicante.

Santacreu Soler, José Miguel. 1986. *La crisis monetaria española de 1937*. Alicante.

———. 1992. *L'Economia valenciana durant la guerra civil: Protagonisme i estanca-*

288                                                   Bibliography

*ment agrari.* Valencia.
Sanz, Ricardo. 1978. *La política y el sindicalismo.* Barcelona.
Sardá, Juan. 1970. El Banco de España (1931–1962). In *El Banco de España: Una historia económica.* Madrid.
Scott, James C. 1985. *Weapons of the weak: Everyday forms of peasant resistance.* New Haven, Conn.
Seidman, Michael. 1991. *Workers against work: Labor in Barcelona and Paris during the Popular Fronts.* Berkeley, Calif.
Semprún, Jorge. 1993. *The cattle truck.* Translated by Richard Seaver. London.
Serrano, Carlos, ed. 1991. *Madrid, 1936–1939: Un peuple en résistance ou l'épopée ambiguë.* Paris.
Serrano, Secundino. 1986. *La guerrilla antifranquista en León.* Salamanca.
*Servicios de Intendencia.* 1938. Madrid? (March).
Simmel, Georg. 1991. Money in modern culture. *Theory, Culture, and Society* 8:3 (August).
Simoni, Encarna, and Renato Simoni. 1984. *Cretas: La colectivización de un pueblo aragonés durante la guerra civil española, 1936–37.* Alcañiz.
Simpson, James. 1995. *Spanish agriculture: The long siesta, 1765–1965.* Cambridge.
Skocpol, Theda. 1979. *States and social revolutions: A comparative analysis of France, Russia, and China.* Cambridge.
Solé i Sabater, Josep M., and Joan Villarroya. 1999. Mayo de 1937–Abril de 1939. In *Víctimas de la guerra civil,* edited by Santos Juliá. Madrid.
Souchy, Agustín, 1992. *Beware anarchist!* Translated by Theo Waldinger. Chicago.
Souchy, Agustín, and Paul Folgare. 1977. *Colectivizaciones: La obra constructiva de la revolución española.* Barcelona.
Souchy Bauer, Augustin. 1982. *With the peasants of Aragon.* Translated by Abe Bluestein. Minneapolis, Minn.
Stone, Bailey. 1994. *The genesis of the French Revolution: A global historical interpretation.* Cambridge.
Suero Serrano, Luciano. 1982. *Memorias de un campesino andaluz en la revolución española.* Madrid.
Tagüeña Lacorte, Manuel. 1978. *Testimonio de dos guerras.* Barcelona.
Thomas, Hugh. 1961. *The Spanish civil war.* New York.
———. 1971. Anarchist agrarian collectives in the Spanish civil war. In *The republic and the civil war in Spain,* edited by Raymond Carr. London.
———. 1976. *La guerra civil española.* Translated by Neri Daurella, 2 vols. Barcelona.
Thompson, E. P. 1975. The crime of anonymity. In *Albion's fatal tree,* edited by Douglas Hay, Peter Linebaugh, John G. Rule, E. P. Thompson, and Cal Winslow. New York.
Tió, Carlos. 1982. *La política de aceites comestibles en la España del siglo XX.* Madrid.
Toribio García, Manuel. 1994. *Andújar en la guerra civil española (1936–1939).* Córdoba.
Tusell Gómez, Javier. 1971. *Las elecciones del frente popular en España.* Madrid.
Ucelay Da Cal, Enric. 1982. *La Catalunya populista: Imatge, cultura i política en l'etapa republicana, 1936–1939.* Barcelona.

Ugarte, Javier. 1990. *El voluntariado alavés en el ejército franquista: Estudio sociológico* (1936–1939). In *Los nuevos historiadores ante la Guerra Civil española*, 2 vols., edited by Octavio Ruiz Manjón Cabeza and Miguel Gómez Oliver. Granada.

Underdown, David. 1985. *Revel, riot, and rebellion: Popular politics and culture in England, 1603–1660.* Oxford.

Universidad de Zaragoza. 1961. *La guerra de liberación nacional.* Zaragoza.

Vallejo Nágera, A. 1939. *La locura y la guerra.* Valladolid.

van Creveld, Martin. 1977. *Supplying war: Logistics from Wallenstein to Patton.* Cambridge.

van Creveld, Martin, ed. 1993. *Feeding Mars: Logistics in Western warfare from the Middle Ages to the present.* Boulder, Colo.

Vila Izquierdo, Justo. 1984. *Extremadura: La Guerra Civil.* Badajoz.

Vilanova, Mercedes. 1995. *Les majories invisibles.* Barcelona.

Vilar, Pierre. 1986. *La guerre d'Espagne, (1936–1939).* Paris.

Villarroya i Font, Joan. 1981. *Els Bombardeigs de Barcelona durant la guerra civil.* Monserrat.

Vincent, Mary. 1996. *Catholicism in the Second Spanish Republic: Religion and politics in Salamanca, 1930–1936.* Oxford.

Viñas, Angel. 1979. *El oro de Moscú: Alfa y omega de un mito franquista.* Barcelona.

————. 1984. The financing of the Spanish civil war. In *Revolution and war in Spain, 1931–1939,* edited by Paul Preston. London.

Viñas, Angel, Julio Viñuela, Fernando Eguidazu, Carlos Fernandez-Pulgar, and Senén Florensa. 1975. *Política comercial exterior en España.* Madrid.

Vries, Lini M., de 1965. *España 1937.* Translated by Carlo Antonio Castro. Xalapa, Mexico.

Whealey, Robert H. 1977. How Franco financed his war—Reconsidered. *Journal of Contemporary History* 12, pp. 133–52.

————. 1989. *Hitler and Spain: The Nazi role in the Spanish civil war.* Lexington, Ky.

Wildman, Allan K. 1987. *The End of the Russian Imperial Army,* 2 vols. Princeton.

Wintringham, Tom. 1939. *English captain.* London.

Woolsey, Gamel. 1998. *Malaga burning.* Reston, Va.

Zúmel, Mariano F. 1986. Cirugía de guerra. In *Los médicos y la medicina en la guerra civil española.* Madrid.

# Index

artillery exchanges: to celebrate Republican
Teruel capture, 176; *desbandada* resulting
from, 223; malfunctions on Andalusia front
(1937–38), 176; ritualization during last
weeks of war, 227; ritualization on the
Jarama front, 157
Asensio Torrado, José, 49, 78, 199, 201, 206
Assault Guards (Republican), 18, 21, 199,
224
Asturian government: rebellion against, 149;
resistance to centralization by, 146–47
Asturian revolt (1934), 21–22
Asturias, Nationalist campaign in, 149–50;
Republican militias from, 89, 93
*automutilados* (self-inflicted injuries), 89, 92,
109, 150, 209, 211–12
Auxilio Social (Nationalist), 95
Azaña, Manuel, 18, 24, 98
Azaña's reforms (1931–32), 18

Badajoz massacre, 47, 48*m*
Bank of Spain currency, 91
Baráibar, Carlos de , 196
Barcelona: bombing raids on, 156–57; fall to
Nationalist troops, 225, 226–27; loss of
electricity supply to, 180, 226; May revolts
(1937) in, 101–3
barter practice, 99–100, 132, 173
Basque Military Tribunal, 92
Basque nationalism, 16, 19
Basque Nationalist Party (PNV), 93
Basque Nationalists, 55
Basque offensive (Nationalists), 49–50
Basque Republicans: British food shipments
to, 93; casualties suffered during Vitoria
campaign by, 89–90; deficiencies in the
northern front defense, 92–93; distrust
between Asturian and Santanderian allies
and, 91; "Iron Ring" defense of Bilbao by,
91; kept separate from Popular Army, 89;
loss of Bilbao and, 93; resistance to
centralization by, 146–47; self-mutilation/
desertions problem of, 92; withdrawal
during Santander campaign by, 148
Battalion Aida Lafuente, 34
Battalion Largo Caballero (Republican), 125
Battalion of Mieres (Asturias), 37
Battle of Brunete, 106*m*, 111–15, 120, 192
Battle of Catalonia, 185*m*, 217
Battle of the Ebro (1938), 190–93

Battle of Guadalajara (1937), 86–88, 104,
106*m*
Battle of Jarama (1937), 82–86, 106*m*,
250n.43
Battle of Madrid (1936): high cost of, 61, 63;
late November battle front of, 62*m*;
Nationalist advance prior to, 57; sites of,
60*m*, 106*m*. *See also* Madrid
Battle of Málaga, 77–78
Bayo, Alberto, 37
Belchite, 118, 184*m*
Belchite massacre, 33–34
Beorleguí, Alfonso, 49
Bernanos, Georges, 33
Bessie, Alvah, 59
*bienio negro* (1934–35), 23, 25
Bilbao: "Iron Ring" defense of, 91;
Nationalist "practical generosity" policy
and, 93–94; Republican loss of, 93
black marketeering: *Etapas* units jurisdiction
over, 167–68; individualism strands
practiced in, 7; proliferation in Republican
zone of, 134; by women, 173
Bolloten, Burnett, 178
Bonald, Louis de, 4
Borkenau, Franz, 39, 222
bread production, 98–99
British foreign aid, 93
British seventeenth-century civil wars, 8, 36,
151–52, 234
British volunteers, 209
Burillo, Ricardo, 201, 206, 270n.266
Buzón, Francisco, 92

Cabrera, Antonio, 35
Cáceres massacre, 81
Calle Muntaner, 157
Calvo Sotelo, José, 25
El Campesino's brigade (Republican), 83
Campo de Gibraltar, 41, 42
*Canarias* (Nationalist cruiser), 42
Canaries (Islands), 45
Casa de Campo, 59, 62*m*, 88
Casado conspiracy (1939), 206, 210, 233
Casado, Segismundo, 114, 210
Casas Viejas rebellion (1933), 21
Catalan front, 224–25
Catalan Maginot Line, 224
Catalan region: failures of Republican
conscription efforts in, 164; nationalism in,